WARBURG INSTITUTE SURVEYS AND TEXTS
Edited by Jill Kraye and W. F. Ryan

XX

T0345598

Foto Giovetti, Mantua

Andrea Mantegna, detail from right-hand segment of the 'Meeting Scene', fresco (painted c. 1474) in the *Camera picta*, Castello di San Giorgio, Mantua (see pp. 92–5). Cardinal Francesco Gonzaga is shown with his father Ludovico Gonzaga, Marchese of Mantua (left), and his brother Protonotary Ludovico Gonzaga (holding his hand, right). The two children are sons of his elder brother Federico, the next Marchese: Francesco, later Marchese (left) and Sigismondo, later Protonotary and Cardinal (centre, holding Protonotary Ludovico's hand).

A RENAISSANCE CARDINAL AND HIS WORLDLY GOODS:
THE WILL AND INVENTORY OF FRANCESCO GONZAGA (1444–1483)

BY

D. S. CHAMBERS

LONDON

THE WARBURG INSTITUTE
UNIVERSITY OF LONDON
1992

© WARBURG INSTITUTE 1992
ISBN 0 85481 080 3
ISSN 0266–1772

Designed and computer typeset at the Warburg Institute and the University of London Computer Centre
Printed by Henry Ling, The Dorset Press, Dorchester, Dorset

Table of Contents

Acknowledgments

This book draws upon work in progress over a long period, and I am indebted to many people. Above all I am grateful to friends in Mantua: first of all, to the staffs of the Archivio di Stato, the Biblioteca Comunale and the Archivio Diocesano, but also I must thank Rodolfo Signorini, Curator of the Fondazione d'Arco, to whom I owe more than I can express for his constant inspiration, learning and warmheartedness, not least his habitual readiness to check a reference or send a photocopy. Likewise I am deeply grateful to another generous friend, Giuseppe Frasso of the Università Cattolica in Milan, who had himself intended to edit the cardinal's inventory, but instead handed over to me not only this commitment but also all his notes, and later read and commented on parts of my text. At the Warburg Institute I am grateful as ever to my colleagues and to the Library. I thank Joe Trapp, for always encouraging my Mantuan researches and for some welcome corrections, and Will Ryan and Jill Kraye, for their patience and painstaking work as editors. To Nicolai Rubinstein I am deeply indebted for his many precious hours devoted to reading the entire book, from which scrutiny it has greatly benefited. Charles Burnett, Charles Hope, Christopher Ligota, Elizabeth McGrath, Nicholas Mann and Anne Marie Meyer have also given valued advice on different points, and I am grateful to Ian Jones for his skill in preparing several photographs. The following list contains the names of others whom I wish to thank for help of various sorts at different times, but I fear it is incomplete: Candace Adelson, Giuseppe Bisaccia, Alison Brown, Clifford Brown, Howard Burns, Claudio Ciociola, Martin Davies, Albinia de la Mare, Simon Ditchfield, Laurie Fusco, Peter King, G. N. Knauer, Michael Koortbojian, Laura Lepschy, Kristen Lippincott, Anna Maria Lorenzoni, Scot McKendrick, John Mallet, Jane Martineau, Mary Ella Milham, Shayne Mitchell, Alessandro Pastore, Marco Pellegrini, Paolo Pissavino, don Giuseppe Pecorari, Judith Pollmann, Ruth Rubinstein, Gertrude Seidmann, Elisabeth Swain, Dora Thornton, Antonia Tissoni-Benvenuti, Caterina Volpi and Nicholas Webb. Finally, I thank deeply Tanya, Serinky and Grusha, for their companionship, lively interest and, on the whole, forbearance.

For the swift provision of photographs and rights of reproduction, I am particularly grateful to the Biblioteca Apostolica Vaticana. Permission to publish the entire text of the inventory has been kindly granted by the Rev. Ordinario Diocesano of Mantua. I would also like to thank the following for supplying photographic material and copyright permission: Archivio di Stato, Mantua (Ministero dei beni culturali); Biblioteca Universitaria Estense; Chester Beatty Library, Dublin; and Foto Giovetti, Mantua.

List of Abbreviations

ASF, MAP	Archivio di Stato, Florence, (Fondo) Medici avanti il Principato.
ASMn, AG	Archivio di Stato, Mantua, Archivio Gonzaga.
ASDMn	Archivio storico diocesano, Mantua.
ASMil, AS	Archivio di Stato, Milan, Archivio Sforzesco.
ASMod, AEC	Archivio di Stato, Modena, Archivio Estense, Cancelleria segreto.
ASP, AGG	Archivio di Stato, Parma, Archivio Gonzaga di Guastalla.
AV	Archivio Vaticano.
b.	*busta* (a box or file).
BAV	Biblioteca Apostolica Vaticana.
BCMn	Biblioteca comunale, Mantua.
BCG, FMD	Biblioteca comunale, Guastalla, Fondo Davolio-Marani.
BMC	*Catalogue of Books Printed in the Fifteenth Century now in the British Museum*, London, 1908–.
BN	Biblioteca nazionale, Bibliothèque nationale.
c., cc.	*carta* (loose sheet or page).
cart.	*cartella* (box file: used in ASMil).
DBI	*Dizionario biografico degli italiani*, Rome, 1960–.
DHGE	*Dictionnaire d'histoire et de géographie ecclésiastique*, Paris, 1912–.
Eubel	C. Eubel, *Hierarchia catholica*, II, Münster, 1901.
GW	*Gesamtkatalog der Wiegendrucke*, Leipzig, 1925–.
I	Inventory (Appendix 2).
PL	J. P. Migne, *Patrologia latina*.
RIS	Rerum Italicarum scriptores, ed. L. A. Muratori.
W	Will (Appendix 1).

Introduction

Hanc itaque gloriam fundatam in quovis genere virtutis a maioribus amplectere et extolle, illustrem fratrem tuum Franciscum Gonzagam cardinalem Mantuanum imitatus, qui unus hac excellenti virtute plus nominis et gloriae sibi in urbe Roma et quoque proficiscitur comparavit, quam omnes simul eiusdem ordinis. Quid sit retinere aurum, quid argentum, quid gemmas, quid annulos, quid vestes, quid chlamydes, quid equos, quid vasa Corinthia, quid Damascena, quid crystallina, quid aulaea, quid peripetasmata, nescit. Multos ex suis tum familiares tum cives ad meliorem fortunam erexit ditioresque sua liberalitate reddidit facietque complures...

> —Bartolomeo Sacchi, il Platina, *De principe* (dedicated to Federico Gonzaga), 1470, ed. G. Ferraù, Palermo, 1979, p. 138.

Franciscus Gonzaga...liberalitate insignis, caritate in suos precipua, erga omnes munificus.

> —Jacopo Gherardi da Volterra, *Diario romano* (c. 1480), ed. E. Carusi, RIS, XXIII, 3, Città di Castello, 1904, p. 124.

This study—built rather necrologically around a will and a post-mortem inventory—investigates the mind, entourage, possessions and final dispositions of a late fifteenth-century Prince of the Church, Cardinal Francesco Gonzaga (1444–1483).[1] Francesco was already by birth a secular prince, being the second son of Ludovico Gonzaga, Marchese of Mantua, and Barbara von Hohenzollern,[2] whose father was John 'the Alchemist', Margrave of Brandenburg. In his second, or ecclesiastical, princely role, from December 1461 onwards, he was one of the earliest of the species of 'political' cardinals sprung from Italian ruling dynasties, and the first of nine cardinals from the Gonzaga family appointed during the next

---

[1] Some basic information about Cardinal Francesco Gonzaga is in Pastor, *Storia dei papi*, II, *passim*, Mazzoldi, *Mantova: La storia*, II, esp. pp. 20–74, and Signorini, *Opus hoc tenue*, *passim*. Full bibliographical references for all works cited in the main text of this book can be found in the Bibliography.

[2] Generally known as Barbara of Brandenburg; I refer to her below usually just as Barbara, since her name recurs so often.

century and a half.[3] As a patron he also played a double role: first, as promoter of the interests of the Gonzaga family and of other Mantuans, particularly in the ecclesiastical sphere,[4] and, second, more on his own behalf, as a conspicuous *mecenate*.[5]

An extraordinary amount of material survives relating to Cardinal Francesco Gonzaga and the personalities of his *familia*, some of whom themselves played a significant role in cultural life and drew their patron into it. Many letters to and from Francesco himself are extant;[6] these are supplemented by hundreds to and from other persons. Only a limited part of this material can be brought into the present discussion, and very little will be said here about the bulk of its subject matter: contemporary political news and diplomacy. The aim of the following chapters is rather to place the will and inventory in perspective, by illustrating aspects of the cardinal's personality, affairs and interests. Preceding the texts, therefore, are discussions of the cardinal's public career and financial problems, and an investigation of what might be called his cultural personality, related particularly to his education, his attitude to books and learning, the literary personalities with whom he was in contact, and his enterprise as a collector and patron. Two final chapters provide an account of events following the test- amentary dispositions made by Francesco on his deathbed, a description and discussion of the will and inventory, and a study of the posthumous admini- stration of the cardinal's affairs. As well as the two principal texts, some letters from the post-mortem period are included as an appendix.

The two major documents presented in this study, cited throughout as W [=Will] and I [=Inventory], are not new discoveries. Eugène Müntz a century ago first drew attention to Cardinal Gonzaga's will and published extracts from it;[7] the inventory has been known about since the 1960s,[8] and was briefly described in a conference paper by Giuseppe Frasso in 1974.[9] Nevertheless, neither of these documents has previously been transcribed in full nor have they been analysed in relation to each other in the wider context of the cardinal's life and testamentary *Nachleben*. Their main interest undoubtedly lies in what they record about the cardinal's collections; not only his gems, bronzes, medallions and *pietra dura* objects, concerning which a separate study has recently appeared,[10] but also

[3] Two detailed studies about the making of comparable cardinals are Picotti, *La giovinezza*, and Pellegrini, 'Ascanio Maria Sforza' (Ascanio became a cardinal in 1484, Giovanni de' Medici in 1489). Partner, *The Pope's Men*, esp. pp. 35–7, 202–6, draws attention to this category among the cardinals.

[4] On Cardinal Gonzaga's dedication to the interests of Mantuans see, for instance, Platina's remark at the end of the quotation from his *De principe* on p. 1, above; on his policy concerning appointments, in which he sought priority in Mantuan benefices for Mantuans but did not share his father's insistence on their keeping residence, see Chambers, 'A Defence of Non-Residence'.

[5] See, for discussion of the meanings of 'patronage', Kent and Simons, *Patronage*, esp. pp. 1–21 (these essays do not, however, cover ecclesiastical aspects of the term).

[6] Few of them autograph, however; see cautionary remarks below, pp. 52–3.

[7] Müntz (who claimed to have found the will in Mantua in 1881), 'Musée du Capitole', esp. pp. 29–31, and more fully in *Les Arts*, III, pp. 297–300.

[8] Meroni (*Mostra*, p. 59) thanks G. Pecorari and R. Zucchi for indicating the existence of the inventory; Zucchi made some use of it in his thesis, *Per una storia della biblioteca dei Gonzaga*.

[9] Frasso, 'Oggetti d'arte'.

[10] Brown, Fusco, and Corti, 'Lorenzo de' Medici'. I am grateful to Laurie Fusco for sending me transcripts of the correspondence she has discovered in Florence and intends to publish in collaboration with Gino Corti, and to Clifford Brown for informing me in August 1989 of the imminent publication of his article. Brown includes some extracts from the inventory (from fols 10^r–12^v and 19^r)—though these selected passages are not given in

books, tapestries, silverware and all manner of other material objects and artefacts which he had accumulated;[11] some of these may not exactly illustrate the selectivity of a connoisseur, though they may be quite suggestive as indicators of mentality.

their original sequence—and many letters published either in whole or part. Four of the same letters occur in Appendix 3 (below), since they are essential to the discussion in chaps. 4–5, the scope of which, however, differs considerably from that of Brown's article.

[11] See Goldthwaite, 'Empire of Things'. The motivations of the clergy as accumulators of 'things' are not, however, discussed in this essay.

Chapter 1: Cardinal Francesco Gonzaga

(i) The Career of Cardinal Gonzaga

Francesco Gonzaga, born on 15 March 1444,[1] was from early childhood intended for an ecclesiastical career. This may have been designed by his parents to avoid the risk of a repeated rivalry between the heir and the second son, as had occurred between his father Ludovico and uncle Carlo Gonzaga,[2] or maybe simply to follow precedent; for another of his father's brothers, Giovan Lucido, the intellectual prodigy, who had been made a protonotary and presumably was expected to rise high in the Church, had died young in February 1448.[3] Francesco was already described by his father as 'our priest' in letters of 1450–2,[4] and although his childish dispositions seemed if anything rather contrary to the clerical life, Pope Nicholas V was persuaded to confer on him the title of apostolic protonotary just before his tenth birthday.[5] The culmination came with the red hat, after sustained pressure upon Pope Pius II from not only Barbara of Brandenburg, but even from Cardinal Nicolaus Cusanus and Emperor Frederick III.

The news of Francesco's elevation was published on 18 December 1461, when he was still only seventeen; Pius II was under no slight obligation after the meeting in 1459 at Mantua of the papal diet intended to rally a crusade against the Turks; but, even so, the appointment of such a young candidate had not been very willingly made and there had even been an attempt to deceive the pope about Francesco's true—and uncanonical—age.[6] The face-saving topos that Francesco looked older than he really was,[7] was used by Pius II[8] and many others, and was even repeated as late as about 1480, when Francesco was already thirty-five.[9] Whether or not he matured quickly, his good looks and geniality soon acquired for him in Rome a far from austere reputation;[10] on the other hand impressions recorded in the latter part of his career suggest at least that he had an

---

[1] 'A dì de domenega xv de marzo 1444 pocho poco inanze xv ory [about 9.30 a. m.] partorì la dita Illustrissima madona Barbara uno fiol…batezà a San Pedro a dì […], e à nome Francescho': Bartholomeo Maloselli, *Vacheto di le memorie* (ASMn, AG, b. 282 bis, c. 36ᵛ), which is the most reliable source for dates of Gonzaga family events of the mid-fifteenth century; cited by Signorini, *Opus hoc tenue*, p. 73 n. 50.

[2] Swain, 'Faith in the Family', p. 181.

[3] The main source on Giovan Lucido is Francesco Prendilacqua, *De vita Victorini Feltrensis dialogus*, ed. Garin, in *Pensiero pedagogico*, pp. 552–667 (606–7). See also Signorini, *Opus hoc tenue*, pp. 71 and 258 n. 13, citing Kristeller, *Iter Italicum*.

[4] Marchese Ludovico Gonzaga to Galeazzo Cavriani, Bishop of Mantua, 31 March 1450, 6 March 1452 (ASMn, AG, b. 2883, lib. 14, fol. 26ᵛ and lib. 19, fol. 5ᵛ); quoted by Signorini, *Opus hoc tenue*, pp. 75 n. 75, 91–2, doc. 1.

[5] AV Reg. Vat. 402, cc. 37ᵛ&38ʳ, dated 11 February 1454.

[6] Signorini, 'Federico III', pp. 247–9; *Opus hoc tenue*, pp. 34–45.

[7] On the *puer-senex* topos see Curtius, *European Literature*, pp. 98–101.

[8] Pius II, *Commentarii*, ed. von Heck, I, p. 449 (lib. VII); trans. Gragg, p. 503.

[9] 'Franciscus Gonzaga…ad cardinalatum assumptus iuvenis aduc, sed in dies ita profecit, ut quamvis sederet inter ultimos patrum, tamen consilio, auctoritate et gratia, vel paucis vel nullis esset inferior…' (Gherardi, *Diario romano*, p. 124).

[10] E.g., the characterization by Gaspare of Verona (d. 1474): 'formosissimum iuvenem, sine dolo malo et omni humanitate refertum, ab universa curia pontificia summe amatum ob facillimos mores suos…' (ed. Zippel, *Vite di Paolo II*, p. 28); a further quotation is given below, p. 37 n. 4.

imposing presence, though the hyperbole of a Ferrarese chronicler in January 1479 may seem excessive,[11] as does the funeral laudation by Giovan Lucido Cattanei.[12]

It is likely that Francesco's ability grew from experience and from heeding the professional advice of skilled members of his entourage. By moving around in Italy (as the Table of Itineraries given at the end of this chapter demonstrates), he must have gained wide knowledge of different persons and places. His earlier years of residence in the papal court, from the end of March 1462, are particularly well documented by correspondence, owing to parental concern for news of his progress. Some of the letters describing his journeys and brief sojourns in different places, including those spent with Pius II in southern Tuscany and Umbria during 1462, are as vivid as the pope's own *Commentaries*.[13] Much less well described, unfortunately, are Francesco's travels with the court of Sixtus IV—again through Umbria—during the summer of 1476.

Cardinal Francesco Gonzaga lived through a period of remarkable change in the style and composition of the papal court. When he arrived in 1462, there were thirty-three cardinals alive (most of them resident in Rome) presided over by the humanist Pope Pius II; in spite of recent increases in the Italian membership of the Sacred College, the Italian-born still did not quite outnumber the seventeen others. Francesco was one of those who switched his vote to Cardinal Pietro Barbo in August 1464,[14] so bringing about—on the whole to his benefit—the seven years of Paul II (1464–71), that eccentric Venetian patrician who managed to combine the qualities of both voluptuary and ascetic. He then lived through all but the final year of the pontificate of the Franciscan theologian Sixtus IV (1471–84), whose election in 1471, with Milanese political backing, he had also helped to bring about,[15] and whose reign saw the Italian majority in the college of cardinals growing fast and government falling largely into the hands of his nephews.

Papal nepotism does not appear to have worried Francesco at all; on the contrary, hearing the news of Cardinal Pietro Riario's death, early in 1474, he declared that he felt the loss as keenly as did Pietro's own brother; indeed he declared he had loved both Pietro and Girolamo Riario since the time their uncle

---

[11] '...la presentia et aspecto suo hè de tanta venustade et gravitade quanto may persona vidi' (Zambotti, *Diario ferrarese*, p. 58.)

[12] Cattanei, *Orationes variae*: see below, p. 93 for the passage in question and for other references to Francesco's good looks. On Cattanei (1462–1505) and his later career in the papal court see *DBI*, s.v.

[13] See Chambers, 'Housing Problems', esp. pp. 26–32; 'Arrivabene', esp. p. 407.

[14] According to G. P. Arrivabene, writing to Barbara on 1 September 1464, he had put the names of d'Estouteville and the cardinal *camerlengo* Ludovico Trevisan first: 'fece el Reverendissimo Monsignor mio in questa forma "Ego F. cardinalis eligo in summum pontificem Reverendissimum d. Rothomagen[sem]. Reverendissimum d. Camerarium. Reverendissimum d. Sancti Marci"' (ASMn, AG, b. 842, c. 331). Barbara wrote to marchese L. Gonzaga on 10 September 1464 that she had been informed (from another source) that 'S. Angelo' (Cardinal Carvajal) had nine votes, whereupon 'el Patriarcha', who had seven, acceded to Barbo: 'doppo, el Cardinale nostro glie dede la sua, che fu casone farlo papa' (ASMn, AG, b. 2098).

[15] According, in particular, to a letter of Giovan Pietro Arrivabene to Barbara, 11 August 1471 (ASMn, AG, b. 844, c. 222) quoted as 'from the Mantuan ambassador' by Pastor, *Storia dei papi*, II, pp. 432–3. The report sent to Milan by Nicodemo da Pontremoli recording how the votes were cast but not specifying each scrutiny, shows 'Mantoa' voted 'ad Rhoanno et vicecancellero' i.e. again for Cardinal d'Estouteville as first choice and for Rodrigo Borgia as second (ASMil, Sforzesco, cart. 68). Cardinals d'Estouteville and Monferrato both cast votes for Francesco.

was still a cardinal;[16] but he was alarmed at first by the increase in numbers,[17] a
fear shared by Jacopo Ammannati, a cardinal of the same vintage as himself.[18]
Their fears were exaggerated, however, because the death rate in the Sacred
College was rapid; when Francesco himself died in 1483, there were actually
fewer cardinals alive than there had been twenty years earlier. On the other hand,
of the total twenty-six in 1483, all but six were Italian. Domination of the Sacred
College by the aristocratic elite of Italy, and of the papacy by Italian political
interests, was well under way by then, and Francesco had made his own contribution to these trends.

Francesco Gonzaga's role in the papal court was never a dominant one, but he
performed the routine duties of a curia cardinal. He had on occasion to take his
turn at solemn liturgical ceremonies; for instance, he chanted the office in the
papal chapel on Christmas Day 1464 (not with great skill, but his shortcomings
evidently amused Paul II).[19] He pronounced the Palm Sunday plenary indulgence
in 1467 outside the church of Aracoeli, in view of the ancient Capitol,[20]
bawled—so Arrivabene implies—a solemn excommunication from the same
place a few days later,[21] and he recited the homily in the papal coronation of the
Emperor Frederick III in St Peter's on Christmas Day, 1468.[22] Whatever his
shortcomings in performance, Francesco seems to have become quite a stickler
for protocol. Agostino Patrizi, papal master of ceremonies since 1468, recorded
as Cardinal Gonzaga's opinion that 'cardinals should always precede the pope',[23]
and when informing his father in March 1477 of the award to him of the papal
honour of the Golden Rose, Francesco was careful to enclose instructions about

[16] Cardinal F. Gonzaga to Duke Galeazzo Maria Sforza, Rome, 26 January 1474: '…dicemo che nui
amassemo strettissimamente la bona memoria del cardinal de San Sisto et esso Conte avanti fussero in stato,
essendo la Sanctitate de Nostro Signore cardinale, che fu a tempo se puoteva iudicare non lo facevamo per
utilitate né fortuna ma per amore vero…successive in ugni lor grado li siamo stati affectionatissimi, e crediamo
de la morte del cardinale havere hauto non minore dolore che lo fratello proprio' (ASMil, Sforzesco, cart. 74).
[17] Cardinal F. Gonzaga to Barbara, 18 June 1473: 'De' cardinali chi cominciano venire da buon mercato, per li
doi exempli che toca la Signoria vostra io già buon pezzo me son avisto che cussì ha ad essere. E credo cum la
gratia de Dio pegioraremo ugni dì più, ma ho fatto pensiere che, se la dignitade del cardinalato invilirà, io me
farò vescovo. Se vescovi seranno abassati, io me atenirò ad cardinalato, perché necessario è che, manchando
uno, sia sublivato l'altro grado' (ASMn, AG, b. 1141, c. 363).
[18] Cardinal Ammannati to Cardinal F. Gonzaga, 11 August 1475: 'Numerus etiam nostri ordinis quantus sit
vides. Tantus is est, ut Episcoporum loco iam habeamur' (Ammannati, *Epistolae et commentarii*, fol. 300ʳ).
[19] Giacomo d'Arezzo wrote to Barbara of Brandenburg, 28 December 1464: 'Lo evangelio cantò lo
Reverendissimo Monsignore nostro et bene vero è che venendo a l'antimo de lo *Ite missa est* fece uno canto de
suo, lo qual Nostro Signore più volte gl'è ricordato subridendo' (ASMn, AG, b. 842, c. 394); Francesco in his
own account admitted 'al *Ite missa est* me imbrattai…durai gran fatica ad ussirne' (ibid., c. 328).
[20] Marasca to Barbara, Rome, 25 March 1467: 'Lo Reverendissimo Monsignore mio dominicha passata
proxima in Palmis, suso il tribunale fatto de nante ad Araceli per la quale se veda verso il Capitolio, e zoso per
le scale, pronunciò la indulgentia plenaria' (ASMn, AG, b. 843).
[21] This letter, of 1 April 1467, to Barbara, must be from Arrivabene, though the secretary for once made an
error, signing it as from the cardinal: 'cussì in vulgare non dico la lesse, ma cridoe come se suol fare in
arengera; bisognoe buon fiato e buona lena e certe, se li mantenne molto bene' (ibid.); however in a letter of 29
March Arrivabene had told her 'la giobia sancta lesse la excommunicatione in vulgare che foe una longa
scrittura, hebbeli buona voce e durolli bene' (ibid.).
[22] G. P. Arrivabene to Barbara, Rome, 26 December 1468: 'Nostro Signore li diede la beretta e la spatha…et
Monsignor mio disse la omelia' (ASMn, AG, b. 843); Pastor, *Storia dei papi*, II, doc. 91, p. 751.
[23] Patrizi, ed. Dykmans, *Cérémonial papal*, I, p. 185.

the reception ceremony it required.[24] It comes as no surprise to find that among his books was a compendium of papal ceremonial.[25]

Francesco also performed such routine duties as proposing or 'relating' candidates for provisions to benefices in the papal Consistory,[26] and welcoming foreign visitors. He was in particularly close attendance during the Emperor's short visit to Rome in the winter of 1468–9, as was only to be expected in view of his widespread German kindred: indeed were it not for Cardinal Francesco Piccolomini, who had inherited Pius II's close German and Imperial connections,[27] Cardinal Gonzaga might instead have been the virtual Cardinal Protector. He had accompanied Frederick III back to St Peter's after his visit to the Scala Sancta and also paid an informal call upon him.[28] He was again prominent during the visit of Duke Borso d'Este in 1471; together with Cardinal Marco Barbo he met Borso at Santa Maria del Popolo and an oration was given from an ornamental pulpit placed between them.[29] Likewise Francesco had frequently to provide social entertainment for fellow cardinals and other prelates, even on occasion for the pope, as happened most lavishly when Paul II chose to visit him in the palace at San Lorenzo in Damaso on the eve of Ascension Day 1468, an occasion almost immediately followed shortly afterwards by entertainment in his second residence, at Sant'Agata, for other guests including the Cardinal Vice-Chancellor.[30] With this powerful figure, Cardinal Rodrigo Borgia, Francesco seems to have been on prudently good if not close terms and continued his mother's custom of supplying him annually with sparrow-hawks.[31]

Among special duties assigned to him was the protectorship of the Benedictine Order of Monte Oliveto, whose mother house at Monte Oliveto south of Siena he visited in the summer of 1462.[32] The monks of this order served his title church of Santa Maria Nuova, and he was sufficiently concerned to take measures protecting them from the mob after the papal election in August 1464, for Cardinal

---

[24] Cardinal F. Gonzaga to Marchese L. Gonzaga, Rome, 23 March 1477: 'io alhora mandarò in nota la cerimonia cum che se haverà ad acceptare...più digna assai che la spada' (ASMn, AG, b. 846, c. 102); see p. 64.

[25] See I 745. Cattanei, *Orationes*, sig. c, stresses that Francesco valued ceremonial.

[26] See below, p. 43.

[27] See Strnad, 'Piccolomini', pp. 227–320 and 350–1 where an undated text is quoted addressing Cardinal Piccolomini as 'parens ac patrona nacionis Germanice'.

[28] G. P. Arrivabene to Barbara, Rome, 1 January 1469: '...Giobia sera el reverendissimo Monsignor mio andoe a visitare Suoa Maiestate la qual in quella hora manzava...entroe Monsignor mio nela camera suoa e li aspettoe forsi un terzo de hora prima che venessi dal luoco dove mangiava. Tandem venendo, Monsignor mio li fece reverentia et abrazaronose insieme' (ASMn, AG, b. 843).

[29] Fabrizio Ariosto's account of Borso's ceremonial entry, in his letter to Ercole d'Este, Rome, 3 April 1471, in Celani, 'Venuta di Borso d'Este', pp. 405–6.

[30] B. Marasca to Barbara, 1 June 1468: 'La vigilia de la Ascensa Nostro Signore venne a cena et a dormire a casa del reverendissimo Monsignore mio cum molte persone, maxime fanti. Se sforcessemo de farse honore, et in vero Sua Reverendissima Signoria ha lo habuto apresso lo pontefice e tuta la corte. Domane Sua Reverendissima Signoria dà dissenare e cena in Sancta Agata al Vicecanzeliero et al Monferrato...' (ASMn, AG, b. 843).

[31] E.g., Cardinal F. Gonzaga to Barbara, Rome, 5 April 1465: '...neli tempi passati Vostra Signoria ha continuato de donare al Reverendissimo Monsignore Vicecancelliere sparavieri...' (ASMn, AG, b. 842, c. 504); cf. G. L. Cattanei to Marchese Francesco Gonzaga, Rome, 9 April 1489: 'El vicecancellero, certamente amico nostro, dice ch'el Cardinale bona memoria solea esser suo fitador de fornimenti da sparaveri ogni anno' (b. 848, c. 30).

[32] G. P. Arrivabene to Barbara, 7 August 1462: 'heri el Reverendissimo Monsignor mio andoe a vedere el monasterio de Monte Oliveto dove foe visto da quelli relligiosi cum gran piacere' (ASMn, AG, b. 841, c. 677); see Table of Itineraries.

Pietro Barbo had been his predecessor as titulary, and a rumour circulated that he had left some of his possessions there.[33] Francesco's further interest in his titulary is little recorded, but he attended in the summer of 1467 the celebration of 'una certa beata' buried there, presumably Francesca Romana (d. 1440),[34] and in 1475 he took his mother's sister, Dorothea, Queen of Denmark, to see the church, including the monks' garden, in their tour.[35] As well as 'protecting' the Olivetan monks, its likely that he also became Protector of the Teutonic Knights.[36]

Francesco sat on the commission of inquiry concerning the canonization of the Franciscan 'seraphic doctor', Bonaventure (1221–74), in progress from 1475 to 1482, though it is not at all clear why Francesco should have been chosen for the job, apart from his possessing the name of the order's founder and the confidence of the Franciscan Pope Sixtus IV; in fact in 1479 and during the final hearings of the case (6 January–24 February 1480) he was not in Rome at all.[37] However, it may have been owing to his involvement in the *processus* that the last of the newly built chapels in the nave of Sant'Andrea at Mantua was dedicated in July 1482 to St Bonaventure, instead of being reserved for the cardinal's own tomb.[38] It must be acknowledged that Francesco contributed also to the cause of proclaiming the infant Simone of Trent, murdered in 1475, a holy martyr to Jewish rituals (in spite of the report of the apostolic commissar, Battista de'Giudici, which tended to absolve the accused of any responsibility for the crime): by supporting Bishop Hinderbach's promotion of the cult, Francesco indirectly helped to foster the persecution of Jews which accompanied it.[39]

Apart from these more religious involvements in administration Cardinal Francesco Gonzaga also had some major political responsibilities in papal service. One of these was his part in the organization of Pius II's abortive crusade against the Turks.[40] Born in the year of the Turkish victory over Christian forces at Varna and the accession of Mohammed the Conqueror as Ottoman Sultan, aged nine when Constantinople fell, and fifteen when Mantua was the seat of the papal diet meant to rally Christendom, it is not surprising that he became so

---

[33] Giacomo d'Arezzo to Barbara, 1 September 1464: '...andando voce che lo Cardinale de S. Marcho havia messo robba nel monasterio de S. Maria Nova, questi andarono lì, over parte de loro...et benché Nostro Signore non ce havesse roba, nondimancho Monsignore Nostro providde che quelli religiosi non hebbono violentia alcuna' (ASMn, AG, b. 842, c. 377).

[34] Cardinal F. Gonzaga to Marchese L. Gonzaga, Rome, 31 August 1467: '...me ne andai a disnare a Sancta Maria Nova per la festa de certa beata de la quale hanno lì el corpo li frati...' (ASMn, AG, b. 843, c. 421). On Francesca see Lugano, 'S. M. Nuova', pp. 139–53.

[35] G. P. Arrivabene to Barbara, 5 May 1475: '...a Monsignore parse monstrarli alcuni luogi et zardini del convento' (ASMn, AG, b. 845, c. 413).

[36] Letter of Barbara, 29 July 1465, (ASMn, AG, b. 2889, lib. 54, fol. 30ᵛ), cited in Chambers, 'Virtù militare', p. 218 n. 39.

[37] Marinangeli,'La canonizzazione di S. Bonaventura', esp. pp. 66–7; Stanislao da Campagnola, 'Le vicende della canonizzazione di S. Bonaventura', esp. pp. 245, 248 (on the first commission Francesco Gonzaga sat with Jacopo Ammannati and Giuliano della Rovere, and was nominated on the commission of August 1479 with della Rovere and Stefano Nardini). This appointment of Francesco is one of the few points about him which Donesmondi, *Storia ecclesiastica di Mantova*, II, p. 60, gets partly right.

[38] Johnson, *S. Andrea in Mantua*, docs. 45, 48, pp. 74–5. See also below, p. 90 n. 302.

[39] There is a grateful acknowledgment to him in the letter from Johannes Hinderbach, Bishop of Trent, to Barbara of Brandenburg, Trento, 29 December 1479 (ASMn, AG, b. 1402, c. 12). On Battista de'Giudici see also I 832; Battista's invective against Platina may imply that anti-semitic attitudes prevailed among some of the antiquarians and humanists in the cardinal's household. Gonzagan support of the cult of Simone is discussed in Chambers, 'Mantua and Trent', pp. 80–2.

[40] Chambers, 'Virtù militare', pp. 216–8.

actively involved. Francesco, who had the previous year taken part in the reception ceremony of St Andrew's Head and met Thomas Palaeologus, Despot of the Morea, was one of the cardinals consulted in the autumn of 1463 about ways and means to raise money for the crusade.[41] Exhorted by Pius II to play the part of 'a new St George',[42] he went back to Mantua that winter; local enthusiasm for the crusade and its taxes was mixed, but the Gonzaga regime was fully committed, and Marchese Ludovico even gave the cardinal two war horses when the latter visited him at Goito in February.[43] Francesco was one of the young cardinals most implicated as a military companion of the pope, obliged to equip his own war galley, and he set sail from Venice, calling at Pola on the way, to join the expedition at Ancona. Its cancellation, owing to the death of Pius II, was a setback also in the cardinal's career. After the election of Paul II he seems to have been less active and mobile for several years, only leaving Rome to make summer excursions into the Alban hills (he was lent, or rented, accommodation at Marino by courtesy of his friends the Colonna) until his appointment as cardinal legate to Bologna, Romagna and the Exarchate of Ravenna in 1471.[44]

The legation of Bologna was a key position in the papal state, and the holder had to play a delicate role in government alongside the dominant Bentivoglio family and the Council of the Sedici, the principal organ of civic authority. The post was normally bestowed on those highest in the trust of popes; among Francesco's recent predecessors were Cardinal Bessarion, from 1450 to 1455, and Cardinal Angelo Capranica from 1458 to 1467, both of whom had acted with considerable tact in supporting the *de facto* domination of the Bentivoglio and respecting the condominium of civic with legatine authority established in 1447.[45] Paul II's known wish to resume direct papal control of Bologna, and recent machinations of the mercenary captain Bartolomeo Colleoni, made the situation at the time of Francesco's appointment particularly delicate. But the pope's death required him to hurry back to Rome after little more than a week in Bologna; when Sixtus IV succeeded Paul in August 1471, a more peaceful prospect lay open, particularly because the new pope had good relations with— indeed some cause for gratitude to—Galeazzo Maria Sforza of Milan, a strong supporter of Giovanni Bentivoglio.

One of the points in recommendation of Francesco as legate must have been his own family's political weight in the region, their good relations with the Bentivoglio and their alliance with Sforza Milan. His legatine faculties were

---

[41] Letters from Rome of Giacomo d'Arezzo, 23 September, and of Cardinal F. Gonzaga to Marchese Ludovico Gonzaga, 5 October 1463 (ASMn, AG, b. 842, cc. 105, 54) quoted in Chambers, 'Virtù militare', p. 216 n. 10.

[42] 'Fate che ne veniati in puncto come un San Zorzo' were the pope's words G. P. Arrivabene reported to Barbara, writing from Nemi, 29 October 1463 (ASMn, AG, b. 842, c. 156); Chambers, 'Virtù militare', p. 216 n. 12. Pius had asked Francesco when he would leave for Mantua.

[43] G. P. Arrivabene to Barbara, Goito 13 February 1464 refers to the gift of 'due corsieri deputati a l'impresa contra il Turco' (ASMn, AG, b. 2402; Chambers, 'Virtù militare', p. 216 n. 19).

[44] The appointment was made on 18 February according to the Acta consistorialia (Eubel, *Hierarchia*, II, p. 41 n. 272) but the bull publishing it was deferred until 3 July: AV, Reg. Vat. 543, cc. 122–5, noted by Zippel, *Vite di Paolo II*, pp. 28–9 n. 5. A bull of Sixtus IV, dated 28 September, renewing the appointment, exists in ASDMn, Fondo Mensa vescovile, Pergamene, b. 2, no. 42.

[45] See in general Ady, *The Bentivoglio*, esp. pp. 48–50. On Bessarion's legation see Nasalli Rocca, 'Cardinale Bessarione', pp. 17–80. A study by Ian Robertson on Paul II and Bologna is shortly to appear in a monograph series of the University of Melbourne.

extended over a wide area of Emilia and central Lombardy, including Mantuan territory, where this superior jurisdiction might well have provoked serious conflict were it not for the fact that he also administered the bishopric of Mantua, and was in general compliant regarding the ecclesiastical policy of his father and of his brother Federico, who succeeded as marchese in 1478.[46] Even so these were times of great political tension. The problem about the future possession of Imola was one of the crises which Francesco faced, and he confessed to Duke Ercole d'Este of Ferrara in May 1473 (when Imola nearly passed to Florence) that he did not know what line to adopt concerning it.[47] But he was on close terms with Sixtus IV's nephew Girolamo Riario, who had been his guest in Bologna early in 1473,[48] and maybe this friendship helped to calm down alarm when Sixtus IV conferred Imola upon Girolamo. Francesco was journeying back to Rome at the time the news broke.[49] He remained in Girolamo's confidence and, to assist him at Imola, tried to recruit a Mantuan for the office of governor there, a man whom he declared would be firm but incorruptible.[50]

Francesco did not remain continuously in residence at Bologna. He was even absent when his position there was enhanced by possession of the bishopric in 1476, an event which was said to have caused popular rejoicing in the streets.[51] However, he did spend fairly long periods in Bologna, or nearby, during 1472–3 and 1478–9. For most of the time he was legate,[52] the work on the spot was done by his *luogotenente*, until 1475 an able canon lawyer from Mantua, Benedetto Mastino,[53] who was succeeded by Giovanni Alimenti Negri from Milan;[54] the auditor or law officer was Alvise Capra.[55] Nevertheless during the periods when he was personally resident at Bologna, Francesco does appear to have taken his

---

[46] See Chambers, 'Defence of Non-Residence', esp. pp. 616–22.

[47] Cardinal F. Gonzaga to Barbara, Ferrara, 25 May 1473: 'Essendo cum questo Illustre Signore in parlamento de' fatti d'Imola…li tochai che non sapeva anchor di certo che forma havesse a pigliare la cosa, né come havessi a governarmi, finché non era a Bologna' (ASMn, AG, b. 1228, c. 937). On the Imola problem in 1473, see Lorenzo de' Medici, *Lettere*, I, pp. 444–6; Robertson, '*Signoria* of Girolamo Riario', esp. pp. 88–95.

[48] G. P. Arrivabene to Barbara, Bologna, 31 January 1473: 'Questa matina aspettiamo qui lo conte Hieronymo a desnare…Monsignor ha terminato de tuorlo in casa, e dàlli doe de le camere suoe'; on 1 February he reported Girolamo's arrival 'qui in palatio, dove li erano apparichiate doe camere de Monsignor per la persona suoa' (ASMn, AG, b. 1141, cc. 284, 286).

[49] Giovanni de la Fiera wrote to Marchese Ludovico Gonzaga, from Rome, 9 November 1473, that he had written to tell Cardinal Francesco of the appointment (ASMn, AG, b. 845, c. 8).

[50] Cardinal F. Gonzaga to Marchese Ludovico Gonzaga, Rome, 19 January 1474: 'Lo magnifico Conte Hieronymo, el qual per mettere buon principio de governo ad Imola ha fatto discorso de trovare qualche huomo de auctoritate et experientia, tale che sia apto a conciliarli quello populo, e darli opinione de buon trattamento, me fa intendere che de presenti non li occorre persona apta a questo suo pensiere e designo se non Messere Amadeo da Castello, consigliere de Vostra Signoria' (ASMn, AG, b. 845, c. 207). He was not appointed; for Girolamo's governors see Robertson, '*Signoria* of Girolamo Riario', pp. 97–8, 115–7.

[51] Giovanni Alimenti Negri to Marchese Ludovico Gonzaga, Bologna, 22 August 1476: 'martedì proxime passato, nel qual pigliassemo la possessione del vescovato sollemnemente *sicut consuetum est*, fuoe fatto in questa citade grandissimo triumpho in sonare campane, fare fuochi, per ugni contrata, cridando tutti "Gonzaga! Gonzaga!" e facendo molti altri signi de alegreza' (ASMn, AG, b. 1141, c. 473).

[52] There is material for a monograph on Francesco's legatine administration, 1471–83, particularly in ASMil Sforzesco 68 (Romagna); ASMn, AG, b. 1141–2 (Bologna); and Francesco's surviving registers (particularly ASMn, AG, b. 3351), on which see below, n. 65.

[53] Giacomo d'Arezzo to Mastino, Rome, 9 August 1471, mentioning Paul II's confirmation of Francesco as legate (ASMn, AG, b. 844, c. 240); against the cardinal's wishes Mastino finally departed for Mantua to serve there as archdeacon: Chambers, 'Defence of Non-Residence', pp. 613–16.

[54] Negri (1439–99) was appointed on 19 June 1475, noted in ASMn, AG, b. 3351, fol. 22ʳ. On his later career see Partner, *The Pope's Men*, p. 162.

[55] On Alvise or Luigi Capra (1434–99) see *DBI*, s.v.

duties seriously, and to have derived some moral satisfaction from so doing. As legate his ecclesiastical jurisdiction extended far and wide, and he made clear his refusal to submit to pressures from the secular authorities—even his own father—where delinquent priests were concerned, priding himself on his clemency.[56]

In 1478–9 he had the task as legate of securing Bologna's dubious loyalty to the pope, during the aftermath of the Pazzi conspiracy and Sixtus IV's war against Florence; nor did he underestimate the difficulties involved, but expressed a belief that the Bolognesi would adjust themselves to events.[57] Although both his brothers Federico and Rodolfo Gonzaga were to serve on the Florentine side, and Giovanni Bentivoglio's pro-Medicean stance was obvious, Francesco seems to have radiated self-assurance and felt that he excelled himself in the discharge of his legatine duties; in a rare admission of private conscience, defending himself against Milanese suspicion of his divided loyalties, he exclaimed that at last he felt justified in holding the exalted office of cardinal.[58] It was no doubt partly thanks to Francesco that Sixtus IV did not enforce his censures against Bologna, and the Milanese agents there seem to have been impressed by his skill in speaking with two voices.[59]

After a difficult year and a half of legatine administration—in the summer of 1479 he had also to deal with an insurrection at Cento, when his suffragan bishop was assassinated[60] —Francesco spent most of 1480 in Mantua; he only returned to Rome in November of that year. In December 1482 he had a new commission as papal legate not only to Bologna but to the papal army then defending Ferrara against the Venetians and was again inspired, with a rather heavy jocularity, to emphasize to his brother Federico that ultimately his loyalty was towards the Church rather than to Mantua.[61] So far as his health permitted he took an active role: he inspected the defences of Ferrara, reported on skirmishes and rumours of attack, and even went out on a night patrol near the enemy lines, boasting in a letter that he was quite prepared to assume the role of a Moses or a Judas Macca-

---

[56] E.g., about a priest, possibly to be deposed, at Rivarolo, the cardinal wrote to his mother from Bologna, 4 November 1473: 'lasciamo stare che sopra la conscientia mia non voria tirarme questo peso quando facessi *de facto* e non *medio iure*; perché se bene ho di altri peccati, almancho sono de tal natura che quando a Dio ne chiamo "Misericordia" non dubito puncto me sono perdonati' (ASMn, AG, b. 1141, c. 259). For another example of his defence of clergy against lay prosecution, see below, p. 55.

[57] Cardinal F. Gonzaga to Marchese Federico Gonzaga, Bologna, 16 July 1478: 'Non sapiamo ne puotemo fare fermo iudicio de questi nostri bolognesi, perché *primum* tra lor sono diversi pareri. *Deinde* comprendemo habiano a mutare pensieri secundo li successi de le cose' (ASMn, AG, b. 1141, c. 516). See also Lorenzo de' Medici, *Lettere*, III, nos 275 and 302, pp. 14 n. 4 and 121 n. 2.

[58] E.g., he wrote, defending himself against Milanese suspicion of double dealing, to Marchese Federico Gonzaga from Bologna, 1 August 1478: '…la stantia nostra qui è procurare de mantenere questa citade come subdita de Sancta Chiesa in buona devotione e fidelitade…in questa terra dove ci conosscemo da tuti e come legato e come vescovo essere bene visti et amati, né altramente ne reputamo qui securi che se fussemo in Mantuoa…e dove fin qui ne reputiamo essere stato forse indigni del capello rosso, ce pareria puoi haverlo meritato, et haverne fatto honore a la casa che ce lo procuroe' (ASMn, AG, b. 1141, cc. 529ʳ–30ʳ).

[59] Lorenzo de' Medici, *Lettere*, IV, no. 30, pp. 58–60; Ady, *The Bentivoglio*, pp. 69–72.

[60] Chambers, 'Virtù militare', p. 219.

[61] Cardinal F. Gonzaga to Marchese Federico Gonzaga, Bolsena, 18 December 1482: '… Quella haverà ad stare sotto la obedientia nostra, e non mancharemo de mostrare quanta sia la facultate d'un legato apostolico, e bisognarà che vui obediate o voreti o no. Mai sì, che per esserne Vostra Signoria fratello, ultra li altri meriti suoi, non mancharemo de darli reputatione et honore nel campo sotto le doe bandiere de Sancta Chiesia e del papa che nui portamo. Pareravi, che nui siamo vechii nel mestiere. Hor assai habiamo mottegiato. L'è verissimo che nui haveressimo molto grato, che la Signoria Vostra se lì puotesse trovare personalmente' (ASMn, AG, b. 544, c. 112; filed as though from Bolzano).

beus.[62] He attended the Diet of Cremona in February 1483, and in the company of Alfonso Duke of Calabria, Ercole d'Este, Lorenzo de' Medici and other notabilities, planned a concerted offensive against the Venetians.[63] His self-assuredness in his role remained great, evidently; he even proposed—claiming it was not from ambition but for the honour of the papacy—that he should be granted legatine powers throughout the whole of Italy.[64] But the strain of continuous military and diplomatic activity may have been altogether too much for Francesco's constitution. Increasingly sick, but attempting still to follow the fortunes of the war of the papal league against the Venetians, which menacingly almost surrounded his brother's territory, he spent his last months incapacitated at Bologna, where he died in October 1483.

In the cardinal's later years personal information about him becomes rather less abundant. His more mature age and the deaths of his father (1478) and mother (1481) account partly for this, since letters tended to be fewer or at least less frank and intimate in content; relatively little original correspondence from Rome survives from his last two years there, 1481–2. On the other hand there are several registers of outgoing letters from the cardinal's chancery which survive, and these greatly supplement our information about his more official business during the limited periods they cover.[65]

(ii) The Milieu of Cardinal Gonzaga

Princes of the Church, like other mortals, cannot be understood in isolation from their human and physical surroundings. A staff of skilled officials and servants and palatial housing were generally considered essential to them if their duties were to be properly performed and their reputations magnified.[66] Some of Cardinal Gonzaga's *familia* were men of high calibre; their letters have already been quoted and their names will continue to appear throughout this study. Biographical details cannot be given in full here but a few individuals deserve to be singled out. Foremost among them was Giovan Pietro Arrivabene (1439–1504), the cardinal's secretary, who was still with him at his death, and whose judicious letters, those written in his patron's name as well as his own, may

---

[62] Cardinal F. Gonzaga to Francesco Maffei, Ferrara, 2 February 1483: 'Nui anche per fare l'offitio de Moisè, e forsi non mancho quello de Iuda Macchabeo, quando fusse bisognato, ne aviammo al rumore' (ASMn, AG, b. 2900, lib. 114, fol. 86ʳ), quoted in Chambers, 'Virtù militare', p. 220 n. 54.

[63] Bonatti, 'Dieta di Cremona', pp. 258–67; Chambers, 'Virtù militare', p. 220.

[64] Cardinal F. Gonzaga to Francesco Maffei, Bologna, 10 Februry 1483: 'E crederessemo in questo caso non fusse fuora de proposito, dicamo a reputatione e favore de la impresa e gloria de la sede apostolica, che *qui preest legatus huic expeditioni* se intendesse *legatus totius Italie*. Il che non dicemo per ambitione ma per augumento de honore de la dicta sede, quando el suo signo et officiale qui fusse de tal nome universal de legatione intitulato' (ASMn, AG, b. 2900, lib. 114, fol. 114ʳ).

[65] ASMn, AG, b. 2896, lib. 96, contains copies of over 560 letters (7 September 1479–13 February 1480); b. 2900, lib. 114 has over 450 letters (25 December 1482–10 April 1483). Another register, b. 3551, records particularly his administrative acts, and contains mandates, faculties, dispensations, letters of safe-conduct etc. issued between 1469 and 1483. It has been listed as the cardinal's legatine register, but the entries begin two years before his appointment to Bologna, and some derive from his authority in Mantua as bishop or as *primicerius* of Sant'Andrea etc.

[66] See, for example, Chambers, 'Economic Predicament', where I drew also upon Paolo Cortesi's *De cardinalatu*, on which see Dionisotti, *Umanisti*, esp. pp. 38–77, also (with extract in translation) Weil-Garris and D'Amico, *Renaissance Cardinal's Ideal Palace*; on *familiae*, see D'Amico, *Renaissance Humanism*, pp. 45–60.

account for a great deal of the respect accorded to the cardinal's mind and judgement.[67] Arrivabene, whose father (Pietro) and brother (Giovanni) were successively chancellors in Mantua, was both learned and efficient. He organized for the cardinal an exemplary writing office, training a number of assistants,[68] but writing most of the cardinal's personal letters in his own elegant hand, and sometimes also the official privileges issued in his name.[69]

A non-Mantuan ecclesiastical lawyer, Giacomo d'Arezzo, was another outstanding and long-serving official of the cardinal; he had formerly been vicar-general of Galeazzo Cavriani, Bishop of Mantua,[70] and after a short period of employment as Francesco's law tutor, he was appointed auditor or principal legal officer of the household in February 1462.[71] Giacomo, like Arrivabene, must have brought credit to the cardinal for his professional skill and also for his perceptive and entertaining letters to Mantua, which survive in abundance from the 1460s. Later on they become rarer; in fact, after 1469, by when he had become master of the household,[72] Giacomo almost fades from view. He accompanied the cardinal to Bologna in 1473, but his services as a jurist cannot have been much needed there, since the cardinal already had a well qualified deputy and legal auditor to order the business of the legation.[73] The only letters of Giacomo written at Bologna which survive are about his private affairs.[74] Back in Rome, there is a letter from him to Barbara of Brandenburg appealing for napkins and table-cloths in April 1475, but this sort of thing was perhaps rather degrading for a distinguished legal mind,[75] and it may be that Giacomo was content to allow his domestic role to be taken over by another individual, Francesco Maffei, who will be discussed below.

On the other hand Giacomo's legal expertise may have remained indispensable until the end, at least in Rome; in support of this is a letter of March 1477 in which the cardinal dismissed the idea that Giacomo might act as tutor to his brother Ludovico the protonotary, on the grounds that he was much too busy in the papal court.[76] Giacomo does not emerge as a personality so distinctly as do

---

[67] See Chambers, 'Arrivabene', *passim*.

[68] These included Aurelio Cornacchia, Bernardino Castigati and Stefano Girello; the latter became head of the legatine chancery at Bologna (ibid., pp. 400–4).

[69] Of two original privileges which survive, with impressions of the cardinal's seal, one dated at Rome 13 May 1475 (appointing Benedetto Mastino vicar-general at Mantua) is written by Arrivabene, the other issued at Mantua, 5 March 1480, is subscribed by him (Biblioteca comunale, Forlì, Autografi Piancastelli, fasc. 121). There are other examples in ASDMn, FCC, Pergamene, b. XXIII, nos 2588, 2590–1.

[70] He is mentioned as holder of this office, e.g., in letters of Marchese L. Gonzaga to the vicar of Revere, 3 April 1459 (ASMn, AG, b. 2886, lib. 32, fol. 65ʳ) and of B. Marasca to Barbara, Pavia, 16 February 1461 (b. 1621, c. 1017).

[71] Barbara to B. Bonatto, Mantua, 15 February 1462: 'ha etiam facto messer Jacomo da Arezo suo auditore' (ASMn, AG, b. 2888, lib. 49, fol. 72ᵛ). See also below, pp. 51–2.

[72] Chambers, 'Housing Problems', p. 22 n. 8.

[73] See above, p. 10.

[74] G. d'Arezzo to Barbara, 8 January 1473; to Marchese L. Gonzaga 31 May 1473 (ASMn, AG, b. 1141, cc. 374, 394).

[75] G. d'Arezzo to Barbara, Rome, 3 April 1475, explains that in the course of a discussion with Giovanni Arrivabene 'hebbi a ragionare secho de li bisogni della casa et infra li altri della grande necessità havevamo de tovale da tavola, guardanappi et tovale da mano per lo tinello de la famegla' (ASMn, AG, b. 845, c. 570).

[76] Cardinal F. Gonzaga to Barbara, Rome, 15 March 1477: 'Rincrescemi quella necessitate imposta a domino Antonio Bonatto di bisognarsi levare dal Reverendo et Illustre domino Protonotario mio fratello, e tanto più che non scio dove ne puoremo voltare a trovarli persona idonea, che certo niuno se ne occorre de presenti, né suso domino Jacobo d'Arezzo bisogna fare pensiere, havendo lui li officii che l'ha in Corte, e di pensieri in la mente che fuora de Corte non se puoriano adempire' (ASMn, AG, b. 846, c. 100).

Arrivabene and Marasca, but he had some distinguished family connections. He evidently enjoyed more prestige by just proclaiming himself to be an Aretine than by using his family name, which was Ottaviani; for he was related to Francesco Accolti of Arezzo, one of the most famous jurists in Italy, through the marriage of his brother (or more probably half-brother) Bartholomeo de Octavianis to Accolti's daughter. This is apparent from a letter in which the cardinal recommended Guido, a nephew of both Giacomo and of Francesco Accolti, who taught canon law at Pisa;[77] not long previously the cardinal had recommended Giacomo to Lorenzo il Magnifico, stressing among his claims for a benefice, his Tuscan origins and manifest goodwill towards the Medici.[78] Giacomo's death had occurred by 14 September 1483, just over a month before that of the cardinal himself; the forebodings of a letter which refers to his age and the gravity of his illness, in spite of the doctors' optimism,[79] are confirmed by a papal bull which, on account of his death, transferred one of his benefices to the cardinal's favoured chamberlain Ludovico Agnelli.[80] The inheritance claims of Gregorio, another nephew of Giacomo's, were supported by Bartolomeo Ottaviani, Francesco Accolti and even Lorenzo de' Medici, who all wrote on his behalf to Marchese Federico Gonzaga.[81]

The third most prominent figure—until he left to enter papal service in 1469—was the earlier master of the household Bartolomeo Marasca (d. 1487), another incessant and lively correspondent of Barbara of Brandenburg, one of the few priests in Francesco's entourage, and also one of the few persons from an unprivileged social background (his father was a fish-weigher in Mantua).[82] According to Bartolomeo Bonatto, the Mantuan ambassador in Rome writing just before Francesco's arrival there in March 1462, the mastership of the household was the most important office in a cardinal's *familia*, far exceeding that of the steward (*senescalco*, *sescalco*, *scalco*), whose only formal duty was to walk before the dishes carried to the cardinal's table.[83] The cardinal's steward until

---

[77] Cardinal F. Gonzaga to Lorenzo de' Medici, Rome, 6 April 1476, where Guido is described as 'nepote del clarissimo doctore messere Francesco et anche di messere Jacopo d'Arezzo nostro auditore e maestro di casa' (ASF, MAP, XLVI, 397). For 'Guitto' or 'Guitton Bartholomei de Octavianis de Aretio' see Verde, *Studio fiorentino*, p. 294; for Accolti see Messina, 'Francesco Accolti'.

[78] Cardinal F. Gonzaga to Lorenzo de' Medici, Rome, 10 January 1475: 'nui impetrassemo questa abbatia per lo eximio doctore messer Jacopo d'Arezzo auditore et maestro nostro di casa, parendone che per essere lui un huomo da bene, come siamo certi sapia la Magnificenzia Vostra, e per essere toscano, è sempre stato buon servitore de la casa vostra' (ASF, MAP, XIX, 450); Chambers, 'Cardinal Gonzaga in Florence', p. 245, n. 19.

[79] Giovanni Arrivabene to Marchese Federico Gonzaga, Mantua, 13 September 1483: 'El protonotario de Arezo era stato mancho male et lo medico ne faceva buon iudicio. *Tamen periculosa est etas*' (ASMn, AG, b. 2430, c. 705).

[80] AV, Reg. Vat. 635, fols. 227ᵛ–9ʳ, dated 18 kal. oct. 1483, i.e., 14 September. The benefice was the archpriestship of S. Maria in Arezzo, to which probably Giacomo was referring in a letter to Marchese Ludovico Gonzaga from Rome, 13 June 1466 (ASMn, AG, b. 843).

[81] Bartolomeo d'Arezzo to Marchese Federico Gonzaga, Arezzo, 21 March 1484 assumes the marchese had heard 'già più tempo fa la morte di messer Jacopo da Reço, maestro di casa…'; Francesco Accolti to the marchese, Pisa, 22 March 1484, justifies by rather sententious references to Cicero and St Paul, his intercession on behalf of Gregorio, his sister's son (ASMn, AG, b. 1102); Lorenzo's letter of 18 March 1484 (b. 1085, c. 90ʳ) is noted in Praticò, 'Lorenzo de' Medici', p. 167.

[82] Chambers, 'Marasca', pp. 265–7; for his zeal in his duties and entry into papal service see also pp. 267–8.

[83] B. Bonatto to Barbara, Rome, 1 March 1462: 'è officio de uno grande impazo, perché bisogna ordeni tuta la casa. Madisì, l'ha questa preheminentia che etiam è il più honorato homo de casa, et quando se manda le famiglie in contra ad alcuno, questo è il più digno, et nel vero se non è persona ben praticha, serà carico al signore, et ne segue de molti inconvenienti nela casa… Et dove è maestro de casa in casa de prelati, l'officio del seschalcho è per niente, se non de andare inanti al piatello. El maestro è quello ordina se faza cussì per el

1468, was a courtly young nobleman favoured by his mother, Baldassare Soardi,[84] whose role seems to have been rather more ample than Bonatto had suggested; whether the office was left empty for a while is not clear, but in his later years the cardinal had as his steward the Paduan humanist scribe Bartolomeo Sanvito.[85]

Another figure whose role in the cardinal's circle was longstanding if elusive, was Ludovico Agnelli, who had entered the *familia* as a well-connected young Mantuan noble in 1460,[86] but in the course of time came to pursue his own career in the curia while still retaining a role as one of Francesco's nominal chamberlains. His advancement seems to have come as part of the reward bestowed on Francesco by the Duke of Milan and by Sixtus IV for his help in the papal election of 1471, when Agnelli was promised the title of apostolic protonotary and a papal governorship, as well as a benefice at Pavia.[87] Francesco wrote strongly in his favour,[88] and the Milanese ambassador's comment seems justified, that Agnelli had unequalled access to the cardinal, his affairs and all his secrets.[89] Agnelli became governor of the Patrimony of St Peter, with its administrative base at Viterbo, and spent at least part of his time there,[90] though he continued to make himself very available for Mantuan or Gonzagan affairs. In the summer of 1478 Agnelli accompanied the cardinal to Bologna and was sent on from there to Mantua to visit the dying Marchese Ludovico.[91] Meanwhile his independent career progressed: he had become a clerk of the Apostolic Chamber in January 1478,[92] and in the winter of 1478 he was sent on a mission to the Emperor, whom he already served as a proctor in the papal court.[93]

Also gaining prominence from about the same time as Agnelli (i.e., after the departure of Marasca) was Francesco Maffei, one of the younger brothers of the

---

signore, cussì per la famiglia, et comitte ali spenditori et altri officiali il comprare de le robe et la dispensatione et li examina' (ASMn, AG, b. 841, c. 539).

[84] Signorini, 'Baldassare Soardi', esp. pp. 155–66.

[85] See below, pp. 59–62, 97.

[86] Protonotary F. Gonzaga to Barbara, Pavia, 22 July 1460: 'torò Lodovico de li Agnelli e Filipo de li Andriasi, li quali me pareno gaiardi ad ugni fatica, como besogna al tempo de lo studio' (ASMn, AG, b. 1621, c. 432, autograph); Agnelli himself wrote to Barbara, from Pavia, 2 May 1461 (ibid., c. 1055). The chronicler Andrea da Schivenoglia wrote of him 'era pure alevato in casa del cardinale' (MS BCMn, 1019, fol. 71ᵛ). He was the son of Carlo Agnelli, *collaterale* or military official for many years in Marchese Ludovico's service. The unsigned article in *DBI* provides little information about his long association with Francesco; more useful on his later career is Partner, *The Pope's Men*, pp. 161–2, 216–17 and *passim*.

[87] G.P. Arrivabene to Barbara, Rome, 11 August 1471: '…a domino Lodovico Agnello ha dato un suo priorato a Pavia di 800 ducati, ditto volerlo fare protonotario et darli el governo del patrimonio' (ASMn, AG, b. 844, c. 222).

[88] Cardinal F. Gonzaga to Galeazo Maria Sforza, Rome, 24 October 1471, urging his admission at Pavia 'per la longa e fidel servitute havemo ricevuto da esso d. Ludovico, el qual è stato xii anni nostro camarero…' (ASMil, Autografi, cart. 68).

[89] Nicodemo da Pontremoli to Duke Galeazzo Maria Sforza, Rome, 25 October 1471: '…gentil persona et veramente nostro. Item, in gratia de Monsignore nostro de Mantoa per modo che ha tutta la cura de li soe secreti et persona sua, in modo che apena poria senza lui' (ASMil, Sforzesco PE, cart. 68).

[90] Agnelli to Marchese L. Gonzaga, Viterbo, 4 September 1473: 'm'è stato necessario esser absente per molti giorni in visitar la provincia' (ASMn, AG, b. 845, c. 114). He evidently retained his interest in the Patrimony; there is a letter he wrote from Civitavecchia, 10 April 1481, to Cardinal Francesco, about the arrival there of a knight of St John who had beaten off a Turkish attacker (copy in ASF, MAP, XXXVIII, 134).

[91] Letters of Cardinal F. Gonzaga to Ludovico and Federico Gonzaga, 7 July 1478 (ASMn, AG, b. 1141, cc. 510–11).

[92] Hofmann, *Forschungen*, II, p. 93.

[93] Cardinal F. Gonzaga to Marchese Federico Gonzaga, Bologna, 18 December 1478 (ASMn, AG, b. 846, cc. 268–9).

apostolic scriptor Agostino Maffei, whose own part in the cardinal's affairs will be mentioned recurrently.[94] It is significant that whereas in the conclave of August 1464 the cardinal had had Arrivabene and Giacomo d'Arezzo as his conclavists,[95] in the conclave of 1471 he appointed Ludovico Agnelli and Francesco Maffei to attend on him.[96] Francesco Maffei's rise and advancement is not easy to document, but a safe-conduct was issued to him by the cardinal on 21 October 1469 as an apostolic scriptor and 'carissimus familaris et continuus commensalis';[97] he ingratiated himself partly by means of the various services he performed for Marchese Ludovico, including business committed to him in the important matter of Sant'Andrea at Mantua.[98] It was perhaps in view of this, that the cardinal granted his request to stay behind in Rome instead of accompanying him to Bologna and Mantua in the summer of 1472,[99] and he evidently enjoyed favour in the circle of Cardinal Pietro Riario.[100] Maffei travelled north the following year, presumably to join the cardinal's household in Mantua, but fell ill on the way, at Cesena.[101]

Some of the difficulty in tracing Francesco Maffei's ascendancy may be explained by the fact that he had not been (as had so many of the cardinal's *familiares*) a protégé of Barbara of Brandenburg, consequently he was under less obligation to write letters to her regularly. Only occasionally is he mentioned in the letters of others, as in the summer of 1476, when Giovan Pietro Arrivabene denied a rumour that he was dead,[102] or in November 1477 when he was named in an official letter of the cardinal as an apostolic scriptor and canon of St Peter's, as well as being the proctor in Rome of Cardinal Jacopo Ammannati.[103] Francesco Maffei seems eventually to have shared, undermined or usurped much of Giacomo d'Arezzo's domestic authority: at the end of 1478 the cardinal actually referred to Maffei as master of the household, when sending him ahead

[94] See below, pp. 45–6.

[95] G. P. Arrivabene to Barbara, Rome, 1 September 1464: 'Quello dì (28 August) al tardo introrono questi Reverendissimi Signori Cardinali in conchiave, e col Reverendissimo Monsignor mio andammo messer Jacomo et io' (ASMn, AG, b. 842, c. 331).

[96] G. P. Arrivabene to Barbara, Rome, 6 August 1471: 'Cum Monsignore mio sono entrati in conclavi domino Francesco Maffei et domino Lodovico Agnelli' (ASMn, AG, b. 844, c. 221).

[97] ASMn, AG, b. 3351, fol. 98ʳ (93ʳ). I was wrong in previously attributing to him a letter of 19 October 1467; this was from a different Franciscus Mapheus: Chambers, 'Housing Problems', p. 23 n. 9.

[98] See Chambers, 'Sant'Andrea', *passim*, and for some of his other services below, pp. 46, 76.

[99] Giovanni Arrivabene to Marchese L. Gonzaga, Rome, 19 July 1472: 'Intendo che in questa partita de Monsignore, messer Francesco di Maffei ha havuto licentia de remanere a Roma, et cussì è restato' (ASMn, AG, b. 2413, c. 535).

[100] Cardinal Pietro Riario wrote on his behalf to Marchese L. Gonzaga, Rome, 10 July 1473, and so did Antonio Venier, Cardinal of Cuenca, describing him as an apostolic scriptor and *familiare* of Cardinal Gonzaga (ASMn, AG, b. 845, cc. 51–3). There are papal letters copied in the registers with the name 'F. de Maffeis', e.g., (1478) AV, Reg. Vat. 582, cc. 17ᵛ, 108ʳ–17ᵛ.

[101] G. P. Arrivabene to Barbara, Marmirolo, 7 August 1473: 'Heri sera, da Rolandino di Maffei se intiese che domino Francesco di Maffei se era infirmato in via, et che se faceva portare da Cesenna a Bologna, dove Monsignor ha scritto ch'el sia acceptato in casa' (ASMn, AG, b. 2415, c. 451).

[102] G. P. Arrivabene to Marchese L. Gonzaga, Narni, 23 July 1476: 'io non ne replicarò altro de domino Francesco Maffei; non fu vero moresse; anti, è sempre stato sano' (ASMn, AG, b. 845, c. 689); Cardinal Arcimboldi wrote to the marchese from Foligno, 2 September 1476: 'Messer Francesco Maffey da Verona ce ha pregato che racommandiamo alla Vostra Illustrissima Signoria Horlando suo patre' (ASMn, AG, b. 845, c. 711).

[103] ASMn, AG, b. 3351, c. 32ʳ.

to Mantua,[104] although by this he may have intended only mastership of the household establishment at Bologna, while Giacomo d'Arezzo remained in the senior role as caretaker at Rome.

During the cardinal's long absence in northern Italy in 1479–80, Agnelli and Francesco Maffei, who meanwhile had both returned to Rome,[105] were the two persons there most in his confidence, judging from his letter register from the second half of 1479. This contains nearly forty letters addressed to Maffei alone, seven to Agnelli alone, and nine addressed jointly to them both (including one in which the cardinal acknowledged their appeal that he should return soon to Rome). On the other hand, there are only two letters addressed jointly to Maffei and to Giacomo d'Arezzo, and only four to Giacomo alone.[106] Agnelli had been instrumental in securing papal absolution for Marchese Federico and Gianfrancesco Gonzaga, who had been excommunicated on account of their military service with Florence;[107] there are various original letters written by him and by Maffei from Rome in 1480, including one in which Maffei notes that Cardinal Rodrigo Borgia had tried to take advantage of him in horse trading.[108] During the cardinal's final period of residence in Rome, his reliance upon Francesco Maffei must have continued to grow; suggestive evidence of this lies in the correspondence while serving in his legation to the papal army engaged in the War of Ferrara; the cardinal's surviving letter register from January to April 1483 contains seventy-eight letters to Maffei, though most of them are about political and military developments rather than domestic or private concerns.[109]

Notably scarce in the cardinal's household, however, were any senior prelates or domestic chaplains. Bartolomeo Marasca, master of the household, may have filled—or tried also to fill—a spiritual role until he passed into papal service in 1469, but evidence suggests that Francesco found the companionship of this unctuous and possibly pederastic priest, a favourite of his mother's, irksome to say the least and as time went on tried to distance himself from him.[110] The nearest person Francesco ever had in the household approximating to the prelate full of gravity and pious counsel so much desired for him by Marchese Ludovico,[111] and a species he declared was hard to find,[112] was—from 1463 to

---

[104] Cardinal F. Gonzaga to Marchese Federico Gonzaga, Cento, 28 December 1478: 'mandiamo de là domino Francesco Maffei, nostro maestro de casa qui, per fare le provisione opportune': ASMn, AG, b. 846, c. 391, dated 1479 *more mantuano* (cf. errors in Chambers, 'Housing Problems', p. 40 n. 130).

[105] G.P. Arrivabene wrote to Marchese Federico Gonzaga, Bologna, 23 May 1479: 'Monsignore mio heri rimandoe domino Francesco di Maffei a Roma' (ASMn, AG, b. 1142).

[106] ASMn, AG, b. 2900, lib. 116, *passim*, and fols 102[r–v] for the letter dated at Bologna 12 November 1479 to Maffei and Agnelli: 'sapiamo che l'uno e l'altro de vui desidera la venuta nostra a Roma. Tamen per lo presente non vediamo modo alcuno.'

[107] Letter of 26 November 1479: ibid., fols 122[v]–3[r].

[108] F. Maffei to Marchese Federico Gonzaga, Rome, 19 July 1480: 'el zè uno cavallo che ha il vicecancellieri, che ne domanda ducati 200...vero è che è caro, che non doveria valere più che cento ducati' (ASMn, AG, b. 846, c. 405).

[109] ASMn, AG, b. 2900, lib. 114, *passim*.

[110] Chambers, 'Marasca', esp. pp. 275–7.

[111] E.g., Marchese Ludovico to Cardinal F. Gonzaga, Goito, 17 April 1462: 'Quattro cose non voglio tacervi. La prima, che vogliati haver in casa uno prelato pratico in corte e bono' (ASMn, AG, b. 2097: draft or copy of letter).

[112] Cardinal F. Gonzaga [autograph] to Marchese Ludovico Gonzaga, Tivoli, 14 August [1463]: 'in questa corte non ge sonno tanti prelati degni quanti forsse existima la Illustre Signoria Vostra, e quelli ce sono non voleno stare com altri' (ASMn, AG, b. 843, misfiled under 1468); cf. Giacomo d'Arezzo's letter to the marchese, Tivoli, 13 August 1463, who confirms '...insino ad hora non gl'è parso trovare tale che satisfacesse

1467—Giovanni Stefano Bottigella (c. 1410–76), a canon lawyer of noble birth from Pavia, who had held various offices in Rome under Pius II.[113] Bottigella had met Francesco at Pienza in May 1462,[114] and again in the autumn at Monte Oliveto, when he wrote, as both his own opinion and that of Cardinal Nicolaus Cusanus, that Francesco was mature beyond his years.[115] He was evidently well known to the Gonzaga family and a particular friend of the cardinal's uncle Alessandro, upon whose death he reported Francesco's sorrow as well as his own.[116] But Bottigella refused to play a leading role in the household,[117] and although he attended the cardinal back to Mantua and in his sea voyage to Ancona[118] and remained with the household at least another three years, he wrote to Mantua only seldom and does not appear to have played a very positive role in the cardinal's affairs. In October 1466 he was appointed Bishop of Cremona,[119] and finally left Rome at Easter 1467.[120]

As time went on, it seems probable that the tone of the cardinal's household became increasingly secular. This is not to say that it lacked clerics. Indeed the will names as many as eighteen persons bearing the prefix 'dominus' before their names (W 26–7). A few of these may have been serious scholars, such as Pietro Marsi, but the majority look at best like administrators with a qualification in canon law, useful to him as supernumeraries of Giacomo d'Arezzo; the more disreputable may have been little else but benefice-seeking parasites. Among the category of clerical administrators were Alvise Capra (1437–99) and Alvise or Luigi Tosabecci, both of whose names will occur in connection with the will and inventory. Capra, originally from Milan, had entered the cardinal legate's administration at Bologna;[121] Tosabecci, however, had a much more long-standing connection with the household; in earlier years he was used occasionally

a la mente della Signoria Vostra', but first mentions the possibility of Bottigella (ASMn, AG, b. 842, c. 227). G. P. Arrivabene reported to Barbara on 18 September that Bottigella had been invited at the time the papal court was at Tivoli (b. 842, c. 148).

[113] Cardinal F. Gonzaga to Marchese L. Gonzaga, Rome, 5 October 1463: 'Io ho tuolto el protonotario Buttigella in casa, parendome persona docta e costumata, et anche vechio cortesano et de bona reputatione…' (ASMn, AG, b. 842, c. 54). On Bottigella see also P. Craveri in *DBI*, s.v., though his Gonzaga connections are not mentioned.

[114] Marasca to Barbara, 14 July 1462 (ASMn, AG, b. 2397).

[115] Unsigned letter to Barbara in his hand dated at Monte Oliveto 5 November 1462 (ASMn, AG, b. 1100, c. 140); of Francesco he declared 'non pare giovene ma vechio sensato', citing in support the 'Cardinale de Sancto Petro ad Vincula, homo sapientissimo'.

[116] Bottigella to Barbara, Rome, 29 January 1466: 'quello sancto homo qual tanto me amava…Il mio…Monsignore ne ha havuto un smesurato dolore et ha rasone, perché li volea bene…' (ASMn, AG, b. 843).

[117] Bottigella to Barbara, Rome, 22 October 1463: 'Aviso bene Vostra Excellentia, che'l Reverendissimo Monsignore prefato non me ha tolto al governo de soa famiglia, né strecto ad questo, perché in vero non saria possibile ad mi, per la complexione mia debile qual non poria patire il caricho di tanta cosa' (ASMn, AG, b. 842, c. 74; similar to Marchese Ludovico [in Latin], ibid., c. 73).

[118] Bottigella to Marchese L. Gonzaga, Rome, 2 September, and to Barbara, 13 September 1464, gives the latter a rather faint-hearted picture of the cardinal, as nervous at sea ('un pocho temete il mare') and sweating in the heat of Paul II's coronation ceremony (ASMn, AG, b. 842, c. 415).

[119] G.P. Arrivabene to Barbara, 8 October 1466, already warned Barbara 'el protonotario nostro ha havuto Cremona' (ASMn, AG, b. 843).

[120] G. P. Arrivabene to Barbara, Rome, 19 May 1467: 'el vescovo de Cremona partì el dì de Pasca per andare a li bagni di Viterbo, dove, dimorato circa quindeci dì, intende de aviarse verso Lombardia' (ASMn, AG, b. 841, c. 666: thus filed owing to misreading of the date as 1461).

[121] In a letter to Girolamo Riario from Bologna, dated 24 November 1479, the cardinal refers to 'messer Alvise Capra canonico ordinario de la chiesia de Milano nostro auditore' (ASMn, AG, b. 2896, lib. 96, fol. 119ᵛ). See *DBI*, s.v., and below, pp. 69, 97–114 *passim*.

as the cardinal's agent travelling between Rome and Mantua,[122] and he is described as a doctor of canon law and auditor of the cardinal, in a letter of appointment dated at Rome 18 September 1476, whereby he was made one of the cardinal's proctors for matters concerning the cathedral of Mantua (of which he was a canon);[123] but how much of his time was spent in the cardinal's immediate entourage is impossible to reckon. A long-standing chaplain of the cardinal—but 'chaplaincies' did not necessarily imply much in the way of spiritual administration—was Stefano Caccia of Novara, an abbreviator of the papal chancery, who seems like Capra and others to have helped to represent the cardinal's good relations with the Sforza regime of Milan.[124] But little has come to light about Caccia or about most of the clerical *familiares* named in the will. One of long standing was Giovanni de la Fiera;[125] another was Ludovico Grossi, who had been made a papal *cubicularius* after the conclave of 1471 and by 1478 had been a chaplain of the cardinal for a long time;[126] his name was rather tainted by scandal.[127]

So far these remarks have been mainly confined to a few leading and professional personalities in Francesco's entourage; there were of course many others at lower levels. The number mentioned by name in the will (W 24–7) amounts to almost seventy, the majority of whom are vaguely categorized as *camerarii* or *familiares* or *continui commensales*, but include servants such as the macebearer and the *credenzario* or keeper of the *credenza* (presumably the cupboards or closets of silverware and other vessels), down to the *sartor, tonsor, botigherio* and *canevario*, not to mention the *apparichiatori* and *parefrenarii*; even so, some individuals must have been excluded—and there is no mention for instance of cooks, scullions and lesser menials. Nor does the will refer to *scudieri*, but these younger lay attendants, 'squires' or perhaps bodyguards, were presumably included under the general category of *familiares*. Often mentioned in the earlier correspondence, *scudieri* continued to wait on Francesco in his later years. In 1479 he wrote of a German *scudiere* who had died suddenly, perhaps infected by plague,[128] and in 1482 he recommended one who had served him for over two

---

122 Cardinal F. Gonzaga to Barbara, 25 May 1466, notes he has heard from Tosabecci and Carlo da Rodiano in Mantua that they had on his behalf asked her for 'el damaschino brochato d'oro per doe dalmatiche' (ASMn, AG, b. 843); on 8 June 1466 he wrote to Marchese Ludovico that 'messere Alvisio Tosabece' would tell him about a lawsuit brought against the mother of 'Francesco de Godini mio famiglio' (ibid.); G. P. Arrivabene to Barbara, Rome, 21 November 1466 noted his return to Rome (ibid.); they both mention his being sent to Mantua with news in letters from Albano, 1, 7 September 1470 (b. 844, cc. 90, 113).

123 ASDMn, FCC, Pergamene, b. XXIII, no. 2588.

124 Cardinal Francesco refers to him 'carissimo nostro capellano' in a letter of 15 April 1472 to Simonetta, and of 3 February 1473 to Duke Galeazzo Maria Sforza (ASMil, Sforzesco, cart. 69, cart. 178). Cardinal d'Estouteville wrote of him to Bona of Savoy, Rome 30 September 1480, as 'abbreviator apostolico et capellano antiquo del…Cardinale di Mantoa…cortesano antiquo et servitore già longo tempo del prefato Monsignore de Mantoa' (ASMil, Sforzesco, cart. 88).

125 See below, p. 116, n. 100.

126 Giacomo d'Arezzo to B. Mastino, Rome, 9 August 1471 (ASMn, AG, b. 844, c. 240); Cardinal F. Gonzaga to Marchese Federico Gonzaga, Bologna 10 October 1478, refers to him as 'mio capellano essendo stato cum nui longamente' (ASMn, AG, b. 846, c. 242).

127 As well as Grossi's illegitimate child, to which Carlo Uberti refers in a letter to Marchese Ludovico Gonzaga, Mantua, 25 October 1471 (ASMn, AG, b. 2413), his provision in 1478 to San Tommaso, Mantua, enforced by the cardinal's authority, provoked scandal (Chambers, 'Defence of Non-Residence', pp. 620–2).

128 Cardinal F. Gonzaga to Marchese F. Gonzaga, Dosolo, 16 February 1479: '…un nostro scudiere todescho el qual, amalato, se mischioe cum tuta la famiglia e sedette la sera suso la nostra sedia presso al fuocho. Lui se ne morse fra doi dì' (ASMn, AG, b. 2104).

years but now wanted to live in a secular court.[129] The *scudieri* had a prescribed place in his funeral procession, following after the chamberlains.[130]

Earlier in 1483, when Francesco as cardinal legate travelled from Ferrara to the Diet of Cremona, his retinue was said to consist of eighty-one persons.[131] No list of the personnel survives from earlier dates, but it is worth noting that when Francesco accompanied Pius II to Viterbo in the spring of 1462, only two months after his first arrival in the papal court, his entourage was much the same size, for the figure then quoted was eighty-two (with fifty-four horses and mules).[132] Some months earlier Bonatto, the Mantuan ambassador in Rome, had been advised by various cardinals that sixty persons and a retinue of forty horses would be the appropriate maximum,[133] and Pius II later quoted the same figures, emphasizing there should be no liveried attendants ('better a virtuous few than a vicious crowd' he warned).[134] In his austere but unimplemented reform proposals, Pius permitted only forty persons and a cavalcade of twenty-four for the cardinals created by himself (previously created cardinals were to be allowed sixty and a cavalcade of forty); his programme would also have proscribed—among other things—superabundant banquets, overstocked libraries, and wall-hangings and decorations which portrayed women or stories without serious moral content.[135] Fortunately for Francesco he did not have to face sacrificing such pleasures, but even from the start, he had disregarded the informal advice passed on by Bonatto about numbers in his household and also flouted the pope's injunction not to clothe his retinue in livery: for his escort certainly travelled to Rome with Gonzaga livery in March 1462.[136] But his transgression of the new norms, by employing between seventy and eighty persons, created no outrageous scandal; indeed, it was not at all excessive by comparison with the average in the early sixteenth century.[137]

---

[129] Cardinal F. Gonzaga to his nephew Francesco Gonzaga, Rome, 13 May 1482, on behalf of 'Francesco da Gazo nostro scudiere' (ASMn, AG, b. 846, c. 497).

[130] See Appendix 3, no. 4. For individuals who were probably *scudieri* see W 24, 26; I 445–7.

[131] 81 *boche* but 71 horses, so P. Spagnoli reported to Marchese Federico Gonzaga, Ferrara, 17 February 1483 (ASMn, AG, b. 1231, c. 180). These figures were modest compared with Duke Alfonso of Calabria's retinue of 207, even if Giovanni Bentivoglio had only 25.

[132] Marasca to Marchese L. Gonzaga, Viterbo, 28 May 1462: 'adviso Quella como se retrova havire otantadoe boche e cinquantaquatro cavalli overo bestie computando le mule e muli' (ASMn, AG, b. 841, c. 741).

[133] Bartolomeo Bonatto to Marchese L. Gonzaga, Rome, 17 December 1461: 'mi sono strecto cum più cardinali per intendere il parere suo…pare che venendo venga honorevole, ma poi assetato, non tenga per adesso più che 40 cavalchature, 30 comuni cavalli et X altre bestie, tra mule et muli da soma; che somamente sono necessarie XX scuderi al più; uno prelato…VI over octo capelani, quatro parefreneri; poi, tra cogo, aparechiatori, spenditori et famiglii de stalla, impire il numero fin a LX boche. Et che supra tuto havesse uno maestro de casa che fusse homo de reputatione' (ASMn, AG, b. 841, c. 287ʳ).

[134] Bartolomeo Bonatto to Marchese L. Gonzaga, Rome, 3 January 1462: '…ch'el non faza livere de recami, né divise a quelli vole siano la famiglia propria del cardinale, perché sono cosse non conveniente a preti, né ad nui piace, et che per niente qua el non passi 60 boche et 40 cavalchature. Serà uno bello stato et mediocre, et serà meglio, et questo il laudamo se fondi in li pochi virtuosi che in li molti viciosi, che quelli pochi li farano più honore' (ASMn, AG, b. 841, c. 486ʳ).

[135] Haubst, 'Der Reformentwurf', pp. 188–91, links the programme with the announcement of the pope's crusading project in the autumn of 1463.

[136] G. P. Arrivabene to Barbara, Florence, 13 March 1462: 'Havendose hoggi a intrare in Fiorenza, el Reverendissimo Monsignore mio fece ordine che ciascuno se mettesse li vestiti e mantelli de la livrea' (ASMn, AG, b. 1100, c. 85), in Chambers, 'Cardinal Gonzaga in Florence', Appendix, doc. 1, p. 88.

[137] Possibly about 150; even the figure suggested by Paolo Cortesi was as high as 140 or 120: see Chambers, 'Economic Predicament' p. 29; Weil-Garris and D'Amico, *Renaissance Cardinal's Ideal Palace*, p. 100 n. 15.

Numbers doubtless fluctuated according to time and occasion, particularly among the larger categories of household staff, the lesser chamberlains (*cubiculari*) and squires (*scudieri*), grooms (*parafrenarii, apparichiatori*) and the rest who made up an armed bodyguard. Their function was certainly not only decorative; they could involve a cardinal's household in little less than street warfare in fifteenth-century Rome, as is recorded between Francesco's household and that of the Venetian ambassador, Niccolò da Canale, in 1465: a micro-historical episode which may be worth recording briefly.[138] A servant of the ambassador had come to collect a horse-cloth, but the cardinal's tailor had not yet finished it, and the tailor's assistant, Guido, knocked the other man's hat off. In return, Guido was attacked near the ambassador's house; he countered this with a sword blow. The cardinal assured the ambassador that Guido, although a Mantuan, was not his servant but the tailor's, and had never eaten nor slept in his house and now was forbidden to enter it. But matters had gone too far. A son of the ambassador had exchanged insults with another of the tailor's assistants; at night one of the cardinal's *scudieri*, Gaspar de la Fiera, was attacked, also an *apparichiatore* called Muzza, caught urinating in the night outside the ambassador's house, was wounded. The cardinal's *mulatieri* then launched an assault; Niccolò da Canale, enraged by these events and by catcalls like 'porci veneciani alla marina', called for a show of force and demanded that eight or ten of the cardinal's servants should be hanged. Matters reached the pope's ears, and it cannot have been easy for Francesco to calm the situation ('Dio sa quanta discrecione ho usato', he wrote).

Probably Francesco's establishment was largest in the middle period of his career, the time when his opulent style was most commented upon; when he arrived at Bologna as papal legate in July 1471 the Bolognese chronicler estimated he had about eighty horses in his retinue.[139] Supposing that their proportion to persons was as at Viterbo in 1462 (and this is also supposing that many travelled by waggon or on foot) the total *comitiva* then would have been well over a hundred, and excluded persons in his service who were not involved in the journey.

* * *

However much importance may be attached to the cardinal's *familia*, it was family in the sense of relatives that dominated Francesco's career and usually—in spite of the scruples expressed about his duty to represent papal authority—determined his priorities: he affirmed in letters this overriding commitment to the Gonzaga regime in a political sense,[140] but sheer affection towards his kindred seems also to have been a mainspring. His mother, Barbara of Brandenburg, the addressee of so many letters from himself and members of

---

138 Cardinal F. Gonzaga to Marchese L. Gonzaga, Rome, 1 June 1465 (ASMn, AG, b. 842, cc. 513–14).

139 *Corpus chronicorum Bononiensium*, p. 430.

140 E.g., to Marchese Federico Gonzaga he wrote from Bologna on 21 July 1478: 'voressimo più presto subire *mortem propriam* che veder in lo stato e casa un minimo disturbo' (ASMn, AG, b. 1141, c. 522); see also the letter quoted above, p. 11 n. 61, and Cattanei's remarks about Francesco's piety towards *parentes* and *patria* (*Orationes*, sig. c iiii).

his entourage, was the central inspiration of this,[141] but towards his father it is clear he was also anxious to be filial and obliging, and not to let their relations be spoilt—for instance—by conflicts between lay and clerical jurisdictions in Mantua,[142] although Ludovico did express himself forcefully against his son's presumption in one particular case, pointing out that it was by virtue of the cap he himself wore as marchese that Francesco got his red hat, and not vice-versa.[143]

This warmth of family feeling was also applied to his younger brothers, each of whom at different times was welcomed as Francesco's guest. Gianfrancesco, who had recently gained distinction for jousting at the court of King Ferrante of Naples, arrived at Marino and then Rome in the autumn of 1466.[144] He had fallen ill and took almost a month to recover,[145] during which time he was looked after with great solicitude by the cardinal, who spent hours at his bedside, ordering warm clothes and other consolations including music to be provided for him.[146] Gianfrancesco was with him again in Rome in 1469,[147] during Francesco's illness in the early summer of 1472 and again for Carnival in 1477.[148] Rodolfo (born in 1451), for whom the cardinal expressed equal tenderness (being worried in 1467 lest he should come to harm as a professional soldier in France and Burgundy)[149]

---

[141] Upon receiving news of Barbara's death Francesco wrote from Rome two grief-stricken letters to Federico; on 16 November 1481 he affirmed his belief '...non vediamo altro refrigerio, se non la consideratione del suo ben vivere, e de la christianissima e devota terminatione suoa...il che ne fa firmamente credere l'anima suoa essere fra li spiriti beati collocata' and on 20 November 'né sapiamo dove voltarne se non al nostro Signore Dio, e pregarlo che se digna tuti nui dare animo patiente a sapere supportare tanta percossa' (ASMn, AG, b. 846, cc. 465^r, 467).

[142] See, e.g., Chambers, 'Defence of Non-Residence', esp. the letter of 31 July 1466 (ASMn, AG, b. 843) at p. 609, App. I, p. 627.

[143] Marchese L. Gonzaga to Barbara, Dosolo, 26 July 1470: '...non deliberamo finché vivemo comportare che né esso cardinale né alcun altro sia signore de Mantua...havemo cussì cara la beretta nostra com'el cardinale el suo capello, perché la beretta nostra ha dato il capello a lui, ma non il suo capello ha dato la beretta a nui' (ASMn, AG, b. 2891, lib. 65, fol. 73^v).

[144] G. P. Arrivabene to Barbara, Marino, 24 August and from Rome, 30 September 1466 (ASMn, AG, b. 843); on 18 October Arrivabene reported his arrival: 'mercorì matina havessemo qui lo Illustre signor messere Zoan Francesco, el qual gionse a Marini prima che de la venuta suoa havessemo certeza alcuna. E stata grande consolatione a lui et al Reverendissimo Monsignore mio...' (ibid.).

[145] Marasca to Barbara, 21 October 1466: 'regratia messer Domenedio che poi se dovea infirmare, è infirmato nele mane del suo Reverendissimo fratello e de tanti soi servitori' (ASMn, AG, b. 843). Various letters from Arrivabene, Marasca, the cardinal's doctor Vincenzo Cerroni, and others, report Gianfrancesco's progress and gradual recovery (ibid., *passim*).

[146] G. P. Arrivabene reported on 28 October 1466: 'El Reverendissimo Monsignor mio gli ha fatto fare una turcha de brocchato d'argento fodrata di martori e zibellini, perché qui non haveva portati panni del verno' (ASMn, AG, b. 843). Giorgio de la Strata wrote on 20 October: 'el ge ha apparato la camera dove el stà tuta de razi, el lecto cum il capelleto glie donò la Illustre Signora Dorothea. Heri matina essendo in lecto lo Illustre messer Zoan Francesco, el Cardinale glie venne apresso et stetero cussì più de due hore a cuzare insieme. L'è certo a tuti nui altri una grande allegreza vederle insieme' (ASMn, AG, b. 843); see also Giorgio's letter of 22 October, below, p. 70 n. 157.

[147] Marasca to Barbara, Rome, 1 January 1469: 'aspetiamo lo illustre domino Zohanefrancesco de zorno in zorno' (ASMn, AG, b. 843); also letters from Gianfrancesco Gonzaga, Rome, 21, 28 February, 8 March 1469 (ibid.).

[148] E.g., letters of Gianfrancesco Gonzaga to Marchese Ludovico, Rome, 31 May and 8 June 1472; to Barbara, Rome, 24 February 1477 (ASMn, AG, b. 844, cc. 325−6; 846, c. 157).

[149] Cardinal F. Gonzaga to Barbara, Rome, 11 March 1467: 'L'è vero che a me piacerìa ch'el fosse bene collocato in qualche digno luoco, e non me despiacerà questo quando le cose de Franza e de Bergogna fossero in più quieto stato...de là, non è usanza de fare presoni ma de amazzare che se piglia; ritrovandose lui novo fra gente incognita me stringe la tenereza de l'amor a temere che non incorresse qualche gran pericolo...se ho questa tenereza non se maravillii Vostra Signoria, essendo dormito cum me tanto tempo et allevato cum me' (ASMn, AG, b. 843).

was his guest in 1476 and from August to October 1477; for part of this time he was lent the use of the cardinal's house at Viterbo.[150]

Later, Francesco's youngest brother, Ludovico (born in 1460), came under his special care, being destined like himself for a career in the Church. Ludovico received the title of Protonotary in the autumn of 1471,[151] at the age of eleven (slightly older than his elder brother had been in 1454), which favour probably represents another gesture of gratitude by the newly-elected Pope Sixtus IV towards the cardinal of Mantua and his family. During his long stay in Mantua in the summer of 1473, Francesco took Ludovico with him to the castle of Marmirolo,[152] and the choice of Bologna (rather than Pavia) for Ludovico's canon law studies was presumably made because of Francesco's position as cardinal legate, although Francesco was not in residence when Ludovico began studying there in 1477.[153] During the cardinal's final period of residence at Rome, in 1481–2, Ludovico lived as a member of his elder brother's household,[154] though he came back to Bologna on his own in the summer of 1482.[155]

There is less evidence of close contact between Francesco and his sisters, but his sentiments towards them were also warmly expressed. In 1467 he was reported to have spoken strong words against Galeazzo Maria Sforza for his jilting of Dorotea, fearing that it would lead to her death,[156] and when this duly happened he was clearly much distressed. He tried to offer his father some spiritual consolation,[157] but confessed to Barbara he could not bear to look often at some handkerchiefs she had sent to him in Dorotea's memory;[158] he also received, and may have specially commissioned, several poems about this tragic event, which remained among his books (I 841–2). Eleven years later, Francesco

---

[150] Francesco Sicco to Marchese L. Gonzaga, 13 August 1477 (ASMn, AG, b. 846, c. 159), and letters from Bartolomeo Riverius to Barbara, Rome, 10 September, and from Rodolfo to Marchese L. Gonzaga, Rome, 2 October 1477 (ibid., cc. 161–2). On the house in Viterbo, see below, p. 26.

[151] Giovanni Arrivabene wrote from Rome, 2 September 1471, 'io spero partirme fra tri zorni et portare le bolle del Illustre domino Lodovico, et me ha bixognato commenciare la cosa fin a fare la supplicatione, perché a farlo protonotario non era dato principio alcuno' (ASMn, AG, b. 844, c. 247).

[152] See below, p. 93.

[153] There exist letters of January-April 1477 from Ludovico and Giovanni Guidotti, his chaplain at Bologna (ASMn, AG, b. 1141, cc. 473–96). Ludovico was also accompanied by Ruffino Gablonetta, whom he describes as 'scholare de rason canonico e familiare mio' in a letter of 14 August 1477 (b. 2418); Ruffino was a nephew of Giovan Pietro Arrivabene, who wrote of him to Barbara on 25 March 1475 as 'un mio nepote...giovene de circa XX anni' (b. 845, c. 464).

[154] E.g., Alessandro Arrivabene to Marchese Federico Gonzaga, Rome, 27 November 1481: 'giunsi qui ad salvamento e ritrovai li Reverendissimo Monsignor Cardinale et lo Reverendo et Illustre Monsignor Protonotario sani benché anchor assai mesti per la morte de la bona memoria de la Illustrissima Madonna commune genitrice' (ASMn, AG, b. 846, c. 420).

[155] Ludovico to Marchese Federico Gonzaga, Cento, 23 August 1482, explaining that he was taking refuge there from the plague scare (ASMn, AG, b. 846, c. 610); there is also a letter dated at Bologna 3 October 1482 (b. 1142).

[156] Giacomo Trotti to Borso D'Este, Rome, 11 April 1467: 'El cardinale de Mantoa a la aperta dice che suo patre nì lui nì alcuno suo fratello nì altri de casa sua mai vorà bene ad Argo [code name for Galeazzo Maria]...l'è stato lui et non altri cagione de la morte de madonna Dorothea sua sorella' (ASMod., ACE, Ambasciatori, Roma, b. 1). On Dorotea see Signorini, *Opus hoc tenue*, pp. 48–51.

[157] Cardinal F. Gonzaga to Marchese L. Gonzaga, Rome, 28 April 1467: '...me persuado sia da la miseria de questo mundo transferita nel choro de le beate virgine' (ASMn, AG, b. 843).

[158] Cardinal F. Gonzaga to Barbara, Rome, 20 May 1467: 'Ringracio Vostra Signoria de questi dece fazzoletti che La me ha mandati per memoria de la benedetta anima de la mia quondam dilectissima sorella, li quali, benché siano belli e molto gientili, nondimeno per adesso ho fatto reponere un puocho da parte, per non havere cagione de vederli molto spesso che me serìa una continua renovatione de dolore' (ASMn, AG, b. 843).

was likewise moved to grief by the death of Cecilia.[159] Meanwhile, he expressed his pride in the nubile attractiveness of Barbarina, describing her as one of the beautiful women of Italy, but concerning his youngest sister, Paola, his humour was less delicate, holding out little hope for her short of a miracle, in an allusion to her physical deformity.[160] This sort of crude joke, even concerning a close relative, may have been typical of him; another was reported by a Milanese ambassador in 1478, comparing favourably the physical handicaps of his father with those of Federico da Montefeltro.[161]

Cardinal Francesco Gonzaga, it needs to be added, was even in the paternal sense a family man. He had a son named Francesco after himself (later nick-named the 'Cardinalino'), who was born, probably in 1477, to a certain Barbara, who subsequently married Francesco, son of Antonio da Reggio (a building contractor and carpenter in Gonzaga service).[162] Just conceivably Barbara was the sister of the chamberlain Carlo Canale, a somewhat opaque character who was later to marry Cesare Borgia's mother.[163] How generous Francesco was to his former mistress is not clear: a letter she wrote after his death to Marchese Federico (asking that a job be found for her husband)[164] may imply that she had resorted to him quite often; but there is no doubt Francesco felt strong paternal affection towards her child. He followed with concern the course of the baby's illnesses,[165] secured his legitimation by the Emperor's authority[166] and lavished gifts upon him, even, in 1478, his house in Mantua, to which was added two adjacent properties bought for 2000 ducats and the country property of Bigarello.[167] To be near his infant's nursery may well have been one of the cardinal's motives for remaining so long in Mantua in 1480; after the death of Barbara of Brandenburg, who seems to have devoted herself to the 'Cardinalino',

---

[159] Cardinal F. Gonzaga to Marchese L. Gonzaga, Rome, 27 April 1478 (ASMn, AG, b. 846, c. 198).

[160] Cardinal F. Gonzaga to Barbara, Rome, 8 July 1474: 'la qual [Barbarina] è de tanto singulare belleza che se puoria mettere a parrangone cum tute le belle donne d'Italia…non so che me posso sperare de quest'altra [Paola] che non è de quella belleza, salvo se quella beata Catherina non havesse operato molto per miraculo.' He added, more charitably, 'è anchora molto tenera' (ASMn, AG, b. 845, c. 230).

[161] Lorenzo de' Medici, *Lettere*, III, p. 53 n. 12.

[162] See Chambers, 'Francesco "Cardinalino"', esp. pp. 5–7. The date of the marriage is unknown, but was before, probably long before, October 1483.

[163] On Canale see *DBI*, s.v. Recently I came upon a possibly suggestive letter of G. P. Arrivabene to Barbara of Brandenburg, Rome, 28 August 1475, quoting the cardinal's reaction to his mother's wish to find a husband for Canale's sister: 'Parlai col Reverendissimo Monsignor mio de quanto la Signoria Vostra me scriveva del maritare la sorella de Canale. La suoa Signoria disse la ringratiassi de la cura pigliava de questa garzona, che tuto sapeva se faceva per amore suo. Per se non haveva designo de darla ad alcuno di suoi, né ad altro…' (ASMn, AG, b. 845, c. 496). Also, once when he heard the baby was ill, it was—significantly, maybe—Carlo Canale whom the cardinal chose to send to Mantua from Bologna, as he wrote on 4 October 1479 to Antonio Bonetto: 'mandamo là Canale, a fine che lui vedesse in che termino el stesse' (ASMn, AG, b. 2896, lib. 96, fol. 49ᵛ).

[164] Barbara 'da Rezo' to Marchese F. Gonzaga, Mantua, 5 December 1483: 'Essendome mancata la speranza del nostro Reverendissimo Monsignore, non scio più dove ricorrermi se non da la Illustrissima Signoria Vostra.' She requested 'che Quella si digni provedere mio marito di qualche officio' (ASMn, AG, b. 2430, c. 445).

[165] Correspondence about the shortcomings of the wetnurse and fear that the child might catch smallpox, continued in October-November 1479 (ibid., fols 50ʳ–131ʳ *passim)*.

[166] Chambers, 'Francesco "Cardinalino"', pp. 7, 31 nn. 17, 18.

[167] Ibid. p. 6, p. 31, nn. 14–16. Bigarello had still to be legally alienated from the *prepositura* of San Benedetto, but for this and the transference of the Mantuan house, the cardinal had been assured by by his sister-in-law Margherita of Bavaria that he had Marchese Federico's approval, according to her letter dated at Goito, 1 August 1478 (ASMn, AG, b. 2895, lib. 88, fol. 33ʳ⁻ᵛ). In August 1479, however, Margherita was alarmed that the cardinal planned to make 'il suo bastardo' his heir: see Chambers, 'Francesco "Cardinalino"', p. 31 n. 17.

he expressed thanks to the marchese for his offer to take on the responsibility, but insisted none the less on making independent arrangements.[168] A knighthood was conferred on the child, who was even brought to visit his doting father at Ferrara, in spite of the war, early in 1483.[169]

As for the physical setting of Cardinal Gonzaga's life, as the Table of Itineraries will show, it very frequently changed. An appreciable amount of his time was spent in different rented accommodation during his first five years in Rome, and in temporary lodgings during his various journeys and vacations;[170] nevertheless before long he accumulated several homes. The villa or *vigna* attached to the church of Sant'Agata dei Goti on the southern slope of the Quirinal Hill was conferred upon him in April 1463,[171] and although it did not meet his need for a base in central Rome fairly near to St Peter's, it was useful as a healthy retreat: he was already there early in May 1463,[172] and continued to make occasional use of it, particularly to escape from summer heat or from health hazards such as plague in the city;[173] he also used Sant'Agata sometimes for entertaining.[174] It must be emphasized, though, that Sant'Agata was a relatively small house, and Francesco never seems to have gone there in winter, except for the patronal feast day, on 5 February.[175] This event Sixtus IV was noted attending in 1482, although there is no suggestion that the pope was received in the adjacent house, which was just a comfortable summer retreat for the cardinal and his favourites.[176]

Meanwhile, in March 1468 Paul II conferred on the cardinal as his main residence in Rome the palace adjacent to San Lorenzo in Damaso (which became his third Roman church),[177] formerly inhabited by the munificent Cardinal Ludo-

---

[168] Cardinal F. Gonzaga to Marchese Federico, Rome, 8 December 1481: 'Ringratiamo etiam grandemente essa Vostra Excellentia de la offerta fatta de tuore Francesco in castello in le camere suoe, et havemo bene gratissimo che Quella per nostro rispecto se digni ricogliere in tal affectione quello suo servitore piccolino…El putto faremo pur governare nela casa che Quella gli ha donata, cum le persone necessarie et cum li ricolti suoi de Bigarello' (ASMn, AG, b. 846, c. 437). See I 435–6, for some nursery furnishings.

[169] Cardinal F. Gonzaga to Marchese Federico Gonzaga, Ferrara, 8 January 1483: 'per fare condure de qua lo nostro Francesco ne siamo rimasi cum la magior admiratione del mundo come de cosa ad nui incognita et inexpectata' (ASMn, AG, b. 1231, c. 3); Pietro Spagnoli recorded his arrival, and the cardinal's delight over the knighthood, in a letter of 24 January (ibid., c. 110). See also below, p. 49.

[170] Chambers, 'Housing Problems', pp. 21–58, *passim*; see also Table of Itineraries. On Francesco's various lodgings in Florence see Chambers, 'Cardinal Gonzaga in Florence', pp. 241–4 and *passim*, and in Ferrara, see below, p. 103 n. 41.

[171] Marasca to Barbara, Rome 14 April 1463 (ASMn, AG, b. 842, c. 186); Chambers, 'Housing Problems', pp. 32–3 and 51, doc. 16.

[172] G. P. Arrivabene to Barbara, Rome, 12 May 1463: '…per pigliare qualche excercitio va a le fiate a quello luoco de Sant'Agatha, el quale, essendo pur remoto da l'altre habitatione come è, li piace summamente, e credo li giovarà' (ASMn, AG, b. 842, c. 145).

[173] E.g., G. P. Arrivabene to Barbara, Rome, 9 July 1474: 'per fugire questi caldi adesso per la magiore parte se sta a Sancta Agatha, che è stantia più frescha' (ASMn, AG, b. 845, c. 153ᵛ); similarly 7, 24 May 1476 (b. 845, cc. 618, 627); 9 July 1477 (b. 846, c. 37).

[174] See above, p. 7 n. 30; also, for example, G. P. Arrivabene to Barbara, Rome, 14 May 1476: 'Monsignor cum circa L. persone se ridusse dominica a Sancta Agata, dove sta più sequestrato da le facende' (ASMn, AG, b. 845, c. 621).

[175] Giovanni Arrivabene to Marchese L. Gonzaga, Rome, 5 February 1475, refers to 'questa sua festa de S. Agata' (ASMn, AG, b. 845, c. 441).

[176] '…exivit pontifex ad Agatense sacellum in Quirinalis collis clivo positum, quod commendatum est amplissimo patri Francisco Gonzage, diaconi cardinali, in cuius coniunctas edes, satis commode constructas, estivo tempore cum carioribus suis, vitandi estus et urbane molestie causa, secedere consuevit' (Gherardi, *Diario romano*, ed. Carusi, p. 36).

[177] Ibid., pp. 37–9.

vico Trevisan, Patriarch of Aquileia, and described in 1462 as 'a paradise'.[178] It was this house which Paul II graciously visited, and where he stayed the night, on the eve of Ascension Day, 1468.[179] More will be said about these Roman houses in another context, concerning building and other works;[180] meanwhile it is important to recognize that San Lorenzo in Damaso became Francesco's main address in Rome and in contemporary sources is always intended rather than Sant'Agata, unless the latter is specifically named.[181] Francesco also bought several small properties in Rome, as his will demonstrates (W 37), but these were presumably for the accommodation of staff or other dependents.

His Mantuan house had been conferred on Francesco as early as 1460,[182] but he had rather less use for it after becoming a cardinal; he stayed more often at his father's castle of Marmirolo, near Mantua, during his return visits and in 1466 had given instructions that his own house should be vacated by all except a care-taker.[183] Since becoming bishop that same year, moreover, Francesco was entitled to use the episcopal palace in Mantua; during his subsequent visits he did so, but also used his own house for entertaining.[184] During his extended sojourns at Mantua in 1479–80 the house was again in full use, and accommodated the nursery household of his infant son, to whom the titulary ownership had been transferred.[185] Perhaps the presence of this infant helps to explain why his solicitous grandmother, the widowed Marchesa Barbara, was moved from Sacchetta to spend the last few weeks of her terminal illness in this house, dying there on 7 November 1481.[186] But the cardinal presumably stayed, or spent more of his time, in the bishop's palace, and his various official letters signed between January 1479 and January 1480 from 'Mantue in domibus residentie nostre' probably refer to this official residence.[187]

Apart from houses in Rome and Mantua, Francesco acquired at different times various other residences. In 1462, to please Pius II, he had bought a site and began building a house in Pienza;[188] and in 1474 he bought from Cardinal Forteguerri a house in Viterbo, perhaps with a view to visit regularly the baths there.[189] As papal legate of Bologna he was entitled to live in apartments provided in the Palazzo Pubblico, which constituted the right-hand block in the

[178] Guido de'Nerli to Barbara, 29 March 1462 (ASMn, AG, b. 841, c. 624, text in Chambers, 'Housing Problems', doc. 3 p. 43).
[179] As well as his letter to Barbara noted above (p. 7 n. 30) Marasca wrote similarly to Marchese L. Gonzaga, Rome, 1 June 1468, and specified ' ... Quella sera che Nostro Signore cenò qui in Sancto Lorenzo, volse che lo Reverendissimo Monsignore cenasse cum seco...'(ASMn, AG, b. 843).
[180] See below, pp. 87–8, 90–1.
[181] Many of the cardinal's official letters (e.g., those registered in ASMn, AG, b. 3351) are dated 'Rome in domibus habitationis [or 'residentie'] nostre apud Sanctum Laurentium in Damaso'.
[182] Chambers, 'Francesco "Cardinalino"', p. 6. Formerly used by the Protonotary Guido Gonzaga, it was situated where the Accademia Virgiliana stands (Pecorari, 'Il palazzo', p. 14). See above, p. 24 n. 167.
[183] See below, p. 40.
[184] Chronicle of Andrea Schivenoglia, 8 October 1472 (MS BCMn, 1019, fol. 71ᵛ); and May 1473: 'si era alozato in lo veschovato de Mantoa, dentro da Mantoa, ma ogne dì si staxia la corte del gardenalo e la corte del lo Illustrissimo messer lo marchexo e di fiolli ogne dì in piaxire e in trionfe' (ibid., fol. 74ᵛ). Letters are signed 'Mantue in nostro episcopale palatio' in August 1473 (ASMn, AG, b. 3351, fols 142ᵛ–3ʳ).
[185] Chambers, 'Francesco "Cardinalino"', p. 6; above, p. 24 nn. 167–8.
[186] Signorini, 'La malattia', pp. 11, 18 n. 47, quotes a copy made after the cardinal's death of the dispositions of Barbara's executors (ADMn, Fondo Capitolo della Cattedrale, b. 15).
[187] E.g., ASMn, AG, b. 3351, fols 44ʳ–74ᵛ.
[188] Chambers, 'Housing Problems', pp. 28–31. It was transferred to Cardinal Ammannati in 1469.
[189] Ibid., p. 38.

same complex of buildings (on the north side of the Piazza Maggiore) from which the secular authority of the Sedici operated. This official residence, complete with courtyard and private garden, had been established in the time of Cardinal Anglic Grimoard in the 1360s, but it had undergone many improvements, particularly c. 1425–8,[190] and Francesco is said to have added some of his own.[191] Many of his letters are signed 'Bononie in palatio residentie nostre', and in was in these imposing premises that Girolamo Riario came to stay with him early in 1473;[192] though for some periods when he was afraid of plague or sedition he preferred to stay in the monastery of the Crociferi (crutched friars) just outside the city,[193] or even at the episcopal castle of Cento. All these different locations will be important to bear in mind when reviewing the cardinal's role as a *mecenate* and collector, and the final disposition of his affairs.

* * *

This outline has not portrayed a prelate of conspicuous spiritual gifts, even though a profound piety was attributed to Francesco in the oration at his funeral;[194] nor will the chapters which follow. Even when stricken by illness or some other personal crisis, Cardinal Gonzaga's religious practices seem to have been limited to conventional, expiatory devotions and observances. In November 1466, when his brother Gianfrancesco was ill, the cardinal vowed to send to the Madonna of Loreto an image, presumably of silver, costing 300 ducats;[195] even before his own illness in the spring of 1472 he was intending to visit Loreto on his way to Bologna.[196] During his illness he made a new vow to the Madonna, and he did in fact stop at Loreto on his journey in July of the same year,[197] one of the few occasions on which he is recorded as having his confessor in attendance, when he made his ex-voto offerings in tangible form.[198] In 1478 he was recommending the Madonna of Loreto to his brother Federico, who promised to comply with a benefaction, although he felt two miracle-working Mantuan

---

[190] Alidosi, *Instruttione*, pp. 116–17; Cavazza, 'Il palazzo', p. 113 n. 2, quotes an extract from a letter of 1428—said to be in the cathedral archives at Siena—from Jacopo della Quercia, praising 'un maestro il qual se chiama Fioravante quale à fatto un palagio bellissimo al cardinale e Lechato in Bolognia, molto ornato…' (I owe these references to Mark Pritchard).

[191] See below, p. 87 n. 283.

[192] Letters in ASMn, AG, b. 1141–2 and registered copies of official acts in b. 3351, esp. fols 66^r–74^r, during 1479. On Riario's visit, see above, p. 10, n. 48.

[193] G. P. Arrivabene to Marchese Federico Gonzaga, Bologna, 25 September 1478: '…per la revolutione de la luna…heri sera se ridusse de foura al monastero di crosari' (ASMn, AG, b. 1141, c. 564).

[194] '…ad extremum usque fati diem nil agere tentasset nisi prius christiano de more psalmos immurmurasset: humilesque Deo preces effudisset…' (Cattanei, *Orationes*, sig. c).

[195] Marasca to Barbara, Rome, 12 November 1466: 'Lo Reverendissimo Monsignore ne ha habuto grandissimo affano, et ha fatto voto al Nostra Donna de Loreto de mandargli una imazene de ducati trecento' (ASMn, AG, b. 843).

[196] G. P. Arrivabene to Barbara, Rome, 30 March 1472: 'Lo viagio nostro serà per la Marcha per andare a Sancta Maria de Loreto' (ASMn, AG, b. 844, c. 304); in a letter to his father of 10 April 1472 Francesco also announced this intention (ASMn, AG, b. 844, c. 336^v).

[197] Bartolomeo Bonatto and G. P. Arrivabene to Marchese Ludovico Gonzaga, Rome, 14 June 1472: '…e raso ch'el sia, andarà ad visitar un luoco di Nostra Donna di consolatione, al qual se ha gran devotione, et nela infirmitate suoa se li votoe' (ASMn, AG, b. 844, c. 322).

[198] G.P. Arrivabene to Barbara, Seravalle, 19 July 1472: 'venerì che staremo a Loreto Monsignore dice volersi confessare e communicare, e per questo ha conducto seco lo confessore suo' (ASMn, AG, b. 844, c. 390); on the ex-votos, see below, p. 84.

Madonnas had almost stronger claims upon him;[199] one of these, the Madonna dei Voti, soon attracted Francesco's attentions as well.[200] The cardinal also professed a special devotion to St Sebastian, probably as a precaution against plague;[201] he visited Assisi in 1472,[202] and again in August 1476 upon the anniversary of Sixtus IV's coronation, but it is not recorded whether the shrine of St Francis, his patron, aroused in him any intense feelings of veneration.[203] He was said to have received the sacraments with singular piety and reverence during a brief remission from his illness, just over a month before he died, and again on his deathbed.[204]

Relics and reliquaries are among the objects (though not in a large quantity) recorded in the inventory, but Francesco's credulity was not unlimited, or at least, seems to have been subject on at least one occasion, to the sceptical opinion of his secretary. This was when they were inspecting some alleged relics at Luzzara and Gonzaga in 1473, and were quite unconvinced about a supposed finger bone of St Catherine.[205] However, it was supposedly Francesco himself who discovered at Mantua, walled-up in the small church of San Paolo adjacent to the cathedral, a further supply of the Holy Blood of Christ (cherished already in the church of Sant'Andrea, and the subject of a famous theological debate during Francesco's first year in Rome).[206] The chronicler Andrea da Schivenoglia gives the date of this discovery as March 1479, without mentioning Francesco, who would, however, have been in Mantua at that time.[207] Francesco may have been eager to enhance the cathedral's reputation as a sacred shrine and to authorize the safe-keeping of the relic in the sacristy, but it was his brother Ludovico who resolved to build a special chapel for it.[208] In fact, Francesco's own religious benefactions and his building activities relating to other churches—which will be discussed later on—all seem to have been on a fairly limited scale.

Francesco received Holy Orders (up to the rank of deacon) from the Bishop of Mantua, Galeazzo Cavriani, on 26 February 1462;[209] and it is possible that he was

---

[199] Marchese F. Gonzaga to Cardinal F. Gonzaga, 19 November 1478: 'ho etiam visto quanto la me scrive de quella corona de Nostra Donna…né è dubio che Nostra Donna, et a S. Maria da le Gratie e a San Petro, monstra di continuo miraculi…nondimanco, se poi parerà pur che se facia il voto de la corona a S. Maria de Loreto, me acordarò sempre ad ogni parere e consiglio d'essa Vostra Reverendissima Signoria' (ASMn, AG, b. 2895, lib. 90, fol. 102ʳ).

[200] See below, pp. 90, 99.

[201] In his letter of 16 March 1473 (see below, p. 89 n. 298) he affirms 'la mia speciale devotione'.

[202] G. P. Arrivabene to Barbara, Foligno, 18 July 1472: 'heri matina andammo ad Assisio ad visitare quella devotione, et hoggi, udita messa a Sancta Maria di Angeli, ritornammo…' (ASMn, AG, b. 844, c. 388).

[203] G.P. Arrivabene to Marchese L. Gonzaga, Narni, 19 August 1476, and Assisi, 26 August 1476 (ASMn, AG, b. 845, cc. 690−1).

[204] Aurelio Cornacchia to G. P. Arrivabene, Bologna, 8 September 1483: 'In quest'hora, che è la XIIIᵐᵃ, vole comunicarse et ha mandato per la famiglia…intendo che è stato una compassione a vederlo, perché s'è ingienochiato et ha tolto lo Corpus Domini cum una devotione mirabile' (ASMn, AG, b. 1142). See also below, p. 97 n. 8.

[205] G. P. Arrivabene to Barbara, Viadana, 15 October 1473 (ASMn, AG, b. 2415, c. 1071); Chambers, 'Arrivabene', p. 417.

[206] Ludovico Gonzaga, Bishop-Elect, to Bernardino Castigati, Sabbioneta, 10 March 1489: '…fecessimo votto de edificare una capella in Santo Piero, dedicandola al Sangue de Christo quale hè in epsa chiessia, che fu ritrovato in Sancto Paulo dalla bona memoria del Reverendissimo Cardinale nostro fratello' (ASP, AGG, b. 41/4, reg. 4), cited in Rossi, 'I medaglisti', p. 28 n. 1; Carnevali, 'Un culto parallelo', pp. 73−4.

[207] MS BCMn, 1019, fol. 84ᵛ.

[208] See Ferrari and Zanata, 'La capella', esp. pp. 83−5.

[209] Signorini, Opus hoc tenue, p. 39, from Schivenoglia, MS BCMn, 1019, fol. 39ᵛ; the chronicler insists that Francesco had received none of the minor orders previously, but if this is so it is difficult to understand why he

eventually ordained priest; he acquired the appropriate liturgical vestments;[210] in 1475 he may have heard the deathbed confession of Cardinal Philippe de Lévis of Arles;[211] but the text is very ambiguous. Even Giovan Pietro Arrivabene fails to clear up the uncertainty; in a letter of 1480 he specifically uses the word 'priest', referring to Francesco, but qualifies it as though he simply meant a cleric and, as such, subject to canon law.[212]

A prince of the Church was not necessarily expected to be an ascetic, an evangelist or a model pastor in order to be considered worthy of his office and status. Francesco Gonzaga had no such qualities, yet neither he nor others excluded the possibility that he might one day become pope; he hinted about this in an autograph letter to his mother, when he was travelling down the Po, bound for Pius II's crusade; the context is obscure, and concerns an unnamed third party; no out-going letter from Barbara clarifies the matter.[213] He mentioned it to his father, too, when trying to allay doubts about his suitability to become Bishop of Mantua.[214] His own election was even considered a possibility in 1471, after Paul II died, although the Mantuan astrologer Bartolomeo Manfredi, asked for an opinion on Francesco's chances, reported that around Christmas 1473 would have been the best time, because the zodiac would then show some of the same features as when he had obtained the red hat.[215]

* * *

This summary may suffice to suggest that even as a fifteenth-century prince of the Church of noble blood, Cardinal Gonzaga was somewhat naive and presumptuous, not to mention worldly; the following chapters will provide further instances of these and other demerits. A low reputation of his character was, thanks to Raffaele Maffei of Volterra, already established in print by 1506; Raffaele (1451–1522)—no relative of Agostino Maffei and his brothers—had lived in the parish of Sant'Eustachio in the 1470s and been attached to the household of Cardinal Giovanni d'Aragona: he must have some first-hand knowledge of Francesco. His characterization is crude but not wholly misleading, and the

---

incurred excommunication in May 1460 at Pavia (see below, p. 51) unless his being a papal protonotary made him liable.

[210] On 25 May 1466 he had written about the fabrics needed for two dalmatics (see above, p. 19 n. 122); on 19 July he wrote to thank Barbara for 'el damascho brochato d'oro e cremesino col cendale per fare la dalmatica, quello friso lavorato d'oro cum la croce de perle in mezo, et un lasso da cane' (ASMn, AG, b. 843). See also vestments and liturgical objects listed in I 372–406. It may be, however, that such items were for the use of his domestic chaplains.

[211] G. P. Arrivabene to Marchese L. Gonzaga, Rome, 10 November 1475: 'Lo cardinale de Arli…heri sera era in termino che medici quasi desperavano de la vita suoa…è gientil signore et supra omnia molto affectionato e fidel al Reverendissimo Monsignor mio, dal qual haveva sempre havuto gran favore per la suoa promotione. E lui stesso lo confessava' (ASMn, AG, b. 845, c. 504).

[212] G. P. Arrivabene to Marchese F. Gonzaga, Sabbioneta, 25 July 1480: 'per essere Monsignore prete, o sia ecclesiastico…' (ASMn, AG, b. 1812), he considered it inappropriate for the cardinal himself to forward a letter concerning a capital crime.

[213] Cardinal F. Gonzaga to Barbara, Corbola 3 August 1464: '… Non staria per questo de acetare el papato, se in me lo volesse dare…' (ASMn, AG, b. 2098). See Fig. 13.

[214] Cardinal F. Gonzaga to Marchese L. Gonzaga, Rome, 19 July 1466: 'Io son qui cardinale e puorìa venir tempo che la sorte tocharìa sopra de me. Doverei io recusar el papato per dir che sia de gran carico?' (ASMn, AG, b. 843, quoted in Chambers, 'Defence of Non-Residence', p. 607).

[215] Manfredi to Barbara, 1 August 1471: 'in quel tempo ritornarà la constellacione quale in el tempo del capello regnava' (ASMn, AG, b. 2413, c. 199).

uncertainty it expresses about the cardinal's intellectual faculties anticipates the essential point behind the discussion which will follow.[216]

The point of this study, however, is not so much to assess Francesco's moral weaknesses and defects as a prelate—about which his own father had been apprehensive from the start—as to examine the attitudes of mind, experiences and resources which made him into a liberal patron, benefactor and collector. If any more positive note can be struck concerning his personality—with the caveat that it is risky to make any pronouncements at all about characters so remote from ourselves in time and setting—it might perhaps be allowed that he seems to have possessed a certain moderation and affability, reckoned to count among the desirable human virtues. Marchese Ludovico Gonzaga had urged upon him in 1462 the need to cultivate such genial qualities,[217] and his success in having done so was stressed in the funeral oration in 1483.[218]

(iii) Table of Itineraries of Cardinal Gonzaga

NOTE: Dates normally refer to nights spent in a particular place (departure from which may therefore have been on the subsequent day); capitalized place names indicate principal or prolonged places of residence. Although some years are shown as spent entirely in Rome (1469, 1474–5, 1481) it should not be assumed that the cardinal made no journeys at all during those years, not even in the vicinity of the city; the fact is simply that the sources examined have not recorded them. All archival references are to *buste* in ASMn AG unless otherwise noted. Places noted as visited by the cardinal should not necessarily be assumed to be the place from which a letter containing the information was written; names of senders, or place names, are sometimes quoted where *buste* do not contain numbered pages.

1461		PAVIA (1621, *passim*)
Dec.	28–9	Milan (1621, c. 991; 1622, c. 423; 1627, c. 237)
	30	Lodi (1622, cc. 521, 523)
	31	Cremona (1622, cc. 522, 525)
1462 Jan.	1	Bozzolo (2397: Card. F. Gonz.; 2097: Marchese L. Gonz.)
	2–	MANTUA (Schivenoglia, MS BCMn, 1019, fol. 38ᵛ)
March	4	Revere (2097: Barbara)
	5	Sermide (ibid.)
	6–7	Ferrara (1228; 2097: Aless. Gonz.)

---

[216] '…Franciscum Cardinalem, a Pio Pont. factum, qui nostra aetate apud Aedis [*sic*] Laurentianas habitabat. Vir iocis et ocio natus: luxu regio, ac praeter facultates alioquin verax et i[n]ter patres consilio aliquando haud inutilis. Decessit admodum iuvenis ex intemperantia' (Maffei, *Commentariorum urbanorum libri*, fol. xlvᵛ). For a brief discussion of Raffaele see D'Amico, *Renaissance Humanism*, pp. 82–5.

[217] '…che siate humano verso ogni homo; che, benché la humanitate sia conveniente a ciaschuno, nientedimanco, chi è nato de bono sangue più se conviene; né natura de gentil sangue per gran dignità se insuperbisse, imo se fa più graciosa e più benigna e magiore commendatione fra li homini…' (letter dated at Goito, 27 April 1462: ASMn, AG, b. 2097); for other passages see Luzio, *L'archivio Gonzaga*, II, p. 49 n. 3.

[218] '…in colloquio et sermone nemo magis affabilis, accessu facilior, vultu amabilior…' (Cattanei, *Orationes*, sig. c iiiiᵛ).

	8	El Pozzo (2097: Aless. Gonz.)
	9	Bologna (1141, cc. 99–102; 2097: Aless. Gonz.)
	10	Loiano (2097: Aless. Gonz.)
	11	Firenzuola (1100, c. 84; 1367; 2397)
	12	Scarperia (ibid.)
	13–15	Florence (1100, cc. 52, 83–6, 101–2, 124)
	16	Poggibonsi (1100, c. 87)
	17–18	Siena (1100, c. 198; 841, cc. 788^r-90^v)
	20	Acquapendente (841, cc. 788^r-90^v)
	21	Bolsena, Viterbo (ibid.)
	22	Sutri (ibid.)
	23–	ROME (841, cc. 552, 791; Eubel, II, p. 36)
May	4	Campagnano (841, cc. 728, 737)
	5	Nepi, Città Castellana (841, c. 728)
	6	Soriano (841, cc. 728, 737^v)
	7–	VITERBO (841, cc. 748–50)
June	24–	PIENZA (Sant'Anna in Camparena) (841, cc. 443–4, 668: *passim*)
Aug.	7	Monte Oliveto (842, c. 703)
Oct.	24–5	Petriolo (1100, cc. 111; 118–9)
	26–	Monte Oliveto (2398: Marasca; 1100, c. 121, 9 Nov.)
Nov.	28	Isola San Secondo (Lake Trasimeno) (1100, cc. 112–3)
Dec.	?–	TODI (1100, cc. 77–9, 10 Dec.)
	20	Avigliano (841, cc. 813; 842, cc. 131, 158, 204)
	21	Orte (ibid.)
	22	Rignano (ibid.)
	23–	ROME (ibid.)
1463 Jan.	1–	ROME (842, *passim*)
May	31	Albano (842, c. 191)
June	30–	TIVOLI (842, cc. 46, 253, and *passim* to 9 Sept., ibid., c. 49.)
Aug.	26–?7	Cavi, Genazzano (842, c. 242)
Sept.	9–13	Frascati (842, c. 49; visited Grottaferrata)
	13–	ROME (842, c. 49 and *passim*)
Oct.	26–9	Nemi (842, cc. 60, 156, 201)
	30–1	Nettuno (ibid., c. 202)
Nov.	1	Rocca di Papa (842, c. 202)
	24?	Florence (2887, lib. 42, fol. 75^v)
	30	Mirandola (2400: Jac. de Folenis: Quistello)
Dec.	1	Quistello (ibid.; also Card. F.)
	2–	Marmirolo, nr. MANTUA (2399: Marmirolo)
	25	Cavriana (2097: Aless. Gonz.)
1464 Jan.	1–	Marmirolo, nr. MANTUA (2402, *passim*)
Aug.	1	Stellata (1228, cc. 483, 485)
	2	Corbola (1228, c. 486; 2098: Card. F.)

	3–5	La Fornace (2098, 2402: Card. F.; 1431bis, c. 546)
	6–7	Venice (1431bis, cc. 544–7; 556)
	8–9	Parenzo (1431bis, c. 557)
	10–?13	Pola (842, cc. 453–4)
	15–18	Ancona (842, cc. 374–5; 454)
	25–	ROME (842, *passim*)
1465 Jan.	1–	ROME (842, *passim*)
July	22	Marino (842, cc. 609, 613)
Oct.	7	Nettuno (842, c. 546)
1466 Jan.	1–	ROME (843, *passim*)
July	19	Marino (843, cc. 33–4, 245)
Aug.	6,22–4	Marino (843, cc. 243–4, 246)
Sept.	22	Marino (843, c. 247)
Sept.	23–8	Nettuno (843, cc. 141; 46)
1467 Jan.	1–	ROME (843, *passim*)
July	1–	Marino (843, cc. 351–2, 538–46: 1, 24, 30 July)
Aug.	1–	Marino (843, cc. 353, 547: 16, 29 Aug.)
Sept.	15	Marino (843, c. 402)
1468 Jan.	1–	ROME (843, *passim*)
June	8–	Marino (843, c. 614; 619: 19 June)
July	1–8	Marino (ibid., c. 614)
Aug.	3–	Marino (843, c. 615; 27 Aug., ibid., cc. 616, 620)
Sept.	6–9	Marino (843, cc. 617, 621–2)
Sept.	22–4	Nettuno (843, cc. 589–90, 632)
1469 Jan.	1–	ROME (843, *passim*)
1470 Jan.	1–	ROME (844, *passim*)
July	9–	ALBANO (844, cc. 34–5, 84)
Aug.	2,31	ROME (844, c. 112)
Sept.	1,15	Rome (844, cc. 40–1)
Oct.	6–	ROME (844, c. 43)
1471 Jan.	1–	ROME (844, *passim*)
July	7	Viterbo (844, c. 267)
	8	Bolsena, Acquapendente (ibid.)
	10	Siena (1100, cc. 556, 558)
	11	Sancasciano (ibid.)
	12–15	Florence (ibid.)
	16	Scarperia (ibid.)
	17	Firenzuola (ibid.)
	18	Scaricalasino (ibid.)
	19	Pianoro (844, c. 167)
	20–8	BOLOGNA (1141, c. 197)
	29	Pianoro (1141, c. 199)
Aug.	4–	ROME (Eubel, II, p. 41; b. 844, *passim*)
1472 Jan.	1–	ROME (844, *passim*)
July	11	Castelnuovo (844, c. 387)

	12	Città Castellana (ibid.)
	13–15	Unknown locations
	16	Foligno (844, c. 388)
	17	Assisi (ibid.)
	18	Foligno (ibid.; c. 392)
	19	Serravalle (ibid.; 390; 2414: Agnelli)
	20	Camerino (ibid.)
	21	Tolentino (844, c. 391)
	22	Macerata (844, c. 393)
	23	Loreto (844, c. 391)
	24	Ancona (ibid.)
	25	Senigallia (ibid.)
	26–7	Pesaro (ibid.)
	28–9	Rimini (844, c. 389)
	30	Forlì (844, c. 394)
Aug.	2–	BOLOGNA (1141, c. 242)
	20	San Giovanni in Persiceto (1141, cc. 249–50)
	21	Mirandola (1339, c. 145)
	22	Bondanello; Gonzaga (Schivenoglia, MS BCMn, 1019, fol. 71^v)
	23	Borgoforte (ibid.; 2414: Bonatto)
	24–	MANTUA (ibid.)
	31	Goito (2414: Card. F. Gonz.)
Sept.	17	Bagnolo (2101, c. 122: Barbara)
	26–	MANTUA (3351, cc. 124^r–127^r; 2413, c. 780)
Oct.	12	Revere (Schivenoglia, MS BCMn, 1019, fol. 74^r)
	13	Mirandola (1339, c. 146)
	17–	BOLOGNA (1141, c. 252)
1473 Jan.	1–	BOLOGNA (b. 1141, *passim*)
May	10	San Giovanni in Persiceto (3351, c. 139^v)
	13	Mirandola (1101, c. 98)
	14	Falconeria, Revere (ibid.)
	15–	MANTUA (2101, c. 424)
	21	Marmirolo (2416, c. 373)
	23?	Revere (2101, c. 488)
	25	Torre della Fossa; Ferrara (1228, cc. 936–7)
	26–	BOLOGNA (1141, cc. 349, 363)
June	22	Torre della Fossa; Ferrara (1141, c. 365; 2101, c. 323)
	24	Revere (1228, c. 938)
	25–	MANTUA (2101, c. 329; MS BCMn, 1019, fol. 76^r)
	26	Cavriana (2415, c. 189)
July	13	Marmirolo (2415, *passim*)
Aug.	2–?3	Reggiolo (2892, lib. 72, fol. 77^r)
	5	MANTUA (3351, cc. 142^r-3^v)

Sept.	12	Gonzaga (2415, c. 35)
	20–	MANTUA (2101, cc. 496–7)
Oct.	13	Luzzara (2101, c. 498)
	14	Viadana (2415, c. 1071)
	15	Dosolo (2415, c. 1071)
	16	Gonzaga (ibid.)
	17–	MANTUA (ibid.; 3351, fol. 18^v)
Nov.	4	San Giovanni in Persiceto (1141, cc. 366, 370)
	8	Mirandola (1339, c. 151)
	?9–13	Bologna
	14	Loiano (845, c. 117)
	16	Scaricalasino (1100, c. 188)
	17	Florence (ibid.)
	21	Siena (845, cc. 116, 117)
	22	Aquapendente (ibid.)
	23	Sutri (ibid.)
	24	Bracciano (ibid.)
	25	ROME (845, c. 10; Eubel, II, p. 43)
1474 Jan.	1–	ROME (845, passim)
Feb.	8	Bracciano (845, c. 127)
	11–12	Viterbo (845, cc. 330–1)
April	1	Bracciano (845, c. 333)
	2–28	VITERBO (845, cc. 333–4)
Oct.	22	Grottaferrata (845, c. 184)
	23	Rocca di Papa (ibid.; 2416, c. 1224)
	25	Frascati (ibid.)
Nov.	7	Ostia (845, cc. 191, 252)
1475 Jan.	1–	ROME (845, passim)
1476 Jan.	1–	ROME (845, passim; Eubel, II, p. 44)
June	10–23	Vetralla (845, cc. 682–5)
July	13	Amelia (845, cc. 687–8)
	23–	NARNI (845, cc. 668–70; 689–90)
Aug.	20–	FOLIGNO (845, cc. 671–9, 690–6)
	22–6	Assisi (845, c. 691)
Oct.	7	Spoleto (845, c. 696; ASF, MAP, xlvi, 413)
	8	Piedaluco (Eubel, II, p. 44)
	10	Rieti (845, cc. 680, 697; Eubel, II, p. 44)
	19	Poggio S. Lorenzo (ibid.)
	21	Nerula (ibid.)
	22	Nomentana (ibid.)
	23–	ROME (845, c. 652; Eubel, II, p. 44)
1477 Jan.	1–	ROME (846, passim)
May	6–22	Viterbo (846, cc. 26, 29, 192)
1478 Jan.	1–	ROME (846, passim)
June	21	Foligno (846, cc. 235, 275)
	22	Nocera (846, c. 275)
	26	Pesaro (846, c. 326)

	27–8	Forlì (ibid.)
	30–	BOLOGNA (1141, *passim*)
Oct.	20	Revere, Sacchetta, ?Mantua (2420; 2421, cc. 246–7)
Nov.	18–	CENTO (846, cc. 25–390, *passim*)
	30	Bologna (846, c. 305; 1141, c. 566)
Dec.	5	CENTO (as above)
1479 Jan.	1–2	CENTO (ibid.)
	3	Bondeno (846, c. 395; 1229, c. 67)
	4–6	Ferrara (1229, c. 66; Zambotti, p. 58)
	7	Figarolo (ibid.)
	8	Revere (ibid.)
	?9–	MANTUA (18 Jan., 3351, fol. 45^v)
Feb.	5	Rodigò (3351, fols 57^v–8^v)
	6–7	Redondesco (2104 (Card. F. Gonz.)
	7	Isola [Dovarese] (ibid.)
	9–11	Bozzolo (ibid.)
	12	Rivarolo (ibid.)
	16–17	Dosolo (ibid.)
	18	Borgoforte (ibid.)
	?19–	MANTUA (ibid.; to 7 Apr, 3351, fol. 65^v)
April	13	Ferrara, Torre della Fossa (846, c. 396; 1229, c. 68)
	14	Bentivoglio (846, c. 397)
	?15–	BOLOGNA (1142, *passim*, from 19 April)
July	?10–	Porretta (1101, cc. 801–3, to 22 July)
Dec.	17–	Ferrara (1229, cc. 69–70)
	20	Felonica, Sermide (2423, Card. F. Gonz.)
21		Revere (2423, Revere)
	22–	MANTUA (2896, lib. 96, fol. 149^r)
1480 Jan.	1–	MANTUA (2896, lib. 96, fols 157 sqq; 3351, fols 77^r–92^r, to 17 Apr.; 2424, *passim*)
July	17–28	Sabbioneta (2104: Card. F. Gonz.; 1812: G. P. Arrivabene)
Oct.	17	Parma (2424: Card. F. Gonz.)
Dec.	1	Ferrara (1229, cc. 134–5)
	2	Bentivoglio (ASMil, Sforzesco, cart. 191)
	3–	BOLOGNA (ibid.)
	14–16	Florence (Landucci, *Diario*, p. 37)
	28–	ROME (Eubel, II, p. 49)
1481 Jan.	1–	ROME (846, *passim*)
1482 Jan.	1–	ROME (846, *passim* to cc. 584, 577, 16 Dec.)
Dec.	18	Bolsena (b. 544, c. 307; filed as 'Bolzano')
	24–5	Florence (2900, lib. 114, fols 2^r, 4^r)
	29–31	Bologna (1142: Card. F. Gonz.; Ghirardacci, p. 226)
1483 Jan.	1–2	Bologna (as above)

	3–	FERRARA (1231, c. 94; 2900, lib. 114, fols. 5^r–128^v, to 20 Feb.; 1231, *passim* to c. 181; Zambotti, p. 131)
Feb.	22	Borgoforte (2431)
	?23–	CREMONA (2431; 2900, lib. 114, fol. 130^r; Bonatti, 'La Dieta', pp. 263–4)
March	2–3	Viadana (2433: Antimaco)
	4–5	Mantua (ibid.)
	6	Governolo, Revere (ibid.: Card. F. Gonz., 7 March)
	7	Bondeno (ibid.)
	8–	FERRARA (2900, lib. 114, fols 130^v–1^r; 1231 to c. 347, 16 April-July, *passim*)
July	17	Sasso (1231, c. 347)
	?18–	Porretta (1231, c. 91; 2430, c. 96; Zambotti, p. 142)
Aug.	4	Oriolo (2430, cc. 696–7)
	5	Vergato (ibid.)
	6	Sasso (ibid.)
	8–	BOLOGNA (1142, *passim*, until death)

Chapter 2: The Financial Problems of Cardinal Gonzaga

In the second half of the fifteenth century a cardinal was expected to live magnificently,[1] particularly if he was the son of a prince. He might go to the other extreme, like the ascetic young Cardinal of Portugal (d. 1459), whom Cosimo de' Medici had held up as a model to Francesco Gonzaga, when the latter visited Florence in March 1462,[2] but no middle course would help in gaining reputation. He was from time to time reminded that austere standards were desirable, as in a long and didactic letter about cardinals' duties addressed to him by Cardinal Ammannati in 1468;[3] but Francesco had little bent for self-mortification, and as his most serious moral imperative was to enhance the prestige of his family, *magnificentia* was the obvious course for him to pursue, and he was acclaimed for it.[4] But the price was a heavy one, and the trouble was that he did not have so much wealth at his command as was generally assumed. After his arrival in Rome in March 1462 he was thought to be so rich that at the time of his mouth-opening ceremony as a novice cardinal, only two of his fellows in the Sacred College gave him presents (Cardinal Mella gave him a bell, and Cardinal Barbo gave him a tapestry bedcover, worth about twenty ducats).[5] The value of the sapphire ring bestowed upon him by the pope during the same ceremony, was likewise carefully estimated—at thirty ducats.[6]

In fact, indebtedness was soon to form a regular pattern in Francesco's life, and his income was never sufficient to meet his desires or needs. It may be argued that these 'needs' were not absolute and arose from the cardinal's simple inclination to live extravagantly; but such an argument begs the question, how was a Prince of the Church expected to live? Within less than a year of Francesco's arrival in Rome, the master of his household was complaining[7] about his

---

[1] See Chambers, 'Economic Predicament'. Müntz, *Les Arts*, III, pp. 39–46, discusses briefly the luxury of some of Francesco's fellow cardinals, particularly of Cardinals Rodrigo Borgia, and Guillaume d'Estouteville.

[2] Letters of G. P. Arrivabene and B. Marasca, Florence, 14 March 1462, and Alessandro Gonzaga, 15 March 1462, in Chambers, 'Cardinal Gonzaga in Florence', docs 3, 4, 7, pp. 250–1, 258.

[3] Ammannati, *Epistolae*, fols 156ʳ-59ᵛ; e.g.: 'Ad pompas et delitias ornamenta cardinalatus non sunt' (fol. 158ʳ).

[4] 'Romae vivit magnifice, ut decet dominos atque principes, ab omni avaritia refugiens' (as above, p. 4, n. 10).

[5] Marasca to Barbara, Rome, 3 April 1462: 'Zamorensis ha donato uno campanello, Sancto Marcho uno panno razo de precio de vinti ducati overo vinticinque ducati' (ASMn, AG, b. 841, c. 684); Cf. Marasca to Marchese Ludovico Gonzaga, Viterbo, 28 May 1462: 'Ugnuno crede che a casa nostra piova dinari e roba, et per questo pareme conoscere puochi presenti siano sta' fatti al Reverendissimo Monsignor mio. De'cardinali, niuno ha presentato, excepto Zamora uno campanello, e Sancto Marco uno celone' (ASMn, AG, b. 841, c. 741). It is not clear whether this *celone* can have been the tapestry bedcover which Barbo provided for the cardinal's first night in Rome, and about which Arrivabene wrote to Barbara on 5 April: '…essendose remandato al Reverendissimo Monsignor de San Marco un panno de rassa che haveva prestato per mettere suso el letto del Reverendissimo Monsignor mio al Populo, non lo volse acceptare, dicendo non l'haveva dato perché li fosse restituto, ma cum animo de donarlo' (ASMn, AG, b. 841, c. 657); *celoni* were of woolen fabric, woven with a colourful pattern (Thornton, *Renaissance Interior*, pp. 77–9).

[6] '…et in questo aprire la bocha, lo sposò como uno zafiro de precio de trenta ducati' (Marasca, as above, 3 April 1462); Francesco himself told his mother in a letter of 2 April that it was worth 40 ducats (b. 841, c. 432).

[7] Marasca to Barbara, Rome, 16 February 1463: 'Per altra mia ho pregato e supplicato a la Excellentia Vostra se digni scrivere al Reverendissimo Monsignore mio, che nelo spendere se voglia regulare et non atendere a li apetiti, maxime de cosse con non ge sieno necessarie né utile tropo. Non perché non volesse Sua Reverendissima Signoria havesse il suo piacere, ma perché a me pare le sue intrate non lo patissa' (ASMn, AG,

spending habits to Barbara of Brandenburg, who joined in the reproaches,[8] but the entertaining was also regarded as a duty, which had to be done with a certain splendour, as the cardinal's auditor remarked.[9] The point was best made by Marasca, when the household was back in Mantua next winter, that although Francesco's blood was noble, his income was not equal to it.[10] In 1474 Giovan Pietro Arrivabene observed that the cardinal was buffetted by contrary winds, on the one hand by his mountain of debts, and on the other by desire to indulge himself expensively.[11] This reputation was to pursue him beyond the grave; Paolo Cortesi, for example, singled out Francesco's inability to control his own squandering by quoting a *bon mot* he allegedly uttered in his own defence.[12]

Nothing like a full and accurate account of the cardinal's income and expenditure can be given. There are no surviving account books, indeed one may question whether any household accounts were kept at all; no individual is named anywhere as having this specific function, and although there were individuals who functioned as *spenditori*,[13] only in a late stage of his career is one mentioned by name.[14] Maybe in earlier days the punctilious Marasca had kept accounts, or his successor as master of the household, the lawyer Giacomo d'Arezzo; but household accounts would in any case represent only a part of the cardinal's budget. Letters provide most of the information available, but they do not furnish regular details and annual summations.

Benefices were generally the main source of revenue for cardinals, whether the major benefices ultimately conferred by the pope and cardinals in consistory, or lesser benefices in the gift of other patrons. Their distribution was always an unfair or unequal business. A papal favourite or nephew, such as Sixtus IV's notorious nephew Pietro Riario, could prosper rapidly, but others might have a long wait and even regard themselves as poor and underprivileged. Such a one was Pius II's favourite, Jacopo Ammannati, who—although he had acquired the bishopric of Pavia, to which Francesco also aspired—together with the pope made light of Francesco's needs on the grounds that he could depend on his father.[15] In spite of this, friendship prevailed, and Francesco in July 1467 even

b. 842, c. 177); see below, pp. 77–8 for Marasca's examples of this acquisitiveness, and for his own household economies, Chambers, 'Marasca', pp. 267–8.

[8] Barbara to Cardinal F. Gonzaga, Mantua, 21 March 1463: '… Haveti pur troppo presto spesi tuti quelli vostri denari, e possemo vi dire che siate stato un pocho mal massaro.' (ASMn, AG, b. 2887, lib. 41, fol. 9ᵛ).

[9] Giacomo d'Arezzo to Marchese L. Gonzaga, Rome, 25 January 1463: 'anchora se sonno fatti alcuni pasti a diversi signori et homini da bene, che erano quasi necessarii a farli splendidamente et cum buono ordine' (ASMn, AG, b. 842, c. 95). On this subject, see (with source material from the first half of the sixteenth century) Byatt, 'The Concept of Hospitality'.

[10] Marasca to Barbara, Marmirolo, 3 December 1463: 'Lo animo suo è corespondente a la nobiltà del sangue, ma le intrate non sonno così…Pur questa matina monstra conoscere in parole che le spese soe siano grande e maiore che le intrate…' (ASMn, AG, b. 2399, Marmirolo).

[11] G.P. Arrivabene to Barbara, Rome 13 December 1474: 'Vedo nel'animo suo combattere doi venti, l'uno de la graveza di debiti che la restringe, l'altro del piacere ha de fare ciascuna cosa qual possa iudicare haverli ad essere grata, e questo la stimula a fare buon pensiere de gratificando' (ASMn, AG, b. 845, c. 199).

[12] '…ut Franciscus Gonzaga senator, qui cum rogaretur cur ceterorum more cogere pecuniam sumptui parcendo nollet, "quoniam" inquit "difficile custodiri potest, quod communi hominum proclivitate expetitur"…' (Cortesi, *De cardinalatu*, lib. II: *De sermone*, fol. LXXXXIʳ).

[13] Baldassare Soardi to Barbara, Rome, 26 December 1462: 'In questa casa poi che se venne a Roma, sono stati undeci spenditori…' (ASMn, AG, b. 841, c. 813ᵛ).

[14] See below, pp. 127–30.

[15] Cardinal F. Gonzaga to Barbara, Sant'Anna in Camparena, 19 August 1462: 'El Reverendissimo Monsignor de Pavia…li aiutava a la gagliarda, et excusandomi io de essere povero, allegorono che se non era riccho de

wrote to Ascanio Maria Sforza interceding for Ammannati to be relieved of taxation.[16]

But there were other problems as well as unequal distribution. Even if title had been acquired to a benefice or a pension upon part of the annual revenue of a benefice, this did not always ensure possession and effective collection of revenues. There might be outstanding debts and would certainly be administrative expenses even if possession was obtained; on the major benefices there would also be substantial service taxes to pay initially. For these and other reasons it is generally difficult to assess benefice income; theoretical income can be computed by trebling the tax valuation (which corresponds usually to the sum obligated or paid to the Apostolic Camera),[17] but this may have been less—or possibly more—than the sum collected in reality. Obviously it was important for a cardinal, or his advisers, to be well informed on the subject, and Francesco, perhaps at the suggestion of his auditor Giacomo d'Arezzo, did obtain or commission a sort of directory, one of his finest manuscripts to survive, in which many if far from all the major benefices of Western Christendom are listed, and many updated valuations of income included. Since the latest date given among these revised entries (under the heading of the bishopric of Avellino) is a papal bull of 9 May 1466, it may be inferred that the manuscript was written fairly soon after then; it is also among the books recorded in his posthumous inventory (I 830).

Cardinal Gonzaga has the reputation of having been a pluralist on the grand scale,[18] but this is rather an exaggeration. The greater number of his benefices were owing less to papal provision than to his family's patronage or political influence in Mantua, and even these did not come easily; there were many disappointments. Francesco's first benefice was the *prepositura* of the monastery of San Benedetto in Polirone. Created in 1441 for an earlier prelate of the family, Guido Gonzaga, it comprised certain estates alienated from the vast landholdings of the famous monastery across the Po about ten miles south east of Mantua.[19] San Benedetto Po joined the reformed Congregation of Santa Giustina of Padua in 1419, on the initiative of Guido, who was its commendatory abbot: some of its lands had meanwhile been transferred to the marchese. Guido died in December 1459, and the *prepositura* was conferred upon Francesco soon afterwards.[20] Its yield varied annually but remained a mainstay of Francesco's income after he became a cardinal. The system of granting short-term leases on some of these estates was adopted, to ensure a more substantial yield, but by 1465 a more

beneficii haveva bene lo Illustre Signor mio patre che era potente e che me aiutarìa' (ASMn, AG, b. 841, c. 461ᵛ). On the preferments of Ammannati, who was free of financial worries only after he obtained the bishopric of Lucca in 1477, see Hausmann, 'Die Benefizien', p. 56.

[16] ASMil, Sforzesco, cart. 62.

[17] See, for the assessments, Hoberg, *Taxae*; for consistorial provisions and taxes, Clergeac, *La Curie*; Lunt, *Papal Revenues*, I, p. 87.

[18] E.g., Hay, *The Church in Italy*, p. 105. Hay also castigates Marco Barbo, in spite of his relatively modest holdings (see Paschini, 'Benefici').

[19] On the *prepositura* see Vaini, 'La collegiata', pp. 335–6. About Guido little is known, though see Donesmondi, *Storia*, I, pp. 362, 393.

[20] Barbara wrote to Marchese L. Gonzaga, 10 December 1459 '…messer Guido protonotario staseva per morire' (ASMn, AG, b. 2886, lib. 37, fol. 132ʳ). Writing from Rome on 14 October 1465 to Borso d'Este of Ferrara, on a matter concerning the *prepositura*, Cardinal F. Gonzaga referred to 'meser Guido mio barba' (ASMod, AEC, Principi, b. 1380B/116).

ambitious scheme was in progress according to which all or part of the annual administration of the *prepositura* appears to have been open to competitive tender.[21]
It is clear that an attempt was being made to increase profit and reduce costs; the
cardinal decided at the same time to shut up his house in Mantua, or rather, to
entrust it to a caretaker, having had an inventory made of the contents.[22]

Francesco had presumed very early on his prospects of obtaining a major
bishopric in Lombardy: Pavia itself was in his thoughts when he arrived there as
a sixteen-year-old law student. He assured his mother that this was not out of
mere ambition or greed and that he had received some encouragement from
Galeazzo Maria Sforza and the famous jurist Catone Sacco.[23] He had no success,
however, until the bishopric of Mantua, or rather its temporal jurisdiction, was
conferred on him in August 1466, after some scruples of his father had been
overcome.[24]

In the lands of the bishopric, like those of the *prepositura*, the cardinal's
deputies did their utmost to increase revenues; the pope was told, before
Francesco's accession, that the income amounted to 4000 ducats annually,[25]
although the tax payable was 400 florins,[26] which assumes an income of only
1200 florins. As a result of the policy adopted, Sixtus IV was informed in 1484
that the value of the bishopric was 2800 florins annually, and even this was more
than double the theoretical figure in the papal tax books.[27] In September 1466 the
cardinal appointed Carlo da Rodiano, formerly his stablemaster, as the steward of
his ecclesiastical lands.[28] As with the *prepositura*, the policy adopted was
annually to lease out parcels of estates to individuals, such as the entrepreneur
Giuliano Lancino, and even to the marchese himself.[29] High prices were de-

[21] Barbara to Cardinal F. Gonzaga, Mantua, 13 November 1465: 'anche de questa medesima oppinione
trovamo el prefato Illustre Signore vostro patre, che la deliberatione presa per vui de affictare questa vostra
prepositura sia bona perché al manco sapereti de quello che ne poteresti valere…' (ASMn, AG, b. 2889, lib. 54,
fol. 73ʳ); and 4 February 1466: 'la prepositura finalmente è locata come da messer Jacomo e Carlo da Rodiano
intendereti' (ASMn, AG, b. 2890, lib. 56, fols 21ʳ⁻ᵛ).
[22] Cardinal F. Gonzaga to Marchese Ludovico Gonzaga, Rome 24 February 1466: 'esendo mo affictate queste
mie possessione, non vorei lì in casa mia tenere altra spesa se non d'uno chi havesse a guardare la casa e
governare quelle puoche massaricie et altro mobile che se lì trova. El me scrisse perhò Carlo [da Rodiano]
questi dì, che del tuto haveva fatto un'inventario e consignato in man de Christoforo, el qual era canevaro. Se
costui è sufficiente son contento che l'habia questa cura; quando non, prego Vostra Signoria che voglia tuore un
puocho de carico in adaptare quelle mie cose e deputarli uno che sia idoneo. A tuto el resto de quelli che
stavano in casa facia dare licentia; perché, come ho dicto, non voglio più tenere lì quella spesa' (ASMn, AG, b.
843).
[23] Protonotary F. Gonzaga to Barbara, Pavia, 6 May 1460: '…usai cum lo Illustre conte Galeazo queste
parole, dicendo che, vacando lo vescovato de Pavia io me raccomandava a la sua Signoria che volesse
sollicitare ch'io puotesse havere questo beneficio, non indutto da cupiditade overo ambitione alcuna, ma aciò se
connoscesse, e maxime in Corte, la estimatione havesse fatto questo Illustrissimo Signore de' fatti mei…hora,
doppo lo mio giongere qua, Messere Cato da se stesso, senza che io ge ne habia parlato, ha scritto a Messere
Andrioto del Maino, exhortandolo e pregandolo che voglia sollicitare che io habia questo beneficio, allegando
lui fra le altre cose lo honore de questo Studio' (ASMn, AG, b. 1621, c. 429).
[24] Chambers, 'Defence of Non-Residence', pp. 606–9.
[25] Cardinal F. Gonzaga to Marchese Ludovico, 15 July 1466: 'La Sanctitate de Nostro Signore me comincioe
a dimandare de la valuta del vescovato, la quale rispuosi essere circa li quatromilia ducati' (ASMn, AG, b. 843).
[26] Hoberg, *Taxae*, p. 74.
[27] Ludovico Gonzaga, Bishop-Elect, to Sixtus IV, Mantua, 3 December 1483: '…ecclesiam mantuanam cuius
fructus uti per conductores ipsorum est duorum milia et octingentorum ducatorum valorem annuum…' (ASP,
AGG, b. 41/3, reg. 1, c. 10ʳ). See also below, p. 113 n. 89.
[28] Schivenoglia, MS BCMn, 1019, fols 46ᵛ–7ʳ.
[29] According to Schivenoglia, in 1469 five of the episcopal *corti* were leased to the marchese and to Giuliano
di Lancino for 3050 ducats (MS BCMn, 1019, fol. 64ᵛ). Writing to Marchese Federico Gonzaga on 27

manded for this privilege, and in 1475 the cardinal even went back on one agreement when offered a higher bid.[30] The policy seems to have been in accordance
with a general trend in northern Italy to permit relaxation of the rules about
alienation of ecclesiastical property in the interest of short term profits for the
Church as well as more efficient exploitation of the land.[31]

Cardinal Gonzaga acquired various other benefices in the Mantuan dominion.
A pension of 100 ducats from the abbey of Felonica (on the south side of the Po,
beyond Revere) had been transferred to him during his first year as a cardinal; in
1467 he obtained complete control of it,[32] and in 1463 he acquired the abbey of
Acquanegra (in the diocese of Brescia).[33] Acquanegra's revenue for tax purposes
was only 127 florins, and there was difficulty in collecting debts, but the same
system of leasing was applied.[34] Two more monastic churches fell to him in
1470: S. Maria della Gerona (in Cremona diocese) and the abbey of Sant'Andrea
in the city of Mantua, which appointment, like the bishopric, had occasioned
some dithering on the part of his father.[35] Sant'Andrea—celebrated in particular
for its possesion of a relic of the Holy Blood of Christ—had, however, for many
years been marked down for refoundation and rebuilding as a secular collegiate
church. The last abbot's intransigence had postponed the realization of this
scheme, but Cardinal Gonzaga soon graduated from abbot to *primicerius* of the
new foundation, and was obliged to contribute not only to the building costs but
also to the diversion of resources to endow new canonries and chaplaincies.[36]
Some portion of the lands of Sant'Andrea nevertheless remained for him to
exploit in the same manner as the other church lands under his control.[37]

The main income-bearing appointments in Italy which Cardinal Gonzaga received thanks to the papacy were the legation (1471) and bishopric (1476) of
Bologna. The legation may have entitled him to an income of over 6000 florins,[38]

September 1479, Giuliano Lancino quoted the sum of 2800 ducats for his *fictanza*, plus another 200 ducats for
the marchese's rights (ASMn, AG, b. 2422). Giuliano, as a leading Mantuan merchant and entrepreneur, himself
deserves a monograph.

[30] Cardinal F. Gonzaga to Barbara, Rome, 14 October 1475: 'havendomi Carlo da Rhodiano fatto relatione de
tuti li partiti se me offeravano in affictare...io tandem haveva concluso per lo migliore et più utile a me de'
darlo a Zohanne de' Strigii per 2400 ducati'; cf. on 18 October: 'La Excellentia Vostra per un'altra mia harà
intieso quanto me mandò ad offerire Ludovico di Ghisi de ficto de la mia prepositura...la conventione per me
fatta cum Antonio Cornachia come procuratore de Zo[an] di Strigi sia per nulla quando se verefichi che
Ludovico voglia dare li 3000 ducati' (ASMn, AG, b. 845, cc. 386, 388).

[31] See Chittolini, 'Un problema aperto'.

[32] Papal letter of 19 October 1462 (ASDMn, Fondo Mensa vescovile, Pergamene, b. 2, no. 36). The
supplication, for this expectative to take effect upon the death of the Cardinal of Genoa (Giorgio Fieschi), had
been signed a year earlier; the abbot objected in vain that the pension had only been granted for that cardinal's
lifetime (Protonotary Francesco Gonzaga to Barbara, Pavia, 2, 14 November 1461, ASMn, AG, b. 1621, cc.
1033, 1132). For the transfer in 1467 see Chambers, 'Sant'Andrea', p. 110.

[33] It was bestowed on him after the death of Cardinal Prospero Colonna (Marasca to Barbara, Rome 26 March
1463; ASMn, AG, b. 842, c. 184). In 1470, however, the cardinal resigned it to his brother Ludovico (letter of
Francesco Sicco, 3 August 1477: ASMn, AG, b. 846, c. 149).

[34] In 1469 Felonica and Acquanegra were said to have been leased to 'uno merchadante che ha nome Ziliano'
(i.e., Giuliano Lancino) for 700 ducats (Schivenoglia, MS BCMn, 1019, fol. 64ᵛ).

[35] Chambers, 'Sant'Andrea', pp. 110–11, also p. 125, doc. 19 (n.b. the date is 16 March, not 21 April as
printed).

[36] Ibid., pp. 99 ff., and esp. pp. 111–14. In a letter of 30 January 1471 the cardinal assured his father he would
contribute 200 ducats a year (ASMn, AG, b. 844, c. 143; ibid., p. 126, doc. 21).

[37] Ludovico Gonzaga, Bishop Elect, noted in June 1484 that the income of the *prepositura* combined with that
of Sant'Andrea had in the previous year amounted to over 3000 ducats (Appendix 3, no. 15).

[38] Gerardo Ceruti to Galeazzo Maria Sforza, Bologna, 3 December 1472: 'in l'ultima congregatione di Sedici
che fu heri mattina, richiesi augumento di provisione, cioè quello che si soleva dare ad legati già bon pezzo fa.

and the bishopric was taxed at 1000 florins[39] so that (on the analogy with Mantua) he may have been able to expect much more than this in practice; on the other hand he may not necessarily have received all of his Bolognese income, either because of his absences or for other reasons, such as the insolvency of the Sedici and their slowness to pay the legate's salary.[40] Both offices of course carried substantial costs of administration; the legation was virtually run by a professional *luogotenente* and the bishopric by a suffragan bishop and the usual officials. Except for the abbey of San Dionigi, near Milan, which the cardinal held from 1471–8,[41] he does not appear to have had other major benefices in Italy.

In Rome Francesco was put in charge of several churches, but they were each worth little; Santa Maria Nuova, his title church, formerly held by Cardinal Pietro Barbo, yielded about fifty ducats a year, which—he was advised as early as January 1462—it was customary to return to the monks there;[42] Sant'Agnese, which was given to him as well a year later, was thought to be worth forty florins;[43] it is unlikely that his third church (received in 1467), San Lorenzo in Damaso, which had to support a body of canons, was very highly endowed, either.[44] He hoped in vain for promotion to one of the cardinal bishoprics; having his eye on Albano after the election of Sixtus IV,[45] and—on the strength of his legatine services—to Tusculum in 1479 and Ostia early in 1483, upon the death of Guillaume d'Estouteville.[46]

In his first years the cardinal received several special subventions from the pope.[47] During the periods when he was resident at Rome he had various additional rights to income: first, a share in the collective revenue of the College of Cardinals, principally derived from the service tax on consistorial provisions to benefices, but this would have varied greatly from year to year.[48] During his first

Et egli n'è compiaciuto. Donde Sua Reverendissima Signoria n'è partito molto contento. L'augumento è mensile da 1 m[ille] ad 1400 de bolognini, che serano l'anno ducati circa 6500' (ASMil, Sforzesco, cart. 178).

[39] Hoberg, *Taxae*, p. 22.

[40] The explanation given by the cardinal for his needing a loan in his letter of 5 December 1479 to Giovanni Tornabuoni: '…et trovarse questa Camera de Bologna indebitata come la è…' (ASMn, AG, b. 2896, lib. 96, fol. 137ʳ). Cf. Cardinal Jacopo Ammannati's experience in the Legation of Perugia, where in 1472 he seems to have received less than half the salary estimated to be regular in 1481–2 (Hausmann, 'Die Benefizien', p. 55).

[41] Chambers, 'Defence of Non-Residence', p. 609.

[42] 'Le intrate di dicto titulo…sono, se non erro, da circha cinquanta ducati, ma ben sottozonse anche dicto Monsignor de San Marco che mai non ge haveva voluto tuor cosa alcuna, e così, credo, farà lo antelato Monsignor nostro…' (Alessandro Gonzaga to Barbara, Rome, 5 April 1462: ASMn, AG, b. 841, c. 800ʳ), quoted in Chambers, 'Housing Problems', p. 24 n. 18.

[43] Marasca to Barbara, Rome, 23 April 1463 : 'Questi dì passati scrisse a la Excellentia Vostra come lo Reverendissimo Monsignore mio havea habuta Sancta Agata in Suburra, lassando li fruti al Cardinale Ruteno, quali sono 40 ducati. Hora li fruti serano pur nostri, et andarano a mantinemento de questa giesia' (ASMn, AG, b. 842, c. 187).

[44] Chambers, 'Housing Problems', p. 38.

[45] G. P. Arrivabene to Marchese Ludovico Gonzaga, Rome, 11 August 1471, mentioned among other vain expectations (such as the rich abbey of San Gregorio in Rome) 'credo haverà anche Albano' (ASMn, AG, b. 844, c. 222); and he wrote from Bologna on 20 January 1473 'De Albano danno speranza per lasciarne qualche puocho de dolce in bocha' (b. 1141, c. 278).

[46] In letters to Francesco Maffei, from Bologna, 23 September 1479 (ASMn AG, b. 2896, lib. 96, fol. 34ʳ), and from Ferrara, 26 January 1483. In the latter case, he complained that the appointment of Cardinal La Balue was unjust ('più novo cardinale de nui') whereas he himself was 'fuora in servitio de la sede Apostolica e non a cose da piacere, immo de molta spesa e periculo' (ASMn, AG, b. 2900, lib. 114, fols 71ʳ–2ʳ).

[47] G. P. Arrivabene reported to Barbara on 26 December 1464 a payment of 300 florins, and on 8 March 1465 one of 100 ducats (ASMn, AG, b. 842, cc. 358, 539).

[48] Clergeac, *La Curie*, pp. 124–9; Chambers, 'Economic Predicament', p. 297.

year as a cardinal the total was over 400 florins,[49] in 1465 his share may have been as high as 1822 florins but by 1470 it was down to 252;[50] and with the number of resident cardinals rising under Sixtus IV the amount of this income each individual received must have fallen. To this has to be added the *propina* or 'tip' which Francesco would have received for his personal effort advocating or 'relating' an individual candidate for a consistorial benefice:[51] he started performing this duty in 1463,[52] and in some years did it quite often (in 1476, for instance, he is recorded as relator nine times),[53] but it is unlikely that these informal payments by the beneficiary's proctor were on a grand scale.

Although Cardinal Gonzaga did obtain a few benefices outside Italy, there were more disappointed hopes than expectations fulfilled. The bishopric of Trent, almost beyond its borders, had in his earlier years been a major objective. An unscrupulous scheme to replace the incumbent bishop—having him kidnapped when drunk and then deposed by the pope—had been the subject in 1462 of Francesco's most carefully reasoned and longest handwritten letter to survive.[54] His hopes of this see were finally frustrated by the election of Johannes Hinderbach, and it is uncertain whether the consolation, that Hinderbach should pay Francesco an annual pension for life of 500 ducats out of the revenues, was ever honoured.[55] Brixen (Bressanone), carrying particularly large revenues, provided another story of frustration in 1464–5; Paul II even appointed Francesco, but the cathedral chapter successfully opposed all his efforts to gain possession.[56] The archdeaconry of Outre-Maine in the diocese of Angers was also conferred on him by Paul II, but it is highly doubtful whether he ever gained possession or received any income from France.[57] The major thrust, however, continued to be to central and northern Europe where the Gonzagas had family connections as well as status conferred by the emperor. The expectations from that direction were

---

[49] G. P. Arrivabene reported to Barbara from Viterbo on 14 May 1462 a payment of 136 florins, and Marasca reported from Rome on 6 January 1463 one of 353 florins, subject to a contribution of 48 florins to the Despot of Morea (ASMn, AG, b. 841, c. 729; b. 842, c. 168).

[50] Antonovics, 'Division Register', n.b. table on p. 101.

[51] Clergeac, *La Curie*, p. 190–2; Lunt, *Papal Revenues*, I, pp. 297–8; Chambers, 'Economic Predicament', pp. 301–2.

[52] Giacomo d'Arezzo wrote to Barbara from Rome on 7 February 1463 that he was to make his début with the abbey of Miramondo near Pavia: 'so certissimo che referirà in bon modo' (ASMn, AG, b. 842, c. 96).

[53] AV, Obl. et Sol. 83 (register of the Camera of the College of Cardinals, 1466–88) *passim*. In 1476, for example, as well as relating various monastic houses in 1476, he undertook Mainz, Meissen, York, Durham, Przemyśl (Poland) and Hamar (Norway).

[54] Cardinal F. Gonzaga to Marchese L. Gonzaga, Todi, 10 December 1462 in ASMn, AG, b. 1100, cc. 77–9; partly published in Meuthen, *Nikolaus von Kues*, pp. 287–9, and in full (where it is also discussed) in Chambers, 'Mantua and Trent', pp. 74–8, 89–92.

[55] Chambers, 'Mantua and Trent', p. 77 nn. 37–8. G. P. Arrivabene wrote to Barbara on 20 April 1466 that Hinderbach was unwilling to pay the pension, though other correspondence suggest arrangements about it were going forward.

[56] See Piccolrovazzi, *La contrastata nomina*.

[57] A bull dated 26 September 1464 (AV, Reg. Vat. 526, fols 169^r–70^v) names the archdeaconry as 'Transmediensis in ecclesia Andegavensis'; Cf. Baldassare Soardi to Barbara, Rome, 24 September 1464 'La Sanctitade de Nostro Signore…ne lo consistorio de heri glie dede uno archidiaconato in Franza de valuta de trecento ducati…' (ASMn, AG, b. 842, c. 276) also Wilhelm Molitor, 26 September (ibid., c. 287: on Molitor see below, p. 44). Giacomo d'Arezzo wrote on 9 October 'Novamente Nostro Signore conferì una prepositura [*sic*] in Francia a Monsignore motu proprio di valuta de ccc. ducati; dicono alcuni che difficil cosa serà haver la possessione, perché lo re Raineri [René of Anjou] ha fatto impresa di quella per un'altro' (b. 842, c. 383^v). Three years later this difficulty had still not been overcome; Cardinal F. Gonzaga to Barbara, Rome, 2 March 1467: 'infra puochi dì spero di mandare uno de miei in Franza per tuore la possessione del'archidiaconato de Andegavia' (ASMn, AG, b. 843).

scarcely hidden; not only was Barbara of Brandenburg in regular contact with her relatives on Francesco's behalf, but for many years the cardinal even had a German notary in his household.[58] Particular hopes were placed in Scandinavia, where Barbara's sister Dorothea was Queen of Denmark. But little came of them; two minor benefices which Christian I had warned the cardinal would only be worth a pittance to an absentee,[59] the provostship of Lund cathedral in Sweden and the nearby priory of Dalby were granted in 1463;[60] but the bishopric of Lund, which was bestowed on the cardinal in 1472,[61] was clawed back by King Christian I two years later, mainly for political reasons, on behalf of the candidate elected by the chapter;[62] there was a written promise, never honoured, to pay the cardinal 4000 Rhenish florins in compensation.[63]

Francesco also tried to obtain benefices in Germany; *prepositure* or provost-ships of the cathedrals of Bamberg and Ratisbon (Regensburg) on which he had expectations were both pursued, without total success, for he was obliged to resign them in return for modest pensions.[64] Francesco does at least appear to have received the payments of his pension on Bamberg, though the sum involved was scarcely worth all the trouble.[65] He also obtained the provostship of Würt-temberg in 1476, thanks to family influence there,[66] and an abbey at Worms shortly before he died;[67] but this was not exactly an abundance of ultramontane benefices.

---

[58] Wilhelm Müller (latinized as Molitor) from Liège.

[59] Christian I to Cardinal F. Gonzaga, Seghebergh, 3 October 1462, in *Scriptores rerum danicarum*, VIII, p. 424; also letter of 14 October 1462 promising the church of Lincop in Sweden (ibid., p. 425).

[60] *Acta pontificum danica*, III, nos. 2288–93, pp. 348–50 (*motu proprio* supplication granted at Tivoli, 23 August 1463, and obligation for payment of annates by Wilhelm Molitor, 20 September 1463).

[61] Bull dated 12 June 1472 in *Diplomatarium diocesis lundensis*, IV, pp. 147–8; with the common services tax obligated on 6 July 1472 by Molitor (AV, Obl. et Sol. 84, fol. 178ʳ). Francesco wrote to Barbara from Forlì, 30 July 1472: 'come sia gionto ad Bologna, intendo de spazare messer Guielmo verso Dacia per mandare a tuore la possessione de quello mio arcivescovato' (ASMn, AG, b. 844, c. 394).

[62] Cardinal F. Gonzaga to Barbara, Rome, 1 May 1474: 'Nel facto de la chiesia Lundense la Maiestate del Re me ha fatto intendere a quanta ruina de tuto lo stato suo resultaria lasciarla andare in commenda et excludere quello electo…la cosa fusse cussì condicionata che io me ne mossi a compassione' (ASMn, AG, b. 845, c. 217).

[63] G. P. Arrivabene to Barbara, Rome, 19 April 1474, gives details of a discussion in which Francesco demanded in vain at least the income of the past two years, estimated at 8000 ducats; 'quasi lacrimando' the king said the net annual income was not more than 600 (ASMn, AG, b. 845, c. 134). A draft or copy of deed in the king's name dated at Viterbo (no day) 1474, undertakes payment in four equal instalments, the first before he left Italy, the last in 1477 (ASMn, AG, b. 2187, c. 1137). Writing to Barbara on 20 April 1475 when the king's chaplain had come to pay money to the Camera Apostolica, Francesco complained that nothing was said about what he was owed; on 22 May he thanked her for instructing her agent Tristano, sent to Denmark, 'per farli ricordo de quelli miei denari' (ASMn, AG, b. 845, c. 367). A reminder sent from Mantua on 23 January 1480 (ASMn, AG, b. 2896, lib. 96, fol. 174ʳ) seems to have had no effect.

[64] Cardinal F. Gonzaga to Barbara, Rome, 3 September 1466: 'Circa questa prepositura de Bamberbo io farò ugni diligentia…la dimandaroe per me e puoi la renunciarò col tempo a Zohanne [Stiber], e tra nui seremo bene d'accordo' (ASMn, AG, b. 843; also letter of G. P. Arrivabene to Barbara, Rome, 25 June 1467: 'credo che hoggi se farà la resignatione de quella prepositura de Ratispona per collui col quale esso messere Giovanni [de la Fiera] haveva concluso in Alemagna. Ha mandato qui el procuratorio e lo modo di pagare li cinquecento ducati. De quello de Bambergo stimo se farà il simile fra puochi giorni' (ibid.). Cf. Gaspar da Verona, citing the confirmation of the pension on Bamberg in July 1470 (Zippel, *Vite*, pp. 28–9, citing AV, Reg. Vat. 536, fol. 34) and in 1472 the bull confirming the pension of 70 ducats on Ratisbon (ibid., from Reg. Vat. 554, fols 131ʳ–2ʳ).

[65] A quittance was issued in his name on 18 May 1478 to Vitus Truchses, provost of Bamberg, for all payments of the annual pension of 60 marks granted on 6 July 1470 (ASMn, AG, b. 3351, fol. 45ʳ⁻ᵛ).

[66] Cardinal F. Gonzaga to Barbara, asking her to send a proctor to his sister Barbarina and her husband Eber-hard, Duke of Württemberg, so that he could get possession, in a letter dated at Narni, 31 July 1476 (ASMn, AG, b. 845, c. 669); he wrote his thanks for this favour on 15 September 1476 (ibid., c. 674ʳ).

[67] AV, Reg. Vat. 632, fols 169ᵛ–70ᵛ; bull dated 17 June 1483.

Not even benefices, offices and lands guaranteed a flow of ready cash. From his first days in the papal court, Cardinal Francesco Gonzaga had depended on private supplements to his funds. The early correspondence is full of direct appeals to his parents,[68] followed reproachfully by their remittances; but he had other irregular sources of money, too.

Francesco soon fell into the habit of borrowing. His first major experience of this was in the summer of 1462 at Pienza, where in addition to the worries of accumulated debt, he was being nagged by Pius II to buy a site on which to build a house as well as to contribute to the military campaign against Sigismondo Malatesta.[69] To raise funds from the bankers, he declared he was ready to pledge his jewels and silver.[70] There was only limited success at first, even an initial refusal from the local agent of the Medici bank.[71] Finally, a messenger sent to Montepulciano by Marasca luckily met a senior official of the Medici bank, who conceded a loan against a mere pledge in writing, on the grounds of Cosimo de' Medici's personal friendship with Ludovico Gonzaga.[72] It was not always to be so easy, though the cardinal continued to trade on his father's credit.

Nevertheless, Francesco soon became beholden to individuals, particularly to the Maffei brothers, members of a Veronese family with roots also in Mantua, who were pursuing their careers in Rome.[73] Agostino Maffei, the eldest, had been in Rome already at the time of Francesco's promotion and on 21 December 1461 had written his congratulations to Barbara of Brandenburg (ASMn, AG, b. 841, c. 368). By 1465 he had a regular arrangement of borrowing from them.[74] In 1466–7 he had to resort both to his father and to the Maffei to deliver him from the clutches of the Medici bank, which was pressing him hard to repay several loans, one of which had been secured by pledging jewels which belonged to the marchese. The details do not need to be rehearsed in full, but both Agostino and Benedetto Maffei had obliged him, drawing upon various capital resources,

---

[68] E.g., Cardinal F. Gonzaga to Barbara, Sant'Anna in Camparena, 19 August 1462, pleads 'tra li denari avancio de la provisione, che sono più de 500 ducati, e li 500 li prestai per el capello, e li 2000, vogliati col tempo…aiutarmi', i.e. for money to build the house at Pienza (ASMn, AG, b. 841, c. 461ᵛ).

[69] Chambers, 'Housing Problems', pp. 28–30.

[70] Cardinal F. Gonzaga to Barbara, Sant'Anna in Camparena, 24 September 1462: 'ho mandato subito messere Bartholomeo Marascha a Pientia per recattarli al bancho de' Medici e di Spinelli. Credo me ne soveniranno, e quando non, tra alcune mie gioiette et argenteri vederò impignandole de ritrovarli' (ASMn, AG, b. 841, c. 478).

[71] Marasca to Barbara, Pienza, 24 September 1462: '…ho ritrovati cinquecento ducati al bancho de' Spinelli… Andai al bancho de' Medici qual similiter se dolseno che tanto fusse tardato, dicendo haverne sborsati otto milia et per lo papa a diversi cardinali…son restato questa note qui in Pienza per andare da matina a Monte Polzano al bancho de' Baronzeli overo mandaro uno mio amico…spero havere lo resto da questi Baronzeli e daròge bon pigno…' (ASMn, AG, b. 1100, c. 110).

[72] Marasca to Barbara, Sant'Anna, 26 September 1462: '…lo principale casetero de Cosmo de' Medici, conoscendo quello amico era andato a Montepolzano, et intendendo la casone, commemorando lui la optima amicicia ha Cosmo cum lo Illustre signore mio signore messer lo marchese, volea per ugni modo servire al Reverendissimo Cardinale de Gonzaga, et così ha fatto. Hozi habiamo habuti cinquecento fiorini de camera da loro Medici, et similiter da' Spinelli. Né l'uno né l'altro ha voluto altro pigno che una police scritta de mi mane e sottoscritta de mane del Reverendissimo Monsignore mio…' (ASMn, AG, b. 2397, c. 983 ['S. Anna']).

[73] See above, pp. 15–16.

[74] Cardinal F. Gonzaga to Barbara, Rome, 2 December 1465, reported 'Messer Augustino di Maffei scriptor apostolico…e tuti suoi fratelli sono mei intimi amici e benivoli' (b. 842, c. 528); likewise to Marchese L. Gonzaga, Rome, 18 May 1467: 'non me manchono de prestarme denari e anche li sono debitor de parichii centenaia de ducati' (b. 843).

including the dowry of Benedetto's wife.[75] In spite of these embarrassments, the cardinal declared to his father that it was not his practice to keep money lying idle, and he would be glad to know what were the prospects of raising a loan in Venice or elsewhere.[76]

Three years later, Agostino Maffei, wrote from his prison in Castel Sant'Angelo (he had been involved with the alleged conspiracy against Paul II) complaining that he had never been repaid and that his relatives needed the money.[77] However, Agostino and Benedetto became complaisant enough after the marchese had made up the interest payment and promised to repay the 2000 ducats, and they agreed to extend the loan.[78] Later that year Agostino Maffei passionately denied that he and his family were a bad influence upon the cardinal.[79] In fact the self-interest behind their readiness to advance money to him is perfectly obvious; Francesco Maffei at about this time seems to have entered the cardinal's household on a regular basis and presumed to suggest that some economies be made.[80]

In the light of his own record, it comes as rather a surprise to learn that after the election of Sixtus IV in August 1471, when the new pope was in a state of anxiety wondering what to do about his feckless predecessor's hoard of jewels and *objets d'art*,[81] Cardinal Gonzaga was appointed (together with Cardinals Bessarion and Angelo Capranica) to a commission responsible for the debts left

[75] The negotiations are best summarized in a letter of Cardinal Francesco to Barbara on 7 June 1467. Initially 2000 ducats had been borrowed on the security of Marchese Ludovico's jewels, requiring 250 ducats a year interest and repayment of half the capital by July 1467; Agostino Maffei had lent 2000 ducats and Benedetto Maffei had lent a further 1000 ducats initially bearing interest at 10%. Francesco wrote to Barbara, Rome, 31 May 1467: '…messere Augustino me ne presta puoi anche mille altri, e mille ne haverò per mezo d'una hereditate de certa donna, la quale gli darà a dece per cento… Messer Augustino di suoi mille non dimanda interesse alcuno, ma quando serà el tempo de restituirli, Vostra Signoria se puoi…fare un dono de qualche argento de cento ducati…' (ASMn, AG, b. 843); see also below, n. 77.

[76] Cardinal F. Gonzaga to Marchese Ludovico Gonzaga, Rome, 9 September 1467: '…non è mio costume de lasciarmi avanzare troppo denari in cassa, anti più presto ho di debiti e non di piccol summa. Se per via del credito mio La puotesse trovare modo de prevalersi, o a Vinesia o altroe, io son contento che là mandi el factore mio, et a mio nome vede de raccatare quanti più denari la può' (ASMn, AG, b. 843).

[77] Agostino Maffei to Marchese L. Gonzaga, Castel Sant'Angelo, Rome, 8 February 1470: 'Circa tre anni fa che el cardinale…mi rechiese volesse prestare ducati doa milia venitiani e rescotere certe giogie…' (ASMn, AG, b. 844, c. 94); on 10 July, having heard that the marchese could not repay half of this sum for a year, he protested: 'Li altri mille, i quali sono denari dotali de la donna de mio fratello miser Benedetto, el Signor Cardinale li promise X per cento, come è ordine e statuto de Roma, non avuto per tre anni se non ducati cento… Anchor lui è stimulato da la donna, et è gravato de famiglia, et à la figliola da maritare' (ibid., c. 95).

[78] Agostino Maffei to Marchese L. Gonzaga, Rome, 18, 26 August 1470 (ASMn, AG, b. 844, cc. 94–7).

[79] Agostino Maffei to Marchese L. Gonzaga, Rome, 26 December 1470: 'Miser Antonio Strozo [Strozzi]…mi aferma essere vero che a la Illustrissima Signoria Vostra è stato persuaso che noi Maffei siamo quelli che mal governa el Signore Cardinale vostro, e che per noi non studia, né da audientia, e fa de molte male spese… O cieche scioche e stolte mente de li homini!…stimano la Illustrissima Signoria Vostra, insieme cum quella del Cardinale esser de pocho iuditio e sentimento, scrivendo ch'el Cardinale si lassi governare a noi, che mai né da voi, né da homo del mondo volse esser governato, e rasonevolmente, perché, nato signore sa più e più vede per esser più l'animo suo elevato che nissuno de noi sui subditi' (ibid., c. 98ʳ).

[80] F. Maffei to Marchese L. Gonzaga, Rome, 9 July 1470: 'ho exortato Sua Reverendissima Signoria a privarsi de parte de tanta famiglia, e *maxime* de quella che *iudicio suo* gli pareva mancho utile. E così insino a questi dì ne sono stati licentiati parechi, como appare per l'inclusa lista, e *etiam* per l'avenire, quanto a me sarà possibile ingegnerò de persuadere che si sminuischa e sia moderata la spesa…ho fatto il debito mio, e pur et non pareria in tutto laudabile ne honore al prefato Reverendissimo Signore, così in uno ponto licentiari molti famigli, sed *paulatim* in modo che *quodam modo* la brigata non comprehenda' (ASMn, AG, b. 844, c. 106).

[81] G.P. Arrivabene to Barbara, Rome, 13 August 1471: 'hoggi la Sanctitate de Nostro Signore ha dato mangiare a tuti li cardinali in castello, e doppo desnare messedorono tuto quello arientiere e gioie cumulate cum tanta anxietate. De denari se parla variamente, et alcuni dicono de grande quantitate, alcuni de puocho numero' (ASMn, AG, b. 844, c. 227).

behind by Paul II.[82] However, since the main assets to be sold were the pope's jewels, perhaps it was for his expertise in this area,[83] rather than for his own experience in money matters that Francesco was chosen.

It would not be possible, nor very enlightening, to document all the cardinal's subsequent credit transactions, but there is no doubt that he continued to meet his needs in the same mode, borrowing far and wide and ultimately relying upon his relatives to foot the bill. For instance, although early in 1473 he had written from Bologna assuring his mother that he hoped to put his affairs in better order,[84] he was seeking a loan—not for the first time, for this bright idea had already been floated in 1469[85]—from the *condottiere* Bartolomeo Colleoni. Although Colleoni apologized that he could not oblige on this occasion, willing though he would have been to lend even as much as 10,000 ducats,[86] he seems to have relented, since a large loan dating from this time was still outstanding many years later, long after his death in 1474.[87] The cardinal even borrowed money from Cardinal Pietro Riario; this sum (1500 ducats) his brothers Gianfrancesco and Rodolfo found themselves under threat of having to forfeit out of income owed to them by the pope for military services.[88] Nevertheless Gianfrancesco was evidently ready to oblige with more, and Marchese Ludovico Gonzaga to underwrite his loan.[89]

[82] Zippel, *Vite*, p. 92n. The evidence is in a papal letter of 1 October 1471 concerning the moneys owed by some of the purchasers, who included the Cardinal *camerlengo* Latino Orsini (AV, Div. Cam. 42, fols 3ᵛ–5ʳ), and instructions of the latter to the treasurer of the Patrimony, Guidantonio Piccolomini, to send the bill for unpaid salaries (previous to Sixtus IV's election) of the castellans of Vetralla and Tolfa to the cardinals 'deputatos super solutione debitorum…Pauli pape ii.' (AV, Div. Cam. 37, fol. 1ᵛ). I am grateful to Simon Ditchfield for pursuing Zippel's references for me.

[83] Cf. below, pp. 79–81.

[84] Cardinal F. Gonzaga to Barbara, Bologna, 26 February 1473: 'io spero de questi denari…in modo che me levarò da le spalle una grande parte di debiti che de presenti me aggravavano, e cum questi di[rigero?] li fatti miei a migliore ordine e forma per l'avenire' (ASMn, AG, b. 1141, c. 292).

[85] Cardinal F. Gonzaga to Barbara, Rome, 18 February 1469: 'Havendo io questi dì scritto a Juliano de Lancino che vedesse de trovarmi in prestito certa summa de denari, etiam cum qualche interesse, me rispuose che, havendo animo de richiedere quelli di Columbi, li quali fanno li facti de Bartholomeo da Bergamo, et havendone parlato cum Vostra Excellentia, Quella gli disse che voleva darmi un migliore adviso, cioè che io proprio li richiedessi esso Bartholomeo, dal qual se rendeva certa per l'amore che ha monstrato a casa nostra seria subvenuto' (ASMn, AG, b. 843).

[86] Colleoni had written to Marchese Ludovico Gonzaga from Malpaga, 4 October 1471, that he was willing to extend the term for repayment of an earlier loan to the cardinal (ASMn, AG, b. 1599) but this time, in a letter dated at Brescia 2 March 1473, explained that he could not oblige him: 'essendo venuto Carlo da Rodiano et havendomi facto intendere el gran piacere che prefata Illustre Signoria haveria servissse el Reverendissimo Monsignore Cardinale suo figliolo de ducati cinquemillia, ho recevuto dispiacere assai nela mente mia de trovarmi a questa domanda in li termini dove mi atrovo.' He nevertheless professed 'quando anche la fortuna mia voglia non solamente offero…5000 ducati, ma 6, 8 et anche Xᴹ' (ibid.).

[87] See below, pp. 128–30.

[88] Odoardus de Bonafrugiis to Gianfrancesco Gonzaga, Rome, 2 June 1473: 'me dice misser Augustino che…S. Sixto disse…essere satisfatto dal Reverendissimo Monsignor nostro, vostro fratello, de 1500 prestatigli, di quali già ne erano passati dui termini per le primi due tercii, et quando non havesse altro modo, se gli pigliaria di denari pertinenti a li Illustri suoi fratelli da la Sede Appostolica, et che de questi iii M. ducati se spectano de pesar, ne piglierìa ducati M. sopra el servito de lo Illustre misser Rodolfo, et poi a la prestanza vel ad altra exbursatione pertinente a Vostra Signoria, se pigliaria li altri 500 per lo resto…' (ASMn, AG, b. 845, c. 20).

[89] The draft or copy survives of a memorandum, dated at Borgoforte 12 October 1473, which was drawn up by Marsilio Andriasi and signed by the marchese. It is addressed to Gianfrancesco Gonzaga: '…essendo richiesto dal Reverendissimo Cardinale mio fiolo che voglia fargli la promessa de ducati cinquemillia d'oro, videlicet ducati 500 [sic] i quali la Vostra Signoria s'è offerta prestarli liberamente per sua cortesia e liberalitate, come ha referito Carlo da Rodiano, son contento, e per questa sottoscripta de man propria me obliga ad essa Vostra Signoria de restituirli dicti cinquemillia ducati ad ogni sua richiesta, purché da lei ne sia avisato et facto provisto de dui mesi inanti…' (ASMn, AG, b. 2187, c. 949).

Ludovico warned Francesco in July 1476, when he was about to obtain the bishopric of Bologna, that he could expect no more subvention from family sources,[90] but notwithstanding this threat, after the death of Ludovico (himself also encumbered by debts) in 1478, the cardinal inherited a share in his dominions, and became the lord of Sabbioneta and other places in the western part of Mantuan territory.[91] In the cardinal's will these lands and castles are cited as though normally income-bearing assets, but their possession may not have improved his financial situation so much as was hoped. He interested himself in them immediately after his return to Mantua in the winter of 1479–80, but money had to be found for their defence,[92] and bad harvests and warfare reduced their yield.[93] After his mother's death in November 1481 he also inherited Villanova and Fossamana, modest properties to the east of Mantua, as well as a quarter of her moveable possessions.[94]

Such windfalls did not provide much relief, and the borrowing had still gone on. The cardinal had jewels in pawn in Venice in 1479 which his creditor there was threatening to sell;[95] a series of letters to Angelo Baldesio, a longstanding Gonzaga agent in Venice, express his alarm and chagrin, and the measures taken to ensure the jewels were not sold.[96] Later the same year he was asking Giovanni Tornabuoni to be patient over payment then due.[97] Even his brother the protonotary Ludovico was squeezed; after Barbara of Brandenburg died, a credit note was found which proved that the cardinal owed him a substantial sum.[98] The state of the cardinal's affairs when he died in 1483 (to be discussed below), with many outstanding loans, including one of 3500 ducats from the Medici bank, unpaid

---

[90] Marchese Ludovico to Cardinal F. Gonzaga, Mantua, 31 July 1476: '…voressemo che ve resporesti a far quello che nui non possiamo, né che c'è lassato fare per non esserne atese le promesse de pagare vostri debiti' (ASMn, AG, b. 2894, lib. 81, fol. 28ᵛ). The cardinal nevertheless lamented to his father in a letter of 19 August 1476: 'le gravissime et intolerabile spese che per questo nostro andare intorno ce bisogna fare, me frustino terribelmente' (ASMn, AG, b. 845, c. 670).

[91] On Ludovico's missing will and the division of territory agreed between the brothers on 3 February 1479 (various copies of the deed in ASMn, AG, b. 20) see Mazzoldi, *Mantova*, I, pp. 36–8; see also Signorini, 'Ludovico muore', esp. p. 111 n. 49 concerning Ludovico's debts.

[92] Cardinal F. Gonzaga to the 'nobles' and men of Isola Dovarese, Mantua, 22 January 1480 (ASMn, AG, b. 2896, lib. 96, fol. 173ʳ).

[93] Carlo da Rodiano to Marchese Federico Gonzaga, 8 August 1482, reported the 'tristissimo recolto' at Rivarolo and Isola (ASMn, AG, b. 2430, cc. 158–9).

[94] ASMn, AN, Estensioni, R 78 (Cornice, 1481): summary of Barbara's will. The contents of Fossamana listed in the inventory after Barbara's death were very meagre; there was a quantity of hay and some goats there (ASDMn, FCC, ser. misc, b. 2/A: inventory, fol. 13 ᵛ).

[95] Cardinal F. Gonzaga to Carlo da Rodiano, Bologna, 14 September 1479: 'el bisogno de riscuotere quelle nostre zoie da Vinesia ne stringe molto, et Angelo [Baldesio] ne sollicita cum farne intendere che chi le ha minacia de venderle, se non se riscuoteno o che al mancho de presenti non se li paghino mille ducati' (ASMn, AG, b. 2896, lib. 96, fol. 16ʳ).

[96] Cardinal F. Gonzaga to Angelo Baldesio, Bologna, 10 October 1479: 'el ce rincresce, et è alieno da la natura e consuetudine nostra, de darve parola se non quanto vedemo haverli fundamento da puoterle cum li effecti verificare, duolendone anche la graveza che vedemo sosteneti per amore nostro nel caso de queste gioie… Pregamovi instrati cum quello gientilhomo a supportarne anchor un puocho…' (ibid., fols 59ʳ⁻ᵛ). On 12 October he again wrote to Baldesio about the jewels 'le quale non voressemo già per cosa del mundo se vendessero'; he had entrusted 'Hieronymo Ranucio, uno di Sedici di Bologna, nostro intimo' to act on his behalf (ibid., fols. 62ᵛ⁻3ʳ); on 17 October he announced that some of the money was to be paid through the Salutati bank (ibid., fol. 67ʳ).

[97] Cardinal F. Gonzaga to G. Tornabuoni, Bologna, 5 December 1479 (ibid., fol. 137ʳ⁻ᵛ).

[98] Among books and other articles in the Cardinal's house in Mantua 'in studio dicte domine in una capsa' was listed 'unum scriptum Reverendissimi domini Cardinalis de ducatis mille in quibus tenetur Reverendo Ludovico protonotario fratri suo' (ASMn, AN, Estensioni, R 78, Cornice, inventory fol. 1ʳ).

debts and unredeemed objects in pawn such as the costly pearl and ruby necklace recently given to the 'Cardinalino',[99] was totally predictable. It points to the conclusion that just as the cardinal's mania for acquisition or collecting had been a heavy drain on his resources, it had contained a speculative element. His need for ready cash may go some way to explain part of his motivation as a collector. The cardinal must have regarded his collector's pieces—including gems, crystal vases and books—in part as material sureties: after all, on his deathbed he assigned them specifically (W 35) for sale to meet outstanding debts.

---

[99] Pietro Spagnoli to Marchese Federico Gonzaga, Ferrara, 24 January 1483, writing about the visit of the 'figliolo de lo Reverendissimo Monsignore mio' (see above, p. 25) added: 'questa matina gli donò una colana de perle belissime da 40 ducati l'una, amezate da certi balassi infilciati inseme, de precio in tuto, secondo sua prelibata Reverendissima Signoria dice, de ducati 1800 etc.' (ASMn, AG, b. 1231, c. 110). On the pawning of the necklace see W 30, and for later references to it, below pp. 100, 104, 117.

Chapter 3: Cultural Profile of Cardinal Gonzaga

(i) Learning, Book Collecting and Patronage of Scholars and Poets

Francesco Gonzaga may in truth have had a rather mediocre mind. He acquired some reputation as a *mecenate* but never as a scholar or intellectual animator; in fact it might be argued that he failed to make as much as he might have done (if better equipped in brain and motivation) of his exceptional advantages. In childhood there is no evidence that he showed signs of special brightness, in spite of being taught by the successors of Vittorino da Feltre, including Ognibene da Lonigo and Platina.[1] He must have soon disappointed hopes that he might prove to be the equal of his brilliant uncle Giovan Lucido, by nature a poet, who as well as being able (allegedly) to recite all the works of Virgil by heart, attained a precocious mastery of civil law.[2] In the autumn of 1458, Francesco's teacher for the previous two years, Bartolomeo Marasca, noted specifically his weak memory and slowness to learn, though he claimed the credit for some recent improvement, and announced plans for practice in Latin conversation and readings of Virgil.[3] His parents, anticipating the papal diet which was to meet in Mantua in 1459, were worried that the young protonotary might damage his own prospects by his intellectual shortcomings and insisted that he should be made to work harder.[4] Giovan Lucido Cattanei at the beginning of his funeral oration declared that Ognibene of Lonigo had first taught Francesco, but gives credit to Marasca for his more intense teaching.[5]

Francesco had some further education in law; in 1459, at the time of the papal diet, he was introduced to the civil law by a Mantuan jurist, Girolamo Preti, who wrote for him an introduction to the *Institutes* (I 863), urging him to learn it by heart; in April 1460 he was sent to extend his law studies at the University of Pavia, accompanied by Preti and several other Mantuan doctors of law. On his arrival there, Francesco was visited by the entire college of jurists, including one of its most distinguished members, Catone Sacco, who made a formal speech of

---

[1] Luzio and Renier, 'I Filelfo', pp. 141–3.

[2] See Francesco Prendilacqua's *Dialogus* in praise of Vittorino, in Garin, *Pensiero pedagogico*, pp. 606–7.

[3] Marasca to Barbara, Cavriana, 31 October 1458, declared he had been teaching Francesco since 9 November 1456. In spite of his 'durecia, debilessima memoria, quali credo siano processe per non essere sollicitato al tempo che se sole o vero per le infirmitade ha havute', Marasca claimed some progress: 'non poria contare tuti le astutie e arte ho usato… È necessario a ciò piglia la consuetudine de parlare latino come altro che como io; vegniamo a Mantoa, unda farò venire amici mei, persone da bene, doe volte e tre la setimana a parlare latino como lui de diverse materie… Per tanto, Illustre Madona, lui vole, et anche a mi pare bene, che livre Virgilio qui, che serà circha a quindese lecione' (ASMn, AG, b. 2393 [Cavriana]); in part cited in Davari, *Studio pubblico*, p. 9. On Francesco's Latin lessons, see also I 835 and Figs 1–2.

[4] Relatively mild letters of exhortation to study, e.g., from Barbara 14 September 1458 (ASMn, AG, b. 2886, lib. 34, fol. 74^v) were followed by others more urgent in tone; e.g., those of 29 October to Francesco ('…sopra tuto ricordati de parlar continuamente per littera perché quando la Corte fosse quy, el serà vergogna a non saper parlare latino e bene; e ricordate che tu sey grande e grosso et hora pare essere uno homo') and to Marasca ('per Dio, non mancati de solicitudine per farlo studiare') to which Marasca's own letter, quoted above, must have been a reply (ibid., lib. 35, fols 5^v–6^r).

[5] Cattanei, *Orationes*, sig. Bviii-ix.

welcome,[6] and a week later promised to dedicate to him a commentary, or the text of his forthcoming lecture course.[7] But attending the lectures of Catone or of other jurists[8] landed Francesco in trouble: he incurred a sentence of excommunication, perhaps on account of his being a papal protonotary or because he already held minor orders. Barbara wrote in alarm to Francesco and Marasca that she had never been warned.[9] His private tutor Girolamo Preti disingenuously denied responsibility,[10] but fortunately the scandal was quickly overcome by means of a papal absolution, with a special dispensation allowing him to attend civil law lectures.[11] Francesco continued to attend the lectures of Catone;[12] he boasted of rising early and in October asked Barbara to lend him some kind of primitive alarm clock.[13] He launched into canon law during his second summer at Pavia, with private lessons from Giacomo d'Arezzo, who reported well of him,[14] and in November encouraged him to attend lectures in that subject.[15] While there is no reason to suppose that Francesco's academic attainment was very high, he was quite self-assertive in Pavian student affairs. He had been a candidate (unsuccessfully) for the rectorship of the *universitas* of jurists in June 1460,[16] and a year later imposed his will on the faculty by having one lecture course moved from the hottest hour of the afternoon to the morning.[17]

---

[6] G. P. Arrivabene to Barbara, Pavia, 27 April 1460 (ASMn, AG, b. 1621, c. 523) and Marasca to Barbara, Pavia, 28 April 1460: 'Io dì de Sancto Zorzo venne la universitade del Studio, et haviano eleto messer Catto Sacho a dire la oratione, e la risposta fece lo Illustre Monsignore mio, io la mandì per messer Stephano Zampo' (ASMn, AG, b. 1621, c. 454). On Catone see, for instance, Vaccari, *Storia*, p. 71; Volta, 'Catone Sacco'; Lublinsky, 'Le Semideus'. Zampo and Antonio Bonatto were among the Mantuan doctors of law accompanying Francesco and were praised by him in a letter to Barbara of 30 April for their performance, probably on the same occasion (b. 2096).

[7] Bartolomeo Marasca to Barbara, Pavia, 3 May 1460: 'heri sera messer Catone fece publicare per tute le scole como a laude de lo Illustre Monsignore protonotario de Gonzaga e marcheso. Vole lunedì cominzare lo titulo *De pactis*, e scrivere sopra vinti quinterni, la quale opera sia intitulata a lo prefato Illustre Monsignore' (ASMn, AG, b. 1621, c. 456); Magenta, *I Visconti e gli Sforza*, I, p. 471, n. 2.

[8] Marasca to Barbara, Pavia, 5 May 1460: 'adesso andiamo a la scola, e qui se comenzia lo tratato de chi in altri mei ho scritto' (ASMn, AG, b. 1621, c. 457).

[9] Mantua, 9 May 1460 (ASMn, AG, b. 2886, lib. 37, fols 84ʳ, 85ʳ, 92ʳ); Mazzoldi, *Mantova*, II, p. 58. See above, p. 28.

[10] Girolamo Preti to Barbara, undated: 'heri io recevey una littera de la Eccelentia Vostra sopra el facto de la prohibitione de lo odire leze civile del Reverendo et Illustre Monsignore...respondo che non me recordo esser me dato aviso alcuno circa ciò...de questa studiar de Monsignor non have' may parlamento alcuno cum Quella salvo quando ge parse che io lezesse la Instituta a la Signoria Sua' (ASMn, AG, b. 1621, c. 547). Preti was reported by Marasca, in a letter of 19 June 1460, to be about to leave Pavia: 'me ne dole asai, perché è homo d'asai' (ibid., c. 478).

[11] Bartolomeo Bonatto to Barbara, Siena, 15 May 1460 (ASMn, AG, b. 1099, c. 598).

[12] G. P. Arrivabene to Barbara, Pavia, 19 July 1460 (ASMn, AG, b. 1621, c. 530).

[13] Protonotary F. Gonzaga (autograph) to Barbara, Pavia, 22 July 1460: '...adesso me levo a setto ore per andare a la schola', and 31 October 1460: 'perché, havendo a levare la mattina a bon hora per intrare a la lectione, puoria accadere qualche fiata domenticarmi in letto, priego Vostra Signoria me voglia mandare il suo svegliarolo' (ibid., cc. 432, 434).

[14] Giacomo d'Arezzo to Barbara, Pavia, 16 July 1461: 'Molti gio[rni] fa l'incominciai a leggere in casa alcuni capitoli in rasgion canonica, e secondo el pare[re] mio questa facultà gli piace non meno che rasgion civile, per la qual cosa comprehendo che per l'avenire farà buno studio in ditta facultà, et maxime che omgni dì cercha com diligentia fornirse de libri necessarii, et novamente ha comperò uno bono et bello libro per presio de ducati ottanta' (ASMn, AG, b. 1621, c. 1050).

[15] Giacomo d'Arezzo to Barbara, Pavia, 6 November 1461: '...gomençò [on 5 November] el prefato Monsignor intrare audire in rason canonica, et secondo el parer mio demostra de bona vogla volerli dar opera, et io colla diligentia debita lo sollecitarò quanto a me serà possibile' (ASMn AG b. 1621, c. 1051).

[16] See Sottili, 'Il palio', pp. 84–6.

[17] Marasca to Federico Gonzaga and Barbara, Pavia, 29 June 1461 (ASMn, AG, b. 1621, cc. 1026–7, cited by Magenta, *I Visconti e gli Sforza*, I, p. 472).

These episodes usefully reveal that self-promotion, family prestige and creature-comfort were already among Francesco's highest priorities. During his last weeks at Pavia he was exhorted by an emissary from his mother, and by Marasca and Giacomo d'Arezzo, to study more seriously and also to make his confession; their reproaches, together with the news from Rome, presumably about the imminence of his red hat, momentarily chastened him.[18]

After Francesco became a cardinal, it was of even greater concern to his parents that he should study; his father pointed out frankly that an unlettered prelate was of no repute at all,[19] although in truth Pius II does not seem to have regarded this as so essential for cardinals of princely blood.[20] Giacomo d'Arezzo, now auditor of the household, wrote what he could in the cardinal's defence, emphasizing his unavoidable distractions, particularly in having to follow Pius II on his travels.[21] In one of his rare autograph letters, Francesco admitted to some shortcomings of his own,[22] and the letter tells its own story, for like other examples of his hand, it is laboriously written and sometimes barely literate. Only one of Francesco's early and personal letters tells us something positive about his mind. For this very long letter to his father, written in December 1462, at least reveals some reasoning power, if somewhat unscrupulous not to mention imprudent reasoning: for Francesco expounded a plot to unseat the Bishop of Trent by kidnapping him.[23] With a few exceptions, most of the autograph letters are addressed to his father, perhaps as a gesture of deference,[24] but they contrast strikingly with the cleverly phrased letters (several hundred of them) elegantly written in the cardinal's name by his secretary Giovan Pietro Arrivabene: very few of these even bear Francesco's signature, apart from one directed to his mother and another to his father.[25] Inevitably the question arises whether these letters may not express more Arrivabene's wit and judgement (they correspond

---

[18] Marasca to Barbara, Pavia, 4 December 1461: 'Certo me dice per quella ambassata essere tanto ben disposto quanto fusse mai. Et cominciassemo a parlare de la confessione quale, credo, tosto farà… Me trovai con messer Jacomo…et deliberassemo parlare tuti dui a confortarlo al ben vivere, al studio, et ad ugni bene. Hane ascultati benignamente, e resposo optimamente. Modo è sopragionto quello se contiene ne le littere veneno da Roma, che tanto lo ha comosso che è in grandi pensieri…' (ASMn, AG, b. 1621, c. 1038).

[19] Marchese Ludovico to Cardinal F. Gonzaga, Goito, 27 April 1462, among other precepts insisted: '…prelato senza littere non può essere reputato' (ASMn, AG, b. 2097).

[20] Haubst, 'Der Reformentwurf', pp. 211–12: 'in filiis tamen regum vel nepotibus ac magnorum principum, quos aliquando pro magna ecclesiae utilitate convenit honorare, mediocris litteratura sufficiat.'

[21] Giacomo d'Arezzo to Marchese Ludovico Gonzaga, Tivoli, 13 August 1463: 'Quanto a lo studio, dice che po' ben considerar la Vostra Illustre Signoria quante incom[modi]tade sonno occorse nelli tempi passati per rispecto della peste, in modo è bisognato [an]dar sempre errando in qua in là. Non nega perhò che alcuna fiata non havesse po[tuto] dare più opera a lo studio non ha fatto, ma di qua inançi, fermandosi li tempi […], spera darà tale opera che merito porrà esser commendato' (ASMn, AG, b. 842, c. 227); he wrote to Barbara, Rome, 2 December 1464: 'Lo Reverendissimo Monsignore nostro heri mandò per mi a posta, dicendome che in tutto hav[erà fatto?] opera a lo studio, et imposime dovesse trovare un libro era di bisogno' (b. 842, c. 393).

[22] Cardinal F. Gonzaga (autograph) to Marchese Ludovico, Tivoli, 14 August (no year given, but it must be—as above—1463): 'me pare habia studiato asai mediocremente al tempo pocho che ho io habuto…' (ASMn, AG, b. 843, incorrectly filed as if written in 1468).

[23] On this letter see above, p. 43 n. 54.

[24] Apart from the two letters mentioned above, and twelve letters from the period before he became a cardinal (in ASMn, AG, b. 1621, 2095, 2096) the following are the total of autograph letters I have found: one to Barbara, 3 August 1464 (b. 2098: see Fig. 13); two to Marchese Ludovico Gonzaga, 23 October, 13 November 1466 (b. 843); one to Barbara, 28 January 1469 (ibid.) and two to Galeazzo Maria Sforza, 24 October 1471, 4 February 1476 (ASMil., Autografi, Cardinali, b. 28).

[25] ASMn, AG, b. 844, c. 35; b. 846, c. 119. Most cardinals' letters do end with autograph signatures.

closely to the many letters Arrivabene wrote in his own name) than his patron's.[26] Cardinal Jacopo Ammannati must, however, be cited, for what appears to be just the opposite opinion; in a letter to Francesco in 1475 he claimed he could detect the latter's own voice even in letters written by Arrivabene, and this may be an important and positive piece of evidence in Francesco's favour. Ammannati also affirms that even if Francesco was no writer, he did read and think for himself.[27]

Nevertheless Giovan Pietro Arrivabene, only four years his senior, was probably the dominant cultural influence upon Francesco. He had been a favourite pupil of Francesco Filelfo, who taught him Greek and nicknamed him 'Eutychius'; in his earlier years he also wrote some Latin poetry.[28] Arrivabene remained with Francesco from before the time he went to study at Pavia, and until his patron's death, and his efficiency as secretary has already been mentioned: his conscientiousness in this role may explain why he seems to have given up his own literary or scholarly ambitions, though he remained an ardent bibliophile and copied books for himself.[29]

Giacomo d'Arezzo, as the leading canon lawyer of the household, must also have exerted some force upon the cardinal's mind; he was nearly as long in his service as Arrivabene. But he is a less obtrusive personality than Bartolomeo Marasca, Francesco's master of the household. Marasca tried sincerely to combine with this office the role of pedagogue and spiritual adviser, but his letters have an unctuous tone, and it is not very surprising if he aroused antipathy. His literary works extended only to sermons and a treatise on dying (thought to be the first written in Italian), and it is unlikely that Francesco found these congenial either.[30] Maybe, for the short while he was with the household, Giovanni Stefano Bottigella exerted some intellectual influence upon Francesco, though his letters do not betray much evidence of his imparting knowledge readily, except once, in offering a cure for stomach-ache.[31]

There were some others in the household whose influence was educational, in different ways. These include Francesco's early humanist tutor, Bartolomeo Sacchi, Platina, whose first release from jail the cardinal secured early in 1465 and who remained a member—not an officer—of his household until c. 1471, except during his second prison term in 1468–9, which also ended thanks largely to Francesco's intercession.[32] Behind Platina and his friends stood the charismatic figure of Pomponio Leto (1427–98). It is difficult to establish any direct contact between Pomponio and Francesco, who successfully distanced himself from the more subversive associations of the 'Academy'. Nevertheless, when he was in trouble, Pomponio claimed that he had composed his Latin poem on the peniten-

[26] See Chambers, 'Arrivabene', esp. p. 404.

[27] 'A calamis non venit sors tua; nec crevit. Melius legendo oculos quam scribendo manum exercere es solitus: et meditari utilius quam atramenta tractare. Dummodo te in tuo secretario agnoscam...' (Ammannati to the Cardinal of Mantua, 11 August 1475, in Ammannati, *Epistolae*, fol. 299ᵛ).

[28] Faccioli, *Mantova*, I, pp. 62–6, II, pp. 62–4; Chambers, 'Arrivabene', p. 399, concerning the *Gonzagidos* and *Carmina ad Pium II*, both of which I suggested Giovan Pietro wrote c. 1459.

[29] Chambers, 'Arrivabene', pp. 418–21.

[30] Chambers, 'Marasca', 1989, pp. 269–77, esp. pp. 274–5; Tenenti, *Senso della morte*, pp. 101–2.

[31] Bottigella to Marchese L. Gonzaga, 21 October 1466, promises to send this remedy from a 'libro de alchune recepte singulare', a book thought to have belonged to King Alfonso of Naples (ASMn, AG, b. 843). He did, however, suggest to Filelfo translating Appian (*DBI*, s.v.).

[32] Chambers, 'Il Platina', pp. 9–19.

tial places in Rome for Cardinal Gonzaga, representing this as evidence of his own moral and religious integrity.[33] In fact—according to the only known and later version of it—the work seems to have been equally concerned with Roman sites which did not have such associations.[34] But the indirect presence of Pomponio in Francesco's mental and social world is undeniable, both before 1468 and in the later 1470s when he presided over the second and more conformist 'Roman Academy'.

Francesco's many associates among Pomponio's 'Academicians' included Agostino Maffei and his brothers, whose money-lending services have already been mentioned. Whether or not unscrupulous in their dealings,[35] the Maffei, particularly Agostino, who was acclaimed by Pomponio Leto as a 'treasury of knowledge' about ancient Rome,[36] were serious bibliophiles,[37] and Agostino, a scriptor of the papal chancery, copied and annotated books for his own library.[38] His familiarity with Francesco is suggested in a letter of December 1470, protesting his own innocence as a bad influence and incidentally pointing to Arrivabene and Giacomo d'Arezzo (also, less convincingly, Platina) as moral mainstays of the cardinal's establishment.[39] He cited as further witnesses in his defence, passages from St Jerome, Terence and Cicero. Neither Bartolomeo Marasca, Giacomo d'Arezzo, nor Giovan Pietro Arrivabene betray much of what they felt about the tone of these more libertine humanists, but they seem to have had only a qualified respect for Platina; although Giacomo d'Arezzo writing in October 1464 praised his literary ability, both he and Arrivabene seem to have accepted that the cardinal's line of defence with Paul II, that Platina was crazy, was just about the truth of the matter,[40] and in 1468 Marasca may even have connived at Platina's second arrest, since it happened when he was having supper in the cardinal's house.[41]

Francesco Filelfo provided the cardinal with a long reading list in 1465, when he was already twenty-one years old. The letter containing it[42] begins with some extravagant compliments proclaiming that he was already learned in civil and canon law and that, thanks to his father, he knew many precepts of the philosophers. He was advised nevertheless to make a point of studying St Jerome's Latin version of the Bible, St Augustine's *City of God* and Gregory the Great's

[33] 'Habetis confessionem meam simul et defensionem quas et defendunt disticha ad singulas stationes a me composita et Cardinali Mantuano dicata…' (MS BAV, Vat. Lat. 2934, fol. 308ʳ), quoted in Zabughin, *Pomponio Leto*, I–II, p. 52. On Pomponio see also the brief account in D'Amico, *Humanism*, pp. 91–102.

[34] Extracts in Zabughin, *Pomponio Leto*, pp. 293–5, nn. 142–8.

[35] See above, pp. 45–7.

[36] In the dedication of his edition of Sallust Pomponio acclaims him 'rerum romanarum thesaurus' (Rossi, 'Niccolò Cosmico', p. 109).

[37] Ruysschaert, 'Recherche des deux bibliothèques', pp. 306–55; 51 books belonging to the (Veronese) Maffei family are identified, many of them first acquired by Agostino or Benedetto.

[38] Agostino's copy of Terence's *Comoediae* is inscribed at the end (MS BL, Add. 14085, fol. 198ʳ): 'Augustini Maffei scriptoris apostolici gratias finito libro referamus Christo' (noted by Ruysschaert, 'Recherche des deux bibliothèques', no. 72, p. 335).

[39] '…el c'è in casa del cardinale misser Zuan Piero homo modesto, grave, prudente e dotto, ecci anchor misser Jacomo d'Arezzo, buono e intendente homo; avete anchor el Platina, de doctrina excellente, e ne le cose corrente universale' (ASMn, AG, b. 844, c. 98ᵛ), letter cited above, p. 46 n. 79.

[40] Chambers, 'Il Platina', pp. 11, 17 nn. 12, 13.

[41] Chambers, 'Marasca', p. 271.

[42] Filelfo to Cardinal F. Gonzaga, Milan, 6 kal. Aug. 1465 (*Epistolarum …libri*, fol. 172ʳ⁻ᵛ); the letter is also mentioned by Bianca, 'Filelfo', p. 210.

De moralibus. Aristotle, Plato and Seneca could be left aside—Filelfo more realistically assured him—so long as Gregory the Great's precepts for a good and holy life were studied. On the other hand, all the works of Cicero were important; and since history is the teacher of life, Filelfo continued, the cardinal should read Livy, Julius Caesar's *Commentaries*, Sallust, Quintus Curtius, the elder Pliny and Plutarch's *Lives*. Filelfo also recommended that he should make an effort to read Greek, perhaps when the weather was bad at Marino or Albano; Arrivabene (Filelfo's own ex-pupil) would give him some help. However, there is little reason to suppose that the cardinal paid much attention to this advice.

Probably Francesco gained a stronger grasp of jurisprudence than of most other subjects. His knowledge in this field also had some scope for practical application, particularly when he came to acquire administrative responsibilities as bishop of Mantua and legate at Bologna. It is surprising that when asked to provide books (presumably law books) for Ludovico, his youngest brother, to start studying at home in 1475, the cardinal had answered he was unable to do so, and that he had only a copy of the *Decretals*, but perhaps this implies he could not spare any of his law books since he might have needed them himself for reference.[43] It may have been in part as a tribute to Francesco's interest in legal studies that in 1476 Ludovico Bolognini (1446–1508) dedicated to him his curious metrical version of Gratian's *Decretum* [I 869]; some years later, suspicion was aroused that Bolognini had written disparagingly about the cardinal, but this proved unfounded.[44]

Moreover, Francesco's letters occasionally record his strong opinions in matters of jurisdiction. For instance, he was inflexible in upholding clerical immunity from secular judgement. Thus he was not in sympathy with his father's determination to have a delinquent priest, the bandit Mandello, put to death in 1477 and even offered to pay for the expense of keeping him in a cage instead;[45] likewise, he wrote from Rome (shortly before his final journey north) expressing his opinion that the defrocking proposed for another priest was a punishment too severe, being equivalent to the death sentence upon a layman.[46] On the other hand one cannot tell whether such pronouncements originated in his own mind or another's; in this particular case, perhaps he repeated the professional advice of his former law auditor at Bologna, the canonist Benedetto Mastino, now Arch-

---

[43] Giovanni Arrivabene (brother of Giovan Pietro) to Barbara of Brandenburg, Rome, 18 November 1475: 'Rincresce a Sua Signoria non trovarsi havere il modo de provedere de libri al Reverendo protonotario suo fratello, che lo faria voluntera, et dice havere solamente le decretale, como per altra mia scrissi a Vostra Signoria, et pareriali che per questo anno se facesse studiare a casa per darli qualche principio de comparere puoi meglio in studio, e fra questo mezo se vedria farli provisione de libri' (ASMn, AG, b. 845, c. 418).

[44] Galeazzo della Rovere, *luogotenente* of Bologna, to Marchese Francesco Gonzaga, Bologna, 7 January 1485: 'sentendo io, che per alcuni era infamiato miser Lodovico de Bolognini, cavalere et doctore integerrimo, che lui in una certa opera sua laudabile e digna, quale al presente ha dato fora, sopra alcuni passi tochava alcune cose in detractione dello honore della felice recordatione e memoria Monsignore Reverendissimo di Mantua… in verità trovo la predicta opera di miser Lodovico netta, pura, et innocente, et in la quale non se trova una parola disonesta…' (ASMn, AG, b. 1142).

[45] Signorini, *Opus hoc tenue*, pp. 61–2.

[46] Cardinal F. Gonzaga to Marchese Federico Gonzaga, Rome, 25 November 1482: 'Et maxime che dal archidiacono nostro de Mantuoa ne fu scritto li havevano dato solum penitentia de pagare cinquanta ducati, di quali la maiore parte era applicata a la fabrica de Sancta Maria lì da li Voti, e da starsi alcuni dì in certo monasterio, che pareva fusse più presto una penitentia sacramentale che iudiciale. La privatione a' preti è come de iure civili ad un laico la morte… Perhò e li sacri canoni e li executori de essi non procedeno a tal acto *nisi ex maxima causa*' (ASMn, AG, b. 846, c. 519).

deacon of Mantua. We may accept quite straightforwardly the remark by Giovanni Bentivoglio, when warned in 1483 that Francesco might not live much longer, that he and the Sedici hoped above all a good canon lawyer could be found, of the right age and moral character, to take over the bishopric—'like this present one of ours'; but even if Giovanni was sincere in his praise of Francesco as a judicious legate and bishop, he probably appreciated him most for his political uses.[47]

* * *

In view of his rather unpromising educational record and the want of direct evidence about any studious bent developing later, it may seem surprising that Francesco Gonzaga became such an avid collector of books. Perhaps the initial incentive depended more upon imitation than intellectual interest: from his earliest years he must have been aware of the libraries of his parents and their friends, and as a young man he was soon able to compare the Gonzaga library with that of the Sforza (ex-Visconti) library in Pavia,[48] and with the book collections of Piero and Giovanni de'Medici which he was shown when he visited Florence in March 1462.[49] Once in Rome he was exposed to the influence of Pius II and of many other bibliophiles and connoisseurs in the papal curia.

The subject of Francesco's book collection has to be introduced here, although it will recur later in connection with the inventory. In boyhood Francesco already employed a scribe, Giuliano da Viterbo, who also worked for Guido Gonzaga (I 815): perhaps he even tried to teach Francesco the art of writing. Three works Giuliano copied for him are recorded in the inventory; two of them survive today. One is an elementary Latin grammar to suit his needs, dated 1457 and possibly composed by Marasca (I 835: Figs 1–2); another was the small copy of Ovid's *Metamorphoses*;[50] the third, a small work on geomancy, the whereabouts of which is unknown (I 894). Francesco made Giuliano one of his closest personal chamberlains at Pavia, in place of one who was sick and negligent, commenting that Giuliano was always alert and interested in his affairs.[51] His first law tutor, Girolamo Preti, was the author of another book written for Francesco as a teaching aid, the introduction to the *Institutes* (I 863) already mentioned. Subsequently

---

[47] G. Bentivoglio to Giangaleazzo Maria Sforza, Bologna, 10 September 1483: 'achadendo el caso del morte sua, *quod Deus avertat*… Questi nostri Magnifici signori Rezimenti et mi desyderamo summamente de potere ellegere uno vescovo bolognese che fusse homo doctissimo in iure pontificio et de età perfecta et de costumi che potesse bene governare le anime de tanto populo, quanto è questo nostro' (ASMil, Sforzesco, cart. 194).

[48] G. P. Arrivabene had written to Barbara from Pavia, 27 April 1460: 'heri lo vescovo de Cremona lo venne a visitare et insiema andorono in castello…e fra l'altre cosse viddi la libraria e relliquie che lì sonno' (ASMn, AG, b. 1621, c. 523; Magenta, *I Visconti e gli Sforza*, I, p. 470, n. 1), and on 23 July 1460: 'heri mattina lo Reverendissimo et Illustre Monsegnore mio disnoe in castello cum lo Illustrissimo Conte Galeacio… doppo disnare introrono in libraria a vedere tanto ornamento et habundantia de libri che lì sonno' (ASMn, AG, b. 1621, c. 531).

[49] Only the poet Giovan Francesco Soardi, among all who wrote to Barbara of Brandenburg from Florence, mentioned in his letter of 15 March 1462 that the cardinal had been shown 'li studii di Pietro e Giovanni belissimi, e gran copia di bei libri' (ASMn, AG, b. 1100, c. 102), printed in Chambers, 'Cardinal Gonzaga in Florence', doc. 5, p. 252.

[50] MS Paris, BN, Lat. 10311 (see I 755).

[51] Protonotary F. Gonzaga to Barbara, 17 May 1460: '…lo levaria de camera et sustitueria uno mio scritore, Juliano da Viterbo, el quale, connoscendolo sollicito e curioso ne li fatti mei, son certo che togliendolo a tal officio faria diligentemente quanto sa partenesse a lui' (ASMn, AG, b. 1621, c. 431).

his canon law tutor, Giacomo d'Arezzo,[52] remarked on his eagerness to buy law books, which is borne out by a letter Francesco sent after returning from a short vacation in November 1461, in which he asked his mother to try and buy for him copies he had seen in Mantua of the Sext and Clementines.[53]

Francesco was also put to use by his parents concerning books. At Pavia, he was urged by his mother to induce Belbello to complete the illuminations in the large missal which had originally been commissioned by Giovan Lucido Gonzaga when studying there. (Instead, however, and on Mantegna's recommendation, it was completed by Girolamo da Cremona).[54] At Rome, within one month of his arrival, he was asked by his father to try and borrow for copying a good Greek text of the Bible, a request which brought him into early contact with Cardinal Bessarion, who offered to lend the Gospels and the Old Testament, though the latter he had left in Florence.[55] Shortly afterwards Bessarion invited the young cardinal to dinner,[56] when the matter, or other matters concerning books, may have been further discussed, though his father's eager response could not by then have been received before the papal court departed for Viterbo.[57] Presumably Francesco had brought with him to Rome whatever books he had already accumulated; at all events, books were left behind there—in Cardinal Prospero Colonna's house—when he went off with the rest of Pius II's entourage.[58] Some of Guido Gonzaga's books passed to Francesco, who planned to get a papal brief entitling him to all of Guido's moveable goods. For example, in December 1463 Barbara was seeking a breviary—in fact, a choir book—of Guido's which she thought was in Francesco's possession.[59] At least two books still extant, which are listed in the inventory of 1483, were Guido's (I 812, 815).

[52] See above, p. 51, n. 14.

[53] Protonotary F. Gonzaga to Barbara, Pavia, 5 November 1461: 'Quando era lì viddi a S. Dominico un bello Sexto e Clementine, quali summamente me piacevano. E perché ho gran desiderio puoterli havere, prego la Vostra Signoria farne fare un pocho de pratica cum li frati e vedere de indurli a vendere questi libri' (ASMn, AG, b. 1621, c. 1128).

[54] Barbara to Protonotary F. Gonzaga, Mantua, 21 June 1460, 10 November 1461 (ASMn, AG, b. 2888, lib. 47, fol. 6; lib. 49, fol. 8) and from him to Barbara, Pavia, 5 November 1461 ('mando a Vostra Signoria quella parte del messale era qua'), 19 November 1461 (ASMn, AG, b. 1621, cc. 1128, 1133), discussed by Meroni, *Mostra*, pp. 55–6; Berselli, 'Messale miniato', pp. 33–4; Pastore and Manzoli, *Il messale*; see I 687.

[55] Cardinal F. Gonzaga to Marchese Ludovico Gonzaga, Rome, 21 April 1462: 'de la Biblia greca ho parlato col Reverendissimo Monsignor mio Niceno, el quale me ha rispuosto che qua non se ritrova havere, se non el Testamento novo, el quale vogliendo io fare transcrivere in Roma me lo prestarà, e cussì ritrovando scriptore lo farò copiare; che l'altra parte, cioé el Testamento vechio, l'ha a Fiorenza' (ASMn, AG, b. 841, c. 438).

[56] Giacomo d'Arezzo to Barbara, 3 May 1462 (ASMn, AG, b. 841, c. 642).

[57] Marchese Ludovico to Cardinal F. Gonzaga, 4 May 1462, informed his son 'haremo a caro, possendose ritrovar in Roma un bono scriptore là, ne voglia far scrivere quella Biblia greca e in carte di capreto…sapiamo ch'el gli è persone doctissime che quando la serà scripta là se poterà fare apontare e coregere dove bisognasse' (ASMn, AG, b. 2888, lib. 46, fol. 23ᵛ).

[58] Francesco da Pavia to (?) Marchese Ludovico Gonzaga, Rome 23 July 1462: '…in cassa de Monsignore de la Columna sono li libri de Monsignore nostro'(ASMn, AG, b. 841, c. 599); Chambers, 'Housing Problems', p. 46, doc. 8.

[59] See above, pp. 26, 39; Protonotary F. Gonzaga to Barbara, Bozzolo, 29 October 1461: 'me parerave fare in questa forma de impetrare uno breve dal papa che in ogne loco che acata di beni mobeli del Reverendo meser Guido che possa conseguerli como cose de lo mio benificio' (ASMn, AG, b. 2096, autograph); Franciscus Gregnanus [da Grignano], Prior of Sant'Antonio in Mantua, to Barbara, Rome, 27 December 1463: 'sopra la facenda del breviario…parlay chon lo Reverendissimo Monsignor mio…non ha may sentito che misser Guido havese altry breviari cha quelly ha al presente la Sua Signoria…hora havendo inteso che non è breviario ma è pur un libro de canto de quelly fu del prefato misser Guido, secundo dice Antonio Donato, piarò il tempo e parlaròne chon la Reverendissima Sua Signoria…' (ASMn, AG, b. 842, c. 81).

It may be that even if Francesco did not greatly appreciate the content of books, he always valued them as fine objects, the skilled work of scribes, illuminators and binders. He appears to have received as a gift from his mother the same large missal (the one decorated by Belbello and others) which probably was the 'messale grande' he had requested in place of a 'messaletto piccolo' which he had given back to her, in May 1467.[60] Francesco was so delighted after the arrival of 'questo suo messale', according to another letter to Barbara, three months later, that he declared every time he went to Marino or came back to Rome he wanted to have it with him.[61] Maybe therefore he did delight more in its script and decoration than in the order of prayers, for which a simple missal would have sufficed.

Similarly, when Francesco asked if he could borrow his father's Aelius Spartianus, it was not only to have the text copied, but also the illuminated portraits of the Caesars, based on Roman medals, which it contained.[62] It is tempting to wonder if the illuminator 'who knows how to draw well', mentioned by the cardinal, could already have been Gaspare da Padova, who in 1484 was to write that he had been in the cardinal's service for over sixteen years.[63] Ludovico's reply was not over-enthusiastic, and he wrote that he himself did not know of anyone capable of doing the job, but he promised a brief loan of the book.[64]

Evidently this was no isolated case of a loan. In 1476 a list was sent from Mantua of books to be recalled, which Francesco was believed to have borrowed.[65] The cardinal denied having borrowed a Suetonius at all, nor did he have a Justin although he admitted he had once had it. What he did have was a copy of a

---

[60] Cardinal F. Gonzaga to Barbara, Rome, 20 May 1467: 'mando a la Excellentia Vostra per Rolandino di Maffei el messaletto piccolo che Quella altra fiata me donoe, e pregola che la voglia mo mandarmi quello altro messale grande che gli ho fatto richiedere, che me ne farà singulare piacere' (ASMn, AG, b. 843). See I 687, but note that Francesco possessed two other missals at the time of his death (I 396, 750).

[61] Cardinal F. Gonzaga to Barbara, 10 August 1467, 'ugni fiata che vado a Marini o vengo qui sempre voglio haverlo drieto, né mai me trovo senza esso' (b. 843). See also, with earlier bibliography: Meroni, *Mostra*, pp. 54–5; Marani and Perina, *Mantova: Le arti*, II, p. 253; Signorini, 'Baldassare Soardi', in Campana and Meldioli-Masotti, *Platina*, p. 164; for a different view, suggesting a third missal was involved, Berselli, 'Messale miniato'; in general, see Pastore and Manzoli, *Il messale*.

[62] Cardinal F. Gonzaga to Marchese Ludovico Gonzaga, Rome, 15 November 1466: '… Gli significo ch'el desiderio mio è stato de haverlo solum per fare cavare copia e del libro e de quelle facie de Imperatori, le quale non trovo qui suso altri Spartiani li quali haverei potuto havere per exemplari. E perché me ritrovo havere copia d'uno miniatore el qual saperà bene ritrare, prego la Signoria Vostra che voglia prestarmelo' (ASMn, AG, b. 843); printed in Luzio and Renier, 'I Filelfo', pp. 136–7 n. 4; Degenhart, 'Ludovico II Gonzaga', p. 209 n. 24. See also I 802.

[63] See Appendix 3, no. 9, and below, p. 62.

[64] Marchese L. Gonzaga to Francesco, Mantua, 25 November 1466 (this reply is not noted by Luzio and Renier): 'havemo ricevuto la littera vostra che ne scriveti circa lo Helio Spartiano, del quale ne parloe Zohanne Arrivabene da parte vostra. Et certo, como gli dicessemo, non è che non ve ne serviamo volontieri, ma considerando che quando ben volessemo farne fare uno cussì digno et bello, non trovaressemo che lo sapesse fare non se ne volessemo privare, ma per prestarvelo, aciò lo faciati transcrivere et tuore quelle facie de imperatori, como diceti, siamo contenti de serviverne et cussì lo havemo facto dare fuori, aciò se tegna modo de mandarvello. Haveremo ben piacere assai gli faciati havere bon riguardo et quando lo haveriti adoperato, ce lo mandiati' (ASMn, AG, b. 2890, lib. 56, fol. 71ʳ).

[65] Cardinal F. Gonzaga to Marchese Ludovico Gonzaga, Rome, 1 May 1476: 'Circa li libri che la Signoria Vostra me richiede per rimetterli in la Suoa libraria, io non me trovo havere quello de XII Cesaribus, ne ho anche a mente haverlo mai havuto. Forsi che ricerchando se trovarà dato ad altro, come etiam lo Iustino che prima stimava fusse presso di me. La chronica vulgare ho bene, e quella mandarò per lo primo victural me accada. De quello repertorio vechio del'Abbate di Nerli non ho anche noticia, ne a le man mie me ricordo capitasse mai. Pur, se tuta volta se trovasse tra altre scripture che anche a Bologna farò cerchare, se mandarà. Da Avignone non confido a questi tempi se puotesse cavare cosa alcuna de privilegii e scripture antique' (ASMn, AG, b. 845, c. 645).

vernacular chronicle (if Mantuan, possibly the rhyming chronicle of Aliprandi) but not the collection by Andrea Nerli, one-time Abbot of Sant'Andrea in Mantua (perhaps meaning Nerli's incomplete *Chronicon* or *Vitae* of the former abbots of Sant'Andrea, 800–1431).[66] Maybe he derived some of his interest in history—as of so many other subjects—from the example of Paul II,[67] though with regard to the past of his native city and forbears, his curiosity had probably been sharpened by Platina who c. 1466 was composing his *History of Mantua*.[68] To cite a further instance, Francesco wrote to his father in 1472 about a medieval document which had come to his attention in Bologna, though his interest in this may have been less historical than on account of its possible use to establish lawful title.[69]

It is not clear whether the cardinal maintained a regular scriptorium in addition to his chancery or whether most of his books were outside commissions, gifts, bequests, or even purchases from booksellers, of whom there was at least one very near to where he lived in Rome.[70] His ownership of one copy of Petrarch's *Sonnets* and *Triumphs* written by the Florentine Antonio Sinibaldi and another by Matteo Contugi of Volterra,[71] who was working in Mantua from 1463–71, points to the varieties of both penmanship and provenance among his books; on the other hand, the sheer number of them might suggest quite a lot of in-house copying. The employment, even in 1460, of Giuliano da Viterbo (unfortunately Giuliano then disappears from view) may imply that Francesco—or perhaps his erudite amanuensis Giovan Pietro Arrivabene—already had the idea of making a specialized scriptorium a part of his establishment. Its reputation may be reflected in the request Felice Feliciano of Verona made to Andrea Mantegna for an introduction to the cardinal, which accompanied a sonnet he wrote in the painter's praise.[72] This sonnet must have been written sometime before the summer of 1465,[73] and probably early in 1462 or in the first half of 1464, when Mantegna would have been able to get directly in touch with him, since Francesco was in or near Mantua.

One of the most significant figures in Francesco's entourage was the prolific humanist scribe Bartolomeo Sanvito of Padua.[74] Sanvito was evidently in Rome by late 1464, and it has been suggested he may have come south with Cardinal

---

66 Begani, ed., *Breve chronicon*.

67 On Paul II's possession of historical works including chronicles, see Weiss, *Un umanista veneziano*, pp. 30–1.

68 See below, p. 65.

69 Cardinal F. Gonzaga to Marchese L. Gonzaga, Bologna, 20 October 1472: 'Essendo trovato presso a certa donna de Bologna questo instrumento cum la inclusa scriptura nel qual se fa mentione de Gonzaga pertinente a casa nostra, m'è stato portato; et io, parendomi pur de qualche importantia et essendo antiquo, perché questo imperatore Henrico primo nominato in esso fue del 920, ho voluto mandarlo a Vostra Excellentia' (ASMn, AG, b. 1141, c. 253). The Saxon Henry I was elected king of the Germans (919), not emperor.

70 E.g., Johannes Hinderbach, Bishop of Trent, wrote in his copy of St Ambrose, *De officiis*: 'Emi hunc librum ab librario sive cartulario illo fiorentino in contrata Sancti Laurentii versus Campum Florum... 1466 de mense martii' (Cortesi, 'Johannes Hinderbach', p. 498 n. 52).

71 See I 762n, and Fig. 7. On Sinibaldi see de la Mare, 'Florentine Scribes', pp. 247–8; on Contugi, *DBI*, s.v.

72 'Felice ad Andrea antedicto, compatre del reverendissimo cardinale mantuano, pregandolo si voglia adoperar per lui di aconzarlo col dito Monsignore secondo il parlamento aùto insieme' (MS Modena, Bib. Estense, α.N.7.28 [Ital. 1155], fol. 7ʳ), published with the sonnet in Kristeller, *Mantegna*, p. 489; cf. Mitchell, 'Felice Feliciano', p. 199, who dated it 1460, which is impossible since Francesco was not yet a cardinal.

73 Signorini, 'Due sonetti', pp. 168–9.

74 On Sanvito (1435–pre-1516), see Wardrop, *Script of Humanism*, pp. 23–35, and research, published and in progress, of Albinia de la Mare, to whom I am grateful for many discussions.

Bessarion or Pietro Barbo, but he was not working there on a permanent basis until 1469–71.[75] Although he seems to have been a free agent who worked for many patrons, Sanvito was certainly engaged in copying or rubricating manuscripts for Francesco.[76] It has recently been argued that Sanvito, like Feliciano, also bound books, both of them pioneering the use of gilt leather and tooled covers with plaquette stamps, relief ornament after or including antique gems, and even a 'Mamluk' style of ornament. Francesco, however, seems to have preferred more conservative bindings in brocade, satin and velvet,[77] as the inventory records; there is no evidence that Sanvito worked for him as a binder as well as a scribe. At a date unknown he had entered the cardinal's household on a more or less regular basis. Sanvito travelled to Bologna with the cardinal in 1478, but he took advantage of this opportunity to go home to Padua and seems to have been left free to work for other patrons.[78] At some point he was appointed the cardinal's steward; even if the domestic duties of this office were only nominal, it did require a fairly regular attendance upon the patron.[79] Sanvito is named as this officer in 1483, and it was he who was sent from Bologna specifically to liaise with the Mantuan court about the cardinal's funeral arrangements; he was also named as a beneficiary in his patron's will.[80] A collector himself, years later, Sanvito recorded that the cardinal had once given him 'a book of recipes' (whether these were medical or culinary is unclear).[81]

The most remarkable of all the cardinal's commissioned books in which Sanvito was involved is the 'Vatican Homer'.[82] The plan was for the Greek text of the *Iliad* and *Odyssey* to be accompanied on facing pages by a Latin translation, and both were to be sumptuously decorated with border illumination and miniature panels illustrating the story (Figs 8–10). Nothing has come to light about the inception of this work, but the Greek text of the *Iliad* was completed by the Cretan scribe Joannes Rhosos, on 30–31 May 1477, and that of the *Odyssey* some time later. The fact that Francesco, in spite of knowing no Greek, should have wanted to have Greek texts, should not cause much surprise; for instance Paul II, like many other bibliophiles, had possesed books in Greek without being able to read them:[83] they were desirable holdings for any prestigious library by this period. Moreover, Rhosos had previously worked for Cardinal Bessarion, with whom, it will be recalled, Cardinal Francesco had been on friendly terms;[84] their contacts continued, for example, both cardinals were delegated, upon the

[75] Alexander and de la Mare, *Manuscripts of Major Abbey*, pp. xxix-xxx; de la Mare, 'Florentine Scribes', esp. pp. 252–3 n. 33 with recent bibliography.

[76] See MSS identified as the cardinal's in List of Manuscripts etc. preceding Bibliography, also I 893.

[77] Hobson, *Humanists and Binders*, esp. pp. 72–3, with acknowledgment to G. Frasso.

[78] Marchese Federico was trying to get hold of him; Arrivabene wrote on 26 November 1478 from Cento that 'Bartolomeo nostro da San Vito' had gone to Padua more than two months previously, but on 3 December that he had returned (ASMn, AG, b. 1142); Chambers, 'Arrivabene', 1984, p. 418 n. 121.

[79] See above, pp. 14–15.

[80] See below, p. 97; W 27; Appendix 3, nos 3–4.

[81] 'A dì X Septembre [1508] ho prestato a M. pre' Zuane che scrive a li monaci de S.ta Justina el libro de le recette che me donà la felice memoria del Cardinale de Mantoa'; [below:] 'recepi dictum librum die 7 dicti.' Transcribed from Sanvito's own *memoriale* (since lost) in De Kunert, 'Un padovano ignoto', p. 12.

[82] MSS BAV, Vat. Gr. 1626–7. See Gianelli, *Codices vaticani*, p. 298; Meroni, *Mostra*, p. 34.

[83] Weiss, *Un umanista veneziano*, pp. 30–1.

[84] See above, pp. 46, 57.

death of Pius II at Ancona, to compose an inventory of the pope's possessions.[85] Can it have been from Bessarion (who, incidentally, had been his last predecessor but one as papal legate at Bologna) that Francesco acquired one of the most curious items, evidently of Byzantine provenance, which is listed in the inventory (I 497): 'a salt-cellar of unicorn horn, with Greek lettering around it, in a small box of gilded silver adorned with the arms of Constantinople'? Upon Bessarion's death (1472) Francesco even entertained some hopes of acquiring his abbey of Grottaferrata;[86] in spite of such a presumption, it might have been from sincere respect for Bessarion's memory that he gave some commissions to Rhosos, an immensely productive scribe, who in 1478 also completed for him the Greek text of the Gospels, with illumination in a Byzantine style.[87] Francesco's reverence towards Bessarion is expressed in one of Paolo Cortesi's anecdotes: according to him, both before and after the Greek cardinal's death, Francesco often pointed out that as Bessarion was praised so much for learning, his example should be seen to justify spending money on it. The story may be fictitious, but it sounds rather characteristic; and Bessarion's death may for a while have invigorated Francesco's conviction that a high reputation could be won from giving support to scholarly projects.[88]

Nevertheless, it does not seem very likely that Francesco conceived unaided the idea of having these parallel texts of Homer written and embellished as a grand work of art. May it not—more probably—have originated in the mind of Giovan Pietro Arrivabene, himself a Greek scholar and active bibliophile? Arrivabene, who evidently admired Bessarion greatly and had his four *Orationes ad principes Italiae* copied by Sanvito,[89] may well have consulted his own former Greek teacher, Filelfo, who was in Rome lecturing at the Studium Urbis between January 1475 and April 1476;[90] Filelfo had acknowledged in the autumn of 1474 that it had been thanks to the cardinal he had been invited there and offered a salary of 600 florins,[91] though this, too, may point to an initiative of Arrivabene's, to prompt the cardinal into speaking on Filelfo's behalf to Sixtus IV.[92] In July Filelfo, writing from Milan, hailed the cardinal 'o et praesidium et

---

[85] Francesco wrote to Marchese Ludovico Gonzaga, 16 August 1464: 'Li Reverendissimi Monsignori Niceno, Avignone [Cardinal Coetivy] et io siamo deputati a fare l'inventario dei beni del papa che se trovarà, et hoggi circa ciò havemo ad essere insieme' (b. 842, c. 459).

[86] Giovanni de la Fiera wrote about this to Marchese L. Gonzaga, Rome, 27 November 1472 (ASMn, AG, b. 844, c. 333).

[87] MS BL, Harley 5790; Meroni, *Mostra*, pp. 37, 59–60; Alexander and de La Mare, *Manuscripts of Major Abbey*, pp. 107, 109; Chambers and Martineau, *Splendours*, no. 26. On Rhosos see Canart, 'Scribes grecs', esp. pp. 67, 79–80.

[88] 'Nam Franciscus quidem Gonzaga, homo nativa benignitate praestans, et quo nemo liberalior est illa aetate iudicatus, cum Bessarionem Nicenum sapientiae gloria praestantem videret constanti omnium celebrari voce saepe dixisse fertur, multo se ante Bessarionis mortem quam postea, opum appetentiorem fuisse verentem ne propter doctrinam tota esset ad illum se conversura civitas, cum intelligeret homines verbo laudare solere sapientiam re autem opum fortunaeque potestate duci' (Cortesi, *De cardinalatu*, fol. XLV^v : lib. II, 'De redditibus cardinalium').

[89] MS BCMn, 909 H 1 35; see *Tesori d'arte*, no. 198, p. 134.

[90] Luzio and Renier, 'I Filelfo', pp. 185–6. Cf. above, p. 55, for Filelfo's advice to the cardinal to try reading Greek.

[91] Filelfo to Cardinal F. Gonzaga, Milan, vi Id. Oct. 1474, prid. Non. Nov. 1474 in Rosmini, *Filelfo*, Supplemento (i.e., appendix containing the later letters of Filelfo from the MS in the Biblioteca Trivulziana, Milan), pp. 370–3.

[92] Filelfo to Cardinal F. Gonzaga, Milan, Idibus Juliis 1474, mentions Arrivabene as his intercessor; Filelfo wrote to Arrivabene himself on prid. Id. Oct. (ibid., pp. 362–3, 374–5).

dulce decus meum',[93] and in a later letter Filelfo even implies that he might have lived in the cardinal's household for a while.[94] However, this involvement of Arrivabene, with Filelfo behind him, in the genesis of the 'Vatican Homer' is only a speculation; Platina, Agostino Maffei, Ludovico Agnelli or others of the cardinal's circle who professed humanist interests may have first put forward the idea. Nevertheless the sequel offers another pointer towards Arrivabene: for just as he later acquired for himself the Greek Gospels (the book contains his name, written in his autograph), he also tried after the cardinal's death to retrieve the unfinished Homer manuscripts.[95] The incomplete Latin translation used for Francesco's *Iliad* has been identified as a reworking of Leontius Pilatus's translation, and is found in several other manuscripts.[96] Francesco later acquired for his library the printed translation (1481) of several books of the *Iliad* by Niccolò della Valle, who had died in 1474 (I 800); but this is quite different from the text in the manuscript.[97] Sanvito has been identified as the scribe of the 'Vatican Homer' Latin *Iliad*, in which nevertheless there are many gaps (much of Books VIII, XII–XV, XXIV). Sanvito did not even begin the Latin text of the *Odyssey*, but it is a reasonable assumption that had he done so, the revised version of a fourteenth-century translation would also have been used for this.

The illumination raises many problems, too. Associated with Sanvito in this and other manuscripts—made for a variety of patrons including King Ferrante of Naples—was an artist exceptionally skilful in the use of classicizing archaeological detail: first designated as 'the Sanvito illuminator', it has been suggested that he might even have been Sanvito himself. Among his masterpieces were the few completed pages in the Latin *Iliad*, on account of which he has also been named 'The Master of the Vatican Homer'.[98] More recently he has been tentatively identified as Gaspare da Padova, who not only came from the same city as Sanvito, but was also recorded as a member of the cardinal's household in his will.[99] The case for Gaspare is strengthened by two letters he wrote early in 1484,[100] which reveal not only that he had been receiving from the cardinal a monthly salary of two ducats for over sixteen years and that he was used by Francesco as an agent to commission work from goldsmiths and to acquire antique objects, but that he also still had the uncompleted Homer in his possession, having removed it from the cardinal's palace for fear of looting when the news of his death reached Rome in October 1483.[101] There was certainly a lot more work on the book needing to be done. Even in the *Iliad* volume, all that had been

---

[93] 15 Kal. Aug. 1475 (ibid., p. 393), see Horace, *Carmina* I.12.

[94] Filelfo to Cardinal F. Gonzaga, Mantua, prid. Id. Maias 1476: 'Usque apud te sum Pater Reverendissime, nam et Romae sum domi tuae, et in presentia remoratus Mantuae…' (ibid., p. 427).

[95] See below, p. 115, also Appendix 3, no. 12.

[96] I am grateful to Dr G. N. Knauer for this and other information arising from his work in progress.

[97] Niccolò only translated Books III, V, XIV and XXII; e.g., his first line of Book III reads 'Et postquam eratas struxere in bella cohortes', cf. MS BAV, Vat. Gr. 1626 (fol. 40ʳ): 'Verum postquam ordinati fuere simul cum ducibus singuli/Troiani…'

[98] Alexander and de la Mare, *Manuscripts of Major Abbey*, pp. 107–10; see also Ruysschaert, 'Miniaturistes "romains"'. For the Latin opening of *Iliad* I (fol. 2ʳ) see, e.g., Alexander, *Italian Renaissance Illuminations*, Fig. XIII, p. 21.

[99] Appendix 1, 27; de la Mare, 'Florentine Scribes', pp. 257–9, and Appendix listing illuminated MSS attributed to him, pp. 285–8.

[100] See below, Appendix 3, nos. 9, 12.

[101] As above, n. 95.

finished on the Greek side was the opening page to Book I (Fig. 8, with three small panels illustrating the narrative, and the elaborate border including two of the cardinal's emblems and his arms at the bottom); on the opening Greek page of *Iliad* Book II (Fig. 9) the text and unfinished illustrations are in a simpler gold frame (the cardinal's *stemma* is nevertheless repeated at the bottom). If the intention had been to continue employing so much gold leaf, it would certainly have become very costly. On the Latin side, as many as four pages have their decoration and illustrations complete; the second example (Fig. 10) shows the cardinal's arms as well as three illustrations apparently by the same hand as those sketched on the facing Greek page. Nevertheless, before it proceeded very far, the programme for the Latin text also seems to have been undergoing revision; there was a limitation of the narrative illustration to one panel.[102] Later pages, with decoration barely sketched in, suggest overall reduction in the scale and high quality of the work.[103] Had the project been continued in the manner that it began, it would certainly have made extraordinary demands upon the artist, in having to invent and execute so many scenes—six to each illuminated opening—quite apart from the rest of the decoration. Assuming that Gaspare was indeed the artist, had he been expected to do the work as part of his salaried duties? If so, he may—quite understandably—have ceased doing it because it would have been so time-consuming and unremunerative. It is also possible that the cardinal had simply lost interest in the project, or any feeling of urgency about it, because of its likely expense and all the other problems involved, during his long periods of absence from Rome since 1478.

Whatever the main reason for the non-completion of his de luxe Homer, Francesco's library, though not to be compared with those of serious scholars in the Sacred College like Cardinals Bessarion,[104] Domenico Capranica[105] or Nicolaus Cusanus,[106] was a much more extensive and intellectually varied library[107] than that, for instance, of the wealthy French cardinal who died in the same year as Francesco, Guillaume d'Estouteville, several inventories of whose books (and other possessions) survive. Of the 249 works (269 volumes) listed as belonging to d'Estouteville, almost all are legal, theological, patristic or devotional works.[108] Our inventory of 1483 lists around two hundred manuscript books, of which only about a dozen are known to be extant, but at least six more books survive which certainly belonged to Francesco, most of them decorated with his coat of arms, and another five are known which may have belonged to him; in all of these, the quality of scribal work and illumination bear witness to the high

---

[102] Lib. II–IV (fols 30^r, 40^r, and the still uncoloured fol. 52^r).

[103] After the—unfinished—introductory page to Lib. VII (fol. 103^r) there is little more except a few rough sketches for architectural borders.

[104] Labowsky, *Bessarion's Library*; Bianca, 'Formazione della biblioteca latina'.

[105] Antonovics, 'Library of Cardinal Capranica'; Luciani, 'Minoranze significative'.

[106] Bianca, 'La biblioteca di N. Cusano'.

[107] On cardinals' libraries generally during this period see Bianca et al., 'Materiali e ipotesi', pp. 73–4. Recent studies of some comparable cardinals' book collections, for which inventories do not survive, include: Torroncelli, 'Note per la biblioteca di Marco Barbo'; Cherubini, 'Giacomo Ammannati'; Strnad, *Francesco Todeschini Piccolomini*, pp. 327–49; Norman, 'Library of Cardinal Caraffa'; for the book collection of Cardinal Giovanni d'Aragona, see de la Mare, 'Florentine Scribes', *passim*.

[108] Müntz, *Les Arts*, III, pp. 285–97; Aliano, 'Testamento e inventari'. For the library of another contemporary French cardinal, see Lanconelli, 'La biblioteca romana di Jean Jouffroy'.

standards of the library, which must have been larger than the inventory suggests.[109]

Francesco evidently acquired a taste for printed books as well as manuscripts; thirteen are listed, although only one which belonged to him has been identified (I 899). The Roman printer Giovanni Filippo de Lignamine, who brought to Mantua the papal emblem of the Golden Rose, as a gift for the marchese, in 1477, was among his protégés.[110] In Bologna Francesco dal Pozzo (Puteolano) of Parma, lecturer in rhetoric and poetry in the university from 1467 to 1477, addressed the cardinal in 1471 as dedicatee of the Bolognese first edition of Ovid (probably the first book printed in Bologna).[111] Puteolano was also tutor to the children of Giovanni Bentivoglio, who invoked the cardinal's name in support of Puteolano's claim upon a Milanese benefice.[112] But neither of these instances proves a very close connection between Cardinal Francesco Gonzaga and Puteolano; Francesco was in Bologna as cardinal legate only very briefly in 1471, just as he was not there at all during 1477 when (in his name) Bolognese citizenship was conferred upon Puteolano.[113] Nor can it be inferred that because as bishop he became ex-officio chancellor of the faculty of theology, he played an active role in sustaining that most revered of disciplines, although one of his very first episcopal acts *in absentia* was the appointment of a notary to deal with faculty administration.[114] But he does seem to have been valued as a figurehead by several Bolognese writers; Ludovico Bolognini has been mentioned, and Benedetto Morando dedicated to him his *De laudibus Bononiae* (I 834).

* * *

Francesco's connections with *uomini dotti* and *litterati* were certainly extensive, although Giovan Lucido Cattanei's funeral oration may have exaggerated his personal commitment.[115] It is recorded in 1476 that formerly he had had an astrologer resident in the household,[116] which may provide a clue to the presence in his library of various books about divination, including translations from the Arabic.[117] But humanist *litterati* were the sort of learned men who seem most to have frequented him. That is not to say that he directly stimulated much in the

---

[109] For a discussion of the books listed, and other matters concerning the inventory, see below, Chap. 4 (i); for extant manuscript books identified as definitely or possibly Francesco's, see below, List of Manuscripts and Unpbulished Sources.

[110] Cardinal F. Gonzaga to Marchese Ludovico Gonzaga, Rome, 8 April 1477: 'A questo è stato electo lo spectabile cavaliere d. Zo[an] Philippo da Ligname, siciliano, scudiere de suoa beatitudine et etiam molto amico mio e gientil persona' (ASMn, AG, b. 846, c. 104). On his publications, see Farenga, 'Le prefazioni'.

[111] The printing company associated Baldassarre Azzoguidi and Annibale Malpigli with Puteolano, who was evidently the corrector and editor. See Sighinolfi, 'Francesco Puteolano', pp. 330–5.

[112] See Ady, 'Francesco Puteolano'.

[113] Letter of 12 December 1477, from Giovanni Alimenti Negri, acting as the cardinal's *luogotenente* (Sighinolfi, 'Francesco Puteolano', doc. V, pp. 460–1).

[114] The letter of appointment in Francesco's name, issued at Narni, 7 August 1476, styles himself 'alme studii universitatis teologorum civitatis bononiensis cancellarius' (ASMn, AG, b. 3351, c. 47ʳ (42ʳ). He issued letters at Mantua on 31 August 1478 and 29 August 1479 delegating his duty to conduct a visitation of the Spanish College (ASMn, AG, b. 3351, fols 47ᵛ, 71ᵛ).

[115] '…hic ingenuorum amator et retributor, hic litteratorum refugium' (Cattanei, *Orationes*, sig. c iiiiᵛ).

[116] G. P. Arrivabene to Marchese Ludovico Gonzaga, Rome, 24 March 1476: 'era morto in palatio da peste messer Orio da Modena astrologo, el qual già stete in casa nostra' (ASMn, AG, b. 845, c. 623).

[117] See below, p. 109, also I 749, 873–94, 896–7.

way of authorship and scholarship. Almost the only works which he clearly did play some part in fostering were Platina's writings of the later 1460s, by providing a roof for the author to write under and probably showing some interest in the subject matter. The *History of Mantua* (*Historia urbis Mantuae*)[118] is the most obvious of these, and Platina had finished the first part of it by early July 1466, when the cardinal took his household on vacation to Marino; the work is dedicated to Francesco,[119] and reaches its climax and end with his appointment to the cardinalate and arrival at Ancona in August 1464.

Rather more problematical are the *De amore* or *Contra amores* and the *De honesta voluptate et valitudine*, although Platina explicitly associated both of these works, too, with the cardinal's 'Tusculan' retreat (surely the Colonna castle of Marino, close to ancient Tusculum, where Francesco spent summer holidays). The problem is that in each case the earliest manuscripts have been found to contain dedications to other persons and appear to be datable to as early as the summer of 1464, whereas Francesco is not known to have stayed in Marino before the summer of 1465 (admittedly he stayed in Albano in June 1463, but as the guest of Cardinal Ludovico, Patriarch of Aquileia, and in 1464 he was neither in or near Rome until the beginning of September). In the case of *De honesta voluptate*, the subject matter, essentially the relationship between food and health, must surely have appealed to Francesco, and the discovery that it is based on the earlier cookery book of Martino, the cook of Cardinal Ludovico,[120] is also interesting in view of Francesco's friendship with that cardinal. It seems possible that either in Rome or when Francesco stayed with the Cardinal Ludovico at Albano in 1463, he or Platina acquired a copy of Martino's cookery book; Platina may have started his work soon after this, but not finished the text, writing to Cardinal Ammannati about the need for editing it during his first imprisonment in the winter of 1464/5 and writing the dedication last of all, in the summer of 1465, when he was staying with Francesco at Marino.[121]

The *De amore* or *Contra amores* gives the cardinal's 'Tusculan retreat' (i.e., Marino) itself as the scene of the dialogue, the first version of which has also been dated to 1465. If the original dedicatee was not Francesco or one of his circle, at least the dedicatee of the revised version (1468) was a member of the cardinal's household, namely Ludovico Agnelli.[122] Finally, Platina also claimed to have written his *De principe* during a holiday sojourn (at Albano) with the cardinal,[123] who is praised in the text;[124] this must presumably have been in 1470, to enable the book to be ready for presentation to Federico Gonzaga the following year. It should be added that Bartolomeo Sanvito was engaged in the writing

[118] The text has not been re-edited since the first edition of Muratori, in RIS, XX, 1731.

[119] Platina to Marchese Ludovico Gonzaga, Rome, 7 July 1466 (ASMn, AG, b. 843), Luzio and Renier, 'Il Platina e i Gonzaga', pp. 434–5; see also Platina, *Lives*, ed. Gaida, *Liber de vita etc.*, p. xv; Ferraù, 'La "Historia Urbis Mantuae"'; Chambers, 'Platina', pp. 13–16.

[120] Milham, 'Manuscripts', pp. 27–9, also 'New Aspects', pp. 92–6.

[121] '...Has ergo rusticationes meas quas hac aestate in secessu tusculano apud inclytum et amplissimum patrem Franciscum Gonzagam' (proemium to Cardinal Roverella, printed in 1498 edn.). I am grateful to Professor Milham, who has revised her previous dating, for discussion of the MS and dedication problems, which will be clarified in her forthcoming edition of *De honesta voluptate*.

[122] A. Tissoni-Benvenuti, 'Due schede', pp. 209–13; Chambers, 'Il Platina', p. 14.

[123] 'Cum essem in Albano vitandi aestus pulverisque causa cum illustri et amplissimo fratre tuo F. Gonzaga cardinali Mantuano' (*De principe*, ed. Ferraù, p. 49).

[124] See the quotation above, p.1.

of both this copy and the revised text entitled *De optimo cive*, to be presented to Lorenzo de' Medici in 1474,[125] so Francesco was probably involved closely in all phases of the gestation of this important work.

Another book which obviously must have appealed to the mind of Cardinal Gonzaga, and in which he was directly involved as an interlocutor in the dialogue it contains, was written by one of the sons of Francesco Filelfo. Giovan Maria Filelfo (1426–80) had been recommended to the cardinal in 1467,[126] and they met at Macerata in 1472, as the text explains. Giovan Maria's dialogue, *De comunis vite continentia*, on the subject of keeping healthy,[127] is mainly a commentary on writings about the same subject by St Basil and St John Chrysostom. Cardinal Francesco Gonzaga and his host at Macerata in July 1472, Bartolomeo Roverella, Cardinal Legate of the Marches, feature as the speakers together with the author. Francesco is made to express, among other views, little faith in contemporary medical science, and this perhaps was a genuine record of his state of mind after his prolonged recent illness.[128] Nevertheless, Giovan Maria does not seem to have gained much tangible favour from the cardinal as a result, for he was still trying to solicit his patronage some years later;[129] nor does he seem to have profited much from his father's connections (already mentioned) with Cardinal Gonzaga. But in any case, even if the elder Filelfo had given him some advice and later obtained his backing to teach at the Studium Urbis, there is no reason to suppose they were at all close; so far as is known, the cardinal was not much interested in Filelfo's scholarly works and did not give him money or even support his angry claims against Meliaduse Cigala for withheld salary payments.[130]

One classical scholar who did gain Francesco's patronage was Pietro Marsi (1442–1512). Marsi (not to be confused with Paolo Marsi) was a friend of Platina, and likewise a victim of Paul II's persecution; he studied with Johannes Argyropulos, transcribed Aristotle's *Ethics* and taught in the Studium Urbis in Rome. On Pomponio Leto's recommendation, Cardinal Ammannati in 1472 had appointed Pietro tutor to his nephew Cristoforo Piccolomini,[131] who had joined Francesco's household probably around the time of his uncle's death in 1479. This may explain how Pietro Marsi came also to be a tutor to the cardinal's youngest brother, Ludovico. Marsi accompanied Francesco to Mantua at the end of 1479, and it may have been then that he composed his brief work on the birthplace of Virgil (printed at Mantua in 1480); he dedicated to Francesco his commentary on Cicero's *De officiis* (I 813) and was still a member of the household when the cardinal died.[132]

---

[125] *De principe*, p. 35; Rubinstein, 'Il "De optimo cive"', p. 137.

[126] Marchese Ludovico to Cardinal F. Gonzaga, 30 May 1467 (ASMn, AG, b. 2890, lib. 59, fol. 37ᵛ).

[127] The unique copy (MS BCMn, 79), is dedicated to Sixtus IV (see also I 772). A note on fol. 96ᵛ records that it was being written in March 1473.

[128] He complains 'solent vehementer errare in quos physicos vocant in exponendis causis morborum' (fol. 9ʳ). Concerning his illnesses see below, p. 96.

[129] He wrote from Mantua on 30 May 1478—just before Francesco himself left Rome—asking Marchese Ludovico for a letter to the cardinal 'che mi favoreggie a Roma' (Luzio and Renier, 'I Filelfo', pp. 195, 193–209 and *passim* on Giovan Maria).

[130] Filelfo to Cardinal F. Gonzaga, Milan, xii kal. Mar. 1477 (Rosmini, *Filelfo*, pp. 429–30); cf. p. 61.

[131] Ammannati, *Epistolae*, fol. 242ʳ; Lee, *Sixtus IV*, pp. 189–90; see also below, p. 91.

[132] Cardinal F. Gonzaga to his *luogotenente* at Bologna, Mantua, 27 December 1479: 'Lo reverendo nostro fratello protonotario da Gonzaga se mostra pur desideroso de continuare lo studio suo sotto don Pietro Marso'

One of the most prominent humanists acquainted with Francesco was Giovanni Pontano, who accompanied Alfonso Duke of Calabria to Ferrara in January 1483 as his secretary; Pontano and the cardinal were recorded having a discussion one morning,[133] but it is more likely that this was about current political matters than moral philosophy, even if Pontano might well—in view of the works he was later to write concerning virtue and wealth—have found Francesco an interesting case for study. So it remains unclear who were the senior scholars Giovan Lucido Cattanei was thinking of when he declared in one of the most enthusiastic passages of his funeral oration that Francesco was a ready listener and participant in learned debate; and there is not much corroborative evidence that Francesco himself displayed such great skills in rhetoric as Cattanei claimed for him.[134]

Neither learned treatises, orations, disputations nor textual commentaries, but rather verse seems to have been the form of expression which most closely linked the cardinal with *litterati*. From his early years in Rome he was a target for neo-Latin versifiers. The ageing and salacious 'Porcellio' Pandoni (c. 1405–85), who had returned to Rome in about 1459, in 1463 addressed himself to Francesco, perhaps encouraged to do so by his patron Cardinal Prospero Colonna.[135] Among his verses in praise of Francesco and the glory of the Gonzaga family, were those relating to the cardinal's summer residence and gardens at Sant'Agata,[136] and—in another—to the antique head of Portia which Porcellio had given to Francesco, probably in the autumn just before he left for Mantua and Pius II's crusade, since the text hints at glories about to be won.[137]

There was no lack of other Latin poets competing for Francesco's notice and addressing verses to him; they included Antonio Geraldini,[138] the elderly Leonardo Montagna (c. 1425–85), a secretary of Alessandro Gonzaga and protégé of Cardinal Ammannati,[139] and the Mantuan Marcantonio Aldegati whose amorous elegies to 'Cinzia' survive, with a dedication to Francesco.[140] Aldegati was at this date a rather obscure figure, though he describes himself as a scholar in a letter

---

(ASMn, AG, b. 2900, lib. 96, fol. 153[r]). See W 27; I 813; also Faccioli, *Mantova*, II, pp. 56, 128 nn. 46–51; della Torre, *Paolo Marsi*, esp. pp. 97–8, 224–5.

[133] Pietro Spagnoli to Marchese Federico Gonzaga, Ferrara, 1 February 1483: 'Questa matina, andando ad casa del Reverendissimo Monsignore lo legato, retrovai lo Pontano, secretario de lo Illustrissimo signor duca de Calabria, esser cum sua Reverendissima Signoria in secreto...' (ASMn, AG, b. 1231, c. 144).

[134] 'Gravia colloquia diligebat, nam a natura sibi insitum erat cum gravioribus maturisque viris, maximis de rebus ratiocinari' (Cattanei, *Orationes*, sig. c i); '...audiebat homo ingenio praesens semper et faceto lepore solers: ac in verborum splendore tonans: compositione aptus: facultate copiosus: remque omnem memoriter exponens' (ibid., sig. c iii).

[135] Pandoni left Rome in 1464, but returned during the heyday of Pietro Riario and lectured in the Studium Urbis (Frittelli, *Giannantonio de' Pandoni*, esp. pp. 63–73, 78–81; Lee, *Sixtus IV*, pp. 185–8).

[136] *De iucunditate de situ Sanctae Agathae* (MS BAV, Chigi J VII 260, fol. 160[r]) noted by Avesani, 'Epaeneticorum libri' pp. 76–7.

[137] MS BAV, Vat. Lat. 1670, fols 77[r–v].

[138] MS BAV Vat. Lat. 3611, fols 21[v]–22[v].

[139] MS Cesena, Biblioteca Malatestiana, XXIX 8; Kristeller (*Iter Italicum*, I, p. 44) notes this as 'Anon., carmina attributed by a later hand to Leon. Montagna'; it includes verses dedicated to Paul II, Cardinals F. Gonzaga, Marco Barbo and others, and is not mentioned in Biadego, 'Leonardo Montagna letterato'. Ammannati thanked Montagna for sending (maybe the same) verses in 1472 (*Epistolae*, fol. 235[r]; Cherubini, 'Giacomo Ammannati', p. 205). On Montagna see also Weiss, 'Lorenzo Zane', pp. 166–8.

[140] Briefly discussed, with note of dedication, in Foligno, 'Di alcuni codici', pp. 72–3. Subsequently noted as lost (Meroni, *Mostra*, p. 88 n. 100) it is in fact MS Boston, Mass., Public Library, F. Med. 126 (see De Ricci, *Census, Supplement*, ed. Faye and Bond, p. 264). The brief quotation below (n. 143) is by courtesy of the Trustees of the Library. I am most grateful to Dr P. Bisaccia for his assistance.

from Ferrara in 1467;[141] he is not known to have been in Rome, but could equally well have met the cardinal in Mantua or Bologna in the early 1470s.[142] The poem contains a barely legible dedication to Francesco at the beginning, describing him as legate to Bologna, so the date must be 1471 or later; there are further allusions to him in lib. II, which—like Porcellio's ode—might seem to allude to earlier times, c. 1463–4, when he had been expected to play a part in Pius II's crusade, but could equally well just reflect the anti-Moslem mood and crusading initiatives of the papacy in the early 1470s.[143] Among other contemporary Latin poets whose writings were represented in Francesco's library were Filippo Buonaccorsi, Cardinal Roverella's secretary, otherwise known as Callimaco (one of the figures most implicated in the conspiracy of 1468), Giovan Pietro Arrivabene's friend Piattino Piatti and Nicodemo Folengo.[144] Since there is no evidence that Francesco tried to discourage such initiatives, some doubt may be cast upon the testimony of Giovan Lucido Cattanei's funeral oration that he had always despised flatterers.[145]

After the sudden death in 1474 of Cardinal Pietro Riario, many of the poet-asters with whom Sixtus IV's extravagant nephew had surrounded himself turned elsewhere for employment, and Francesco may have been eager to inherit some of Pietro's reputation for a *liberalitas* quite unprecedented in scale and character. The example and moral legacy of Pietro Riario must have had a wide and lasting resonance; Cardinal Jacopo Ammannati was one of those who expressed uncensorious wonderment, composing an essay in the form of a letter about it intended for Francesco's eyes, but apparently never completed and sent.[146] As well as Giovan Antonio Campano and others,[147] among Pietro Riario's literary protégés who gravitated towards Francesco was Paolo Emilio Boccabella (Emilius Romanus). He may have been introduced earlier by Platina, Porcellio or others of the Roman 'Academy', but it was in Bologna, where—in spite of his advancing years—Boccabella had come to study law in 1476,[148] that he made a bid for Francesco's attention. Two years later he hailed with laudatory if vacuous verses the cardinal legate's return to that city and also composed facile verses in honour of members of Francesco's entourage, including Giovan Pietro Arriva-bene and the protonotary Ludovico Gonzaga, and his two most important officials

[141] This letter to Marchese Ludovico Gonzaga from 'Marcus Antonius de Aldegatis de Mantua scolaris', Ferrara, 4 April 1467, mentions his friendship with the Florentine exile Lorenzo Strozzi (ASMn, AG, b. 1228, c. 605). On Aldegati (or Aldegatti) and his later works see Faccioli, *Mantova*, I, pp. 66–7; II, pp. 56, 127 n. 44.
[142] A letter signed 'Marcus de Aldegatis' dated 21 June 1471, no place given but probably Mantua, relates to military service (ASMn, AG, b. 2412). Foligno, 'Di alcuni codici', p. 73, suggests a connection with Ludovico Aldegati, the cardinal's suffragan bishop of Mantua and bishop of 'Lamone' (Lamus, in Anatolia, *in partibus*) apppointed in 1473 (citing Schivenoglia, MS BCMn, 1019 fol. 76ᵛ).
[143] Among the concluding lines are: 'Tu decus imperii Romani Gloria gentis/Gonzagae Cardo et maximus ecclesia es/Te metuunt Arabes, metuunt tua nome Teucri/… (MS cited above, unnumbered folios).
[144] See I 842–6. On Piatti see Simeoni, 'Un umanista milanese' (cited in Chambers, 'Arrivabene', p. 405).
[145] '…adulatores bilinguis, delatoresque ut perniciosam pestem detestebat' (Cattanei, *Orationes*, sig. c i).
[146] Ammannati, *Epistolae*, fols 272ᵛ-273ʳ. For other admiring assessments see Zippel, 'Un apologia dimenticata'; Farenga, '"Monumenta Memoriae"'.
[147] In Campano's *Epigrammatum libellus* dedicated to Pietro Riario there is a piece dedicated to the Cardinal of Mantua (MS BAV, Vat. Lat. 2874, fol. 24ʳ); also one in an anonymous collection of a member of the same circle (MS BAV, Ross. 1129, fol. 15ᵛ).
[148] *DBI*, s.v. (though his dates are not established), also remarks by Tissoni-Benvenuti, *L'Orfeo*, p. 47.

at Bologna, the *luogotenente* Giovanni Alimento Negri, and the auditor Alvise Capra.[149]

Also in or on the fringe of the cardinal's entourage from the mid-1470s was the Paduan Niccolò 'Cosmico', another member of the Pomponian circle, a friend of Giovanni Lorenzi, Cardinal Marco Barbo's secretary and a student, like Poliziano, of the Greek teacher Demetrius Chalcondylas. By 1476 Niccolò was in Rome, possibly teaching grammar and living in the house of Agostino Maffei, whom he described as his Maecenas.[150] Niccolò's advice was sought concerning the cardinal's programme for mural paintings in December 1479, and the link with him seems to have come through Francesco and Agostino Maffei.[151] Since Niccolò was an active pederast and flaunted the fact in his love poetry, it would hardly have done for him to have dedicated his verses to the cardinal. There is no evidence, however, that he was even a *commensalis*; he seems just to have been a fringe member among that gifted group of Paduans—including Sanvito, Gaspare and Hermes—who did much to determine the cultural tone of the cardinal's household in his later years.

Another Niccolò, apparently a poet from Pietro Riario's circle, who became one of Francesco's close and most favoured household chamberlains, was Poliziano's friend Niccolò da Piacenza; Protonotary Ludovico wrote to Marchese Federico Gonzaga from Rome, 4 May 1484, on behalf of Niccolò as the late cardinal's *cameriere*, 'antiquo servitore…et in vero singularmente amato'.[152] Also—though very near to the end of the cardinal's lifetime—the Florentine Bernardo Bellincioni (1452–92) joined the number of attendant poets or would-be protégés. In April 1483 he sent to Marchese Federico Gonzaga a copy of a poem which he claimed to have written when the cardinal was staying in Giovanni Tornabuoni's house in Florence the previous December.[153] Bellincioni later composed a poem about the death, or rather the after-life, of Cardinal Gonzaga, in which his soul is described as soaring like a bird to be received by St Peter in heaven and presented to his father and mother, his three prematurely deceased sisters and other relatives.[154]

Whether Francesco actually read the books he owned is another matter; he possessed some eye-glasses (I 91; 477), but—although spectacles were in fashion[155]—these *occhiali* might have been more used for peering at cameos, coins and illuminations than for reading. However, Cardinal Ammannati's remark about Francesco's reading should be borne in mind,[156] and since there is evidence

---

[149] Several collections survive of Boccabella's *Carmina*—lib. II and lib. V of which were dedicated to the cardinal (see I 839).

[150] Rossi, 'Niccolò Lelio Cosmico', esp. pp. 108–12; in a letter from Rome, which he was hoping to leave, dated 8 April 1477, he asked Alessandro Strozzi to send letters care of 'misser Augustino de' Maffei, il quale mi è mio Mecenate et habito cum lui' (ibid., p. 151); see also *DBI*, s.v.

[151] Ibid., p. 111; see below, pp. 86–7.

[152] ASMn, AG, b. 847, c. 50. See W 26 and below, p. 74.

[153] Bellincioni to Marchese Federico Gonzaga, Milan, 23 April 1483: 'in questa sarà interchiusa una chanzona ch'i' feci al nostro Ilustrissimo monsigniore chardinale de Mantua, et sendo sua Signoria in Firenze, in chasa di Giovanni Tornaboni, del mese di dicembre…et avendone io perduta chopia l'ò ritrovata qui' (ASMn, AG, b. 1628; cf. Luzio and Renier, 'Del Bellincioni').

[154] Bellincioni, *Rime*, ed. Fanfani, pp. 150–9.

[155] Ilardi, 'Eyeglasses', esp. pp. 345–8, concerning orders for them in 1462–6 in letters to and from Nicodemo Tranchedini da Pontremoli, Milanese ambassador in Florence.

[156] See above, p. 53.

that he did borrow books, it may be assumed perhaps that his purpose was sometimes to read rather than simply have them copied, as in the late example of his request to borrow a copy of the *Apologues* by Bartolomeo Scala (I 761). Even so, it may be that he continued to enjoy books most of all as visual objects and acquired knowledge from them mainly through having passages read aloud, though there is no evidence that Giovan Pietro Arrivabene or others performed this additional service for him. Poetry at least he enjoyed aurally, hearing it sung to the accompaniment of lute playing, and he possessed several song-books. Francesco evidently delighted in music, both for pleasure and therapy: he provided it, for instance, to soothe his brother Gianfrancesco when the latter was ill in Rome.[157] In the summer of 1470 he invited the blind poet Francesco Cieco da Firenze to perform for him at Albano and warmly commended him for his vocal clarity and skill on the lute.[158] Two other Florentine singers were much favoured by both Francesco and his father: Baccio Ugolini, a bizarre figure who also acted as a diplomatic go-between, described by Marchese Ludovico Gonzaga in 1471 as no less the cardinal's favourite than his own,[159] and Malagigi, by whose playing and singing Francesco wished to be soothed at the baths of Porretta in 1472,[160] and by whom Ludovico was also entertained.[161]

Cardinal Gonzaga also developed a taste for more elaborate musical spectacles. This may have had something to do with the influence of Cardinal Pietro Riario; admittedly Francesco had been out of Rome during most of Pietro Riario's heyday, but he no doubt heard about the style of entertainment favoured by the pope's nephew; one of Riario's banquets even took place in Cardinal Gonzaga's house in Rome, borrowed for the occasion during his absence in the summer of 1472.[162] This presumably was the house at San Lorenzo in Damaso although the less palatial house at Sant'Agata cannot be wholly excluded seeing that the event took place during the heat of July. While Marchese Ludovico evidently disapproved of Pietro Riario's luxurious style of living,[163] reports of the

---

[157] Giorgio de la Strata to Barbara, Rome, 22 October 1466: 'tuto il zorno non se li parte da canto, et cercha de darli ogni appiacere, hora in far cantare, sonare et altre piacevolece' (ASMn, AG, b. 843).

[158] A safeconduct and licence for this performer to return home was dated at Albano, 9 September 1470 (ASMn, AG, b. 3351, fol. 9ᵛ); he should be distinguished from another, more celebrated blind singer from Ferrara (see Frasso, 'Un poeta improvvisatore').

[159] Marchese Ludovico to Cardinal F. Gonzaga, 27 August 1471 observed that 'el Baccio nostro…non è manco vostro che nostro' (ASMn, AG, b. 2892, lib. 69, fol. 35ʳ). On Baccio see Del Lungo, *Florentia.*, esp. pp. 307–12; Luzio and Renier, 'I Filelfo', pp. 144–5; Lorenzo dei Medici, *Lettere*, I, no. 240, p. 268 n.1.

[160] See below, p. 79 n. 235, for the famous letter of 18 July 1472, which specifies 'de Malagise pigliarò piacere del sonare e cantare suo, et a questo modo me serà più facile ad lasciare lo sonno'. On Malagigi see also Del Lungo, *Florentia*, pp. 304, 313.

[161] 'Malagigi de Florentia' to Marchese Ludovico, dated (without day) June 1473, commented on Eleonora of Aragon, Ercole d'Este's betrothed, 'la sposa mi pare di comune belleza o qualche cosa meno' (ASMn, AG, b. 1101, c. 99); about his therapeutic singing to the marchese, Marsilio Andriasi wrote to Barbara from Goito, 10 February 1474: 'a le xiiii o circa, [Ludovico] se pose suxo il lecto et dormitte una hora, poi fece cantare Malazise' (b. 2415, c. 1226).

[162] Giovanni Arcimboldi, Bishop of Novara, to Duke Galeazzo Maria Sforza, Rome 26 July 1472. The dinner for the French ambassador, 'in casa de Mantoa' (which was decorated 'de veluti e tapezarie et de altre cose et ornamenti degnissimi…et una credenza de argenti molto degna et bene apparata et richa': it is not clear whether these were Francesco's or Pietro's furnishings) included 'l'istoria de Jason' in edible form, presumably made of sugar (ASMil., Sforzesco, cart. 70), partly published by Motta, 'Un pranzo dato in Roma'; noted by Cruciani, *Teatro*, p. 166, who discusses comparable occasions.

[163] Marsilio Andriasi to Barbara, Borgoforte, 29 August 1473: '…de quella lecti de velluto per questa venuta di San Sixto et cetera, Sua Signoria [Ludovico] me ha risposto che a casa sua non se usano simile lecti…né gli

entertainments, including mythological inventions, which he sponsored, must have excited curiosity equally in Rome, Bologna and Mantua.[164] Francesco himself gave a New Year dinner in Rome in which role reversals and other charades added to the entertainment. Among the guests were the Milanese ambassadors (Sacramoro, bishop of Piacenza, and Agostino Rossi) and the cardinal's brother Rodolfo. A good-looking young chamberlain called 'Brugnullo' presided at the head of the table,[165] dressed up in clothes belonging to the cardinal.[166] A mock disputation was held, and then a battle, between the Virtues and the Vices, in which the Virtues (personified by more of the cardinal's *familia* dressed and made up as women) were victorious.[167]

But the most famous of literary and musical spectacles sponsored by Cardinal Gonzaga was Poliziano's *Fabula de Orpheo*, the date and occasion of which has never been definitely established.[168] The first printed text of *Orfeo* (1494) includes a letter of Poliziano to Carlo Canale, the chamberlain already mentioned in connection with the cardinal's mistress Barbara and their child;[169] knowledge of that story may well have titillated Poliziano's imagination, but it would be safer not to suggest allusions to it in his version of the myth of Orpheus and Eurydice. Although undated, this letter refers to the cardinal as though still living, so it must have been written over eleven years before the text was printed. Canale recalls that Poliziano had written *Orfeo* hurriedly in two days, amidst constant upheavals (*continui tumulti*), under pressure from the cardinal who had also insisted that it should be in Italian rather than Latin.[170] For the part of Orfeo Baccio Ugolini was named in the *intermezzo*, where Orfeo, seated upon a mound, played his lyre and sang Latin verses in praise of the cardinal (defying the patron's stated preference for Italian).

There is evidence that both Poliziano and Baccio Ugolini were in Mantua in the first half of 1480. During the previous year, Poliziano had lost the favour of

---

farà tante representatione, perché di qua non sònno quelle nymphe, driade, nayade et napee...' (ASMn, AG, b. 2415, c. 32ʳ), cited in Signorini, 'Ludovico Muore', pp. 111–12.

[164] E.g., G. P. Arrivabene to Barbara, Bologna, 22 February 1473: 'da Roma non se ha altro di nove se non che in questo tempo là non se fa altro se non sonare, cantare e ballare, e tutta la corte sta occupata in maschere e feste' (ASMn, AG, b. 1141, c. 291), or Giovanni Arrivabene to Barbara, Mantua, 19 June 1473: '...essendomi mandato copia del triumpho et pasto facto per Monsignor de S. Sixto a la Illustrissima sposa de Ferrara, aciò che la Vostra Illustrissima Signoria habia da legere et possia considerare le fatiche e spese de Sancta Chiesia, m'è parso mandargela alligata, rendendomi certo ne debba pigliare piacere, et da Marsilio et Aloviso, chi sono buon fabulisti, poterà chiarirse de quelli versi gli sono et del misterio suo' (ASMn, AG, b. 2416, c. 290).

[165] Perhaps Floramonte Brognolo, who is mentioned as 'nostro cameriere' in a letter from the cardinal dated 17 September 1480 (ASMn, AG, b. 2424); he is named in the will (W 27). On his later career see *DBI*, s.v.

[166] '...el Cardinale fece un rey suo camarero ciamato Brugnollo...questo Brugnollo pare dolce et suave, che è bello giovane senza barba, et de la bella persona. Questo re era obedito et reverito quanto è la Vostra Excellentia in cassa vostra per quella sera, et anche el Cardinale gli volle bene, perché quello tal Brugnollo lo merita. Lo rey sentava in capo di tavola, vestito d'una turcha de zetonino raxo cremessino, quale turcha era del cardinale, una collana d'oro teneva al collo cum uno pendente assay bello...' (Johannes Marcus to Galeazzo Maria Sforza, 2 January 1476, ASMil., Sforzesco, cart. 80), published in 'Cena e rappresentazione'; extract in Huelsen et al., *Sant'Agata*, p. 75 n. 1; Cruciani, *Teatro*, pp. 171–2; Tissoni-Benvenuti, *L'Orfeo*, p. 47 n. 41.

[167] '...fatta la cena se fece una representatione assay bella de le virtute, como sono contrarie a li vicii. E quivi venerono tute le virtute vestiti ad modo femenille cum volti contraffati et depinti; et detro gli sequiva li vicii, e qui se fece una disputatione inante a lo re utrum se doveva atachare a la vita epicuria overo acostarse a le virtute. E qui se ballò cum spade in mano li viciosi, et le virtute abateno li vicii...' (ibid.)

[168] Picotti, *Ricerche umanistiche*; Tissoni-Benvenuti,'Il viaggio', and *L'Orfeo* (which supersedes previous editions).

[169] See above, p. 24.

[170] Text reprinted in Tissoni-Benvenuti, *L'Orfeo*, p. 136.

Lorenzo and Clarice de'Medici; when Lorenzo went on his secret mission to seek a unilateral peace with King Ferrante of Naples, not only was he excluded, but he may have felt that, as a former favourite, Florence was unsafe for him in such uncertain times, so he set off on travels in northern Italy.[171] When he came to write his *Apologia* (dated at Mantua 19 March 1480) Poliziano told Lorenzo, who was by then triumphantly back from Naples, that he had been spending more time at Mantua than elsewhere and enjoying the company of Baccio Ugolini and others.[172] On 21 April 1480 he was issued at Mantua with a letter of chaplaincy from the cardinal, giving safe-conduct for himself and two other persons;[173] this was in fact a quite standard form of protection which does not imply particular familiarity and what journey it anticipated is not clear; it was not until August that Poliziano was back in Florence.[174] Baccio, meanwhile, who had recently been serving as Florentine agent in Bologna, had come to Mantua in December 1479, and when the cardinal himself prepared to follow by water, he sent a letter asking that Baccio should come to meet him with the *bucintoro*.[175] Although Baccio returned to Florence in late March (bearing with him Poliziano's *Apologia* to Lorenzo de' Medici), he was back in Mantua by 26 April, again in Florence a month later, but by 30 May once more leaving for Mantua, from where he wrote to Lorenzo de'Medici on 12 June.[176]

In light of these facts, limited though they are as evidence, Picotti's view has long prevailed that the first performance of *Orfeo* took place at Mantua some time in the first half of 1480, during Poliziano's presence there, and with Baccio performing. Picotti suggested a number of possible occasions, including a visit of Giovanni Bentivoglio in early February, but was disinclined to date the event before Poliziano's letter of chaplaincy and safe-conduct was issued in April. He therefore came down in favour of June, when Baccio was back in Mantua, and the betrothals were to be celebrated of Francesco Gonzaga (the cardinal's nephew, later marchese) to Isabella d'Este and of Chiara Gonzaga to Gilbert de Montpensier; but he acknowledged there were problems about his choice, since these celebrations did not happen at all as planned.[177] It is difficult to understand why so much importance need be attached to the cardinal's letter of 21 April, which was not particularly significant as a token of recognition or of initial favour by a patron to an artist. Of the alternative dates suggested before Baccio began his series of journeys to and back from Florence, Shrove Tuesday, 15 February, when the cardinal is known to have given a dinner party,[178] seems

---

[171] Picotti, *Ricerche storiche*, pp. 58–63, 95.

[172] 'Mantuae plurimum fui…cum multis aliis…tum in primis Nicolao Cesaris filio Baccioque Ugolini' (Picotti, *Ricerche storiche*, p. 64, and doc. V, p. 81).

[173] ASMn, AG, b. 3351, c. 97^r; the discovery was made by Picotti, *Ricerche storiche* pp. 95–6.

[174] Picotti, *Ricerche storiche*, pp. 67, 100.

[175] Ibid, pp. 59 n. 3, 98–9; Cardinal F. Gonzaga to Gianfrancesco Strata, Bologna, 12 December 1479: '…mandarà Baccio gioso nel bucintoro' (ASMn, AG, b. 2896, lib. 9, fol. 145^v). Picotti mistranscribed the addressee's name as 'Sante'.

[176] Picotti, *Ricerche storiche*, p. 99.

[177] Ibid., pp. 100–3. Picotti is generally followed by Pirrotta, *Li due Orfei*, pp. 8–9.

[178] Cardinal F. Gonzaga to Protonotary L. Gonzaga, Mantua, 8 February 1480: 'Per el pasto nostro che serà martedì proximo, al qual havemo convitati li Illustri Signor Marchese et altri nostri fratelli, et hora invitamo la Signoria Vostra, pregamo Quella, puoi che l'è fuori et in paese, dove è buon cacciare et ucellare, che voglia

much the most likely occasion.[179]

Recently it has been objected that the *Orfeo* cannot have been performed at all in the first half of 1480, since the court was still in mourning owing to the death the previous October of Marchese Federico's wife, Margherita of Bavaria.[180] But in practice some relaxation of mourning may have been allowed, just as, for instance, a dispensation had been imposed on Paola Gonzaga, some months after Marchese Ludovico's death, rather against her own wishes, so that she could dance and otherwise celebrate her marriage at Bolzano in November 1478.[181] Such a relaxation seems to have been sufficient at least to permit some entertainment on occasions which had no official importance, such as New Year or Carnival—otherwise the cardinal could hardly have been planning to hold his dinner party, at which the widower was to be guest of honour; nor, for that matter, unless the mourning had been relaxed, could illuminations and other rejoicings have been ordered on 25 March 1480 as a celebration of the peace just negotiated between the Italian powers.[182] Admittedly the *Orfeo* might seem to have been a peculiarly indecorous entertainment at this time, not least because in Poliziano's version of the legend, Orfeo, having lost Eurydice, resolves in future to confine his erotic pleasure to his own sex (neither appropriate, therefore, with respect to the marchese's recent widowerhood nor to the forthcoming marriages, let alone to the cardinal's renunciation of Barbara, his mistress and the mother of his son).[183] But during Carnival many taboos may have been lifted.

The Mantuan imagery in the ode to the cardinal (whose promotion as pope is confidently predicted), with the swift-flowing Mincio and nearby waves of the Po acclaiming their Maecenas, seems also to presume that he is in Mantua, or recently arrived there. The Bacchanal song at the end carries the authentic flavour of Carnival celebration.[184] It is almost inconceivable that with Baccio under their roof the Gonzagas could have resisted the temptation to hear him perform again, or the simultaneous opportunity of seeing the performance of a *fabula* devised by Poliziano.

Speculation no doubt will continue. An earlier date for Poliziano's composition has been urged on account of its similarities with the *Stanze* and it has been suggested that the text only *implies* that Baccio was *intended* to sing the Ode in praise of the cardinal, not recording definitely that he did so, and it may have been written and sung earlier, or interpolated later. But if the theory is valid that the text as printed was a version preserved by members of the cardinal's household, it would seem stranger for the Ode to have been inserted later, rather than preserved as a part of the record of a performance by Baccio which actually

mandare qualche selvatigine, fasiani, perdice, et altri ucelli che ad Essa pariranno essere convenienti et apti' (ASMn, AG, b. 2896, lib. 96, fol. 189ʳ); paraphrased by Picotti, *Ricerche storiche*, p. 101 n.4.

[179] It is favoured by Vitalini, 'A proposito della datazione', and by D. Mattelini in a forthcoming article.

[180] Tissoni-Benvenuti, 'Il viaggio', pp. 368–82; *L'Orfeo*, pp. 62–3.

[181] Stefanino Guidotti to Marchese Federico Gonzaga, Bolzano, 16 November 1478: 'disseno havere impositione...di cavargli il corrotto de le veste negre e vestirla di colore...conveniente a tal atto e iocundità e festa' (ASMn, AG, b. 544, c. 71); Billo, 'Le nozze di Paola Gonzaga', pp. 7, 13.

[182] Picotti, *Ricerche storiche*, p. 101; ASMn, AG, b. 2038–9, Gride (1478–88), fasc. 7.

[183] See above, p. 24.

[184] Vitalini, 'A proposito della datazione', pp. 249–50. Carnival at Bologna was described as 'li dì bacchanali' (with relief that they were over, so that serious study could be resumed) in a letter of 23 February 1477 from Giovanni Guidotti, chaplain to protonotary Ludovico Gonzaga (ASMn, AG, b. 1141, c. 487).

occurred.[185] Some may still think that the Ode's allusions to Francesco as a future Mantuan pope fit best with late July 1471, when Paul II's illness and death had raised that faint prospect; but this goes back a long way in the debate.[186] The main objections are that Francesco had arrived in Bologna on 20 July 1471 after only a brief stop in Florence;[187] even if Baccio was high in Gonzaga favour then as a performer,[188] Poliziano would have been only seventeen. Moreover the cardinal had almost immediately to hasten back to Rome, having heard of the pope's death and the forthcoming conclave to elect his successor; he would have had no time at all for festivities in Mantua or Gonzaga, where his father was staying. The most that can be said is that a visit might have been intended, but would have had to be cancelled. It cannot be excluded that *Orfeo* was staged in the course of a banquet at Rome[189] (in the style of the New Year occasion of 1476) sometime in 1476–7, but a performance in Mantua, probably in Francesco's house there, on the last day of Carnival in 1480, still remains likeliest.

There is no point here in pursuing the problem further; it should only be noted how little else there is to connect Cardinal Francesco Gonzaga with Poliziano. No correspondence between them has come to light, and no predilection of the cardinal for Poliziano's writings emerges from the list of his books in the inventory. The connexion, such as it was, probably depended on Giovan Pietro Arrivabene, in praise of whose learning Poliziano dedicated a Greek epigram, and to whom in 1491 he wrote recalling his gratitude for help at a difficult time of his life. He may well have been alluding in that letter to the winter of 1479–80 when he had been deprived of his security in Florence.[190] Another special link was probably the cardinal's chamberlain Nicolò da Piacenza, to whom Poliziano addressed adulatory Latin verses, complimenting him on his charitable and benign demeanour, as well as their mutual celebration of Cardinal Gonzaga's role as a modern Maecenas towards poets.[191] The *Orfeo* was certainly the most important work of literature produced under the aegis of Cardinal Gonzaga, and on the testimony of Poliziano's letter to Canale, he had played an important part in its inception; but it was the music which Francesco may have enjoyed most of all, and that is irretrievably lost.

(ii) Collecting and the Visual Arts

Just as imitation of his parents, his preceptors and his peers may largely explain Francesco Gonzaga's interest in books and literary culture, so may it account for his collecting of antique objects, coins and medals and engraved gems, and of jewels, tapestries, miscellaneous works of art, artefacts and 'scientific' curiosities. Again, his interest was probably stimulated by early impressions:

---

[185] Cf. Tissoni-Benvenuti, *L'Orfeo*, pp.174–6, and Maier ed., *Stanze*, pp. 95–6, 102–3.
[186] It was Del Lungo's argument, who narrowed the date to between 18–22 July (*Florentia*, p. 320), refuted by Picotti, *Ricerche storiche*, pp. 89–93.
[187] For his movements see above, Table of Itineraries.
[188] Picotti, *Ricerche storiche*, p. 100, and see above, p. 70.
[189] Tissoni-Benvenuti, *.L'Orfeo*, p. 68. Her alternative suggestion that it was performed at Bologna is less convincing, in view of the tense political circumstances and fear of the plague during the cardinal's residence there in 1478–9.
[190] Picotti, *Ricerche storiche*, p. 65; Chambers, 'Arrivabene', pp. 404 nn. 36–7; 431 n. 191.
[191] Picotti, *Ricerche storiche*, p. 65 n. 3; Tissoni-Benvenuti, *L'Orfeo*, pp. 46–8; see also above, p. 69.

Gonzaga family collections, including those of his deceased uncle and model, the protonotary Giovan Lucido,[192] contact with distinguished visitors to Mantua, particularly during the papal diet of 1459, or the viewing of notable collections before and after his arrival in Rome. He was shown Piero de' Medici's collections in Florence in March 1462,[193] and in Rome was soon swept into the company of eminent collectors and connoisseurs, notably some of the cardinals who had recently been entertained by his parents in Mantua.

Among these cardinals was Prospero Colonna, with whom Alessandro Gonzaga, Francesco's uncle, was particularly friendly. Alessandro stayed in Prospero's house when he came to Rome with the young cardinal in March 1462.[194] Francesco became a favourite of Cardinal Prospero Colonna,[195] and was evidently much upset by his death a year later,[196] when he served as one of his executors.[197] Cardinal Pietro Barbo also made Francesco and his uncle and younger brother welcome, offering at once to show them his 'things', by which Alessandro assumed he meant his medals, silverware and other precious objects,[198] and remained particularly benevolent towards him;[199] so, above all, did that Paduan Cardinal Ludovico Trevisan, Patriarch of Aquileia, whose style of living was the most lavish in the Sacred College of his time,[200] and from whose collections, after his death, Paul II enriched his own.[201] Alessandro Gonzaga was impressed by Ludovico's garden,[202] though his principal menagerie was at Albano, where he kept peacocks, Indian hens and Syrian goats.[203] Francesco over

---

[192] On Giovan Lucido's coin collection, seen by Ciriaco d'Ancona at Pavia in 1442, see Müntz, *Les Arts*, II, p. 173; Weiss, *Renaissance Discovery*, pp. 167–8.

[193] G. P. Arrivabene to Barbara, Florence, 14 March 1462: 'andoe Monsignor a visitare Petro, chi era in letto pur per gotte, e qui li forono monstrati medaglie, camaini cum diversi intagli, vasi e molte belle gioie'; Gianfrancesco Soardi to Barbara, Florence, 15 March 1462: 'Poi gli monstroron le camere e studii di Pietro, che si sta nel letto, e le zoglie sue che sono medaglie d'oro, d'argento e di ottone, chamaini di precio di ducati 800 alcuni di essi, e vasi belissimi a mio iudicio, di bone pietre o di cristallo ornatissime d'argento, perle e altre pietre fine' (ASMn, AG, b. 1100, cc. 83, 102); Chambers, 'Cardinal Gonzaga in Florence', pp. 250, 252.

[194] Alessandro Gonzaga to Barbara, Rome, 24 March 1462: 'Monsignor nostro me habia dato licentia che stia in casa del prelibato Monsignore de Colona, cum tutta la mia brigata' (ASMn, AG, b. 841, c. 791ʳ).

[195] E.g., Marasca to Barbara, Rome, 27 April 1462: 'Monsignor è stato con Monsignor Colona et ha cenato seco' (ASMn, AG, b. 841, c. 687).

[196] Marasca to Barbara, Rome, 26 March 1463: 'se comenza conoscere quanta perdita habiano fatti quelli a chi volea bene questo signore, et se alcuno era amato da lui era Monsignor mio, quale per insine a questa hora ho veduto piangere più volte' (ASMn, AG, b. 842, c. 184).

[197] G. P. Arrivabene to Barbara, 14 April 1463: 'El Reverendissimo Monsignore mio…ritrovase molto occupato per il spazamento de questa famiglia de la bona memoria del cardinale Colona, ch' è quasi ugni dì li executori conveneno insieme' (ASMn, AG, b. 842, c. 141).

[198] Alessandro Gonzaga to Barbara, 30 March 1462: 'Monsignor de San Marco ha visto tra li altri cardinali Monsignor nostro e così lo Illustre Meser Zoan Francesco e mi, cum tante cordiale proferte quanto dir se potesse…anche fi un parlare, como a dire ch'el ne haveria volentera monstrato de le sue cose. Non so mo se fossero medaie, arzentaria o altra cosa' (ASMn, AG, b. 841, c. 798ʳ).

[199] Marasca to Barbara, 6 January 1463: 'questo cardinale de Sancto Marco gli mostra singulare affectione, e non cessa laudarlo e acarezarlo, et publice et private' (ASMn, AG, b. 842, c. 167); G. P. Arrivabene reported on 27 April 1463 that Francesco had recently dined with Barbo (b. 842, c. 143).

[200] Paschini, *Lodovico Cardinal Camerlengo*, esp. pp. 216–33, for his relations with scholars such as Guarino da Verona, Poggio Bracciolini and others.

[201] Ibid., pp. 209 and 235–6, for an extract concerning items of silverware bought from the executors for 1000 gold florins by Paul II, 26 April 1465. A previously unknown inventory of this lavish cardinal's possessions is shortly to be published by Edward Butterfield.

[202] Alessandro Gonzaga to Barbara, Rome, 30 March 1462: 'Lo venere sopranominato andassemo a disnare cum Monsignor Camerlengo, el quale ce dette un disnare solennissimo soto una sua loza adherente a un bellissimo zardino che'l ha, nel quale sono mille zentileze facte de erbe polidissimamente, galea, nave, pavoni, leoni e più altre belle cose…' (ASMn, AG, b. 841, c. 795ᵛ).

[203] Pius II, *Commentarii*, ed. von Heck, II, p. 703 (lib. xi); transl. Gragg, pp. 158–9.

the next two years came to know him well. He was particularly attentive when Francesco fell ill in March and May 1463,[204] and after his recovery entertained him at Albano.[205]

Nor was it only Francesco's fellow cardinals who inspired him as a collector, particularly of antiquities; in his own household he had the modest example of Giovan Pietro Arrivabene, who had two signet seals made for himself from ancient intaglios;[206] and there were members of Pomponio Leto's circle also in attendance. Porcellio Pandoni, as has already been noted, gave to the young cardinal an antique head, supposedly of Portia, probably in the autumn of 1463.[207] Possibly this was among the marble antiquities which Francesco arranged to be conveyed to Mantua that winter and showed to his father.[208] Probably Agostino Maffei and his brothers, while helping to keep Francesco in funds, also fostered his cupidity to possess such rare objects. Francesco Maffei was a ready supplier of semi-precious stones, and on this account ingratiated himself with the marchese, promising in 1470 to get permission to send him pieces of porphyry and serpentine (he apologized that in the meantime he could only send two salami sausages),[209] and over a year later keeping his promise and also sending a tablet of alabaster incised with the Gonzaga arms.[210]

Even if his mind had not been dazzled by the example and inducements of other collectors and connoisseurs, Cardinal Gonzaga would have been dull indeed had he not responded to the visual relics of antiquity surrounding him. His titular church, Santa Maria Nuova, was just near the arch of Titus and the Colosseum; San Lorenzo in Damaso, where he had his principal residence from March 1468, was on the site of the Theatre of Pompey. Within a week of arriving in Rome he is known to have visited ancient sites as well as churches,[211] and no doubt this was only the first of many such expeditions; on a later occasion, for

[204] Cardinal F. Gonzaga to Barbara, 14 March 1463 (ASMn, AG, b. 841, c. 99); G. P. Arrivabene to Barbara 14 May 1463: 'el Camarlengo…ugni dì lo manda a visitare' (b. 842, c. 140).

[205] G. P. Arrivabene to Barbara, 9 May 1463, notes the invitation; Marasca to Marchese Ludovico Gonzaga, 31 May 1463, records Francesco's presence at Albano (b. 842, cc. 144, 191).

[206] Chambers, 'Arrivabene', pp. 402, 404 and pl. 2.

[207] 'Marmoreum caput Portie uxoris Bruti et Catonis filie/que morte viri audita, sumpto carbone vivo periit…/Dono datum amplissimo patri et domino F[rancisco] Gonzage Diacono Cardinali/ex Porcelio poeta laureato. Sic illum alloquitur', followed by verses in Francesco's praise (MS BAV, Vat. Lat. 1670, fol. 77ʳ), cited in Weiss, *Renaissance Discovery*, p. 197. See also above, p. 67.

[208] Cardinal F. Gonzaga to Marchese L. Gonzaga, Marmirolo, 20 May 1464: 'heri gionsero li mei muli, et hanno portato quelle teste e sepulcro de marmore, li quali domane farò portar lì, e venirò anche io a monstrargeli' (ASMn, AG, b. 2402).

[209] Francesco Maffei to Marchese L. Gonzaga, Rome, 23 May 1470: 'mando a Vostra Illustrissima Signoria para dua di sumate…Non mando al presente porfidi né serpentine, perché anchora non si ha potuto haver licentia de Nostro Signore' (ASMn, AG, b. 844, c. 105). The two pairs of 'sumate' I take as meat, i.e., 's[al]umate'; cf. Ludovico Agnelli to Marchese Francesco Gonzaga, Rome, 18 March 1493, promising 'vinticinque presutti e vinti sumate' (ASMn, AG, b. 849, c. 377).

[210] Francesco Maffei to Marchese L. Gonzaga, 16 August 1471: 'Mando…dui tondi di serpentina e una tavola d'allabastro cum l'arma de la Illustre Signoria Vostra intagliata. Le qual cose, benché siano di picciol precio…, supplico a Quella se degni acceptare la sincera fede e bona voluntate del suo servitore' (ASMn, AG, b. 844, c. 259).

[211] G. P. Arrivabene to Barbara, 1 April 1462: 'hoggi el dicto Reverendissimo Monsignore è cavalchato per Roma a vedere alcune chiesie e molte antiquitate' (ASMn, AG, b. 841, c. 656); cited by Esch, 'Mauern bei Mantegna', p. 319.

example, he may have accompanied his brother Gianfrancesco on a ride to visit the Baths of Diocletian.[212]

Whether Francesco accompanied Pius II on a famous archaeologizing tour,[213] which included visits to Albano and Lake Nemi, in the second half of May 1463, is uncertain; Pius records taking three of the cardinals with him, but Francesco (it may be recalled that he had recently been ill) is not named in the pope's account,[214] nor is the papal trip mentioned in any letters of Francesco or his domestic officers. Francesco did visit Cardinal Ludovico, the Patriarch of Aquileia, at Albano, but it seems to have been after Pius II had returned from his trip;[215] he went to Nemi the following October, and Marasca recalled Cardinal Prospero Colonna's project to raise the Roman galley submerged there.[216] Francesco spent much time in the Alban hills and the nearby seacoast during the summers which followed. On one trip to Nettuno, even if Francesco's main purpose was to hunt, the extent of Giovan Pietro Arrivabene's knowledge about the remains of the Roman port at Anzio and villas in the vicinity suggests that an expedition to these ancient sites had been made.[217] In the autumn of 1473 Francesco was keen to make a private visit to Padua;[218] whether this was to pursue antiquarian interests is not recorded; but he cared, for instance, about Roman inscriptions sufficiently to possess at least one collection of them in his library. This appears to have been the lost sylloge of classical inscriptions in Italy made by Ciriaco of Ancona;[219] another manuscript (which does survive), containing inscriptions collected in Rome, probably the sylloge of Nicola Signorili, may also have belonged to him.[220]

Francesco's ardour for acquiring finely wrought objects and curiosities, new as well as ancient, had already in February 1463 drawn reproachful comments from Marasca, his penny-pinching *maggiordomo*; other members of the household, he complained, incited Francesco by describing—for instance—mirrors and furs they had seen on sale; just recently the cardinal had been tempted to acquire some elaborate silverware, including vessels which had formerly belonged to Alfonso

---

[212] Marasca to Barbara, Rome, 25 November 1466: 'Lo Reverendissimo Monsignore è sano, et similiter lo Illustre messer Zohanefrancesco, quale hozi è cavalcato a le terme de Dioclciano' (ASMn, AG, b. 843).

[213] So Esch assumes: see above, n. 211.

[214] Pius II, *Commentarii*, ed. von Heck, II, pp. 702–11; transl. Gragg, pp. 758–66.

[215] Francesco was still in Rome on 22 May, when he wrote to the marchese (ASMn, AG, b. 842, c. 41); Marasca's letter to Marchese Ludovico Gonzaga, dated 31 May (b. 842, c. 191), quoted in Chambers, 'Housing Problems', p. 33 n. 83, informing him that Francesco was at Albano and that it had been difficult to get a message to the pope in Rome.

[216] Giacomo d'Arezzo to Marchese L. Gonzaga, Nemi, 26 October 1463: 'è andato ad uno luogo chiamato Nemo delli Colomnesi, per andare poi a Rocha de Papa'; and Marasca to Barbara, Nemi, 29 October 1463: 'hozi, se partemo de qua da Nemo, posto suso lo laco in che è quella nave quale già volse cavare il cardinale [Prospero Colonna] bone memorie, et andemo a Neptuna, terra suso el lito del mare e lì staremo tri giorni, poi lo Reverendissimo Monsignore se drizarà a Rocha de Papa' (ASMn, AG, b. 842, cc. 116, 202).

[217] G. P. Arrivabene to Cardinal Jacopo Ammannati, letter dated 4 October at Rome, probably in 1467: 'Dominus meus ad xi kalendas octobris ex more suo Neptunam accessit... Magna ibi supersunt adhuc antiquitatis vestigia et praecipue portus Antiaris...Ibi aliquot dies morari institueramus, et eos piscatione, venatione, aucupio, quorum omnium larga facultas est, laetissimos agere...' (Ammannati, *Epistolae*, fol. 140ʳ). The letter is mentioned in Faccioli, *Mantova*, II, p. 59; Chambers, 'Arrivabene', p. 405 n. 40.

[218] G. P. Arrivabene to Barbara, Viadana, 15 October 1473: 'Monsignor sta in proposito di andarsene puo per nave cum quatro o cinque a Padoa incognito' (ASMn, AG, b. 2415, c. 1071).

[219] I 821; Frasso, 'Oggetti d'arte e libri', p. 144, drew attention to it.

[220] MS Utrecht, University Library, 764; van der Horst, *Manuscripts*, p. 48, fig. 713–14; see below, List of Manuscripts.

of Aragon, King of Naples: among these desirable pieces were two flasks, a fruit dish and an exotic salt cellar in the form of a castle on the back of an elephant.[221] He appears to have been continually on the look-out for objects either to acquire for himself or else to give to his parents;[222] sometimes his presents were living creatures, such as the camels and an unbaptized Turkish slave sent in 1474.[223] Francesco himself did not emulate the Patriarch of Aquileia in having a menagerie of live curiosities, although that cardinal had once sent him as a present a white ass and an 'Indian hen';[224] but he evidently had dogs—dogleads and a dog's collar are listed in the inventory (I 614, 621, 679); he once sent Barbara one of his lapdogs as a gift and advised that it should be frequently washed but underfed.[225] When in *villegiatura* at Marino he also took delight in a pet goldfinch.[226] But mainly it was antiquities—such as a small antique vase he had described and then sent to his mother in October 1472[227]—and other decorative objects that he collected or gave as presents. Even at the distracting time of his last departure from Rome, bound for the War of Ferrara, he had left instructions for others to seek out ancient coins for him.[228]

Among the more ingenious artefacts which the cardinal possessed were an astrolabe and several time-keeping devices (I 465, 113, 684). He evidently found clocks particularly fascinating. In 1467 he entertained in his household a certain craftsman from Ferrara, whose skills intrigued him; the man presented him with two clocks and other devices he had made; Francesco later recorded that he had rewarded this man with money and some valuable cloth.[229] In September 1479 he

---

[221] Marasca to Barbara, 16 February 1463, complained of Francesco's spending money 'de cosse non ge sieno necessarie né utile tropo'; he informed her 'ultra che lui veda, l'uno de' famigli dice "ho veduti lì tali spechii", l'altro dice "ho trovato marteri overo foini per grando merchato"; l'altro questo, l'altro quello. E como sente, presto vole… Ulterius lui havea quasi fatto mercato de dui fiaschi de arzento, de una frutarola, de uno salino suso uno castello posto suso uno elefante, pur de arzento dorato circa quatrocento ducati, a termene ho tanto zanzato a recordange che non ha uno pizolo in cassa… pur ha lassati questi vasi, et invero se quello gli havesse voluti lassare a undese ducati la libra, pocho me haveria giovato el mio dire. Questi sono vasi che furono del Re Alfonso' (ASMn, AG, b. 842, c. 177). On tapestries intended for King Alfonso of Naples, which Francesco acquired, see I 201.

[222] E.g., to Barbara he sent with a letter from Rome, 14 September 1464, four leather *spalliere* (ASMn, AG, b. 842, c. 310); from Bologna, 17 October 1472, he wrote to her 'per Philippo di Andriasi mando a la Signoria Vostra quello vasetto antiquo del qual gli rasonai, che credo per esser pur de foza singulare li serà gratissimo' (b. 1141, c. 252); according to a letter from Rome, 22 May 1474, he had sent her then 'una arca de Noé' (b. 845, c. 219).

[223] Cardinal F. Gonzaga to Barbara, Rome, 11 October 1474: '…un presento per parte mia de marito e moglie et una figlioletta cameli, e d'un schiavo turco… Lo schiavo non è bategiato. Quella e del baptismo e de liberarlo o non, ne farà la voluntate suoa' (ASMn, AG, b. 845, c. 245).

[224] Marasca to Barbara, Rome, 13 June 1463: 'novamente ha mandato a donare uno asenello biancho et una galina de India al Reverendissimo Monsignore mio' (ASMn, AG, b. 842, c. 192).

[225] Cardinal F. Gonzaga to Barbara, Tivoli, 5 September 1463: 'mando a Vostra Signoria uno de li mei cagnolini, qual credo li piacerà e reussirà molto bello se Essa lo farà spesso lavare e tenere netto; nel mangia[re] non se li vol dare se non pane e anche temperatamente perché non cresca troppo' (ASMn, AG, b. 842, c. 269).

[226] Platina, *De honesta voluptate*, lib. v, 12, as indicated by Professor Mary Milham (see Chambers, 'Il Platina', p. 14 n. 27).

[227] Cardinal F. Gonzaga to Barbara, Bologna, 17 October 1472: 'Per Philippo di Andreasi mando a la Signoria Vostra quello vasetto antiquo: del qual gli rasonai che credo per esser pur de foza singulare le serà gratissima' (ASMn, AG, b. 1141, c. 252).

[228] See letter of Gaspare da Padua, 28 February 1484: below, Appendix 3, no. 9, and the letter of Giuliano di Scipio, cited below, p. 83 n. 256.

[229] '…attestamur quod de anno mcccclxvii…cum ad nos venisset magister Marcus Ragnerius de Milano habitator Ferrarie et nobis duo horilogia et quedam alia opera pulcra donasset. Nos delectati admodum eius virtutibus et artificio tenuimus ipsum apud nos Rome per plures dies, et demum discedenti a nobis tum contemplatione…domini ducis Mutine et Regii, tum ob virtutibus suis et precipue eius in nos fidem et

wrote from Bologna that he was searching in vain for a clock for his brother Federico; he mentioned that a year before he had sent a small one to Barbara of Brandenburg; he would find out if a clockmaker at Ferrara had any in stock.[230]

One figure stands out above all the rest as the connoisseur who most deeply impressed Francesco: Cardinal Pietro Barbo, Pope Paul II. Even if, after his elevation, Paul became inaccessible and inscrutable—Francesco was among those who testified to this[231]—he seems to have remained quite cordial in attitude towards Francesco, at least as a fellow collector. How much he and Paul saw of each other's collections of medals, bronzes, engraved gems and other fine objects can only be a matter for speculation; but almost certainly Francesco copied from Barbo the method of displaying some of his finest cameos on silver tablets inscribed with his arms; the pope had sixty such trays, Francesco had at least twenty.[232] Some, but it cannot be shown how many, of Paul's specimens eventually passed into Francesco's hands. A number of them are recorded in his keeping on 30 November 1471, four months after the pope's death; these he may have obtained for inspection with a view to purchase.[233] Since he was one of the cardinals made responsible for discharging the deceased pope's debts,[234] he was in a good position to purchase such precious objects for himself; likewise there can be no doubt about the provenance of the cameo in a ruby setting showing the head of Pope Paul (I 540) or—a rather less valuable item—the copper ring with Pope Paul's arms upon it (I 586).

Frustratingly little has come to light about Francesco's acquisition of individual items, but it is evident that his collection was by the early 1470s already remarkable, when it was probably in order to show and discuss some of the most recent acquisitions that he was so eager to have a conversation and meeeting with Andrea Mantegna, anticipating boredom at the spa baths of Porretta in the summer of 1472.[235] It has to be added that this famous encounter and connois-

---

affectionem, volentes personam suam ut decebat honorare, eidem magistro Marco de nostra mera liberalitate, non ob precium vel mercedem alicuius rei ab ipso habito, donavimus et nomine vere donationis tradidimus centum et vigintiquinque florenos auri papales in pecunia numerata, et insuper pannos sericos et laneos usque ad valorem aliorum vigintiquinque... datum Rome in domibus residentie nostre xviiii martii 1470' (ASMn, AG, b. 3351, fol. 102^r).

[230] Cardinal F. Gonzaga to Marchese Federico Gonzaga, Bologna, 24 September 1479: 'El ne rincresce de non trovarne horilogio alcuno accomodato da puoterne servire la Signoria Vostra, secundo lo desiderio suo. Ritrovamone solum un grande, desatto da portare, el qual è anche mal ad ordine. Un piccolino, che havevamo l'anno passato, donammo a la Illustre madonna nostra matre. Mandaremo a Ferrara a vedere se per ventura quello maestro chi sta lì ne havesse de' fatti, e trovandone uno, ne forniremo la Signoria Vostra' (ASMn, AG, b. 1142).

[231] E.g., Cardinal F. Gonzaga wrote to Marchese L. Gonzaga, Rome, 31 July 1466: 'li modi e pratiche de questo Nostro Signore sono tanto profunde e secrete che ad ugniuno danno da pensare assai' (ASMn, AG, b. 843).

[232] Müntz, Les Arts, II, pp. 223–36; for Francesco's twenty silver tavole see I 572.

[233] They included 'uno cammeo grande cum testa de donna cum lo pecto'; 'uno calcedonio cum testa de Alexandro', 'una Faustina amantata' and 'uno cameo grandicello cum testa de Tiberio et bello' (Müntz, Les Arts, II, pp. 117–18); cited by Weiss, Renaissance Discovery, p. 197. See also Pastor, Storia dei papi, II, pp. 438–9.

[234] See above, p. 46–7.

[235] Cardinal F. Gonzaga to Marchese L. Gonzaga, Foligno, 18 July 1472: 'Lo arivare mio a Bologna credo serà a li cinque o sei de avosto, dove non intendo de fermarme più che doi dì, et andarmene al bagno, dove per havere qualche solatio e transtullo ad fugire lo dormire, come è necessario in quello luoco, prego la Signoria Vostra che li piacia ordinare che Andrea Mantegna e Malagise lì vengano e stiano continuamente cum me. Cum Andrea pigliarò spasso de monstrarli miei camaini e figure de bronzo et altre belle cose antique, sopra le quale

seurs' conversation at Porretta did not in fact take place, because when the cardinal arrived at Bologna his doctors advised against going on to take the waters at Porretta;[236] just conceivably Mantegna came instead to see him at Bologna, but there is no evidence of this. Nevertheless, the expression of his wish for such a meeting is perfectly valid for the record, almost as valuable as if it had actually happened.

The cardinal's fascination for uncut precious stones—of which he had some in his possession from the very beginning of his career[237]—may have been in part owing to their aesthetic appeal and also to their supposed amuletic powers, about which he could have learned much from his copies (I 804–05) of Pliny's *Natural History* (lib. xxxvii) and Albertus Magnus' *On Minerals*,[238] and from other books (e.g. I 765, 831). Years later, his brother Ludovico was the proud possessor of a gold chain on which were two of the cardinal's stones which were valued as amulets: an alectorius, held to be effective in preserving friendships, and a jacinth (*iacintho*), which was believed to ensure honourable regard and to afford protection against poison; but the lapidaries cite multiple magical properties for most of the stones they list.[239] Such associations were part of the common currency of ideas prevailing in the court of Rome and elsewhere, and it seems relevant here to mention a passage in the unpublished dialogue, *De dignitate cardinalis*, ascribed to Cardinal Jean Jouffroy and dedicated to Cardinal Bessarion in 1468, which contains a defence of curial splendour: this describes the gems on the new tiara of Paul II, with quotations from Pliny and Solinus concerning their talismanic properties.[240]

Francesco evidently appreciated, too, the use of precious stones as medical remedies, to be taken internally. He possessed a piece of bezoar (a stone secreted within the body of certain animals), which also was to pass to his brother Ludovico (I 587)—and he swallowed a small dose of it during one of his gravest illnesses, as an antidote to suspected poison.[241] His cherished piece of unicorn (W 21; I 608), really narwhal whale, also comes into this category of natural objects

---

studiaremo e conferiremo de compagnia…'(ASMn, AG, b. 844, c. 392); Del Lungo, *Florentia*, p. 306; Kristeller, *Mantegna*, doc. 45, p. 527, and frequently quoted elsewhere.

[236] G. P. Arrivabene to Marchese L. Gonzaga, Bologna, 2 August 1472: 'Questa matina circa le xii hore per la gratia de Dio siamo entrati in Bologna cum grande demonstratione d'amore de tuto questo populo, e lo Reverendissimo Monsignore mio…haveva terminato partire giobia per aviarse al bagno, ma perché sento doppo siamo arrivati messer Bavera dissuadere il bagno, che non intendo anchor per qual cagione, se attenderà prima de consultare bene e maturamente la cosa' (ASMn, AG, b. 1141, c. 242); also he wrote on 3 August to Barbara: 'Questa matina, etiam cum consentimento di medici, ha terminato solum de pigliar questa purgatione, puoi bevere qui tre o quatro giorni l'aqua, senza andare là suso al bagno, et puoi fin a xv dì, di venire de là' (ibid., c. 243); Barbara had already been advised in the postscript to a letter (signature missing) dated at Mantua 1 August: 'me pareria che, se per questo anno el potesse uscir senza bagni, el lo vole fare…questo non è el suo anno da bagni' (b. 2413, c. 868).

[237] See above, p. 45 n.70.

[238] Albertus Magnus, *Book of Minerals*, esp. II, 2: 'Precious Stones and Their Powers', pp. 68–126.

[239] Ludovico Gonzaga to Marchese Francesco Gonzaga, Quingentole, 6 August 1495; 'mando a vostra Illustrissima Signoria una catenella d'oro cum uno electorio et uno iacinto; lo electorio era de la bona memoria del Cardinale nostro et ha virtù a conservare li amici' (ASMn, AG, b. 2448). See, for instance, Evans, *Magical Jewels, passim*; Thorndike, 'Unpublished Minor Works' (referring to some texts with both Roman and Mantuan associations); Tomasoni, *Lapidario estense*, for the many powers ascribed to these and other stones.

[240] Miglio, 'Vidi thiaram', esp. pp. 141–5.

[241] B. Bonatto and G. P. Arrivabene to Marchese L. Gonzaga, 15 May 1472: 'li hanno dato un puocho de belzoar havuto dal papa che è una pietra contr'al veneno, la qual se raspa e dassi bevere o in aqua o in brodo' (ASMn, AG, b. 844, c. 310).

valued not only on account of rarity and beauty but also for their prophylactic and medical powers.[242] In addition the cardinal's (relatively small) collection of holy relics should be mentioned in this context, rather than related to his religious beliefs: the tooth of Sant'Apollonia, for instance, kept in an ornamental purse (I 601), must have been cherished as a protection against toothache.

But as well as visual appearance and benign magical power, cash value was also something which a collector like Francesco bore in mind: rare stones in particular were handy as semi-liquid capital, usable as credit pledges when money was needed at short notice. He evidently developed a dealer's sense of market values and could keep a cool head in bargaining, though he was no match for Paul II. In 1467 Francesco had the idea of selling to the pope one of his father's largest rubies, thinking it would appeal to him for his grandiose tiara.[243] Although he could show him only a drawing or paper cut-out of its shape, he expected a good offer, and tried to play on the pope's cupidity by a warning that Galeazzo Maria Sforza wanted the ruby too. These tactics failed, however; Paul kept his offer low and the sale fell through.[244]

Among the more spectacular and lavish furnishings which the cardinal had at his various establishments, or transported between them on his journeys, were his numerous tapestries and carpets, wall hangings, woven panels to place on or behind seats, beds and tables, as well as floor coverings. On account of both the quality and quantity of these, he quickly gained a reputation in the papal court: Pius II marvelled at the display of them at Viterbo in May 1462.[245] In Rome at the time of the Emperor Frederick III's visit in 1469, Francesco's display was reckoned by his secretary to be the best;[246] and on a social occasion shortly afterwards his tapestries were specially praised together with the rest of his ever growing store of costly furnishings.[247] When the cardinal arrived at Bologna in July 1471, amazement was aroused at the scale and splendour of his retinue and

---

[242] See I 608n, also e.g. Franchini et al., La scienza a corte, pp. 115–21, on pieces of 'unicorn' in Gonzaga collections. Barbara of Brandenburg had a piece, too, which she bequeathed to Marchese Federico Gonzaga in 1481: see Signorini, 'La malattia', pp. 13 and 20 n. 70. An item possessed by Gianfrancesco Gonzaga in 1496 is listed in his inventory as 'uno alicorno da nachara' (BCG, FMD, b. 23, c. 23ᵛ).

[243] Cardinal F. Gonzaga to Marchese L. Gonzaga, Rome, 23 November 1467: '…me venne in mente de quell'altro bello ballascio in tavola, el qual credo tuorìa voluntiera, perché cadeno molto bene in queste mitre, e già la Suoa Beatitudine ve ne ha posti de molto belli, et assai li piaceno quando sono in tavola, et in alcuni gli ha speso de molti denari' (ASMn, AG, b. 843).

[244] Cardinal F. Gonzaga to Marchese L. Gonzaga, Rome, 18 January 1468: 'Questa sera doppo el consistorio monstrai a Nostro Signore quella forma del balascio…e disseli anche, secundo me referì el Bonatto, com'el Duca de Milano ge l'haveva richiesto cum grand'instantia… Suoa Sanctitate puoteva per questa forma vedere la grosseza de la zoia e la condicione, presupponendo puoi che de colore era avantagiata et non haveva defecto alcuno. Volse allora monstrarmene cinque di suoi, che sono molto belli, non in tuto grossi come questo, ma ge n'è de centocinquanta, sesanta fin in ottanta caratti, e demum me concluse che, s'el Duca lo vole e falli tal precio, che li venga meglio dargelo, non vole già fare danno a Vostra Signoria che, per quanto se comprenda, essendo in la perfectione se dice, non haveria suoa Sanctitate animo de spenderli più che da cinque in seimilia, né anche vorìa affirmare de seimilia, se prima non lo vedesse' (ASMn, AG, b. 843).

[245] '…cardinalis mantuanus longum vie tractum cohoperuit et nobilissimis adornavit historiis quas peritissimi textores pannis appinxere divitibus' (Pius II, Commentarii, ed. van Heck, lib. viii, II, pp. 500–1; transl. Gragg, p. 553).

[246] G. P. Arrivabene to Barbara, Rome, 1 January 1469: '…le vie apparate ornatissimamente, ma la nostra vinceva tuti li altri apparati' (ASMn, AG, b. 843).

[247] Giovanni Arrivabene to Barbara, Rome, 10 January 1469: 'El reverendissimo Monsignore mio fece domenica passata la cena a quelli tri cardinali…et ge erano altri prelati…et fece un digno comito nel quale se vide un bellissimo apparato de tapezaria et argentero, et tutavia se attende a multiplicarlo.' His letter of 5 January refers to a banquet for Cardinals Borgia, Monferrato and Barbo (ASMn, AG, b. 843).

possessions, and this was recorded in local chronicles. One chronicler even specified some of the 'histories' on the tapestries, particularly the ones portraying legends of Alexander the Great, which were hung round the garden or courtyard of the legate's residence.[248]

The provenance of these tapestries is uncertain. Many were probably made in Tournai or Arras and might have been imported directly or though Venice; the 'Alexander the Great' pieces might have been similar in design to the famous narrative tapestries acquired in 1459 by Philip the Good Duke of Burgundy from Pasquier Grenier of Tournai: during the same year members of the Grenier family at Milan showed Duke Francesco Sforza a 'designum' for Alexander tapestries.[249] Francesco may have acquired others by gift or purchase, such as the four pieces originally made for Alfonso of Aragon, King of Naples (I 201), though he sometimes sold pieces of his own, perhaps just to raise cash; he had received a woven bed-cover from Cardinal Barbo early in 1462,[250] but at the time of his departure to Bologna, just shortly before Paul II died, Francesco had managed to sell the pope some satin hangings or coverlets—not including (presumably) the bed-cover given in 1462—for what seems a very high figure.[251] Finally, some of the cardinal's pieces may even have been made by Flemings in Mantua, so might some of his carpets: in 1473 Francesco sent from Bologna one of his servants (called 'Barisano') to Mantua to learn carpet-weaving.[252] He was still acquiring tapestries not long before his death, as references in his will (W 21) and various entries in the inventory indicate (I 204, 297, 330, 334, 461). The silverware and costly dishes and vases were likewise a source of wonderment when Francesco arrived in Bologna; there were vague if astounding estimations of their value.[253]

To draw a distinction between objects acquired for use, pleasure or decorative display, and objects acquired for financial investment, is difficult. Almost any portable item had some cash value which might in some circumstances be exchangeable for money. Even clothes or pieces of material (items which, as will be seen, occupy a large part of the cardinal's inventory) were sometimes turned to this account, as when the cardinal proposed distributing them in lieu of out-

---

[248] '...messer Francesco da Gonzaga cardinale...intrò in Bologna...a dì 21 de lulio a ore 12, et venne con bela conpagnia de chortexani et preti: havea circha 80 cavali in soa corte... Nota che'l dito avea più de 300 lire d'argento in taze, bazili, brunzi et confetiere con altri vasi, et tanti panni de razo lavorati de seta e d'oro estimati più de 10 milia duchati. Tute le stantie soe erano adobate de tali panni; fra li altri li era uno ne'l'orto con la istoria de Alixandro Magno contra del re Porto de India con gente d'arme da cavalo et da piede tuti armati et alifanti con castele adosso et li omini che conbateano; con molti de loro, feriti de vertuni, pareano essere vivi, li omini e cavali tanti erano naturalmente bene lavorati: era una belessa et alegresa de core a vedere tanti beli lavori d'oro e di seta' (*Corpus chronicorum Bononiensium*, IV, p. 429).

[249] Forti Grazzini, *Arazzi a Ferrara*; Roblot-Delondre, 'Sujets antiques'; Biscaro, 'I paramenti', p. 194 n. 1; I am grateful to Candice Adelson and to Scot McKendrick for references, some from the latter's PhD dissertation (see Bibliography below).

[250] See above, p. 37 n. 5.

[251] '...si pagano al cardinale Francesco Gonzaga duc. 724 ad introitum a Sanctissimo d. n. papa, pro valore certi paramenti de setani raso chremosino unius lecti' (ASV, Introitus et Exitus, 486, c. 197b), cited in Zippel, ed., *Vite*, p. 190 (M. Canensi).

[252] Cardinal F. Gonzaga to Barbara of Brandenburg, Bologna, 1 February 1473 (ASMn, AG, b. 1141, c. 285); Braghirolli, *Della manifattura di arazzi*, p. 34 and *passim* on Flemish tapestry weavers in Mantua.

[253] Cf. the description, in general less specific than that of the other Bolognese chronicler quoted above, n. 248, but which notes 'una credenza de argento estimata di valore di 20,000 ducati' in Ghirardacci, *Historia di Bologna*, pp. 207–8, quoted by Brown, 'Lorenzo', p. 86 n. 1.

standing wages owed to his household staff,[254] or when his brother Ludovico gave instructions in the spring of 1484 that the excavators or seekers whom he hoped would bring to light for him some pieces of antique sculpture, should be rewarded with articles of clothing.[255]

* * *

It is difficult to show that Cardinal Francesco Gonzaga played a specially active part in commissioning and collecting contemporary works of art, with the possible exception of illuminated manuscripts. In any case it is unlikely that such commissions would have been set down in legal contracts: for example, according to Gaspare of Padua, writing after the cardinal's death, the work that the goldsmith Giuliano di Scipio did for him was normally ordered informally without any notarialized agreement.[256] Only a few references to objects specially designed for him have come to light: nothing is known, for example, about the origin of his silver seal (I 104), of which several impressions survive. It shows the Madonna and Child with saints Benedict and Bernardino within a Mantegnesque architectural framework:[257] the choice of saints is a bit surprising, though St Benedict may have been used because of the *prepositura* of San Benedetto in Polirone, and St Bernardino because he was Franciscan. Francesco's roving acquisitiveness and the sheer quantity of fine objects described in the inventory suggest that many objects were made to order, but the correspondence is usually unhelpful. To start with, there is no evidence, apart from intrinsic probability, that he was ever a patron or customer of Cristoforo di Geremia, the celebrated Mantuan goldsmith and dealer in Roman antiquities, who in 1462 had been attached to the household of Cardinal Ludovico Trevisan while remaining in touch with Marchese Ludovico Gonzaga,[258] and who, after a period in Florence, returned to Rome where he worked for Paul II.[259] Francesco can be shown to have employed only a former apprentice of Cristoforo, Gian Carlo Zentelisia,[260] to make horse trappings.[261]

---

[254] Cardinal F. Gonzaga to Carlo Rodiano, Bologna, 7 September 1479: 'havemo facto un pensiero, non trovandone el modo de puotere dare le page a denari a la nostra famiglia, et essendo pur lei bisognosa de vestirse per questa vernata, di trovare tanti panni a credenza che suppliscano al bisogno, e dargeli cum computargelo perhò al conto de la provisione suoa. Faressemo stima che tu comprasti octo pezze buone de panno, de lxx bianche e quatro de queste ne faciasti tingere in scarlatto, e quatro in pavonazzo chiaro, cerchando de essere bene servito de le tincte...' (ASMn, AG, b. 2896, lib. 96, fol. 2ᵛ).

[255] Ludovico, Bishop-Elect of Mantua, to Ruffino Gablonetta, Rome, 9 June 1484: 'puollo molto ben servire uno zuppone di seta et a quelli marangoni che levaranno e portaranno a casa esse statue o capi uno pare de calze a ciascun' (ASP, AGG, b. 41/3, reg. 1, c. 169ʳ).

[256] '...perché el ditto maestro non fece mai merchato né pacto con la bona memoria de lo Reverendissimo Monsignore di cosa che lui li facesse' (See Appendix 3, no. 12).

[257] Fig. 4. See also *Tesori d'arte*, no. 139, p. 112; below, p. 92 n. 317.

[258] Rossi, 'Cristoforo di Geremia', with Geremia's letter of 6 April 1462 (ASMn, AG, b. 841, c. 596), informing Marchese Ludovico Gonzaga that he was sending him the *saliera* he had ordered, and four antique heads.

[259] Müntz, *Les Arts*, II, p. 44; Rossi, 'Cristoforo di Geremia', p. 411.

[260] First heard of in a letter of Marchese Ludovico to Cristoforo di Geremia, Belgioioso, 19 October 1463, containing recommendations for Zentelisia 'qual ha uno poco de designo et vene lì per imparar' (both letters cited in Rossi, 'Cristoforo di Geremia', p. 411).

[261] Cardinal F. Gonzaga to Barbara, Rome, 7 December 1476: 'ho visto la richiesta me fa Vostra Signoria de ritenere el Zentilisia a quella opera suoa de cofani...benché l'havesse in le mani da finirme certi fornimenti

There is some tangible evidence about objects which Francesco donated to churches. In 1468 he was concerned that the reliquary of the Holy Blood at Sant'Andrea in Mantua needed to be replaced[262] and the following year he bought or ordered for this purpose a gold chest or coffer and glass receptacle; they were evidently made in Venice, for Francesco proposed sharing the cost with his father and elder brother by means of grain shipments there from Mantua, a scheme which failed to gain the marchese's approval.[263] Nor is it known from whom he commissioned various other sacred objects: the gold reliquary containing a piece of the Cross, sent to his cousin Margaret of Denmark, Queen of Scotland, in 1471,[264] or the chalice and votive image of the Madonna which he presented in person at the shrine of Loreto in 1472;[265] or the many gifts, including tableware and altar furnishings, a jewelled cross, a fragment of the True Cross and a crystal reliquary with a thorn from Christ's crown which he presented after 'a copious but not ambitious' banquet for King Christian I of Denmark in 1474.[266]

Only a little more is known about a few more private commissions later in his career. There was a purse of black material worked with gold, ordered on his behalf from the Pollaiuolo brothers by one Niccolò di Cesari, agent of the Salutati bank in Rome, and forwarded to him at Cento near Bologna on 2 January 1479.[267]

From the same time is a letter about a candlestick the cardinal had commissioned, using as intermediary 'Hermes', the enigmatic Hermes Flavio de Bonis of Padua. This *famiglio*, still a member of the household in 1483 (W 27), had been the friend or lover of Girolamo Riario's Adonis-like page Alessandro Cinnuzzi of Siena, whose death in 1474 was lamented in verses and possibly

---

miei da cavallo, nondimeno resto contento che rimanga ad ugni commandamento de Vostra Excellentia' (ASMn, AG, b. 845, c. 656).

[262] Cardinal F. Gonzaga to Barbara, Rome, 19 January 1468, without being explicit about his intention, required her 'fare vedere la cassa dove se teneno in Sancto Andrea li tabernaculi del Sangue de Christo e de la spongia, e voglia fare mensurare la largeza, alteza e longeza de essa cassa, et anche la longeza e grosseza di tabernaculi, e dignisi advisarmene' (ASMn, AG, b. 843); noted by Carnevali, 'Un culto', p. 73.

[263] Marchese L. Gonzaga to Barbara, Florence, 11 August 1469: 'L'è venuto hozi a nui Carlo da Rodiano el qual, tra le altre cose ne ha dicto da parte del Reverendissimo Cardinale nostro, come novamente ha comprato una cassetta et uno bichero d'oro bellissimo per reponere el Sangue de Cristo da Mantua, et che l'ha facto uno suo pensero che per pagare questa casseta gie dagamo cento o cinquanta moze de frumento del nostro, vui cento del vostro, e Federico cinquanta del suo. Quanto è per nui, ge habiamo risposto che non gie ne daressemo grano, perché meglio ne pare dalle intrade nostre attendere a pagare nostri debiti che fare simile spese ... prefato cardinale ha facto promessa per tuto septembre proximo de darli seicento moza di frumento per condure a Vinesia in pagamento de le predicte cose' (ASMn, AG,, b. 2891, lib. 63, fol. 73ʳ).

[264] G. P. Arrivabene to Barbara, Rome, 30 January 1471: 'Lo Reverendissimo Monsignor mio manda a donare a la regina de Scotia del ligno della croce ligato in oro per cosa di devotione' (ASMn, AG, b. 844, c. 217).

[265] G. P. Arrivabene to Barbara, Pesaro, 27 July 1472: 'andammo ... giobia a Sancta Maria de Loreto, e lì suoa Reverendissima Signoria satisfece a li voti suoi, offerse lo calice per se, nel qual è argento per cento ducati senza la factura e l'oro, et una imagine de Nostra Donna altra fiata votata per lo Illustrissimo Zoan Francesco quando fue amalato a Roma' (ASMn, AG, b. 844, c. 391).

[266] G. P. Arrivabene to Barbara, Rome, 19 April 1474: 'dominica matina Monsignor mio andoe a levarlo [i.e., the king] da casa, e menollo qui a desnare, dove era fatto splendido e copioso apparato, ma non ambitioso ... Doppo lo disnare, Monsignor li donoe tre belli muli di soma cum tre para de casse de la quale ve n'è una per altare, cum toto lo fornimento da la messa, et una per tavola da manzare. E dedeli uno crosetta gioiellata de precio de 150 ducati, et un puocho di ligno de la croce, del qual li fece la experientia sul fuoco. E per la regina una spina de la corona di Christo in un vasetto di cristallo; al Duca de Saxonia un' altra crosetta ...' (ASMn, AG, b. 845, c. 134).

[267] The purse is described as 'una scharsella di raxo nero spagnolo lavorata chon oro' (Covi, 'Nuovi documenti', pp. 64–5, 70–1).

commemorated on a medal designed by Hermes himself.[268] Although Hermes was a goldsmith, the extant correspondence does not throw light on any of his own works done for the cardinal, only upon his role—like that of Gaspare da Padova—as an expert adviser and go-between; this he also performed with regard to the cardinal's domestic building plans in the winter of 1479–80.[269] The candlestick episode throws some light upon Francesco's procedure in such matters; it was not his custom, he wrote, to haggle with artists, but he could not accept a price so unreasonable (more than double the six ducats suggested by the expert valuers).[270]

Francesco was, however, anxious to support the goldsmith Bartolomeo Melioli, who had evidently come to work for him in Bologna in 1479, when the cathedral chapter in Mantua, angered by this absence, threatened to cancel a contract with the artist.[271] How much Francesco commissioned from Melioli is not known; only one item in the inventory is attributed to him by name (I 120), but it may be inferred that other decorative pieces and repairs to silver objects were by his hand.

No documentation has been discovered about any work Francesco commissioned from the versatile Mantuan artist Sperandio Savelli, in particular his medal,[272] showing the cardinal's head on the obverse with the inscription 'Splendour of Liberty and of the Roman Church' and upon the reverse an enigmatic *impresa* including a lynx, pyramid and martial paraphernalia, which also appears on at least two of the cardinal's manuscripts.[273] All that is sure is that Sperandio was in Bologna from July 1478 onwards, produced medals for members of the Bentivoglio family and leading Bolognese personalities, and that the cardinal's brother Ludovico later recalled that Francesco had favoured him.[274]

---

[268] Patetta, 'Di una raccolta', pp. 167–9. The medal, of which an exemplar was recorded by Armand, had inscribed on the reverse HERMES. FLAVIUS. APOLLINI SUO CONSECRAVIT.

[269] E.g., the cardinal's letter to Francesco Maffei, 28 January 1480: 'per la fabrica te haressemo mo aviato Hermes…' (ASMn, AG, b. 2896, lib. 96, fol. 172ᵛ; see also below, p. 91). Hermes's horse is listed in the inventory (I 921); for his subsequent career as a 'carissimo famigliare' of the Bishop-Elect Ludovico Gonzaga, see Rossi, 'I medaglisti', pp. 26–38, and as *inzegnero* of Ludovico's chapel of the Holy Blood in Mantua cathedral, see Ferrari and Zanata, 'La capella del "Sangue di Cristo"', p. 83.

[270] Cardinal F. Gonzaga to his *luogotenente* in Bologna, Mantua 20 January 1480: 'Havevamo fatto fare lì per lo mezo de Hermes un candeliere, la manifactura del qual havendo lui fatta estimare da maestri de l'arte, fu taxata a sei ducati. Pare ch'el maestro ne dimandi mo XIIII e altramente non lo voglia dare. Sapeti bene che non è nostra consuetudine de assutiliare queste cose, né de ritenere ad altri la sua mercede. Pur quando vogliono ussire tanto del honesto, non ce pare de comportargelo…' (ASMn, AG, b. 2896, lib. 96, fols 171ᵛ–2ʳ).

[271] Cardinal F. Gonzaga to the chapter canons, Bologna, 21 October 1479: 'nui sentemo che a Bartholomeo Miliolo havevati dato a lavorare e fare un certo tabernaculo, lo quale lui etiam haveva tuolto a fornire secundo eravati rimasti da accordo. N'è ditto mo che per l'absentarse da Mantuoa e venire suo qua, havevati animo de fare provisione d'altro maestro che lo expedesse, che a lui molto rincresceria, e a nui chi non voressimo ch'el nostro, havendo levato di là, li risultasse in danno…' (ibid., fol. 69ᵛ).

[272] Figs 5–6; Hill, *Corpus*, no. 390e; Chambers and Martineau, *Splendours*, no. 44, p. 130; Chambers, 'Virtù militare', pp. 221–3, where I suggest it might allude to Francesco's military legateship in the War of Ferrara; Bazzotti, 'Imprese gonzaghesche', pp. 155–7, prefers a Platonic meaning, citing St Paul, Corinthians, I. xiii. 12 and other sources.

[273] MS Dublin, Chester Beatty Library, W. 122, fol. 3; also in the left-hand margin on the first page of Greek text in the cardinal's *Iliad*: MS BAV, Vat. Gr. 1626, fol. 1ᵛ: see Figs 3, 8.

[274] Ludovico Gonzaga, Bishop-Elect of Mantua, to marchese Francesco Gonzaga, Quingentole, 11 February 1495 (?): 'esso fu sempre molto grato et accepto alla pia memoria del cardinale nostro, et io conseguentemente l'ho amato et estimato'; quoted from U. Rossi by Venturi, 'Sperandio', p. 395; the date and location of this letter in ASP, AGG need to be checked. On Sperandio's other Bolognese medals see also Venturi, p. 394; Hill, *Medals*, pp. 52–4.

Francesco's interest in commissioning works of art could sometimes be sporadic or dilatory. This was apparently the case with the 'Vatican Homer'; likewise with his mother's tomb.[275] A marble funerary monument to Barbara was to have been erected in front of a reconstructed shrine of St Anselm in Mantua cathedral; this was her wish and in accordance with a discussion which Marchese Federico remembered having with Francesco himself. But although Mantegna made a drawing for it, the cardinal allowed the matter to slide for over a year. He had not replied from Rome when a decision was already needed early in 1482, nor in July when he was reminded about it; in December 1482 Federico complained that he still needed the cardinal's opinion, not wanting to go ahead with anything he did not like. It was only in February 1483 that Francesco at last wrote that he liked Mantegna's drawing,[276] but he seems to have taken no steps to encourage the project, which was never carried out.

That Francesco could, however, be prescriptive and concerned about the details of a design is shown in the case of a silver belt which he ordered for his infant son,[277] and just before his final departure from Rome at the end of 1482 he had asked Gaspare da Padua to commission a porphyry spice-grinder or pepper-mill from Giuliano di Scipio, the goldsmith who had worked formerly for Paul II and was also a dealer, or even a faker, of antiquities. Gaspare wrote about the uncompleted pepper-mill some months after the cardinal's death, and mentioned incidentally that there had been no legal contract ('el ditto maestro non fece mai merchato né pacto') which may suggest that Francesco's *committenza* tended to be informal or unbusinesslike and therefore went unrecorded. Gaspare also mentioned that Giuliano di Scipio had sold medals and jewels to the cardinal; indeed, he probably had for a long time been one of his main suppliers.[278]

Only seldom does one find trace of a painter in Francesco's household. Andrea Mantegna's assistant and fellow-antiquarian Samuele da Tradate is probably the Samuele who died under the cardinal's roof in Rome in October 1466 (see I 773), but there is no supporting evidence that Samuele had been working for him. A certain 'Zohanne Alvise' named in 1479 as 'our painter' is very likely the same Giovan Luigi de' Medici, apparently a Mantuan, who in November 1484 was commissioned by Protonotary Ludovico to submit a design for a bronze tomb of Barbara of Brandenburg; however, the cardinal's letter, from Bologna, does not clarify whether Giovan Luigi had been working for him in Mantua, Bologna or Rome.[279] If it was at Rome, he might have been engaged on the mural painting *in*

---

[275] Evidence from the 'Terminationes commissariorum' (ASDMn, FCC, Miscellanea, b. 2/A), is in Resti-Ferrari, 'Spigolature', pp. 275–8; see also Signorini, 'La malattia mortale', pp. 11, 29 (doc. 8).

[276] '1º Febbraio 1483: Lo Reverendissimo Cardinale ha risposto al fatto de far la sepultura che lo designo ge mandassimo de d. Andrea Mantegna ge piace…'('Terminationes', fol. 35ʳ), Resti-Ferrari, 'Spigolature', p. 278.

[277] Cardinal F. Gonzaga to Bonetto, Bologna, 7 September 1479: 'Mandamote…uno centurino tuto de argento per lo nostro putino, al qual, se li passetti seranno troppo distanti l'uno da l'altro, puorai farne fare de novi, tramezarli et adaptarlo in modo che lo possa portare' (ASMn, AG, b. 2896, lib. 96, fol. 1ᵛ).

[278] Gaspare da Padova to Marchese Federico Gonzaga, Rome, 28 February, 29 March 1484, in Appendix 3, nos 9, 12; Giuliano di Scipio himself wrote to the marchese on 1 May 1484, of his outstanding claim 'havendo servito et venduto certe gioye et medaglie alla bona memoria del Reverendissimo Monsignore fu lo cardinale de Mantua…delle quale remasi ad havere da Monsignore ducati octantaocto' (ASMn, AG, b. 847, c. 49). On Giuliano di Scipio see Müntz, *Les Arts*, II, pp. 117–18; also above, p. 83.

[279] Cardinal F. Gonzaga to Carlo da Rodiano, Bologna, 21 October 1479: 'devi ricordare che nui altre volte donassemo a Zohanne Alviso nostro depintore ducento ducati per maritare alcune sue sorelle' (ASMn, AG, b.

graffito which the cardinal commissioned for his garden walls: no other painter's name has come to light.

This garden project amounts to the only programme of painting which can be attributed to the cardinal, and the correspondence about it is in the same letters which refer to some domestic building works (discussed below), in the later months of 1479. His gardens were, for their own sake, cherished by Francesco; in his letter of 19 November to Maffei he mentioned the pomegranate trees that he had planted with his own hand, which he was angered to hear had been cut down, and ordered cypresses, pines, new pomegranates and other trees to be planted there. He also mentions the small secret garden (*horticello picolino*), which had space for little more than a bench to sit upon, and where no trees should be planted.[280] The new amenity, however, was to be a series of paintings upon the walls within the garden. Francesco's selection of stories for this scheme all came from Ovid's *Metamorphoses*. He required the battle of the Lapiths and Centaurs for the walls of the secret garden, the story of Theseus for the outer wall of the labyrinth (and the death of the Minotaur within it), and near the exit of the garden he wanted the fable of Meleager or the hunting of the Caledonian boar—all rather violent scenes, which might well appeal to a member of the Gonzaga family, reared to a delight in blood sports.[281] Francesco wanted Nicolò Cosmico to advise on the names of the Lapiths and the Centaurs, and also about whether Hercules should be represented in the legend of Meleager; Francesco could not, therefore, have bothered to look up the *Metamorphoses* for himself, where there is no question of Hercules's presence. But there is little reason to suppose Francesco had the right qualities of mind to devise iconographical programmes. According to Paolo Cortesi, a particularly mean neighbour of Francesco's (apparently in the Campo dei Fiori neighbourhood) once asked him to suggest an unexpected subject for a painting for his house and was simply told to commission a personification of liberality.[282]

For which of the cardinal's various gardens were the murals intended? Obviously not for the one attached to the legatine residence in Bologna, although according to one (rather later) Bolognese source in 1478 Francesco was indeed developing the garden there.[283] It has been assumed that the garden in question was the one at Sant'Agata dei Goti, which had been celebrated even before Francesco's tenancy there and became even more famous under his successors, particularly thanks to the improvements of Cardinal Niccolò Ridolfi.[284] But a stronger possibility remains—particularly as the cardinal's letter does not name Sant'Agata, as most letters do when referring to his second residence—that the

---

2896, lib. 96, fol. 69ᵛ); for the letter concerning Barbara's tomb, see D'Arco, *Delle arti*, II, pp. 18–19, doc. 20; Signorini, 'La malattia mortale', p. 29, doc. 9; on Giovan Alvise de' Medici see also Thieme and Becker, *Allgemeines Lexicon*, s.v.

280 ASMn, AG, b. 2896, lib. 96, fol. 125ʳ; Chambers, 'Housing Problems', appendix, doc. 27 p. 57.

281 Cardinal F. Gonzaga to Francesco Maffei, Bologna, 4 December 1479 (ASMn, AG, b. 2896, lib. 96, fols 136ʳ–7ʳ), text in Chambers, 'Housing Problems', appendix, doc. 28, pp. 57–8 and part in Rossi, 'Niccolò Lelio Cosmico', p. 111.

282 'Franciscus Gonzaga homo munificus et excellenti gratia senator dicenti, nescio cui, avara cupiditate ceco, velle se domum suam, quam in foro Olitorio haberet, aliquo inusitato picture genere ornare, "Pingere" inquit "liberalitatem iube"' (Cortesi, *De cardinalatu*, lib. II 'De sermone' ['Facetie et ioci'], fols lxxxv ᵛ–lxxxvi ʳ).

283 Ghirardacci, *Historia di Bologna*, p. 218: 'Di quest'anno il cardinale legato di Bologna fece minare alcune case che erano a canto il palazzo de'signori, et in dirizzò un bellissimo giardino et lo cinse di alte mura.'

284 Coffin, *The Villa*, pp. 183–4.

murals were meant to be at San Lorenzo in Damaso,[285] where there was also a *loggia* and garden: features which had been admired by Alessandro Gonzaga in 1462 and served the cardinal well when he was convalescing from illness in 1472.[286] That extensions were intended for this garden may be implied by the cardinal's purchase with his own money of a house *beyond the garden* of the house at San Lorenzo in Damaso;[287] and further points strengthen the argument that this was the garden in question. The same correspondence also includes references to domestic building works which seem to have been at San Lorenzo in Damaso,[288] and suggestive references to the garden in the church building accounts for 1481 have also come to light. These mention a direct access to the garden from the church and that the two sacristies overlooked the garden, so it was necessary to provide non-see-through windows of oil-cloth to avoid scandal being aroused by the sight of the cardinal taking a stroll.[289] Why Francesco's perambulations should have scandalized the canons of San Lorenzo in Damaso must be left to the imagination, but an extensive garden, with follies and mythological decorations, for a palace so centrally situated in Rome and adjacent to a titulary church, may have been thought unusual and incongruous, and maybe this was in part why the clergy were shocked as they peeped from the sacristy windows.

Meanwhile, there is little to record that Francesco owned or appreciated panel paintings. The inventory contains only two such items: a pair of small devotional paintings 'in the Greek manner' (I 598)—perhaps even Greek icons, a large variety of which Paul II had collected,[290] and from or through whom Francesco may have acquired this pair. The only panel painting by a famous artist that Francesco is known to have acquired is a Madonna by Botticelli. He received delivery of this *tondo* in September 1477, payment for it (40 gold ducats) having been made through the Salutati bank;[291] it may even have been a gift from Benedetto Salutati, who was a neighbour living near Sant'Agata.[292]

It is all the more surprising that Francesco's role as a *committente* and connoisseur of architecture and painting was very limited, in view of his personal relations with two such major figures as Leon Battista Alberti and Andrea Mantegna. Alberti, who was in Mantua in 1459–60, had congratulated the marchese

[285] Chambers, 'Housing Problems', pp. 57–8.
[286] For Alessandro's letter see above, p. 75 n. 202; G. P. Arrivabene writing on 3 June 1472 told Barbara 'al disnar se veste, e descende in la logia suoa del giardino…' (ASMn, AG, b. 844, c. 317); on 8 June he was again reported to be in the garden (b. 844, c. 326).
[287] '…domus post ortum domus habitationis Rome Sancti Laurentii in Damaso': this was to be sold according to the cardinal's will (W 37).
[288] See below, p. 91.
[289] 11 September 1481: '…pro evacuatione Navi repleta immunditiis versus Portam Orti Domini Cardinalis'; (1 Oct 1481): 'pro tribus Fenestris impannatis…una in Sagrestia magna, et alia in parva, et alia una supra ubi sunt mantici, et hoc ne videret[ur?] Cardinalis deambulans per Ortum, quod scandalum…generaret' (Valtieri, 'La fabbrica del palazzo', p. 22 n. 21; San Lorenzo in Damaso, pp. 15–16).
[290] Müntz, Les Arts, II, pp. 202–6.
[291] Covi, 'A Documented Tondo', suggests that it may be the 'Virgin in Adoration' in the Museo Civico, Piacenza. However, this is impossible to reconcile with the recently argued case for dating the picture 1483–7, on iconographic and stylistic grounds (Pronti, 'Nuove acquisizioni', who seems unaware of Covi's article).
[292] Benedetto's house in Rome is mentioned by Ludovico Gonzaga, Bishop-elect of Mantua, writing on 25 May 1484 to the future Marchese Francesco: 'Io etiam mi son sequestrato e riducto in Roma bene in un luoco un puoco remoto chi è de Benedetto Salutati, et appresso a Sancta Agatha, chiesia che fu de la bona memoria del Reverendo Monsignore Nostro' (ASP, AGG, b. 41 (3), reg. 1, c. 154r).

upon Francesco's elevation in December 1461, reflecting (as no one else did) that such a virtuous young cardinal would set a good example to his elders and that he hoped to see him soon in Rome.[293] Since Alberti was living more in Rome than elsewhere for much of the next decade, there can be little doubt that he sometimes frequented Francesco's household, even if there is no record of direct contact between them. When Luca Fancelli was sent from Mantua to Rome in October 1464 to consult Alberti about the church of San Sebastiano, Francesco was asked to provide hospitality for Luca for a month and a half,[294] and a few months later the marchese asked him to offer Alberti all possible favour.[295] When one of the cardinal's chamberlains, Filippo Andriasi, returned to Mantua in 1468, he brought with him some drawings by Alberti:[296] but neither of these episodes tells us anything about their relations.

The building project at Sant'Andrea in Mantua, in which from 1470 the cardinal was involved as titulary abbot and then as *primicerio* of the new collegiate foundation, might have led to some direct collaboration, had not Alberti's death intervened. Francesco negotiated with Sixtus IV the permission to rebuild, and expressed his urgent wish that the work should go ahead and not become a never-ending project like the cathedral of Milan; he also undertook to pay his contribution to the building costs.[297] But in general it seems he was perfectly content to leave the project, including approval of the architectural design, to his father, whose taste and judgement in such matters was well known. Francesco's only recorded opinion of any building in which Alberti had a hand in the design was about the church of San Sebastiano at Mantua, and this well-known remark (which might really have been the jest of Arrivabene, who penned the letter) that it might resemble a mosque or a synagogue rather than a church, sounds like jocular disparagement.[298] When he stayed with the Servite friars at the Annunziata in Florence in 1473 no comment by him is recorded[299] about the *tribuna* there designed by Alberti and paid for by Marchese Ludovico Gonzaga,

[293] L. B. Alberti to Marchese L. Gonzaga, Rome, 24 December 1461: 'Io me rallegro chon gli altri vostri servidori della dignità quale ha nuper chonseghuita Monsignore el cardinale vostro figlio per più respetti. Et certo, dovemo noi altri essere lieti, però che quando fra e nostri maiori saranno simili homini degnissimi e modestissimi la chiesa di Dio sarà chon più reverentia e maiestà presso di chi debba reverirla…spero vedere qui assiduo Monsigniore, a chui porto somma reverentia e affectione, per vostro rispetto e per sua virtù' (ASMn, Autografi, b. 7).

[294] Marchese Ludovico Gonzaga to Cardinal F. Gonzaga, 18 October 1464 (ASMn, AG, b. 2889, lib. 51, fol. 95ᵛ).

[295] Marchese L. Gonzaga to Cardinal Francesco Gonzaga, Mantua, 5 January 1465: 'Siamo certi sapiati quanto messer Babtista de li Alberti sia nostro, e per nui in questo tempo passato se sia operato in darne el modo et la via a la fabrica del nostro San Sebastiano…haremo a caro che anche vui per rispecto nostro lo habiati per ricomandato e ge prestadi ogni favor possibile' (ASMn, AG, b. 2889, lib. 52, fol. 35ᵛ); Braghirolli, 'Alberti a Mantova', pp. 12–13.

[296] The return of Andriasi, 'buono e fidel servitore' was announced in the cardinal's letter to Barbara, Rome, 5 June 1468 (ASMn, AG, b. 843); Filippo Andriasi wrote to Marchese Ludovico Gonzaga from Revere, 9 August 1468: 'Qui alligata mando a la Vostra Illustrissima Signoria alcuni designi quali me dete messer Babtista de li Alberti a Roma; Quella me perdoni se son sta' tardo a mandarli' (ASMn, AG, b. 2409, c. 173).

[297] See the correspondence, particularly the cardinal's letters of 30 January 1471 and 15 January 1472, also the marchese's draft letter of 2 January (Chambers, 'Sant'Andrea', pp. 211–14, and documents 21–3).

[298] Cardinal F. Gonzaga to Marchese Ludovico Gonzaga, Bologna, 16 March 1473: '…per essere fatto quello edificio sul garbo antiquo non molto dissimile da quello viso fantastico de messere Baptista di Alberti io per anchora non intendeva se l'haveva a reussire in chiesia o moschea o synagoga' (ASMn, AG, b. 1141, c. 305; Davari, 'S. Sebastiano in Mantova e Luca Fancelli', p. 94).

[299] Chambers, 'Cardinal Gonzaga in Florence', pp. 243 nn. 23, 24.

and among his books no copy is recorded of Alberti's treatise *De re aedificatoria*, nor of any other of Alberti's writings.

In fact there are very few building works at all with which Francesco can be credited, even in Mantua. Apart from his initial contributions to the new Sant'Andrea, he arranged for roof repairs carried out at Marmirolo in May 1473,[300] since he himself had been lent the use of the marchese's country residence there. He became more directly involved with Sant'Andrea after Marchese Ludovico's death, when he was in Mantua in 1480. In September 1480 he was trying to expedite the work there and uncovered some sharp practices among the contractors supplying building materials;[301] and during 1481–2, although in Rome, he is likely to have been responsible for the decision as to which patron saints the nave chapels should be assigned on completion.[302] But concerning the fabric of Sant'Andrea, Marchese Federico, who held the *iuspatronatus*, seems to have been the person most involved in the decisions just as his father had been. Similarly, with regard to the cathedral, although Francesco was bishop, it was to the marchese that the chapter addressed itself about the chapel of the Madonna dei Voti (a devotional image which, the crowds testified, had been working miracles since 1477),[303] under construction in 1480–81.[304] Although Francesco was to remember this Madonna dei Voti in his will (W 10), he does not appear to have taken a close interest in building the chapel; likewise, although it was allegedly he who had discovered the new supply of the Holy Blood, it was his brother Ludovico who made the vow to build the new chapel for it.[305]

Elsewhere, the building of the cardinal's house in Pienza in 1462–3 was begun to keep Pius II satisfied, but soon abandoned;[306] works in Rome do not seem to have amounted to much beyond small modifications and repairs. Francesco had his arms affixed to the facade of his title church in Rome, Santa Maria Nuova,[307] and initiated some repairs in 1468 either at Sant'Agata or San Lorenzo in Da-

---

[300] Vasić Vatovec, *Luca Fancelli*, p. 377.

[301] Cardinal F. Gonzaga to Marchese Federico Gonzaga, Mantua, 11 September 1480: 'mandammo hoggi de novo per lo massaro e presidenti de la fabrica, per corregere ugni errore, chi in summa se li trovasse, e dare tuta volta migliore ordine al governo de essa per l'avenire. Havemmoli tuti insieme e maestro Luca [Fancelli] cum lor…' (ASMn, AG, b. 2424); Johnson, *S. Andrea*, appendix II n. 43, pp. 73–4, publishes the full text but with some misreadings, also the related letters of 9, 10 and 12 September from Luca Fancelli and Marchese Federico Gonzaga.

[302] Johnson, *S. Andrea*, docs 45, 47–8 pp. 74–5 from records of the notary Fenino dei conti Capralba (but see above, n. 301).

[303] Marani, in *Mantova*, II, pp. 87–91.

[304] There are two letters extant of the chapter to Marchese Federico Gonzaga; one of 19 September 1480, proposing that work should continue on the roof, to provide protection from the weather: 'l'è finito quello puocho principio de la fabrica a quella capella di Nostra Donna di voti in San Pedro, secundo il disegno de la bona memoria de lo Illustrissimo signor vostro patre, cioè quelli quatro archi dove va suso la cuba sopra l'altare di Nostra Donna' (ASMn, AG, b. 2424); Gaye, *Carteggio*, I, p. 263; and the other of 10 September 1481, about the canons' need for a new cemetery as a result of the works: 'Havendo nui bisogno de tirare del cimiterio nostro vechio una quantità di terra sacrata adunata quando si fecero i fondamenti de la capella nova de la Nostra Donna…' (b. 2424).

[305] Carnevali, 'Un culto', pp. 73–4; Ferrari and Zanata, 'La capella del "Sangue di Cristo"', pp. 83–5. See above, p. 28 n. 206.

[306] Chambers, 'Housing Problems', pp. 28–31.

[307] Marasca to Barbara, Sant'Anna in Camparena, 23 August 1462: 'Ho ricevuto da Roma el designo de le arme novamente compite nela fazata de Sancta Maria Nova como per usanza fanno cardinali a le chiese de soi tituli' (ASMn, AG, b. 841, c. 708); Chambers, 'Housing Problems', p. 28 n. 51.

maso,[308] but these works cannot have been of great significance. He has been credited with a radical restoration of the church of Sant'Agata, but this is based only upon a notarial document of 1527 which transcribes a deed dated 19 May 1475 about the sale of some of the church's property for a round figure. This alienation of land was justified by the urgent need of money to pay for repairs, as the roof and other structural parts were on the verge of collapse.[309] But there is no evidence that they were carried out, much less that they were on the scale suggested. On the other hand, there is evidence, from the recently discovered *Libri dei fabricieri*, of various improvements at the church of San Lorenzo in Damaso during Francesco's period as its titular patron, though how much was owing to his initiative and how much owing to the canons who served the church is another question. In 1479 the *piazza* (*platea*) in front of the church was repaved and the main doorway was reconstructed; in 1481 the other doorways were also improved with marble cornices, the floor of the portico was paved, and the great organ was repaired; in 1482 several carved marble stoups for holy water were installed.[310]

In 1479 there is also evidence of domestic building works in progress, apparently at San Lorenzo in Damaso. This location, rather than Sant'Agata, is not specified in the correspondence, but as a rule when Sant'Agata is intended and not the cardinal's principal residence, it is named; in any case the details are more suggestive of the larger premises at San Lorenzo in Damaso rather than the retreat on the slopes of the Quirinal. Francesco's letters about these works, addressed from Bologna to Francesco Maffei, reproach him for spending too much.[311] Much of the cardinal's anger was about the construction of a spiral staircase which he pointed out was impractical, but he refers to the eleven rooms on an upper floor, and rooms specifically allocated to his nephew Protonotary Ludovico Gonzaga and to one Cristoforo (probably Cristoforo Piccolomini),[312] who would hardly have had permanently designated quarters in the limited accommodation of Sant'Agata, where there were (or in 1463 had been) only four rooms and a reception hall upstairs.[313] Moreover, a written tradition records that in 1480 it was impossible to enter the interior of the bell tower at San Lorenzo because of a breach authorized by Maffei.[314] In conclusion, Francesco was mainly fussing about the cost in these letters of 1479–80, and expressing anxiety that the master of his household was exceeding both his instructions and the

---

[308] Letter of 26 August 1468 in Chambers, 'Housing Problems', p. 39 n. 129.

[309] Huelsen et al., *S. Agata*, pp. 173–4, for the relevant part of the 1527 contract. In the same book (p. 101) is the unsupported statement that there exists a 'stemma del card. Gonzaga nelle volte delle navatelle della chiesa'.

[310] Valtieri, *San Lorenzo in Damaso*, pp. 13–18, 181, and *passim*.

[311] Letters of 18 November and 4 December 1479 in Chambers, 'Housing Problems', appendix nn. 27–8, pp. 56–8.

[312] The nephew of Cardinal Jacopo Ammannati, he was named by as 'mio cameriere dilectissimo' in a letter from Cardinal Francesco to Marchese Federico Gonzaga, Bologna, 16 September 1479 (ASMn, AG, b. 1142); he is also named in W 27.

[313] B. Marasca to Barbara, Rome, 14 April 1463: 'C'è la casa cum doe camere terrene e loza. De sopra sonno doe camere e sala' (ASMn, AG, b. 842, c. 186); also Chambers, 'Housing Problems', p. 32, doc. 16.

[314] '…non poterat ascendi in Campanili ex parte interiori propter facturam factam per Dominum Franciscum Maffeum' (Valtieri, *San Lorenzo in Damaso*, p. 14, quoting the manuscript history of G. Bitozzi, fol. 30).

available resources: the tone of the letters is not exactly that of an enthusiastic building patron.[315]

* * *

Andrea Mantegna's relations with the cardinal were without doubt much closer than Alberti's. Although in 1482–3 Francesco was so slow to acknowledge and approve Mantegna's drawing for his mother's intended tomb,[316] and although there is no record of the court painter doing any work directly for Francesco—it is, however, just possible that Mantegna had designed the cardinal's seal[317]—the two shared a passion for collecting and talking about antiquities.[318] Their social familiarity can be illustrated in the summer of 1472 when Mantegna planned a supper party for Francesco and members of his household, asking the marchese to permit him to hunt quail and pheasants for the occasion,[319] a concession which others entertaining the cardinal at this time had received.[320]

It is well known that Mantegna painted two portraits of Francesco (and there may have been others),[321] though neither of them was commissioned by him or done at his expense. The first time was when he was still a boy, perhaps painted from life soon after the artist arrived in Mantua in 1459–60 and probably before Francesco left for Pavia in April 1460. This is the small portrait now in Naples,[322] where Francesco appears a modest, subdued-looking youth. The clothes he is wearing, including a cap or bonnet, must have been assumed in Mantua to be appropriate to his ecclesiastical rank as a protonotary (they resemble what his younger brother Ludovico would later be shown wearing in a medal of 1475).[323] This portrait is entirely undocumented, though it might have been meant as a present to some person unknown or perhaps as a souvenir portrait for his parents to keep when he went away. The other portrait, which if not painted until 1474, when the work was completed, could at least have been drawn from life in either the summer of 1472 or the following year, is the full-length figure in the 'Meeting Scene' of the *Camera picta* in the Castello di S. Giorgio at Mantua; a detail of

---

[315] Chambers, 'Housing Problems', pp. 40–1; see also above, pp. 87–8.

[316] See above, pp. 85–6.

[317] *Tesori d'arte*, no. 139, p. 112; see above, p. 83, and Fig. 4.

[318] See above, p. 79 n. 235.

[319] Mantegna to Marchese L. Gonzaga, Mantua 21 September 1472: 'Aviso la Vostra Illustrissima Signoria chome io ho deliberato dar disnare al Reverendissimo C[ardinale] et a li suoi, di fuora al bastion. Ma sencia l'altorio di la Excellencia Vostra, non ne poria haver honore, a la quale ricoro si voglia dignare far hocelare, ch'io habia de le quagle et eciam qualche fasan, quela quantità parerà a la Vostra Illustre Signoria che sia convenga. Et questo el domando di gratia. De le altre cose son preso che proveditto, e questo bisogneria per sabato prosimo per la dominica che viene' (ASMn, AG, Autografi, b. 7); Kristeller, *Mantegna*, doc. 48, p. 528.

[320] In a letter of 16 September 1472 Francesco thanked his father for this (ASMn, AG, b. 2413, c. 779). The round of banquets and festivities held in the cardinal's honour is recorded by the chronicler Andrea Schivenoglia (MS BCMn, 1019, fol. 76ʳ).

[321] E.g., the unidentifiable 'retrato di Monsignor Cardinal Francesco vechio' noted in an inventory of moveables which had belonged to the son of Gianfrancesco Gonzaga at Sabbioneta, dated 1 July 1540 (ASMn, AN, pacco 4950, notary Federico Gorni). I owe this reference to Clifford Brown.

[322] Lightbown, *Mantegna*, cat. no. 12, pp. 410–11.

[323] Hill, *Corpus*, no. 195. The medal, attributed to Melioli, shows a protonotary's tasselled hat below the portrait.

Mantegna's masterpiece which dominates one of its walls and has assured, more than anything else, the cardinal's fame.[324]

What was Mantegna meaning to express about the cardinal in the *Camera picta*? The iconography of the room as a whole need not concern us here, but this particular question does demand a brief discussion. One fact he was obviously wishing to record for posterity was the cardinal's comely appearance, his rubicund good looks and imposing physique: observations about which were made not only in his early youth,[325] but also later in his life. In July 1473 when he was staying near Mantua at Marmirolo, having taken his youngest brother Ludovico as companion there[326]—a fact with possible significance for the brothers' joint appearance in Mantegna's picture—a prominent Mantuan chancery official, Zaccaria Saggi, thought Francesco's appearance more striking than ever.[327] Zaccaria had a close acquaintance with Mantegna, and it was he who in November 1475 described the *Camera picta* as the most beautiful room in the world.[328] In 1479, Francesco was described with even more hyperbole by a Ferrarese chronicler as endowed with the bearing of an emperor and a swelling chest like a cuirass.[329] Francesco's amazing good looks were further commemorated in Cattanei's funeral oration, where a story is told that in the Jubilee of 1475 crowds of all nations flocked to gaze upon him.[330] Mantegna was making in paint rather similar observations, while also demonstrating that the cardinal personified the ecclesiastical dimension of Gonzaga authority together with the young protonotary Ludovico.

Whether or not the 'Meeting' alludes to a particular event in the cardinal's life has been endlessly discussed. The ingenious and strongly sustained explanation of Rodolfo Signorini is that the major theme is the well documented meeting between father and son on 1 January 1462 at Bozzolo, when the (newly appointed) cardinal was returning from Pavia via Milan to Mantua, and Ludovico

---

[324] See the Frontispiece.

[325] See above, p. 4 n. 10; cf. Bartolomeo Bonatto to Barbara, Goito, 8 December 1463: 'Heri la Sua Signoria [Marchese Ludovico] vite el Reverendissimo Cardinale in campagna, el quale è bello come una perla, ma ad mi pare magro' (ASMn, AG, b. 2399).

[326] Cardinal F. Gonzaga to Barbara, Mantua, 13 July 1473: 'Io me ne vado questa sera a Marmirolo, e cum esso me meno lo Reverendo Protonotario nostro…lo vicario de Marmirolo venne qui a farne una gran duoglianza, mostrando che, andandoli el protonotario el non puoria restarli lui, per havere doe figliole giovene' (ASMn, AG, b. 2416, c. 287). The vicar, Hector de Sichis wrote to Barbara complaining of the inconvenience to himself (b. 2415, c. 454), but it is clear from what Antonio Bonatto wrote to her on 14 July that Ludovico did join the cardinal there: 'Credo che Vostra Signoria ha intexo como lo Reverendissimo Monsignore Cardinale ha menato cum se a Marmirolo il protonotario; quanto sia al proposito di esso prothonotario per lo imparare e dare opera al studio suo Vostra Signoria lo intenda bene…pur me rincresce sanza caxone si desvilgii et perda el tempo' (b. 2415, c. 464).

[327] Zaccaria Saggi to Galeazzo Maria Sforza, Goito, 26 July 1473, expressed the good wishes of Marchese Ludovico and all his sons 'e maxime il Reverendissimo Monsignore Cardinale, il quale… è più bello ch'el fusse may' (ASMil., Sforzesco, cart. 396).

[328] ASMn, AG, b. 1625, c. 107, cited in Signorini, *Opus hoc tenue*, doc. 23, p. 305.

[329] '…hè uno homo beletissimo de anni 50 [*sic*] o lì circha, homo de gran statura, corpo robustissimo, de occhi eminenti, de aspecto venerando, de una facia da Imperatore, de uno pecto da coraza; la presentia et aspecto suo hè de tanta venustade e gravitade quanto mai persona vidi…' (Zambotti, *Diario ferrarese*, p. 58).

[330] 'Accedebat enim facies eximiae formae virilitatis plena…non enim mortalem hominem, non terrenum, sed quamdam divine formositatis imaginem conspexisse fatebantur…nam superiore (ut passim dicitur) iubilei tempestate infinita…multitudo numquam Roma in patriam ut fertur rediiset…nisi prius occupatis propriae domus foribus Franciscum ad saturitatem admirari, intueri, contemplarique licuisset'(Cattanei, *Orationes*, sig. ciiiᵛ).

was on his way to Milan to see the ailing Duke Francesco Sforza.[331] It would be wrong to apply unhistorical criteria of narrative to expect unity of time and place; no matter, therefore, that the participants had to be updated to their 1473–74 appearances, and others introduced (for instance, the Emperor and the King of Denmark, also the two children), who had nothing to do with the central story, i.e., the 1462 meeting. Signorini also links this 1462 event with happenings in the court scene (which Mantegna had completed by 1470) and suggests the whole scheme must have been drawn up before Mantegna had started work in 1465. This reading is in many respects attractive and convincing, except for those who refuse to accept that a particular, historical meeting was intended at all.

Even assuming that there was a historical incident underlying the *storia*, it might still be objected that by 1465 the encounter at Bozzolo would have seemed rather remote and not particularly memorable. At the time the programme was (presumably) devised, before Mantegna started work in 1465, other meetings in the countryside might have seemed more meaningful. During the prolonged visit of the cardinal to Mantua and its vicinity in 1463–64, there had been various encounters outside Mantua between Francesco and his father and brother. When he arrived in early December 1463, the first meetings[332] were, because of plague quarantine rules in force, necessarily in the country, where grooms and dogs might well seem more fitting to the scene than at Bozzolo on the road from Milan. Remembering the cardinal's commitment to the crusade, the presentation of a pair [*sic*] of war horses at Goito could well be cited in this context; so could some of the details which have been interpreted in support of the 1462 story: the fact that Francesco is not wearing official regalia, apart from a *mozzetta*, and that his skull-cap appears to be white rather than the red which Paul II later prescribed;[333] the crescent moon and sun on the horse's trappings,[334] and the minuscule figures of the Magi hastening to Bethlehem.[335] In fact the latter details would be even more pointedly significant in this reading. Mantegna is known to have himself expressed support for the cardinal's mission to raise money for Pius II's crusade, offering—if only he were paid his salary—to make an increased contribution beyond the thirtieth part required of him.[336] One might go further, and even suggest that in depicting Pius II's 'new St George' setting out from the Castello di San Giorgio, Mantegna might have recollected Pisanello's scene, not far away in the church of Sant'Anastasia at Verona, of St George with his horse setting off to fight the dragon.

It will be objected that the Crusade was called off, and the cardinal never earned his triumph, so what would have been the point of commemorating it

---

[331] Signorini, 'Lettura storica'; *Opus hoc tenue*, pp. 113–81, esp. pp. 127–41. Disagreement has been expressed by Lightbown, *Mantegna*, pp. 110–11.

[332] E.g., G. P. Arrivabene to Barbara, Marmirolo, 8 December 1463: 'havendo heri scritto lo Illustre Signor messer lo marchese che sul tardo veneria in campagna per vedere el Reverendissimo Monsignor mio, montassemo a cavallo, e pocho de là da le teze de Bosello trovassemo Sua Signoria, con la quale esso Monsignor stete circa doe hore, e ne la partita terminorono anche hoggi de essere insieme' (ASMn, AG, b. 2399). Cf. the letter of B. Bonatto, Goito, 8 December, cited above, n. 325.

[333] Signorini, *Opus hoc tenue*, pp. 148–9, does not rely overmuch on the evidence of dress, but makes some valuable observations.

[334] Signorini, *Opus hoc tenue*, p. 202.

[335] Ibid., pp. 150–1. Painted out in the recent conservation work, they have now been unconvincingly restored.

[336] A. Mantegna to Marchese L. Gonzaga, Goito, 26 April 1464 (ASMn, Autografi, b. 7); Kristeller, *Mantegna*, doc. 22, p. 423; Chambers, 'Virtù militare', p. 216.

afterwards; that he ought to have been shown in armour and riding gear, while other more explicit allusions should have been included; there are a host of counter-arguments. But the point of this digression is rather to suggest that the Meeting Scene might have carried multiple associations by the time it was finally painted and revealed in 1474. Francesco could not have seen himself in the *Camera picta* before he returned to Mantua in the winter of 1479–80; unfortunately no letter has come to light recording what he thought of it, but considering his lack of enthusiasm for the Palazzo Schifanoia in Ferrara,[337] in spite of its recent fresco decorations, and his complete silence about the Sistine Chapel, perhaps he was little moved even by the *Camera picta*.

[337] See below, p. 103 n. 41.

Chapter 4: The Death and Posthumous Affairs of Cardinal Gonzaga

(i) The Will, Death and Burial of the Cardinal

Cardinal Francesco Gonzaga had been lying ill in Bologna for over two months by the time his will was signed, sealed and witnessed on 20 October 1483, one day before his death. Concerning this last illness there is no need to enter into detail; it must have related to the chronic stomach or liver disorder from which he had suffered recurrent attacks over many years: in Rome in the spring of 1472 he had been so ill that his recovery was then considered a miracle;[1] in 1479 he had gone to Porretta to seek a cure, and earlier in 1483, during his period of service as military legate at Ferrara, he was frequently reported to be ill;[2] but this time the complications of his jaundice became too great to overcome.[3] On 20 October Arrivabene wrote to the marchese that his life was despaired of.[4] The explanation of the death given later implied that his exertions as papal legate in the War of Ferrara combined with the perilous spa waters of Porretta, to which he had again resorted in July, ultimately had been to blame.[5]

The will is a very long and specific document, and it seems inconceivable that the contents could have been dictated on the cardinal's deathbed; presumably it had been under preparation for some time,[6] and all that was finally needed was copying-out and authentication by a notary in the presence of witnesses, which took place in the cardinal's palace at Bologna on the given date. In fact although it was duly recorded that the testator was still in his right mind, he was too weak to sign the will himself, which had to be done on his behalf by the domestic scribe, Aurelio Cornice (W 49). Aurelio was probably a brother of Antonio Cornice or Cornacchia, who had acted at the death of the cardinal's mother,

---

[1] Gianfrancesco Gonzaga to Marchese L. Gonzaga, Rome, 11 May 1472, wrote that the pope sent hourly inquiries, and 'heri in la Missa, havendo sentito lo caso, fece bene quatro voti a quatro sancti'; Bartolomeo Bonatto and Giovan Pietro Arrivabene next day, however, reported the fever gone and 'lo stomacho assetato' thanks to the doctors and the 'gratia concessa dal celo per intercessione de Nostra Donna e suoi sancti e tanti universal preghiere fatte da ciascuno' (ASMn, AG, b. 844, cc. 322, 307). See also above, p. 27.

[2] Pietro Spagnoli wrote to Marchese Federico Gonzaga, Ferrara, 8 January 1483 that the cardinal 'molestato dal suo stomaco' could not attend the council of war (ASMn, AG, b. 1231, c. 103); on 9 February and 10 April he again mentioned this illness, and on 27 April Girolamo Stanga wrote 'gli è sopravenuto un poco de opilatione che pare sia suo mal vecchio che gli à lassato una certa gialdeza negli ochi et la persona' (ibid., cc. 165, 231, 276).

[3] There are abundant letters, particularly from G. P. Arrivabene and Protonotary L. Gonzaga, also from doctors, recording his illness since July 1483, in ASMn, AG, b. 1142 and b. 2105.

[4] 'Ad me…pare che Monsignor mio Reverendissimo sia in pessimo predicamento e da puoterne fare puocha speranza, vedendolo tanto annihilato' (ASMn, AG, b. 1142).

[5] Marchese Federico Gonzaga to Barbarina Gonzaga, Duchess of Württemberg, 18 January 1484: 'Lo Illustrissimo Monsignore Cardinale nostro fratello per certa sua indispositione de zaldezza contracta in Ferrara dove per le guerre et in favore de quello Illustrissimo Signore Duca faceva residenzia per la sede apostolica, essendo Sua Signoria andato al lugio a li bagni de la Poretta per liberarse aciò che poi el se potesse transferire in campo cum nui altri signori, li sopravenne, ritornando dal bagno a Bologna, uno pocho de febre cum alcuni dolori, che a principio parse farne non molto caso…poi li sopragiongeva qualche maligno accidente che lo atterrava…' (ASMn, AG, b. 2899, lib. 116, fol. 50^r-v). See also Chambers, 'Virtù militare', p. 221.

[6] Licence to make a will had been granted by the pope, as recorded in a subsequent brief dated 23 October 1483 addressed to the—by then deceased—cardinal: AV, Arm. XXXIX, reg. 16, fol. 60^r.

Barbara of Brandenburg, two years previously.[7] Two of the executors named in the will were members of the cardinal's staff with him at Bologna: Giovan Pietro Arrivabene and Alvise Capra.

On 21 October the cardinal's condition had worsened, and he was persuaded to take the sacrament: Arrivabene's letter on that day provides a rare reference to his devoutness.[8] He died the same night, and plans had to be made immediately by Arrivabene and Capra, the executors on the spot, in consultation with Protonotary Ludovico Gonzaga, about transporting the illustrious corpse home to Mantua.[9] The journey, with the coffin borne on a cart and escorted by the household, is recorded in letters from Arrivabene[10] and also from the young Protonotary Sigismondo Gonzaga, who had been at Carpi on his way to Bologna when he heard the news, and met the cortège at Modena.[11] Meanwhile, the cardinal's steward, the scribe Bartolomeo Sanvito, had been sent ahead to give instructions about the procedures thought appropriate by the executors and by Ludovico. A letter outlining the order of procession to be followed in the reception at Mantua was sent by the marchese's son Francesco who, in Federico Gonzaga's absence, appears to have been put in charge.[12] Further discussion was anticipated about the precise arrangements required in order to conform with customary practices in the court of Rome. Sanvito, Giovanni Arrivabene (recently appointed as the cardinal's estate manager in Mantua),[13] and two Mantuan officials, the *massaro* or fiscal administrator of the city and the *collaterale* or military administrator, Be Agnelli, were to meet and discuss the details, though clearly the protocol could not be quite the same as when a cardinal died in Rome.[14]

On the evening of 26 October the procession entered Mantua, and the bier was received at the church of San Francesco, where the cardinal had expressed his wish to be buried among his Gonzaga ancestors (W 2). First came the mace-bearer, Francesco Godini,[15] and the bearer of his red hat, then the principal *familiares* and family mourners, led by Protonotary Ludovico Gonzaga and Fran-

---

[7] Antonio wrote for Marchese Federico Gonzaga a summary in Latin and another in Italian of Barbara's will, and one of the post-mortem inventories made in November 1481 (ASMn, AN, Estensioni notarili, R. 78, A. Cornice, 1481); see also Signorini, 'La malattia', esp. p. 20 and app. 3, pp. 21–6.

[8] G. P. Arrivabene to Marchese Federico Gonzaga, Bologna, 21 October 1483: '…ce parse de farlo communicare, e cussì in quest' hora […] ha tuolto cum grandissima devotione lo Corpus Domini…li indicii et argumenti de morte multiplicano, per modo che tememo de perderlo presto' (ASMn, AG, b. 1142).

[9] G. P. Arrivabene to Marchese Federico Gonzaga, Bologna 22, 23 October 1483, in Appendix 3, nos 1–2; Protonotary Ludovico Gonzaga wrote on the same day to the marchese (b. 2105).

[10] Letters of 24 October from Correggio (Appendix 3, no. 3) and 25 October from Gonzaga (b. 2432).

[11] He received there the condolences of Eleonora Duchess of Ferrara and her daughter Isabella, and then joined the escort back to Mantua by way of Correggio and Gonzaga: Sigismondo Gonzaga to Marchese Federico Gonzaga, letters of 22 and 23 October from Borgoforte and Modena (ASMn, AG, b. 2105); on 25 October he wrote from Gonzaga 'questa sera siamo alozati a Gonzaga con il corpo, dove non habiamo ritrovato provisione alcuna; domane disenaremo qui et poi se aviaremo per venir a Mantuoa, et essi ordinato intrare la sera da meza hora di notte e sepelir il corpo a Sancto Francesco' (b. 2432).

[12] Letter of Francesco Gonzaga in Appendix 3, no. 4. Marchese Federico Gonzaga had written to Francesco from Revere on 24 October informing him of his uncle's death and requiring him to assume mourning: 'vogliamo che subito vedi farti vestire de verde scuro secundo usanza' (ASMn, AG, b. 2105).

[13] Cardinal F. Gonzaga to Marchese Federico Gonzaga, Ferrara, 5 March 1483: 'Essendo successa la morte de quondam Carlo da Rhodiano, havemo dato lo medesmo governo de le terre e beneficii nostri a Zohanne Arrivabeno' (b. 1231, c. 26). On Giovanni see also Chambers, 'Arrivabene', pp. 414–16 n. 87.

[14] See for Roman custom Patrizi, *Cérémonial papal*, I, pp. 221–30.

[15] See W 24; I 633; also a letter of Cardinal F. Gonzaga to Eleonora of Aragon, Duchess of Ferrara, dated at Bologna 31 August 1479, which mentions he is sending 'Francesco de' Godini nostro cameriere e maciere' (ASMod, AEC, Principi, b. 1380B/116).

cesco, the future marchese. Others followed in order of dignity and consanguinity, and 'all Mantua' was said to be present.[16] However, because of the war situation—and the War of Ferrara had reached a crucial point, with the loss of Asola on 11 October and Mantuan territory directly threatened by the Venetians on two fronts[17]—there were some notable absentees, namely all three of the cardinal's other brothers. Marchese Federico was at Revere resting on his laurels; Gianfrancesco, lord of Rodigò, was on the eastern frontier at Sermide;[18] and Rodolfo could not attend because he was serving with the enemy and, being subject to ecclesiastical penalties, had had to be excluded from any bequest under the cardinal's will (W 17). How soon the funeral and burial took place is not clear; normally a deceased cardinal would lie in state for over a week of ceremonies; but a week had already passed since his death, and it was necessary to bury the body as soon as possible, as Giovan Pietro Arrivabene had written on 22 October. On the other hand, the young Francesco's letter of 27 October, already quoted, refers to the customary week of liturgical ceremonies meant to begin on the following day, and the cardinal had expected that all the proper observances should be kept (W 39).

Some attempts had been made to discover in advance the contents of the will. The marchese had even proposed that Francesco should interrogate Giovan Pietro Arrivabene about it, but this had been in vain.[19] Arrivabene and Capra had reported on 27 October that now they had duly delivered the cardinal's body to the church of San Francesco, they were ready to read the will; they had been prepared to come to Revere for this, but had now heard the marchese himself was coming to Mantua.[20] On 29 October they appeared before the marchese and in the presence of Bartolomeo Castigati, as presiding notary, the will was opened and read.[21] All this was while the funeral ceremonies were still proceeding; their culmination, Giovan Lucido Cattanei's oration in praise of the deceased, took place over two weeks later, but perhaps the occasion for this was not the inhumation but a subsequent requiem mass.[22] The cardinal had simply prescribed that he should be buried near to the tomb of his father, in the family chapel in San Francesco; that he should wear a ring on which was set a *turchina*, and a gold brocade cover should be used for the bier and afterwards be presented to the friars; subsequently an inscription should be set up to his memory (W 2–4). Giovan Pietro Arrivabene had expected the coffin to be placed in a temporary grave

---

[16] Letter of Francesco Gonzaga, 27 October 1483, in Appendix 3, no. 6.

[17] See Mazzoldi, *Mantova*, II, pp. 43–4.

[18] Letters from him at Sermide from October 1483 to January 1484 survive in ASMn, AG, b. 1800.

[19] Marchese Federico to Francesco Gonzaga, Revere, 25 October 1483: 'Nui intendemo che el Reverendissimo quondam Monsignor cardinale nostro fratello et tuo barba ha facto in questo suo ultimo testamento, ma non havemo anchor potuto sapere alcuna particularità d'esso, el che assay desyderamo. Perhò te imponamo che como da te non monstrando havere commissione da nui circa ciò, vedi de intrare in rasonamento sopra questa materia cum messer Zoan Petro Arrivabeno, interrogandola minutamente del tuto, et de quanto recavarai ce ne renderai subito avisati' (ASMn, AG, b. 2105). Cf. Sigismondo Gonzaga to the marchese, Mantua 28 October 1483: 'circa el testamento dicono non poterne parlare sub fide loro, et ch'el testamento è sigillato cum nove sigilli' (ibid.). Seven of these seals, minutely described, were of the witnesses (W 49–50).

[20] Appendix 3, no. 5.

[21] ASMn, AG, Libri Decretorum 21, fols 27^v–29^r; cf. also W 52.

[22] The date of the oration was 13 November, according to the text: 'Acta Mantue in templi Sancti Francisci idibus novembris 1483': see above, p. 5 n. 12 and *passim*.

until the new tomb was ready;[23] nothing more has come to light about such a monument, except a reference in the will of Francesco 'Cardinalino' in 1511.[24]

The provisions of the will can be summarized briefly. The other two executors whom it named (W 45) were meanwhile Ludovico Agnelli and Francesco Maffei; the marchese was required to give all the executors full assistance (W 43). By way of sequel to the burial instructions were certain legacies for pious—or at least ecclesiastical—purposes. First, an 'enrichment' was proposed for the *prepositura* of San Benedetto (W 5), but this was nothing more than the enfranchisement of the estate of Bigarello, the use of which had been conferred upon the cardinal's infant son several years previously and was now intended to become his freehold.[25] The sum of 7000 ducats rather optimistically earmarked to pay for Bigarello was to be found out of the 3000 ducats about to be paid by Gianfrancesco, together with the cardinal's share of the unpaid dowry of his mother Barbara of Brandenburg, amounting to 4000 ducats, which the marchese was expected to produce. This first provision of the will was to lead later to complications and considerable ill feeling within the family. Second, there were bequests amounting to 3600 ducats to the cathedral of Mantua (W 6–8) to pay for masses for the souls of his parents and himself (on the vigil of the anniversary of his death the cathedral clergy were to go in procession for this purpose to San Francesco). This fund his brother Gianfrancesco was obliged to oversee, while his son was to remunerate the friars of San Francesco (W 9) rather more modestly for celebrating the anniversary of his death at their high altar (this first anniversary may indeed have been celebrated, in 1484, with Bernardino da Feltre as its celebrant).[26] The cathedral was also to receive the cardinal's legatine cross and a silver candlestick bearing the figures of Adam and Eve, and for the chapel of Santa Maria dei Voti a ruby ring was designated for the Madonna's crown (W 10–12).

By these provisions the testator does not perhaps display outstandingly disinterested generosity towards the Church, and it is notable that no legacy was made to the collegiate foundation of Sant'Andrea in Mantua (perhaps the cardinal considered he had already contributed more than enough to its building fund), nothing for any educational or charitable institution and nothing to any church or monastery outside Mantua. (One might add that no chaplain, confessor or professionally holy person is anywhere named as a beneficiary of the will.) The main ecclesiastical preoccupation expressed was that Agnelli and Maffei, and also the marchese, should petition the pope to concede that Protonotary Ludovico Gonzaga might succeed to the administration of the bishopric and Sigismondo to the *prepositura* of San Benedetto, or to hold these benefices for at least six years; also that income in hand from the cardinal's benefices should be used to pay off debts (W 41–2): another provision that before long led to trouble. Meanwhile the accumulated income from a pension on a reserved (and unnamed) benefice formerly belonging to Cardinal Hessler,[27] a sum of 600 ducats, said to be in the

---

[23] Appendix 3, no. 2.
[24] Chambers, 'Francesco "Cardinalino"', pp. 51–2.
[25] See above, p. 24.
[26] Meneghin, *Bernardino da Feltre*, p. 69 n. 64.
[27] Hessler, a great pluralist, had for long been the protégé of the Emperor Frederick III for the red hat; he was eventually created a cardinal on 10 December 1478. Francesco does not appear to have done much to help in his

hands of Francesco Maffei, was to be paid back, except for 100 ducats concerning the use of which Arrivabene, Capra and Aurelio Cornice were supposed to have special instructions (W 33).

It is significant that Francesco the 'Cardinalino' (now aged about six) was the first-named beneficiary of the will, and his name recurs in it more often than does that of any other member of the Gonzaga family. The cardinal entrusted the child to Protonotary Ludovico Gonzaga and Giovan Pietro Arrivabene as guardians (W 31), and appointed two other persons with the task of looking after him and his interests (W 31, 32), commending him also to the marchese's special protection (W 43). A priority reiterated in the will was that the estate of Bigarello, already conferred upon him, should be freed of any obligation to the *prepositura* of San Benedetto Polirone (W 5); he also bequeathed to the 'Cardinalino' the nearby estate of Fossamana (W 29) and a few of his valuables. Thus, he required (W 30) that the ruby necklace Giovan Pietro Arrivabene had been asked to pawn for 1000 ducats 'only a few days before' should be redeemed for the sake of the 'Cardinalino'; the latter was also to have a piece of unicorn's horn and some newly acquired bed hangings and other pieces of tapestry (W 21).

Finally the cardinal appointed his younger brother Gianfrancesco as his universal heir (W 44). In addition to a personal legacy of three silver goblets (W 16) he left Gianfrancesco his share of the paternal inheritance, but this also carried an obligation to set aside 12000 ducats from income to meet various commitments. Thus Rivarolo, Sabbioneta and the fishpond of Comesachio were to pass to Gianfrancesco; but the funeral expenses had to be found from this source of income, as well as some of the money intended for the *prepositura* (W5, 36, 39): a rather badly drafted provision, which later led to dispute.

There were various other individual legacies. To his elder brother, Marchese Federico Gonzaga, the cardinal made the generous bequest (W 15) of one of his finest cornelians in a silver case, a silver wine-cooler, pieces of 'unicorn' and his entire collection of bronze figures and images (I 85, 564, 492, 539). Rodolfo, the next brother, was to receive nothing (W 17), as already mentioned, though his illegitimate son Hector was to get some silverware (W 22). The youngest brother, Protonotary Ludovico Gonzaga, was to receive (W 18) some silver basins, including one for shaving, also a missal and a diamond ring. It is remarkable that no legacies were provided for either of the cardinal's two surviving sisters (perhaps because they were married?) nor for any of his nieces. A religious office book (W 19) was designated (perhaps not very suitably) for Francesco, heir to the marchesate, while his son Sigismondo, who was just beginning his clerical career, was to have the cardinal's copy of the *Decretals* (W 20). These are the only books reserved for special bequests, although a clause in the will specifies the need to return a book the cardinal had borrowed (W 34). Other items designated for individuals are the cornelian with the head of Julius Caesar for Alfonso Duke of Calabria (W 13), a dark-coloured horse to be returned to Girolamo Riario (W 14), which is not identifiable among the horses listed in the

promotion, but mentioned in a letter to Duke Ercole d'Este of Ferrara, dated at Mantua 3 January 1480, that Hessler was coming on to Ferrara on his journey to Rome (ASMod AEC, Principi, b. 1380B/116). On Hessler, see Hollweg, *Dr Georg Hessler*; Strnad, 'Der Apostolische Protonotar'. Possibly the benefice in question was the cathedral provostship of Worms: see Strnad, pp. 43, 49.

inventory, the silver ink-stand for Giovan Pietro Arrivabene (W 23) and the mace to be given to its habitual bearer (W 24).

Only two of the cardinal's servants were named to receive small money legacies (W 25). Ten of the chamberlains (those who were—presumably—in fact rather than just in title servants of the chamber) and three serving boys were to share in all the cardinal's clothes and household bedding (W 26), to be sold and the proceeds divided by the executors. These together with the rest of his *familiares* (nearly fifty are named), including the elite of professional members, were to share the silverware, except whatever was designated in particular bequests (W 27). Tapestries, carpets, horses and mules and other effects (but not the silver already mentioned, nor the books) were, once enough money had been realized to pay outstanding wages and salaries, also to be distributed among members of the household, according to merit, length of service and other criteria left to the discretion of the executors (W 28).

Finally, the most valuable items the cardinal had collected—gems (the cameos mounted on silver trays as well as other cameos and intaglios which were loose), antique and *pietra dura* vases, books—were reserved to pay off debts (W 35). Also intended to pay off debts were the proceeds from the sale of two pieces of property the cardinal had acquired in Rome, but which he emphasized he had bought with private money (W 37).

(ii) The Inventory: Its Compilation, Function and Limitations.

The inventory is dated, without reference to place, on 27 October 1483, i.e., on the day after the cardinal's retinue arrived in Mantua with his body and two days before the will was opened. It is not a room by room inventory, nor is it arranged under headings which classify the objects.[28] It is written throughout in the hand of Giovan Francesco Strata, a chamberlain whose name often occurs in correspondence of the previous four years and who must have been closely in the cardinal's confidence, often entrusted with special journeys and commissions.[29] Strata's signature appears on the inventory together with the signatures of two other *familiares*, Cosmo Andriasi (another long-serving chamberlain)[30] and the less easily identified Alessandro Secco.[31] It is authenticated at the beginning in the hand of Giovan Pietro Arrivabene to whom it was presented in the presence of Alvise Capra; Arrivabene's emendations, and others in Capra's hand, will be discussed later.

A number of questions arise. Does the inventory represent only the possessions in the legatine palace at Bologna at the time of the cardinal's death, so that one must assume that Strata and the other two *familiares* who signed it—having been instructed by Giovan Pietro Arrivabene and Capra—were left behind for a day or two to list all the items to be dispatched? This seems unlikely since

---

[28] Cf. for instance the inventories of Cardinal Pietro Barbo (later Paul II) published by Müntz, *Les Arts*, II, pp. 181–287; these do not specify rooms, but do classsify objects under some general headings.

[29] E.g., letters to Alfonso Duke of Calabria and to Barbara 9 September 1479: 'Zo. Fr. Strata mio cameriere' was to be sent to Tuscany to consult Marchese Federico Gonzaga (ASMn, AG, b. 2896, lib. 96, fols 6ᵛ–7ᵛ).

[30] E.g., Cardinal F. Gonzaga names him in a letter from Bologna, 1 November 1478, as 'nostro cameriere' (ASMn, AG, b. 846, c. 251).

[31] I have not found Secco (or Secho) named in correspondence, but see I 937.

Arrivabene insists in his letter of 22 October that all the *familia* were leaving together to accompany the cardinal's body to Mantua.[32] It hardly seems possible that they could have done the listing hurriedly on 22 October, immediately after the cardinal's death, before packing and loading everything onto carts and mule-back for the journey of about sixty miles. It is possible that, in the listing, they also made use of earlier inventories; but even so, it would seem likeliest that the final list was drawn up only after arrival at Mantua, when it was dated. In this case, it would represent the cardinal's possessions in Mantua, together with those brought from Bologna, united on 27 October; in fact the listing may not all have been completed on that day, for the date only appears at the beginning, not the end of the document.

Over the years Cardinal Gonzaga had certainly transported much of his movable property away from Rome. Mention has already been made of the large amount he brought to Bologna when he arrived for the first time as papal legate, in July 1471, most of which he must presumably have left behind when, less than two weeks later, he had to travel back fast to Rome for the conclave.[33] When Francesco returned to Bologna in 1472 he evidently kept close to his person some of his most treasured antiquities, jewels, gems, bronzes, coins and medals;[34] this was probably usual, for security reasons, and because in any case they were easily portable. Bulkier things, however, had been dispatched directly to Mantua through Ferrarese territory.[35] He had again sent ahead many goods when he returned to Bologna in 1478.[36] There is once more no evidence that he took much back on his winter journeys to Rome in 1473 or 1480; moreover, he had deliberately moved many of his effects from Bologna to Mantua, where he had his private house as well as the bishop's palace in which to store them, during the winter of 1478, when he evidently wished to lend whatever was required for the wedding celebrations of his brother Gianfrancesco. This removal was also a precaution, since the risks in Bologna to the legate's person and property were high during the aftermath of the Pazzi Conspiracy, when his immediate task was to try to retain Bolognese loyalty to the papacy and to discourage support of Florence. Other things he had stored in 1478 in the castle of Cento, which he held by right of his title as archbishop of Bologna,[37] though in fact some of his silverware was stolen from there.[38]

---

[32] Appendix 3, no. 1.

[33] See above, pp. 5 n. 15, 9, 81–2, 96.

[34] Cf. the famous letter from Foligno dated 18 July 1472 (above, p. 79 n. 235), which refers to 'miei camaini e figure de bronzo et altre belle cose antique'.

[35] Cardinal F. Gonzaga to Marchese Ludovico Gonzaga, Macerata, 22 July 1472: '…me accaderà mandare li mei muli, li quali haranno roba pur de qualche valore, per lo dominio del duca Hercule' (ASMn, AG, b. 844, c. 393).

[36] Giovanni Arrivabene to Marchese Federico Gonzaga, Bologna 26 June 1478, noted (although the cardinal himself was not yet beyond Pesaro) 'giongeno li carriagi et robbe sue' (ASMn, AG, b. 1141, c. 575).

[37] Gerardo Ceruti to the Duke of Milan, Bologna, 1 November 1478: 'Monsignore ha cavato del palazo de Bologna sue zoye, arzenti et tapezarie. Maestro Hieronymo dice ne vol mandare parte ad Mantua per le nozze del fratello. Il resto metterà in la roccha de Cento, dove Sua Signoria se vole riddure' (ASMil, Sforzesco, cart. 188).

[38] Cardinal F. Gonzaga to Marchese Federico Gonzaga, Bologna, 3 June 1479: 'Essendo nui questa vernata proxima a Cento, uno fante del castellano nostro lì, nominato el Fornaro, robboe de la credenza nostra certi vasi nostri de arzento fra li quali era una bella nappa, come più diffusamente puotrà intendere Vostra Signoria da Rizardo, exhibitore de la presente, nostro credenciero' (ASMn, AG, b. 1142).

His anxiety to avoid the expense of endlessly carting possessions around Italy, and to concentrate most of them at Mantua, is implied in a letter to Francesco Maffei later the same year.[39] In December 1479, before his departure for Mantua, he sent ahead more of his possessions.[40] One may infer that the cardinal kept relatively few of his possessions at Bologna after that time; he was hardly there again, except for a day or two in transit, until the last two and a half months of his life; nor is it likely that he had brought much with him to Ferrara, or accumulated many new things to furnish the house he was lent when resident there as military legate from January to June 1483.[41] Presumably whatever he did have in Ferrara would have been dispatched back to Mantua, when the remaining members of his household were sent home early in August of 1483; he had been intending to go to Mantua himself, in any case, and had stopped in Bologna after his course of Porretta waters only because recurrent illness made him too weak to travel.[42]

In conclusion, it seems most likely that this was a composite inventory, recording what was brought from Bologna and what was in the bishop's palace and the cardinal's private house in Mantua, too. The cardinal's house in the *contrata Griffonis*, which he had only kept sparsely furnished in the 1460s,[43] had doubtless been much enriched during his visits in the 1470s, and it was sufficiently well-furnished for Barbara of Brandenburg to be moved there in her last illness; she died in this house on 7 November 1481.[44] Possibly some of the contents inventoried after her death had in fact been the cardinal's, but—leaving aside this intractable problem—among the quarter of her movables which he was allotted as his share of the inheritance and which were held on his behalf by Antonio Bonetto, a number may be identifiable with items in his own inventory of 1483. These included eight books and some miscellaneous decorative objects,[45] though there is no trace of others, such as the gilded figure of St George with a pearl on the tip of his lance;[46] on her deathbed Barbara had expressly said

[39] Cardinal F. Gonzaga to Francesco Maffei, Bologna, 23 September 1479: 'venendo de là, nui non voressemo già al buon tempo essere puoi constretti ad ritornarne de qua, perché a nui seria troppo desconzo a portare suso e giuso tanta robba, e seriane una spesa intolerabile...'(ASMn, AG, b. 2896, lib. 96, fol. 33ᵛ).

[40] Cardinal F. Gonzaga to Jacopo Trotto, Bologna, 11 December 1479: 'Nui cominciamo a mandare inanti duoe nave carichi de forcieri, panni de rasso, balle et altre robbe nostre e de la famiglia nostra verso Mantuoa' (ASMn, AG, b. 2896, lib. 96, fol. 144ʳ).

[41] Before ever arriving there he had, interestingly, rejected an offer of the Palazzo Schifanoia, writing to Giovan Francesco Strata from Rome on 7 December 1482: 'Schivenoia è molto lontana e mala stantia da inverno. El c'è ditto de la casa di Trotti e del vescovato. Vedi mo tu, dove te parirà fare migliore designo' (AS Mod, AEC, Principi, b. 1380B/116). In fact Strata settled for the Trotti palace, as J.B. Cusanus wrote to Duke Giangaleazzo Sforza, from Ferrara, 3 January 1483: '...fu accompagnata Sua Reverendissima Signoria da la Illustrissima Madama et da nuy altri ambasciatori al suo alogiamento, quale è la casa de li magnifici Polantonio et maestro Jacobo Trotti, casa belissima et molto commoda' (ASMil, Sforzesco, cart. 329).

[42] Francesco Gonzaga to Marchese Federico Gonzaga, Mantua 8 August 1483: 'Ceterum qui s'era dicto ch'el Reverendissimo Monsignore Cardinale non veneva a Mantua e se ne andava adritura a Sabioneta. Doppo ho inteso come pur Sua Signoria Reverendissima venirà a Mantua et de ciò Giovanni Arrivabeno ne ha littera qual de commissione de Sua Signoria li fa apparechiare per el vivere suo, et dice aspettare hogii la famiglia che Sua Signoria haveva lassiato a Ferrara' (ASMn, AG, b. 2430, c. 714).

[43] See above, p. 40.

[44] See above, pp. 24, 97 n. 7; Signorini, 'La malattia mortale', p. 11.

[45] See I 90–1, and for the books, below, p. 107 n. 57. Among other items was a *galea* and an *ovarolo*, and from Barbara's house at San Giorgio, near Mantua, 'uno spechio grande' (ASDMn, FCC, ser. misc., b. 2/A 'Inventario de le cose', fols 2ᵛ, 33ʳ).

[46] Listed in the inventory of the house as 'Sanctus Giorgius pedester cum una perla in capite bastoni aurati' (ASMn, AN, Estensioni, R. 78, [A. Cornice, 1481], inventory, fol. 1ʳ), and in the record of distributions, as 'un

that she wished Francesco to have the various costly trifles (*jocalia*) which he had previously given her,[47] but there is no clue as to which these items were. In general it is not possible, nor would it be very enlightening, to identify from the cardinal's inventory the various rings, loose pearls and rubies, ornamental cups and various vessels, textiles, spoons, mattresses and other things which he may have received from his mother's estate. Many of these effects may have just remained in the house as apparently did the cradles of the 'Cardinalino' (I 435–6); Giovanni Arrivabene was taking measures for its security in October 1483, as worsening news about his patron arrived.[48]

That the inventory consisted of possessions in several different houses, brought together in some haste and confusion, seems also to be suggested by the absence of any headings as to particular rooms, cupboards, chests etc where objects were kept; but that it certainly included what there was in Bologna is clear from the inclusion of some items which the cardinal had recently had in use or near to hand. The bequests in the will are so specific that one is tempted to think that many of these cherished things had been under the cardinal's eye as he dictated his wishes, and they are all specific objects which can be found in the inventory, apart from the pearl and ruby necklace left to his infant son and namesake, which was in pawn (W 30).

On the other hand, the inventory cannot possibly include whatever possessions of the cardinal still remained in his two houses at Rome; so—even if most of his more portable objects had travelled with him and were concentrated in Mantua—the inventory has to be disregarded as a total statement of his goods and chattels. Even though the news of his death travelled quickly, so that one of the named executors, Ludovico Agnelli, wrote from Rome only four days later to express his sorrow,[49] there was not conceivably time for a list of possessions there to have arrived in Mantua by 27 October. One entry seems to present a difficulty, since it enumerates three old mattresses from Sant'Agata (I 182), the cardinal's second residence in Rome. The best explanation would seem to be that these mattresses had already been brought from Rome the previous winter, but in some way (perhaps from a previous, administrative inventory) were still identifiable by members of the household as bedding from Sant'Agata. One may wonder why three old mattresses had to be brought from Rome at all, but Cardinal Gonzaga seems to have been rather short of bedding; there are only thirteen other mattresses (eight of them small) and a feather bed listed in the inventory.

San Zorzo dorato cum una perla in capo la lanza', valued at 1 *lira*, 10 *soldi* (ASDMn, FCC, ser. misc., b. 2/A, 'Inventario de le cose', fol. 3ᵛ).

[47] 'Et quia nonnulla jocalia dono habuita praefato Reverendissimo domino cardinali filio suo, ut ibi asseruit, voluit et mandavit quod in optione ipsius…sit eligere ipsa iocalia' (Latin summary of Barbara's testamentary wishes in ASMn, AN, Estensioni, R. 78 [A. Cornice, 1481], fol. 5ʳ).

[48] Giovanni Arrivabene to Marchese Federico Gonzaga, Mantua, 22 October 1483: 'Io qua attendo a le commissione me sono mandate et a provedere al bixogno de quello poterà accadere et a la conservatione de le cose de casa' (ASMn, AG, b. 2430, c. 710).

[49] L. Agnelli to Marchese Federico Gonzaga, Rome, 25 October 1483 (b. 846, c. 654).

(iii) Description of the Inventory

The order of contents promised at the beginning of the inventory is not followed consistently, although some rough groupings of types of object do in practice emerge. No locations or valuations are given, and only on the first two pages are weights given of the objects listed (I 1–104); later on (I 240–339) some measurements in *braccie* are included of pieces of cloth, tapestry and carpets etc. It is written throughout in the same hand, that of Giovan Francesco Strata, and authenticated at the beginning by Giovan Pietro Arrivabene, on behalf of the other executors. Arrivabene and Capra appear at different times to have gone through the inventory, making a few corrections, indicating items which were designated in the will as special bequests and checking off others.

The inventory begins with silverware (I 1–120), some of the entries containing more than one object, as for instance the fifteen *tondi* bearing different *historiette* (I 83), or the twenty bread knives with silver handles, some imperfect (I 120). Most of the items are silver or silver gilt; only a few are described as made of gold alone: a water jug, a wine goblet and a spoon and fork (I 35–8). There are some objects, probably from the cardinal's *studio*, with particular functional uses, such as the silver seal (I 104), bell (I 96) and ink-stand (I 73), but most of them seem to constitute the contents of the *credenza*: objects for domestic use, entertainment and ornament, such as plates, flasks, candlesticks, jugs, dishes, basins and many types of drinking vessel. Some of these were pieces of elaborate design: for example, *bicheri* decorated with animals or nymphs (I 16, 17) or the big silver-gilt candlestick made in the form of a tree with Adam and Eve (I 106). There are as many as seventy-one spoons, thirty-two knives (in addition to the bread knives mentioned) and twenty-one forks.[50] Liturgical silverware is listed among the rest; there is not much of it, but mixed up with the items from the *credenza* are a chalice and paten (I 98), a holy water vessel with a broken spurge (I 77), the legatine cross (I 105), part of another cross (I 101) and a gold *anchonetta* containing relics (I 92).

The next section (I 121–70) lists clothes and bedding (I 171–97). Such things hardly constitute part of the cardinal's collections in the proper sense of the word, though some items may be of interest to historians of dress, and it has to be remembered that finely tailored pieces of silk, damask and fur were certainly material objects of value and desirability, also of use for purposes of payment or reward.[51] Among other articles from the cardinal's wardrobe listed here are his two mantles (*gabani*) 'in the Bruges style' (I 162, 164), his seventeen rose-coloured birettas (I 196) and two pairs of rose-coloured stockings, one long, one short (I 168, 170).

Then follow tapestries and other decorative hangings; the subjects they illustrate are given in many cases and complement the short list of the astonished Bolognese chronicler in 1471.[52] It is strange perhaps that none of these items were reserved for special bequests since they were among the cardinal's most spectacular articles of decoration: some of them certainly ended up—whether

---

[50] Assuming that *forcine, forcelle* and *forchette*, not to mention *pironi*, are all of the same species.
[51] See above, pp. 78 n. 229, 83 nn. 254–5.
[52] See above, pp. 81–2.

bought from the estate or appropriated—in the possession of his brother Gianfrancesco. Some stories on the larger tapestry panels are scriptural, including
Solomon, Joseph, Abraham (eight), Judith, Cyrus and Ezechial; others showed
maidens (four), wine-harvesting scenes (seven) and Achilles (two). Other tapestry panels listed include (I 198–9) two of Alexander (presumably those noted in
1471), two of Solomon (I 200, 217; there is also an embroidery of Solomon, I
218) and one each of the following: Augustus, the Paschal Lamb, and
another—probably similar—entitled 'Sine peccato est', the Creation of the
World, Christ in the Garden, Christ bearing the Cross, Christ on the Cross, the
Assumption. Pieces of tapestry and embroidery to cover the seats or back-rests of
benches (*spalliere*) are listed showing the virtues, the sciences and the planets,
also two of St Anthony; doorhangings (*portiere*) include a woman on horseback,
the Annunciation, Perseus, Argos, a boy, Gideon, Augustus and a lion. Three
bore Gonzaga emblems (two of the marigold, one of the turtledove); two were
simply of leaves and flowers. There were also a large number of non-figurative
items, all in green. Carpets (I 292–342) follow next, some specified as floor and
some as table or chest coverings; then come bed canopies and coverings
(I 343–54).

The inventory then becomes very miscellaneous. There are cushions, more
clothes, and what appears to be the contents of the cardinal's chapel: ecclesiastical vestments, altarcloths and other sacred furnishings including an old missal
(I 396)—separated from the rest of his books—an ivory box to contain the Host
and an ivory icon (I 417–18). Then there are silk handkerchiefs, fine linen cloths
and sheets, also riding equipment, including saddles and stirrups, some items
with names of members of the household as their users, and the cardinal's own
cuirass (I 442), helmet and other armour (I 443), suggestive reminders of his
recent duties as legate in the War of Ferrara,[53] and the breastplates of several of
his attendants (I 444–7). Also listed is a *pavaglione* or bed-tent given by Duke
Alfonso of Calabria (I 433), and among other interesting objects which appear
are an astrolabe (I 465) and two pen-sharpeners (I 471–2).

Strata and his colleagues at this point (I 468) seem to have reached the treasure
chests. There are vessels, vases and cutlery again, but these are objects of greater
rarity and value than the silverware listed earlier, objects fashioned from precious
stones and rock-crystal, often with jewelled and gold mountings: true collector's
items, of the sort described in a letter to Isabella d'Este in 1502 as 'cose rare e da
signori'.[54] Some may have been antique or imitation antique, some Byzantine in
origin or imported from the eastern Mediterranean. There was, for instance, the
salt-cellar of horn (*alicorno*) inscribed in Greek letters in a silver casket (I 497);
among the most elaborate pieces were a crystal jug inlaid with gilded parrots and
enamelled with a pearl on the top (I 502), and another salt cellar, this one of
jasper ornamented in gold with six serpents at the base, two rubies, two sapphires
and nine pearls (I 494). Though described as if functional, mostly of these items
were probably more ornamental than useful, even the two pen-sharpeners, one
with the handle of cameo and silver gilt, and the other of jasper (I 471–2). There

[53] See Chambers, 'Virtù militare', pp. 219–21.
[54] Francesco Malatesta to Isabella d'Este, Florence 27 April 1502, published from ASMn, AG, b. 1104 by
Brown, 'Little Known Letters', p. 197.

are seventy entries in this sequence, though again some are multiples, such as the four crystal spoons and two crystal forks with silver gilt handles (I 532, 534). The bronzes (I 539) follow as a single entry, unfortunately without any description of individual pieces or even their approximate number; they are followed by gems, cameos and intaglios, and for these the inventory does provide not only number (over 500) but particular descriptions.

It is a remarkable collection, even if not so big as that of Pietro Barbo. Two hundred and seventy-two of the gems were loose, including one with Barbo's own head as Paul II (I 540), another with the head of Julius Caesar which was left to the Duke of Calabria (W I3; I 542) and the only one of the lot which has been identified in an existing collection, the so-called 'Felix gem', which had formerly belonged to the same pope (I 564). The description of it in the inventory does not identify the mythological story, but Strata and his colleagues probably did not have sufficient learning, let alone available time, for this. Among mounted cameos (I 569–72) were fourteen on gold rings, eight on a square silver mirror and others upon plaques or trays (two of these are specified as made of jasper, with respectively twenty-four and sixteen cameos upon them), a tray of prasma with eighteen cameos and twenty silver trays (*tavole*) bearing the cardinal's arms, inset with cameos: a method of displaying such gems copied from the collection of Paul II.[55] One may assume that these items were the pride of the cardinal's collection, and the category of highest monetary value, the implications of which will be discussed later. The list of odd jewels which follows is significantly short: eleven items, mostly mounted on rings, including a gold ring with Francesco's arms on it (I 582) and another ring with the Barbo arms (I 586).

After these exceptional treasures the inventory again becomes miscellaneous. There are more pieces of cloth and silk, cushions, including two feather cushions *de stomacho* (I 639), which may relate to the cardinal's years of suffering from stomach illness;[56] pants in a bag (I 636); two dog leads made of silk and a dog collar (I 621, 679), a sand clock (I 684), the mace (I 633), a copper inkwell (I 591) and a prized piece of unicorn's horn (I 608; cf. 86). There are also two small icons, which presumably are paintings, the only paintings in the entire inventory (I 598).

Then we reach the cardinal's books (I 687–901). Including the missal listed earlier (I 396), the inventory contains altogether 215 titles or 222 individual volumes (twelve of them printed); five of the books were noted as borrowed (subsequently restored to their owners), so the totals should discount these. Seven titles can be identified with relative certainty among the books which the cardinal had been allotted as part of his share of his mother's property after her death.[57] A total of over two hundred books was a relatively large collection, considering, first, that the list is certainly incomplete, and second, that Cardinal Gonzaga was not himself a scholar. It may be compared to the libraries of a number of contemporary cardinals, unfavourably of course with those as learned as Bessarion, whose library, bequeathed to San Marco in Venice, had risen to 1024 books by

---

[55] See Müntz, *Les Arts*, II, pp. 223–36.
[56] See above, p. 96.
[57] See I 694, 713, 716, 738, 770, 852–3. The eighth book, 'un libreto de le stationi de Roma', valued at 1 *soldo* (ASDMn, FCC, b. 2/A, 'Inventario de le cose', fol. 14ʳ), does not appear in the cardinal's inventory.

his death in 1472, or even to Domenico Capranica's bequest of 387 books to his newly-founded college.[58] Cardinal Marco Barbo was said to have had about five hundred books, and more in commission when he died in 1491.[59]

The books are listed very roughly in groups according to subject, which may suggest they were assembled hastily from the shelves and chests. By a crude classification according to subject matter they reach the following group totals:

1. Religion (Bibles, sermons, breviaries, service books, lives of saints, patristic, theological and miscellaneous devotional works): 66

2. Classical literature in Latin (poetry, moral philosophy, orations, dramatic works, ancient history, grammar etc); Greek texts in Latin translations; commentaries on texts, including modern humanistic ones: 45

3. Medieval and humanistic Latin literature (including moral treatises, historiography, poetry etc): 26

4. Vernacular (Italian) literature: 13

5. Law (civil and canon law texts and commentaries): 17

6. Science, i.e., medicine, astronomy (excluding texts from antiquity, except through Arabic versions), minerology etc: 39

7. Miscellaneous: 9

There are many texts missing which one might readily have expected to find. For instance, only one work by Aristotle is named, the *Ethics* (I 900); Plato is only represented by a commentary on the *Timaeus* (I 824); but what is even more striking is the absence of writings by contemporaries with whom the cardinal was well acquainted. There are only two of Filelfo's works (I 720, 722) and one of Pius II's (I 828), and neither Arrivabene's *Gonzagidos* nor Marasca's *De arte bene moriendi* are listed,[60] nor anything by Platina except for his *Lives of the Popes* (I 747)—and these authors were members or former members or close associates of members of the cardinal's own household. Not only are Poggio Bracciolini and Flavio Biondo of Forlì absent, but so are Alberti and Poliziano. Meanwhile there are the books, already noted, which the cardinal is known to have possessed but which are absent from the inventory: above all, the two volumes of the incomplete Vatican Homer.[61] Most of these, presumably, would have been among the items of property left behind in Rome.

After the books comes a list of fourteen mules and eleven horses (I 902–36), with the names of the animals and of some of the members of the household who rode them. This was a very modest stable for a cardinal, and probably reflects the limitation and immobility of his establishment in the last four months of his life. In his earlier years it had been very different. Following the item of a chest containing five cases of medals (414 in all, but their metal is unspecified), the main inventory ends with the autograph signatures of Strata, Andriasi and Secco.

After these signatures, however, a further section begins, which suggests that the compilers in their haste had overlooked various other receptacles containing small articles of value. First to be added were a large quantity of 'medals'

[58] See, for these and other cardinals' libraries, the bibliography noted above, p. 63.
[59] Letter believed to be from Cosimo Orsini, Abbot of Farfa, to Giovanni Pico della Mirandola, Rome, 19 March 1491: '…roba, cioè libri, per octo milia ducati. Ha circha cinquecento volumi de libri, e anchor non si sa che se ne abbi ordinato: sono boni e belli libri' (Zippel, 'La morte di Marco Barbo', p. 493).
[60] See above, p. 53.
[61] See above, pp. 60–3, and, in general, the list of Manuscripts and Unpublished Sources, below.

(I 938–45), some of which were possibly antique coins. In a silver clock case (perhaps I 573) forty-seven 'gold medals' were counted; there were eleven more, of unspecified metal, in a small paper bag (*cartozeto*) and 281 small silver medals in a wooden box. In another container there were two cases and a *busoleto* (a small receptacle or urn) with fifty-one silver medals inside, and a further quantity in a damask bag. The only medal individually itemized is 'the large one of Constantine' (discussed under I 942). There are no other clues as to what any of these medals were; remarkably there is no mention at all of Sperandio's medal of the cardinal himself,[62] which may strengthen the argument that it was a commemorative medal made after his death, although there is no other evidence in support of this. The total number of Francesco's 'medals' is 929; this is a huge figure and does suggest that many were Roman coins, which it is known he collected.[63] Even if many of the items were coins, as a numismatic collection it would have been roughly equal in size to the vast hoard of Cardinal Pietro Barbo before he became pope.[64]

More gems follow next (I 946–53). A chest, possibly a small one, is listed with four cases containing over two hundred cameos and cornelians; and twenty-nine rings are listed, some of them of gold and with cameo settings. Gianfrancesco Strata's signature alone ends this section.

A further addendum, also signed by Strata, must have been written later, in or after December 1483, when Giovan Pietro Arrivabene had gone to Rome, for it inserts some additional items from another inventory, made by Arrivabene, of certain valuables he had taken with him.[65] Evidently a few more miscellaneous articles belonging to the cardinal had come to light in the meanwhile, and it was thought useful to transfer the details to the master inventory. This section (I 954–60) itemizes a small leather case containing many loose stones, some of them incised, fourteen gold rings, a copper ring with a glass intaglio, a pearl on a silver mounting and other miscellaneous things such as a rose-coloured mule-cloth, and a piece of the barber's equipment. Strata signed this section, too, as well as the final postscript, where some riding-gear is noted as missing (I 961–6).

Quite a number of unexpected sides to Francesco's personality and interests are revealed from this inventory, even if partially incomplete. The proportion of astronomical books is surprising. Even if he had consulted astrologers and been fascinated in general with divination,[66] it is a big step further to have been a collector of translations from learned Arabic texts, and it raises the question of who can have been advising him, or whether such books were among those acquired involuntarily, either by gift or bequest or from the books of Guido Gonzaga. The relatively large number of titles which concern medicine, surgery and the preservation of health is rather less strange, in view of the Gonzaga family's preoccupation with and experience of chronic ailments and inherited disease: Francesco himself was recurrently ill.[67]

---

[62] See above, p. 85. Possibly it was counted among the 'cose de bronzo' (I 539).
[63] E.g., above, p. 78 n. 228.
[64] Weiss, *Un umanista veneziano*, p. 28; *Renaissance Discovery*, p. 168.
[65] See below, pp. 114–15.
[66] See above, p. 64.
[67] See above, pp. 66, 96, and Luzio, *L'archivio Gonzaga*, II, p. 48.

On the other hand, it is perhaps surprising that the inventory contains no reference to antique marble sculptures or fragments, of which the cardinal was without doubt a collector. It should be pointed out that such articles would have been exceptionally heavy and fragile to transport around Italy, and so they may have been among the principal valuables left behind in Rome; even so, it is remarkable that they are never mentioned in letters as saleable assets. Some perhaps had been displayed in the gardens at San Lorenzo in Damaso and at Sant'Agata, remaining there as semi-permanent fixtures. It is possibly significant that early in 1484 Marchese Federico Gonzaga was instructing his ambassador to see what things of this sort could be acquired from Cardinal Rafaelle Riario, the new incumbent at San Lorenzo.[68]

* * *

Some explanation needs to be given of the marginal notes to the main text, or those of them not made in Strata's hand. Presumably those made by Giovan Pietro Arrivabene were made soon before his departure in December to Rome (which will be discussed below) and mainly signify collations with the will, noting the various items designated as bequests which may have been handed over immediately to the legatees, as well as those he had taken charge of himself (signified by the initials 'Jo. p.'). The other annotator's hand, which is sometimes confusingly similar (though he usually runs together Arrivabene's initials so that they read as 'Jop'), can be identified as that of his fellow-executor in Mantua, Alvise Capra.[69] Capra's emendations were clearly made later and certainly after mid-July 1484, for they twice refer to Federico Gonzaga as the late marchese (I 539, 564); one of them refers to an item having been held by Arrivabene and handed over to Protonotary Ludovico Gonzaga, who had it in Rome (I 82); there are also notes of sales and other dispositions. Precisely when Capra was making his emendations is not clear, though he can hardly have done so later than the second half of November 1485 when he was again serving the papal legation at Bologna, now held by Cardinal Ascanio Sforza.[70] Also difficult to explain are the various symbols which appear in the left hand margin throughout the inventory (no attempt has been made in the present edition to reproduce these gnomic crosses, circles and other signs). They are probably the record of successive checkings, or perhaps of sales or availability for sale of different objects.

(iv) Problems of the Cardinal's Heirs and Executors

Many problems were to follow after the publication of the cardinal's will. What follows is an account, so far as sources permit, of the sequel: the administration of his estate and difficulties which the inheritance encountered.

---

[68] Marchese Federico Gonzaga to Stefanino Guidotti, Mantua, 12 March 1484: 'Desyderassimo grandemente havere qualche bella et bona testa de preda de quelle antique lì de Roma, perhò vogliamo usati ogni arte et industria in vedere de recavarne, se possibile serà, dimandandone in nomine nostro ad Reverendissimo Cardinale de San Zorzo' (ASMn, AG, b. 2900, lib. 117, fol. 66ʳ).

[69] See both their signatures on the text of the letter of 27 October 1483, in Appendix 3, no. 5.

[70] *DBI*, s.v., also information from Marco Pellegrini.

Presumably Giovan Pietro Arrivabene and Alvise Capra, the two executors of the will present in Mantua at its opening on 29 October 1483, made an initial distribution of legacies, such as the items bequeathed to Marchese Federico and other members of the Gonzaga family, and to the corporate beneficiaries in Mantua, the cathedral clergy and the friars of San Francesco. But it must have been difficult for them to estimate the extent of either the assets or the debts; their difficulty was aggravated by distance, by the fact that some of the cardinal's possessions—and many of his debts—were in Rome, as were their two co-executors, Ludovico Agnelli and Francesco Maffei.

For their part, Agnelli and Maffei had acknowledged by letter their responsibility to oversee the redistribution of Cardinal Gonzaga's benefices, particularly to bear in mind his hope that Ludovico should succeed him in the bishopric of Mantua.[71] The cardinal, who could not of course bequeath his benefices but only express pious wishes about them, had implied that Ludovico should also get the *prepositura* of San Benedetto in Polirone (W 41) together with the retention of those benefices which he (Ludovico) had held previously. Ludovico's nomination to the bishopric was published in bulls dated, if not yet delivered, 27 October;[72] and Marchese Federico wrote to Sixtus IV on 6 November, thanking him and announcing that Cristoforo Arrivabene, a canon of Mantua, was coming to urge other favours[73]—but the pope resolved on a different distribution of the benefices. This was more favourable to the marchese's son Sigismondo and to several of the cardinal's protégés, including the two executors in Rome. Thus the Protonotary Sigismondo—though only fourteen years old—was to succeed his uncle in the *prepositura* of San Benedetto and the *primiceriato* of Sant'Andrea, while Ludovico Agnelli was to have Felonica, Francesco Maffei the abbey of S. Maria della Geronda and Agostino Maffei the archpriestship of Ostiano.[74] While Sigismondo's appointment may have met with approval, the gains at Ludovico's expense by two of the cardinal's executors were less well received.[75]

[71] Capra and G. P. Arrivabene on 27 October 1483 (Appendix 3, no. 5) mention a letter from Rome dated 23 October that they had already received; likewise, F. Maffei to Marchese Federico Gonzaga, Rome, 18 November 1483, declared that he himself, with Agnelli, had been to see Sixtus IV about the bishopric being transferred to Ludovico, even before having confirmation of the cardinal's death (ASMn, AG, b. 846, c. 662).

[72] Eubel, II, p. 204; papal bulls of 6 kal. Nov. in ASDMn, Fondo Mensa Vescovile, Pergamene, b. 3, no. 57, to the clergy of Mantua; no. 58, to the bishops of Cremona and 'Lamola' (i.e., Aldegati, suffragan bishop of Mantua and bishop of Lamus *in partibus*), bearing the signature, with another apostolic scriptor, 'Ben[edictus] de Maffeis'; and no. 59, to the vassals of the bishopric.

[73] ASMn, AG, b. 2899, lib. 113, fol. 11ʳ.

[74] These subsequent provisions to benefices, so Francesco Maffei (as an interested party) wrote in the letter of 18 November quoted above, had been made entirely on the pope's decision (ibid.). A papal bull announcing Sigismondo's appointment, addressed to the bishop of 'Lamola' and the archdeacon and archpriest of Mantua, dated 6 kal. Nov. (27 October) and countersigned 'expedita quinto Kal. Decembris A. de Maffeis' (27 November), also a papal brief (likewise bearing Agostino Maffei's signature) addressed to Marchese Federico Gonzaga, dated 29 October 1484, informing him of the appointment of Sigismondo, are in ASMn, AG, b. 3328; cf. letters from Agnelli and from Agostino Maffei, 29 October (b. 846, cc. 658, 659).

[75] On 7 November Stefanino Guidotti wrote from Loiano, on his way to Rome, that the successful intrusion of Agnelli and Francesco Maffei 'summamente mi dispiaque, parendomi ch'el seria stato bene ad ogni altro cortesano che a loro che voleno esser tenuti di casa' (ASMn, AG, b. 846, c. 617); Agostino Maffei, who on 18 November wrote in turn denouncing Ruffino Gablonetta (Ludovico's auditor) for trying to get hold of the cardinal's benefices (b. 846, c. 661), defended himself in a letter of 26 November (b. 846, c. 669). Guidotti, on the other hand, expressed pleasure on behalf of Sigismondo, whose bulls, he wrote on 11 December, he hoped shortly to forward (b. 846, c. 632).

Meanwhile, another letter from Maffei confirms that there certainly were some valuable possessions of the cardinal still in Rome: for he claims that by following instructions he had redeemed some jewels which were in pawn, but that he claimed for himself 1258 ducats, which sum he (or perhaps one of his brothers) had previously advanced; at all events, Maffei refused to part with the jewels.[76] This demonstrates that the cardinal's valuables had served to stave off foreclosure by his creditors for years and had all long been as much a financial as an aesthetic investment.

Francesco had approved when Cardinal Rafaelle Riario became the new Apostolic Chamberlain early in 1483,[77] without suspecting how soon his palace at San Lorenzo in Damaso would also fall into Riario's hands.[78] Riario took possession—improbably—fourteen hours after the cardinal drew his last breath in Bologna; but as looting had been anticipated at San Lorenzo in Damaso in the event of his death, it may be that Maffei and other former members of the household had already stored elsewhere items of the cardinal's property remaining there or at the villa residence of Sant'Agata; an initiative of this sort taken by Gaspare da Padova has been mentioned earlier.[79]

Marchese Federico Gonzaga also had, however, a responsibility to ensure that the executorial business was properly discharged, under the terms of his brother's will (W 43), and it was partly owing to him that Sixtus IV issued two briefs early in December 1483, one to Protonotary Sigismondo, as the new holder of both the *prepositura* and of Sant'Andrea, releasing these benefices from their share of liability for the cardinal's debts, and the other to the marchese. The pope now prohibited any further distribution of assets before the creditors had received their due.[80] Clearly there would be no difficulty in finding purchasers for Francesco's

---

[76] Francesco Maffei to Marchese Federico Gonzaga, Rome, 24 November 1483: 'Cristoforo Arrivabene mi ha detto che ha comissione de Vostra Illustrissima Signoria de scodre certe zoie che fureno de la bona memoria del Cardinale. Io ge le ho proferte, pagando quello sono in pegno, etiam cum el satisfarmi a me de quello ho ad havere, che mi pare rasonevole, che montarà in tuto circha 1258. Vero è che le cose valeno molto piú. Io lo scrito a questi signori executori che facino che sia pagato da loro non posser haver una risposta' (ASMn, AG, b. 846, c. 665). In another letter, dated 26 November, Maffei referred to letters from Arrivabene and Agnelli 'domandate certe zoie o pegni...li rispusi che non credea che Vostra Illustrissima Signoria mi volesse tore quello havea ad havere' (ASMn, AG, b. 846, c. 666).

[77] Cardinal F. Gonzaga wrote to Girolamo Riario, Ferrara, 7 February 1483: 'Piacene bene la provisione [after Cardinal d'Estouteville's death] de la casa e del offitio del camarlengato fatta in persona del Reverendissimo Monsignore nostro cardinale de San Zorzo' (ASMn, AG, b. 2900, lib. 114, fol. 109ᵛ).

[78] Schiavo, *Cancelleria*, pp. 42–3, cites the bull of 18 October 1483 (AV, Reg. Vat. 646, cc. 175–6) which transfers the palace, referring to Francesco as 'forsan iam obitum'; Riario's taking possession is mentioned in Bitozzi's MS history of San Lorenzo in Damaso, fol. 7, cited by Valtieri, *La Basilica*, p. 182.

[79] See above, p. 62, with reference to Gaspare's letter (Appendix 3, no. 12).

[80] The original brief addressed to the marchese, dated 10 December 1483, is in ASMn, AG, b. 834, c. 297. On the privilege for Sigismondo, Stefanino Guidotti had written from Rome on 18 November, 'hozi messer Francesco Maffei, che par haver inteso per altri da Mantua la novella de quelli seimilia ducati de la gravatione di benefitii etc el si offerisce cum bon mezo de aiutar la cosa per modo che se si desse uno mille ducati a la Sanctità de Nostro Signore ch'el revocaria quella concessione per breve'(ASMn, AG, b. 846, c. 620). On 7 December 1483 Stefanino wrote: 'hozi tandem seriano spazati i dui brevi...per la liberatione di quelli benefiti del Illustre e Reverendo Monsignor mio prefato vostro fiolo, uno directo a sua Reverenda Signoria de la gratia fatta motu proprio, l'altro directo a Vostra Excellentia exhortatorio che la sia o deputati che si sia chi invigilet a non lassar distrahere quelli beni mobili del Reverendissimo condam [*sic*] Cardinale Mantue, e che la curi o faci havere cura che creditori siano satisfatti cum manco danno de la heredità che si possa, e questo ha fatto Sua Sanctità perché l'era persuasa che, fazendo Vostra Illustrissima Signoria render bon conto a chi ha manezata la roba, ge seria apresso a satisfare ai debiti' (ASMn, AG, b. 846, c. 631).

miscellaneous hoard;[81] soon after sending this brief, Sixtus, in conversation with the Mantuan ambassador, recalled that the deceased cardinal had often assured him that he had more than sufficient capital in *beni mobili* to pay off all his debtors.[82]

Against this backgound, Giovan Pietro set off for Rome,[83] while Capra stayed behind in Mantua, having authorised him and the other executors to act on his behalf.[84] Giovan Pietro took many objects either listed as bequests or regarded as saleable, corresponding probably to those which are marked with his initials, in Capra's hand, in the inventory. According to a letter he wrote on 26 December,[85] he understood that his mission was to make contact with the other executors and arrange the settlement of debts. He had been surprised to learn of the brief inhibiting the executors sent to the marchese. Another purpose was to advance Ludovico's claim to the bishopric on more favourable terms; indeed Ludovico insisted that it was the main purpose.[86]

Ludovico was beginning to feel alarmed; not only had he litttle prospect of immediately succeeding his brother in the cardinalate,[87] but even his succession to the bishopric, recommended in the will, was proving difficult; he had expected to get immediate enjoyment of the income and not to have been faced with any conditional obligation to meet past debts of the cardinal: later he claimed that he had not known that the clause to this effect had been inserted in the will (W 41) and expressed bitterness about the unfair advantage conferred upon Sigismondo.[88] Out of compassion, he claimed in his letter of 7 December from Mantua, he had already taken in many members of the deceased cardinal's household but could not pay them anything without this income.[89] Ludovico's letters were to express mounting suspicion and bitterness, particularly against the Maffei brothers,

---

[81] E.g., Antimaco to Marchese Federico Gonzaga, Milan, 22 November 1483, mentioned that Ludovico Sforza was asking about the 'mobile et robe': '…me dimandò se gli erano belli tapeti da tavola' (ASMn, AG, b. 1628).

[82] Stefanino Guidotti to Marchese Federico Gonzaga, Rome, 15 December 1483: 'L'altro breve è diretto a Vostra Excellentia, el qual exhorta quella voglia abrazar il carico di voler far che li creditori siano pagati, e di beni mobili se l'è posibile, ché la Sanctità Sua dice ch'el Reverendissimo quondam Monsignor Cardinale disse più volte ch'el havia tanto di capitale in beni mobili che pagariano tuti i debiti soi' (ASMn, AG, b. 846, c. 633).

[83] Ludovico Gonzaga to F. Maffei, Mantua, 3 December 1483, noted Arrivabene's departure on that day (ASP, AGG, b. 41/3, reg. 1, fol. 7ᵛ).

[84] ASMn, AN, Estensioni, R. 80 (A. Cornice, 1483), deed dated 26 November 1483, drawn up in the cardinal's house *in contrata Griffonis*, authorised them to sell goods to raise money, particularly to pay the salaries of the *familia* and the cost of their clothing for a month in mourning.

[85] Appendix 3, no. 7.

[86] Ludovico had sent letters dated 3 December to the pope, to Cardinal Rafaelle Riario as camerlengo and to the other cardinals (ASP, AGG, b. 41/3, reg. 1, fols 9ᵛ–10ᵛ). He wrote to Arrivabene on 7 December that the matter of the bishopric 'fu la principale causa per la quale fui mandato' (ibid., fol. 12ᵛ). Meanwhile Marchese Federico wrote to Agostino Maffei on 4 December that his acquisition of Ludovico's former benefices was, on account of the debts left by the cardinal, 'tutto l'opposito de quello che era il desiderio nostro'; he wrote similarly to Francesco Maffei (ASMn, AG, b. 2899, lib. 113, fols 63ᵛ–5ʳ).

[87] S. Guidotti to Marchese Federico Gonzaga, Rome, 18 November 1483, reported that Cardinal Riario had warned 'queste sono cose che non si fanno ogni dì né molto spesso' (ASMn, AG, b. 846, c. 621).

[88] Appendix 3, no. 15.

[89] Ludovico Gonzaga, bishop-elect, to G. P. Arrivabene, Mantua, 7 December 1483: '…la graveza a me imposta per dicto vescoado de pagare sei milia ducati in satisfactione de debiti de la bona memoria de Monsignore Reverendissimo, e quantità de spesse che a me è necessario de fare per la molta famiglia che ho a le spalle, de la quale grande parte è de quella de la prefata, che sono huomini da bene, virtuosi, e chi per compassione e quasi debito ho racolti, facendoli etiam intendere che de li fructi del vescovato predicto del anno presente a me, non me intra né quatrino per havere havuto lo prelibato Monsignore li denari de questo anno' (ASP, AGG, b. 41/3, reg. 1, fols 12ʳ–13ᵛ).

considering as he did that his ecclesiastical career and financial interest had been ill-served and obstructed by them.[90] It is clear from the correspondence that the papal bulls had been held up, and he had not yet obtained full posesssion.

Marchese Federico Gonzaga remained uneasy about his deceased brother's estate. In early January he wrote to the executors, insisting that all sale or distribution of the cardinal's goods should be suspended and that the items which Giovan Pietro Arrivabene had taken to Rome should be inventoried and returned to Mantua.[91] Agnelli, Arrivabene and Maffei replied jointly that they would obey these orders and would dispatch copies of the two inventories, the list of items brought to Rome, and the list (presumably the master inventory, the one which survives) also containing the articles still in Mantua 'di quelle che sono di qua, quante di quelle di là'.[92] They even offered to resign, not being able to act simultaneously in Mantua as well as in Rome, where they had other commitments; Agnelli did in fact obtain papal permission to appoint a proxy in Mantua, his brother Be Agnelli.[93] Meanwhile, Stefanino Guidotti, still in Rome as the Mantuan ambassador, wrote in early February that he had failed to get any satisfaction from the executors; he explained that Francesco Maffei was holding on to some of the jewels,[94] though others were in the hands of a Milanese merchant.[95]

On 14 March 1484 Arrivabene wrote about all these matters in greater detail,[96] and at the same time he wrote a letter to Capra (which does not survive) in which he explained that because of illness he had been unable to act immediately. He now enclosed copies—unfortunately missing—of two inventories, one of them simply a list of the objects he had brought to Rome, as requested by Agnelli and Maffei. Arrivabene explained that the items intended exclusively for the *camerarii* of the cardinal had been kept apart from those intended jointly for the *camerarii* and other members of the household, which were left behind in Mantua in the charge of his brother Giovanni. He declared that the executors had appointed three persons to agree on the prices to be asked and that accounts were being properly kept. Giovan Pietro furthermore argued that it would make more sense to carry on the administration at Rome rather than at Mantua, since more of

[90] He made hostile remarks, e.g., in his letter to Francesco Maffei of 27 November 1483, ASP, AGG, b. 41/3, reg. 1, fol. 4[r] or to Giovan Pietro Arrivabene of 13, 24 January (fols 54[v], 67[v]–8[v]), 12 March 1484 (fols 105[v]–6[v]): 'la iniquitate de essi Maffei'; or to Marchese Federico Gonzaga, 14 April 1484 (ibid., fols 125[r]–6[v]).
[91] Marchese Federico Gonzaga to L. Agnelli, F. Maffei and G. P. Arrivabene, Mantua 10 January 1484: 've advisiamo et comettiamo che debiati soprasedere et non procedere piú ultra circa la alienatione de li beni del prefato quondam Monsignore, cussì de quelli che vui Messer Zoan Petro haveti portati lì a Roma, come tutti li altri che lì o altrove se ritrovassero, et vogliati transferirvi qua ad nui… Et sopra ciò aspetiamo risposta da vui per il presente cavallaro che vui havemo driçiato a questo effecto, et da vui, Messer Zoan Petro, la copia del inventario facto per vui de li beni et heredità del prefato quondam Monsignore' (ASMn, AG, b. 2900, lib. 116, fol. 33[v]).
[92] Appendix 3, no. 8.
[93] Papal brief dated 16 February 1484 confirming that his brother should act for him 'quia in agendis Mantue circa executionem testamenti… personaliter interesse non potest' (AV, Arm. XXXIX, reg. 16a, fol. 36[v]).
[94] S. Guidotti to Marchese Federico Gonzaga, Rome, 8 February 1484: 'Questi executori del testamento qua sono stati insieme doe volte, dove hano vogliuto che sia presente, per esser poi informato de le cose. Hano ateso di voler cavar di mane a messer Francesco Maffei certe gioie che lui dice esser in pegno a la usura, tamdem comprendessi che lui le ha in mane' (ASMn, AG, b. 847, c. 113[r]).
[95] '… Ritrovano uno merchadante chi è creditor di essa heredità di circha ducati mille, el quale vole riscodere lui etiam queste zoie per mille altri che sono in pegno, e tenersile presso a se senza altra usura, finché lui sia satisfatto in tuto, o che parà altro miglior assetto a Vostra Excellentia. Credo perhò più chiaro ne scriverà messer Zoan Pedro…' (ibid., c. 113[v]).
[96] Appendix 3, no. 10.

the debts were there; he proposed that the marchese could appoint someone to ensure everything was done correctly.

Arrivabene's inventory of the objects he had brought to Rome was presumably the one mentioned on the last page of the original or master inventory of 27 October (I 954–66), in order to indicate some variations or omissions, and a check by Giovan Francesco Strata, using Arrivabene's inventory as control, may explain the placing of the initials 'Jo. p.' beside so many items, though a quantity are also noted in the margins to be in the keeping of 'Jo. F.' or 'Jo. f.' (was this Gianfrancesco Gonzaga, the cardinal's brother, or Giovan Francesco Strata, the *camerario* and compiler of the surviving inventory?). Finally, it must be remembered that there may even have been a third inventory: of the possessions which had been all the time in Rome. For Arrivabene goes on to mention other *beni mobili* from, presumably, the cardinal's two Roman houses, at San Lorenzo in Damaso and Sant'Agata: many beds and mattresses and other household goods 'che erano qui in casa'. Of these he had never seen an inventory, though he was prepared to give Francesco Maffei the benefit of the doubt in having had one made and sent to Mantua. Presumably these objects included the missing books already mentioned, the statuary and other objects of value, in addition to all sorts of household bric-à-brac. Moreover, there were certain items which were in other hands: the jewels which Maffei was keeping and two *confectieri* worth 300 ducats, which had been in pawn for four years and had accumulated interest amounting to 500 ducats.

A few days later Guidotti confirmed some of these problems in a letter and complained that he too was being molested by creditors, so that the marchese ought really to appoint someone to supervise these matters together with the executors.[97] He referred in particular to the *roba mobile* and the need for the bedding and other items to be sold, mentioning also the jewels which Francesco Maffei had retained, including a diamond worth 1000 ducats. Giovan Pietro Arrivabene, having recovered his health, does seem to have become more active at this time, as we learn from the letter of Gaspare da Padova on 29 March. He reported Arrivabene's attempt to retrieve from him the cardinal's incomplete bilingual and illustrated Homer, and, when he failed to get possession of these unique manuscripts, his refusal to pay Gaspare what was owing to him on the grounds he had insufficient authority to do so.[98]

No complete list of the debts owing seems to have been available; indeed details about some of them only enter into the surviving correspondence at irregular intervals, in some instances years later. Among the first is the claim of Francesco Maffei already mentioned; one of the last to emerge was a sum of 674 ducats apparently owing to Baccio Ugolini;[99] but various other associates or even members of the household also claimed that the cardinal owed them money—beyond, presumably, their back wages, which the will took into account. For instance, 500

---

[97] Appendix 3, no. 11.
[98] See above, p. 62, and Appendix 3, no. 12; on his recent illness, see above, p. 114.
[99] Onofrio Tornabuoni to Lorenzo de' Medici, 21 January 1489, mentions 'il credito di Giovanni [Tornabuoni] e del Baccio Ugholino, che sono quelli di Giovanni ducati 3500, e 674 quelli del Baccio' (ASF, MAP, XXVI, no. 513); Brown, 'Lorenzo', p. 100.

ducats was owing to Giovanni de la Fiera;[100] there was also the modest claim of twenty-two ducats for services rendered by Gaspare da Padova;[101] later it emerged that two of the chamberlains, Carlo Canale[102] and Carletto Franzoni,[103] both claimed considerable sums which they had formerly advanced to their patron. Among other minor claimants who presented themselves was one Alvise Vismara, who visited Ludovico at Bracciano in August 1484 and expressed a wish for settlement in goods rather than cash; he was not anxious to have cameos or jewels (the valuation of which he said he did not understand) but fancied some of the tapestries, including the scenes of Alexander the Great, presumably the same pieces so much admired at Bologna in 1471.[104] The cardinal's standby creditor of years past, Agostino Maffei, even put in a claim for a mule which he said he had lent to one of the cardinal's servants during the journey from Bologna back to Rome (perhaps, therefore, as long ago as December 1480?), but this individual had sold it for fifty ducats and subsequently alleged he had given Agostino a horse in exchange.[105] In contrast to such relatively trivial claims, however, the outstanding debt which continued to loom most seriously was the loan of 3500 ducats from the Medici bank, which Arrivabene had mentioned in his letter of 14 March 1484.[106]

The cardinal's brothers (apart from the excluded Rodolfo) were all deeply concerned about the administration of the estate; and each one was anxious to disclaim any obligation to meet the debts out of his own portion of the inheritance. Marchese Federico, however, seems to have been freed of his special responsibilities by a further papal brief and not to have persevered with his proposal that everything should be sent back to Mantua. The main burden was transferred to Gianfrancesco as the universal heir and heir to Sabbioneta and the rest of the cardinal's paternal inheritance. Gianfrancesco himself makes all this clear in a letter to Marchese Federico dated 25 May 1484, in which he also proposed to take charge himself of those inventoried chattels which Giovan Pietro Arrivabene had left in Mantua in the care of his brother Giovanni.[107] Perhaps, if the 'Jo. Fr.' initials against items do refer to him, they indicate precisely what these chattels were.

[100] S. Guidotti to Marchese Federico Gonzaga, Rome 15 December 1483 (as above, n. 82): 'prego ben la Excellentia Vostra che operando che creditori siano pagati, la si digni haver tra primi racommandato messer Zohan da la Fiera che de' haver ducati 500…' Giovanni de la Fiera, a canon of Mantua cathedral, had been the cardinal's vicar for the church of San Lorenzo in Damaso: he is so named, for instance, in letters of 9 February 1477 and 26 February 1478 (ASMn, AG, b. 3351, cc. 30^r, 41^{r-v}). He is named in the will as a *continuus commensalis* (W 27); G. P. Arrivabene had written to Barbara from Rome, 7 October 1467, 'messer Zohanne è venuto a stare in casa' (b. 843). He was a papal master of supplications, 1465–85 (Hofmann, *Forschungen*, II, p. 85).
[101] Appendix 3, no. 9, and letters of Marchese Francesco to S. Guidotti ('vogliamo che trovati esso Gasparo qual ne fi ditto alozia ne la casa che era de esso Monsignore Cardinale') and G. P. Arrivabene, also to Gaspare da Padua himself, Mantua, 16 March 1484, insisting that payment to Gaspare should be made quickly (ASMn, AG, b. 2900, lib. 117, cc. 81^r, 82^{r-v}); cf. above, pp. 62, 83, 86.
[102] Appendix 3, no. 21 and below, p. 127.
[103] Appendix 3, no. 27, 30 and below, p. 129.
[104] Appendix 3, no. 18; cf. above, p. 82.
[105] Agostino Maffei to Marchese Federico Gonzaga, Rome, 18 December 1484: '…fui a Bologna con sua Reverendissima Signoria et a la retornata nostra a Roma, essendo nui gionti a Fiorence, imprestai ad Ioanfrancesco da Rodiano una mia mula learda per andar a Mantua…' (ASMn, AG, b. 847, c. 97).
[106] Appendix 3, no. 10.
[107] Appendix 3, no. 13.

Meanwhile Ludovico also involved himself closely in the executors' affairs. He had come to Rome himself in April 1484,[108] mainly, it would seem, to clear up remaining problems about the bishopric, which he did at last legally obtain,[109] and in the hope of advancing his greater ambition, to acquire the red hat.[110] On this expectation, he pointed out, also depended many of Cardinal Francesco's former servants.[111] However, because of the plague scare and general state of insecurity in Rome, by the beginning of June Ludovico had taken refuge at Bracciano, as the guest of Virginio Orsini. At the same time (i.e., from May to early July) Arrivabene was absent in Naples on a diplomatic mission for the pope;[112] Ludovico, who had money problems of his own,[113] took the liberty of discussing all the financial problems of the cardinal's executors, though admittedly in his role as a guardian (together with Arrivabene) of Francesco 'Cardinalino' he did have some direct involvement. Thus, on 8 June, he wrote to Arrivabene expressing sympathy for him as an executor harrassed by creditors, a special concern about the 1000 ducats needed to redeem the necklace bequeathed to the 'Cardinalino' and some anxiety that the expense of mourning clothes for the household should be paid off.[114] The following day he also wrote to Gianfrancesco, asking him to attend to these payments and to regard the 'Cardinalino' with special favour, pointing out that some of the territorial income he had inherited from the cardinal was, under the terms of the will (W 36), intended for such purposes.[115]

Evidently Gianfrancesco made avuncular professions of love towards the 'Cardinalino' and expressed himself willing in principle to accept his responsibility. This transpires from another letter, written to him over a month later by Ludovico.[116] Gianfrancesco's side of the correspondence does not survive, but it may be that he had again insisted as a precondition that he must have possession of all the remaining goods of the cardinal or a record of what had happened to them; for Ludovico went on to ask in this same letter if he wished to have the inventory (yet another inventory) of those books and a small amount of

---

[108] On 27 March 1484 he wrote to Giovan Pietro Arrivabene and to Ruffino Gablonetta that he was about to leave Mantua (ASP, AGG, b. 41/3, reg. 1, fols 119^v–21^r); on 14 April he was writing to Marchese Federico Gonzaga from Rome (ibid., fols 125^r–6^r).

[109] On 9 April Ludovico wrote from Rome to the Bishop of 'Lamola' (Aldegati) reappointing him suffragan, (ibid., fol. 135^r); on 4 May to Benedetto Mastino about the canonical terms of his provision (ibid., fol. 135^r); on 14 May 1484 he took his oath in the presence of Cardinal Francesco Piccolomini (ASDMn, Archivio della Mensa vescovile, sez. 1, pergamene, b. II no. 62). He remained unconsecrated, i.e., 'Bishop-Elect'.

[110] Marchese Federico Gonzaga had already written on 18 February 1484 asking the pope to confer the cardinal's hat upon Ludovico (ASMn, AG, b. 2900, lib. 117, fol. 15^r).

[111] Ludovico wrote to his brother-in-law Duke Eberhard of Württemberg on 13 June 1484 that he had had to refuse many 'viros sane probos ac virtutibus at moribus preditos…quibus tamen locum in domo mea convenientem promisi postquam (si Domino placuerit) ad cardinalatus dignitatem promotus fuero' (ASP, AGG, b. 41/3, reg. 1, fol. 179).

[112] Chambers, 'Arrivabene', p. 423.

[113] He alludes to them, e.g., in a letter of 8 June from Bracciano to Ruffino Gablonetta (ASP, AGG, b. 41/3, reg. 1, fols 172^r–3^r).

[114] Bishop-Elect Ludovico Gonzaga to Giovan Pietro Arrivabene, Bracciano, 8 June 1484: 'ho molto bene intieso la graveza che haveti a le spalle de satisfare tra li debiti che se hanno ad pagare de la bona memoria del Reverendissimo Monsignore nostro, a doi a li quali non si può dare dilatione. L'uno è per li panni negri tuolti a li funerali per termino de Aprile proxime passato; l'altro de li mille ducati accatati sopra la colona del puttino a termino per tutto magio o giugno' (ASP, AGG, b. 41/3, reg. 1, fol. 167^v).

[115] Appendix 3, no. 14.

[116] Appendix 3, no. 16.

silverware, which he, Ludovico, had taken from Giovanni Arrivabene (presumably before setting off for Rome in March 1484) with an obligation either to
return them or pay the purchase price.

Ludovico wrote much more about the cardinal's estate and the obligations of
his brother Gianfrancesco (rather than of himself or the bishopric) in a long letter
to his auditor and agent Ruffino Gablonetta.[117] In it he divulged his recollection
of some last thoughts of the cardinal, who apparently had confided to Ludovico
that he estimated that he had assets worth 60–70,000 ducats, including the unpaid
share in the maternal dowry, and the sum owing him since 1474 by King Christian I of Denmark.[118] The total, so the cardinal had reckoned, should be adequate
to cover all his debts and to leave some money in hand. There was the obligation
to find 7000 ducats to buy the freehold of Bigarello for the 'Cardinalino', but this
Ludovico insisted the marchese was bound to furnish, i.e., by paying over 3000
florins of the same dowry money and the debt from Denmark, which he somewhat vaguely quotes once as 4000 and once as 5000 florins. Ludovico reiterated
that it was Gianfrancesco who was legally obliged to pay off the miscellaneous
debts, but it should be perfectly possible for him to do so from the proceeds of
goods and chattels in his keeping. In a postscript to the same letter Ludovico
added a most interesting breakdown of estimates.

By this reckoning, the total debts amounted to not more than 20,000 ducats.
Such a sum may seem a heavy burden for a cardinal to leave to his heirs, but it
was little beside, say, the figure of 95,000 ducats of debt which Cardinal Pietro
Riario had left behind in 1474—the figure recalled by Girolamo Riario in the
course of a conversation about Cardinal Gonzaga's debts back in November
1483. Indeed, Girolamo had insisted that Francesco's executors should easily be
able to meet these debts, just as he himself had paid off Pietro's, and that there
was no case for supporting an appeal to the pope to waive the obligation imposed
on two of the former cardinal's principal benefices in Mantua, the very obligation—in so far as one of these benefices was the bishopric—which Ludovico
was disclaiming.[119]

In the same letter to Ruffino Gablonetta, Ludovico then gave a most illumina-
ting account of the cardinal's various assets. He set aside the silverware, clothes
and other items left collectively to members of the household, i.e., the things left
in Mantua in the hands of Giovanni Arrivabene. Gianfrancesco Gonzaga, he
assumed, had 4000 ducats' worth of articles in hand, which evidently included
the tapestries; the gems and other valuables were expected easily to realize the
rest of the money needed. The sums which Ludovico quotes are remarkably low.

---

[117] Appendix 3, no. 15.
[118] See above, p. 44.
[119] S. Guidotti to Marchese Federico Gonzaga from Rome, 18 November 1483: ' … Ultimo gli dissi di quello
gravamento havea imposto la Sanctità del Nostro Signore sopra la prepositura e primiceriato di pagare quelli
seimillia ducati, e come se la Sanctità Sua havessi inteso che di beni del patrimonio suo si potessi pagare come
esso Reverendissimo Cardinale grava lo herede, che forsi Sua Sanctità non ge lo haveria concesso, attento che
pocha serà la entrata di quelli benefitii per le guerre e mal ricolti, e lo pregai per parte de la Excellentia Vostra
che mi aiutassi a persuadere a la Sanctità del Nostro Signore che per quella rata desgravassi essi benefitii di
tanto carico. Sua Illustre Signoria molto familiarmente me rispose: "Meser aciprete … a me non pare honesto
far questa dimanda … s'el fessi al senno mio il faria conto ch'el cardinale vivesse anchora dui over tri anni a
pagar questi debiti, perché mi recordo quando morite la bona memoria del mio fratello el si ritrovò debito
nonantacinquemilia ducati, et io per amor suo tra lo mio soldo e provisione e pigni che misi a lo interesso, pagai
in dui anni ogni cosa…"' (ASMn, AG, b. 846, c. 618).

The precious vases and other such objects are quoted as likely to raise 2000 ducats; the books 1000 ducats—a very low sum compared for instance to the 8000 ducats estimated in 1491 as the value of Cardinal Marco Barbo's 500 books;[120] the jewels were said to be worth 2000 ducats, and the gems (for the acquisition of which he says that the cardinal spent 20,000 ducats) were expected to fetch 11,000 ducats. If Ludovico is right in these assessments, it would seem he was implying either that Cardinal Francesco Gonzaga had usually paid too much for everything, or else that the collectors' market was glutted in the summer of 1484, perhaps also depressed by the contemporary insecurity in Rome.[121] Maybe, too, when a large collection came on the market, it was normal for the selling party to sustain losses of up to fifty per cent, whereas the seller of an individual rarity could name whatever price he wanted if the moment was right and a collector's cupidity was aroused sufficiently. Selling prices may have been very fluid; but even if risky, this does not mean that the whole business of collecting was unsound as a form of investment.

In spite of all this optimism, among the largest and most urgent single debts mentioned both in Giovan Pietro Arrivabene's letter of 14 March 1484 and Ludovico Gonzaga's letter of 26 June remained the outstanding loan from the Medici bank.[122] The vital point about this was that some of the gems had been deposited as security against the 3500 ducats borrowed; as noted already, Giovan Pietro Arrivabene had in December taken with him to Rome—among other things— many of these most valuable and portable assets of the deceased cardinal, hoping to realize there the best possible price, since it was stipulated in the will that they should be set against the debts. He had, however, been harrassed for payment by the Rome agents of the Medici bank, who were threatening to take legal proceedings which would incur excommunication for the guarantors of the loan, including Arrivabene himself. Alternatively, they assured him, Lorenzo de' Medici would be interested in buying the gems for a fair price.

In his letter of 14 March Arrivabene does not tell everything about this which he might have done, and more is recorded in recently discovered correspondence between Antonio Tornabuoni in Rome and Lorenzo de' Medici in Florence. This illustrates quite specifically Lorenzo's interest.[123] As early as February Antonio Tornabuoni had been in touch with Arrivabene, and since Agnelli was soon going to pass through Florence, it was expected that he could bring from Rome some of the gems on approval; Lorenzo de' Medici was particularly interested in the six silver trays of mounted cameos and loose intaglios which he had seen previously, perhaps during one of the cardinal's visits to Florence, or he may even have seen some items during his visits when in the cardinal's company at Ferrara and Cremona in February and early March 1483.[124] Meanwhile, it has also emerged that Alfonso Duke of Calabria, who already had one of the best cameos as a

---

[120] See above, p. 108, n. 59.

[121] See Pastor, *Storia dei papi*, II, pp. 569–75.

[122] Appendix 3, nos 10, 15; above, p. 116.

[123] See Brown, 'Lorenzo', *passim* (anticipated in 1983 by the same author's short article 'Questions of provenance', pp. 102–4). Some of the correspondence discovered by Laurie Fusco and Gino Corti is incorporated in Brown's long article of 1989; their essay 'New Documents for Lorenzo de' Medici as a Collector of Antiquities and Rare Objects 1465–92' is forthcoming.

[124] See Table of Itineraries; Lorenzo had arrived at Ferrara in February.

legacy (W 13; I 542), was interested in purchasing other pieces in the collection. According to Tornabuoni, Arrivabene had shown him fourteen of the tablets and told Agnelli to find out what Alfonso's intentions were.[125] Giovan Pietro Arrivabene had tried to arouse Tornabuoni's interest in some of the other articles left behind in Mantua,[126] and there was even a suggestion that if it turned out the value was much greater, Lorenzo might pay off the sums of money which the cardinal owed to the Guild of Bankers as well as to Baccio Ugolini.[127] Arrivabene undertook to send the selected gems on approval to Florence; on his own authority, apparently, he sent a servant with the key to the strong-box and a list (presumably based on his own inventory already mentioned). The loose gems were therefore inspected in Florence, but no purchase was made.[128] Lorenzo had been disappointed not to find an intaglio he particularly fancied, which depicted a scene with four horses (the quadriga); months later, Tornabuoni and Arrivabene were again searching for it in vain.[129]

Not surprisingly, some alarm began to spread in the family. Since Gianfrancesco was insisting that he himself should now have control of the cardinal's remaining assets, it stood to reason that he should try to regain the gems. Ludovico, some of whose letters during the summer of 1484 have been quoted already, wrote from Bracciano on 26 July that he and Giovan Pietro Arrivabene had just had a long consultation with an agent of Gianfrancesco.[130] Arrivabene had agreed to hand over the gems, being only too anxious to release himself personally from the obligation to the Medici bank under the terms of which he faced the dreaded possibility of excommunication. He had, therefore, undertaken to try to gain the bank's agreement to the gems being placed in Ludovico's charge for two months, during which time they hoped that Gianfrancesco could negotiate with the Medici bank to try and reach a satisfactory settlement by other means. Should this not succeed, and should it also transpire that he was not wholly exonerated from the risk of excommunication, Arrivabene would resume the safekeeping of the gems. Two weeks later, on 10 August, Ludovico also wrote to Antonio Tornabuoni,[131] begging him to accept other valuables of the deceased

[125] Antonio Tornabuoni's letters to Lorenzo of 10, 21 February 1484 (ASF, MAP, LV, nos 29, 28); 6, 10, 13, 20, March 1484 (ASF, MAP, LV, nos 7, 15, 37, 357), 26 March (ASF, MAP, CXXXVIII, no. 227) and 31 March 1484 (MAP, XXXIX, no. 205). All but the letter of 21 February (which declares that already 'Il prothonotaio Angniello sarà istato con V[ostra] M[agnificentia]') are in Brown, 'Lorenzo', pp. 92–4. In the letter of 10 March it transpires that Alfonso 'n'aveva viste xiiii tavolette e detto le voleva'.

[126] Antonio Tornabuoni to Lorenzo de' Medici, 13 March 1484: 'Diciemi anchora detto messer Gianpiero che a Mantova sono rimasti cierti altre chose e certi vase, che s'ànno pure a vendere per paghare i debiti di Monsignore' (ASF, MAP, LV, no. 37; Brown, 'Lorenzo', p. 94); in his letter of 20 March (see below), Tornabuoni also mentions that Arrivabene 'm'aveva detto che a Mantova era rimasto non so che vasi belli et altre choxe'. On 24 March (MAP, XXXIX, no. 192A) he assured Lorenzo that Arrivabene would send 'un suo fidato' to Florence 'e tutte quelle chamei e altre cose'.

[127] Antonio Tornabuoni to Lorenzo, 20 March 1484: '...che gli ànno a dare al Arte del Chanbio e ciert'altri di Baccio Ugholini' (ASF, MAP, LXXIII, no. 357); Brown, 'Lorenzo', p. 94.

[128] Tornabuoni's letter of 31 March (ASF, MAP, XXXIX, no. 205); Brown, 'Lorenzo', p. 94.

[129] Letter of Tornabuoni, 1 September 1484: 'sono dipoi istato con messer Gianpiero...non v'abiamo trovato lo 'ntaglio che voi domandate. Èvene bene una pichola, in sulla quale è 4 chavalli, ma non v'è ruote;' also his letter of 9 October (ASF, MAP, XXXIX, nos. 308, 346); Brown, 'Lorenzo', p. 94.

[130] Appendix 3, no. 17; Brown, 'Lorenzo', pp. 95–6.

[131] '...fustive contento de acceptare per modo tante robbe, a computo del credito del bancho, che fussero equivalente per la mitade de tutta la quantitate o circa, e del resto fare aspetto uno anno, absolvendo tamen hora domino Zoan Petro da ugni obligatione e restituendo li camei ad esso oratore' (ASMn, Fondo D'Arco 85, fol. 127); Brown, 'Lorenzo', p. 96.

cardinal to discharge half of the outstanding debt and promising cash to cover the rest of it within one year, and to Arrivabene, assuring him of Gianfrancesco's serious intent to purchase.[132] But Gianfrancesco evidently failed to intervene effectively; and something even more irregular was to happen in October 1484, when Antonio Tornabuoni sent 144 stones to Florence for a second inspection, so that Lorenzo could look for the intaglio with the quadriga;[133] this time it was done without even the knowledge of Arrivabene, who had gone to Mantua in order (so Tornabuoni thought) to discover if the new marchese, Francesco Gonzaga, would buy the gems.

A curious silence regarding the cardinal's estate seems to fall upon the surviving correspondence in the later months of 1484 and throughout 1485. Perhaps this had something to do with the accession as marchese of the young Francesco Gonzaga, or to the fact that Ludovico returned to Mantua at the end of September 1484,[134] and Giovan Pietro Arrivabene returned not long after him,[135] so that all the persons most closely involved were for some while able to communicate more informally on their home ground.

* * *

It is not the purpose of this study to pursue for its own sake the after-history or dispersal of the cardinal's special collections, nor to attempt to trace what became of any other of his assets. Nevertheless, something more can be added, by way of sequel, before returning to the general probems of the inheritance and the unsettled debts.

The papal brief banning further alienation of the cardinal's goods in December 1483 implied that some items had already been sold or given away, and although the sales noted against items in the inventory are not dated, some of these may have taken place in Mantua perhaps as early as November 1483. Although Giovan Pietro Arrivabene had already been planning a sales campaign early in 1484, the correspondence of Ludovico and Gianfrancesco from May of 1484 onwards proves that many items were not yet sold, but there was an expectation this would soon be happening, so at some earlier point the papal prohibition on sales must have been lifted. Perhaps it was at the time that Marchese Federico had been relieved of his responsibility concerning the executors' business, and that Gianfrancesco apparently had come to accept his obligations as the universal heir. Alvise Capra's cryptic signs in the left hand margin of the inventory may also

---

[132] '...per satisfare a lo Illustre Signor Zoan Francesco mio fratello circa'l desiderio de suoa Signoria de havere li camei, e per liberare nui de la obligatione che haveti col bancho de' Medici, cum summa contenteza mia voria voluntieri che la richiesta quale facio ad Antonio Tornabuoni havesse luoco' (ASMn, Fondo d'Arco 85, fols 128–9).

[133] Tornabuoni's letter of 9 October (ASF, MAP, XXXIX, no. 346); Brown, 'Lorenzo', pp. 94–5: Brown comments 'Tornabuoni shiped [sic] to Mantua a leather box containing 103 cornelians and a sack containing another 41', but obviously Tornabuoni sent them to Florence, not Mantua. These items correspond to I 947, 954.

[134] On 10 September Ludovico wrote to Giovanni Arrivabene about his imminent departure from Rome; on 22 September writing from Florence he expressed uncertainty about the protocol for his reception in Mantua as a prototary and bishop-elect; by 9 October he was addressing letters from Mantua (ASMn, Fondo d'Arco 85, fols 155, 158, 166).

[135] Chambers, 'Arrivabene', pp. 423–8. Apart from a mission to Milan in late December, Arrivabene was in Mantua from October 1484 to late February 1485; he then returned to Rome as Mantuan ambassador.

date from this period, and the references (already mentioned) to Federico as the deceased marchese. In two of his letters of 10 August from Bracciano, Ludovico referred to a sum of money either in the Gaddi bank or with Giovan Pietro Arrivabene, representing the proceeds of *robbe vendute* out of the cardinal's estate; this was the balance after the salaries still owed to the household had been paid and was believed to be about 300 ducats, the sum which Ludovico himself claimed he needed for his journey back to Mantua.[136]

Close relatives and members of the cardinal's household were among the purchasers. Gianfrancesco Gonzaga stated in January 1487 that he had bought some of the cardinal's posessions left in Mantua, all for a fair price;[137] these may include some of the articles which he took from Giovanni Arrivabene's custody at the end of May 1484,[138] including tapestries, the proceeds from sale of which were earmarked in the will (W 28) for the benefit of the chamberlains of the household.[139] Some of these and also some books listed in Gianfrancesco's own post-mortem inventory of 1496 almost certainly were among the cardinal's former possessions.[140] But Gianfrancesco did not obtain or retain custody of everything, for in November 1486 he had mentioned that the executors had charge of the remainder of the cardinal's goods.[141]

There seems to be little doubt that Ludovico, thanks to the friendly offices of Giovan Pietro Arrivabene, acquired various items in the summer of 1484; one example recorded in the inventory is a large silver *bochale* with gilded handles (I 82); indeed it may be that some of the cardinal's possessions had been stored by Arrivabene in the house Ludovico rented in Rome. The correspondence between Ludovico and Ruffino Gablonetta refers to his desire for books to read during his sojourn at Bracciano, and some of the books mentioned seem to correspond very closely to books in the cardinal's library; if not those books themselves, they might have been copies previously made from them.

Ludovico particularly wanted two books of geomancy, one large, one small: according to the inventory, the cardinal had no less than four books on the subject, one—copied by Sanvito—specified as large (I 893), and another—in the hand of Giuliano da Viterbo—specified as smaller (I 894), as well as another smaller one (I 897), and one which was borrowed (I 896). He also asked for the *Bosadrello* (cf. I 823), and two books on dreams (I 757, 758).[142] He reproached Ruffino in a subsequent letter for not forwarding the large book on geomancy and added more requests; for a Hyginus (cf. I 883, 887), a Vitruvius (not represented in the inventory) and 'lo canzoniere nostro', which is more probably a song-book than the collected verse of Petrarch, although the compound title had already

---

[136] Appendix 3, no. 19. He wrote similarly to Gianfrancesco Cataneo (ASMn, Fondo d'Arco 85, fols 131–2).

[137] Appendix 3, no. 24.

[138] Appendix 3, no. 13.

[139] See also Ludovico's reference to the tapestries in Appendix 3, no. 18.

[140] BCG, FMD, b. 23. Some of the items most clearly identifiable have been cited in notes below items in cardinal's inventory. A few other miscellaneous items, listed in 1496, must undoubtedly have been Francesco's, e.g., 'due bacine grande laborate a cistello cum l'arma del Cardinale cum dui bronzini grandi' (fol. 16ᵛ), but in most cases it is impossible to be so certain of the provenance. A description of Gianfrancesco's inventory is being prepared by Clifford Brown.

[141] '…hanno tutta la robba ne le mane' (Appendix 3, no. 23).

[142] Ludovico Gonzaga to Ruffino Gablonetta, Bracciano, 13 June 1484: 'Le turche nostre tutte vogliamo presso di nui qui. Mandaticele adonque quanto più presto sia possibile, e cum esse li duoi libri de geomantia, lo grande e lo picolo, lo Bosadrello da li dati e li duoi libri da li Insomnii' (ASP, AGG, b. 41/3, reg. 1, fols 178ᵛ–9ʳ).

been used in an early printed edition. Ludovico added that he would like to have some other books for light reading and for study, suited to his place of recreation at Bracciano.[143] Ruffino still failed to send the right books, and Ludovico wrote again with some irritation; though the text of his letter is ambiguous, the description he gives seems to refer to the book of geomancy rather than the 'canzoniere' (specifying, to clarify his request, that 'the small one was bound in red leather and in script almost like that of Sanvito').[144] Although Ludovico had to apologize about the 'canzoniere' since he had in fact left it in Mantua,[145] in the end he got the books he wanted.[146]

As to other items which passed into Ludovico's possession—apart from the direct bequests—he apologized to his niece Chiara (who was in fact only five years his junior) that he did not have any of the gems, which were Gianfrancesco's property, but he did have a number of antique medals, which he would divide with her and her husband Gilbert de Montpensier.[147] It is unfortunate that he was not more specific about which medals he had, though some years later he mentioned in a letter that he was sending to Gianfrancesco the medal with the cardinal's own portrait on it, i.e., the famous one by Sperandio,[148] and regretted that he was not himself eminent enough to be commemorated in this fashion,[149] overlooking the fact that a medal had been struck in his own honour in 1475.[150] Gianfrancesco's inventory of 1496 records that he possibly had two copies of the medal of the cardinal.[151]

For his part, meanwhile, Giovan Pietro Arrivabene certainly bought some of the cardinal's books; the marginal notes in the inventory which record his initials do not necessarily imply that these books he had taken to Rome all passed into

---

[143] Letter of 24 June 1484: 'Lo libro grande de giomantia non ne haveti mandato secundum ve richiedemmo. Mandatice quello, lo canzoniere nostro, lo Vetruvio, lo Higeno e qualche altro libretto che vi parà essere apto e conveniente per questo luoco da piacere e da studiare, qualche operetta piacevole e delectevole' (ibid., fol. 192ᵛ).

[144] Letter of 29 June 1484: 'Lo libro di giomantia quale ce haveti mandato non è quella che nui volevamo, ne anche lo canzoniere. Questo è di littera buona e coperto de raxo alexandrino, quello è grande, né ha tanti puncti quanto ha l'altro chi è picolo, et è coperto de corame rosso e scritto de la littera quasi conforme a quella de Sanvito. Dicemo però lo grande e non lo picolo, perché non credesti de haverlo mandato' (ASMn, Fondo d'Arco 85, fol. 3).

[145] Letter of 4 July 1484 (ibid., fol. 14).

[146] Letter of 7 July 1484 (ibid., fol. 21).

[147] Ludovico to Chiara Gonzaga, Mantua, 21 January 1485: 'Rincresceme e duole summamente che io non habia camei da satisfare a la richiesta de Vostra prefata Signoria. Quelli de la bona memoria del Reverendissimo Monsignor Cardinale sono de lo Illustre Signor Zoan Francesco suo barba e mio fratello. Io non ne ho alcuno, et da vendere non se ne trovano. De le medaglie che ho, quale sono puoche, a la tornata de lo Signor Conte suo consorte gli ne mandarò la parte suoa, e farò da buon fratello che partirò per mitade. Voria bene haverne assai e belle, perché tanto più vontieri farìa la divisione. Acceptarà la Signoria Vostra lo buono animo mio, e non risguardarà a la quantitate né qualitate de esse medaglie. Pregola bene sia contenta de haverme excusato de li camei, de' quali veramente non ne appare veruno, come ho dicto, da vendere' (ASMn, Fondo D'Arco 85, fol. 365); Brown, 'Lorenzo', p. 96.

[148] See above, p. 85; also Figs 5–6.

[149] Bishop-Elect Ludovico to Gianfrancesco Gonzaga, Ostiano, 13 August 1488: 'mando alla Signoria Vostra la medaglia della bona memoria di Monsignore, e questa è unica de quante ne habbi. Io non sono anchora stato di tanta auctorità che me hanno sculpite in metallo come li altri, e perhò ne son per hora privato di quelle' (ASP, AGG, b. 41/3, reg. 3, unnumbered pages).

[150] See above, p. 92 n. 323.

[151] 'Una altra bolza cum medaye de diverse stampe de ramo…et ultra due altre medalie a la stampa del cardinale Mantuano' (BCG, FMD, b. 23, fol. 9v). However, this may just mean two of the cardinal's medals.

his own library, but he recorded the price he paid for one book,[152] and he wrote his name in two others.[153]

Another rare instance of the recorded selling of some miscellaneous items from the inventory is found at a much later date, when the executors or guardians of the 'Cardinalino' decided to realize cash on two of the items bequeathed to him. One was the so-called piece of unicorn or, rather, narwhal whale horn (W 21; I 608), about which Ludovico wrote to Giovan Pietro Arrivabene's secretary in January 1489, to say that it was being sent to him in Rome. Ludovico may have been keeping this large object himself or else had recently retrieved it from the Cardinalino's household; he was careful to send it in one piece, as breaking it into two would reduce the value, and had entrusted it to the Medici bank's agents in Florence as the safest carriers.[154] Cardinal La Balue of Angers had expresssed interest in acquiring it, but a better offer, 500 ducats, had been made by a Venetian merchant. Ludovico admitted he would have liked to buy it himself, but could only have offered 100 ducats; presumably Arrivabene agreed to the sale. The other item to be sold was the crimson tapestry bed-hanging (*sparaviero da letto*: W 21; I 461). As late as May 1490, Marchese Francesco Gonzaga himself was negotiating to buy this, for a price estimated by his aunts Antonia and Caterina Gonzaga. Arrivabene understood the price offered to be 250 ducats; he expressed some uncertainty about the rightfulness of this transaction, but hoped the cash could be well employed for the beneficiary.[155] In fact the marchese had first quoted the sum on offer as 200 ducats and later reduced it to 150 ducats.[156]

Of all the assets assigned for sale to meet debts, the gems remained the most marketable and sought after. At the end of 1485 Marchese Francesco at last expressed his serious wish to buy them.[157] Early in January 1486 Arrivabene wrote that the period of the pledge to the Medici bank had now expired.[158] Apparently Lorenzo de' Medici, who had been ill, was still willing to buy some of the items, and a tentative approach had been made through Baccio Ugolini; but he had only offered 4100 ducats, which the executors considered too little. Arrivabene therefore urged the marchese to buy them for himself at that price, so that they could be kept in the family; he only needed to pay off the debt to the Medici bank, i.e., he needed to find 3500 ducats in cash, and the executors could wait for the rest of the price to be agreed. Francesco concurred, but seems to have done nothing more about it, perhaps having difficulty in raising the 3500

---

[152] Filippo Barbieri, *Discordantiae…Sibyllarum*, Rome (Giovan Filippo de Lignamine), 1481, in BAV, Incun. IV. 29. This is probably I 899. Arrivabene wrote inside that it cost 5 *carleni*. See Farenga, 'Le prefazioni', p. 410.

[153] I 812, and the Greek Gospels, not in the inventory: MS BL, Harley 5790.

[154] Appendix 3, no. 28; there is a similar letter to Bernardino Castigati, also one to Angelo Tovaglia asking him to pass on the horn to Onofrio Tornabuoni, and another to O. Tornabuoni, all dated 12 January 1489 (ASP, AGG, b. 41/3, reg. 3).

[155] G. P. Arrivabene to Marchese Francesco Gonzaga, Rome, 15 May 1490 (ASMn, AG, b. 848, c. 287), quoted in Chambers, 'Cardinalino', p. 9 n. 33.

[156] Marchese Francesco Gonzaga to Ludovico Gonzaga, 20 April (also to Giovan Pietro Arrivabene), and 29 May 1490 (ASMn, AG, b. 2903, lib. 134, fol. 46^v; lib. 135, fol. 37^v).

[157] Letter to G. P. Arrivabene, Mantua, 11 December 1485 (ASMn, AG, b. 2902, lib. 126, cc. 56^v–7^r; Brown, 'Lorenzo', p. 96).

[158] Appendix 3, no. 20 (Brown, 'Lorenzo', p. 96). This and the following letter from Arrivabene are of such importance in clarifying the story that I have retained them in spite of recent publication by Brown.

ducats.[159] Two months later Arrivabene still urged him to act and tried to encourage him with the idea that Giovanni Tornabuoni did not want his nephew Lorenzo to have these valuables;[160] but he awaited Francesco's instructions in vain.[161]

Arrivabene revealed more in his letter of 14 February to the marchese.[162] It will be remembered from the correspondence early in February 1484 that some of the cardinal's valuables had been pawned to a Milanese merchant in Rome;[163] Arrivabene now let it be known that the executors had pledged three of the tablets of cameos, those mounted on jasper and prasma (I 569–71), with the Milanese merchant, against repayment of another debt of the deceased cardinal, this one for 1100 ducats. These tablets he described enthusiastically: the jasper was like a mirror in which you could see your face reflected, he told Francesco, quoting the valuations for each plaque and every individual cameo. Marchese Francesco expressed more interest in acquiring these items, hoping to finance the deal by means of certain assignments or credits which he was claiming from the Sforza government.[164] It seems to have foundered on this point, just when the marchese had been convinced by Arrivabene's argument that Gonzaga family honour required he should have these mounted cameos in his possession.[165] He was still pursuing the matter in the middle of May 1486, after the Milanese merchant had procrastinated; but these gems presumably stayed in the latter's hands, while the others remained with the Medici.[166]

---

[159] Marchese Francesco Gonzaga to G. P. Arrivabene, 21 January 1486: 'dicemovi in resposta che nui siamo contenti torre essi camei ligati in tavole et quelle altre robbe depositate per 4100 ducati offerti dal magnifico Lorenzo, al qual nui vederemo provedere per il credito del bancho di 3500 ducati, parendone conveniente et anche honesto che nui siamo preferiti e del pretio compiaciuti che altri voleno dare, ad ciò che le cose remangano in casa' (ASMn, AG, b. 2902, lib. 126, fol. 71ʳ⁻ᵛ); Brown, 'Lorenzo', p. 97.

[160] G. P. Arrivabene to Marchese Francesco Gonzaga, Rome, 5 March 1486: '…se gli serà parso de mandare qua la provisione di ducati 3500, o darli qualche ordine a contentarli, se attenderà ad tuore le cose in nui per farne la voluntà de Vostra Signoria, la qual etiam del resto fin a la summa de 4100. Credo facilmente haverà cum Baccio Ugolini ugni commodità del tempo per li suoi 600. E li executori in questo ne faranno totalmente la voluntà de Vostra Signoria. El più forte è de provedere per principio a li 3500, li quali etiam attengono principalmente a Zohanne Tornabuoni, zio del magnifico Lorenzo, el qual non ha mai visto voluntiera che Lorenzo li piglii. Et harà molto più caro lo contentassimo del denaro che che la vendità andasse inanti a qualunque precio se fusse, forsi dubitando che Lorenzo non la facesse seco troppo a la domestica…' (ASMn, AG, b. 847, c. 507); Brown, 'Lorenzo', p. 98, with the last sentence omitted.

[161] In a letter of 26 March 1486, Arrivabene wrote that he was still awaiting instructions to proceed (ASMn, AG, b. 847, c. 523).

[162] Appendix 3, no. 22 (Brown, 'Lorenzo', p. 97).

[163] See above, p. 114.

[164] In a letter of 11 March the marchese instructed Arrivabene 'che quando esso mercadante volia piliare de la assignatione che habiamo a Milano per lo servito nostro, li attenderemo et tuoremole'(ASMn, AG, b. 2902, lib. 126, fol. 90ᵛ). Arrivabene had gone in vain to Milan in the winter of 1484–5 concerning this credit (Chambers, 'Arrivabene', pp. 424–7), and there are letters of Zaccaria Saggi and the merchant Niccolò Magiolini about unsuccesful attempts in March 1486 to raise money on the strength of it (ASMn, AG, b. 1629, cc. 180, 313).

[165] Marchese Francesco Gonzaga to Zaccaria Saggi, Ferrara, 23 April 1486: 'Essendo li dì passati per lettere de messer Zoan Petro Arrivabene avisati che in mane de certo mercadante milanese in Roma se retrovavano tre tavole de disape adornate de camei, che furono de la bona memoria del reverendissimo Monsignore Cardinale, nostro barba defuncto, consignate a lui per uno suo credito haveva cum la heredità, e intrassimo in pensiere de haverle ad ciò che, essendo pur cosa bella et honorevile, remanessero in la casa… Hora, messer Zoan Piero ne risponde dicto mercadante scrivere ad uno suo fratello nominato Evangelista Arzone, che da nui intenda la conditione de queste assignatione' (b. 2902, lib. 127, fols 13ᵛ⁻14ʳ); Brown, 'Lorenzo', p. 98; also Saggi's reply of 28 April (ASMn, AG, b. 1629, c. 208).

[166] Marchese Francesco Gonzaga to G. P. Arrivabene, Gonzaga, 18 May 1486: 'scrivessimo a Milano per quelle tre tavole ornate de camei che furono de la bona memoria del Reverendissimo Monsignore cardinale nostro barba. Ne rispouse Zacharia nostro oratore havere parlato cum el mercadante là e informato de la

It is clear that in the world of connoisseurs, rumours went on flying around wildly as to the whereabouts and purchasability of the cardinal's collections. Even King Matthias Corvinus of Hungary wanted to put in a bid in 1488, though his wife Beatrice d'Aragona assumed, first, that the marchese had possession of all the cardinal's valuable objects; then, she acquired incomplete information about their being offset against debts and silverware taken by members of the household; finally, she heard something about the cameos being in the hands of Lorenzo de' Medici.[167] Eleonora's reply of 30 April was discouraging about the medals and tantalizing about the cameos;[168] but on 13 October she explained that they were not in Lorenzo de' Medici's hands, nor did the Medici bank have the freedom to dispose of them;[169] indeed, Giovanni Tornabuoni had sent the cameos back to Rome.[170] It may be that Lorenzo had, after all, acquired just a few of the medals and intaglios some time earlier, and possibly a couple of the tapestries, but remained unwilling to commit himself to the larger consignment of gems.[171]

In 1488 hopes were again raised that Gianfrancesco Gonzaga would buy back the gems, and Baccio Ugolini acted as intermediary.[172] Arrivabene still had a threat of excommunication hanging over him for non-fulfilment of the pledge to the Medici bank;[173] but by January 1489 the executors, who were said to have accepted some payments for their co-operation, seem to have been ready to surrender the right of redemption. However, four months grace was allowed just in case Gianfrancesco still wanted to buy in the gems.[174] That they were held in Rome meant that they were not confiscated with other Medici possessions in Florence after the revolution of November 1494 which explains why Piero de'

conditione de quelli nostri assigni, disse volerne dare aviso al fratello a Roma. Attenderemo in che se risolveranno' (b. 2902, lib. 127, fol. 25^r).

[167] Letter of Beatrice to her sister Eleonora d'Este, Vienna 20 February 1488, asking her as the marchese's sister-in-law to try to arrange a purchase of the 'bellissime medaglie d'argento et d'oro antiquissime, et similmente camei, pur bellissimi, quali forono del Cardinale de Mantua morto' (ASMod, AEC, Principi Esteri [Ungheria], b. 1622/3), in Brown, 'Lorenzo', p. 98. The rest of this correspondence in the Este archives, originally published in Hungary, is also included by Brown.

[168] '…havea una grande quantità de medaglie de argento et mettallo, et havendo, dopoi la sua morte, lassato molti debiti, et potissimum de li soi familiari, loro tolseno in pagamento quelle erano de argento et le altre se distribuiteno, in modo che non se ne ritrova alcuna al presente. Sua Reverendissima Signoria havea etiam de digni et bellissimi camaini et in grande numero…valeno circa da 14 in 18 mila ducati…sono de le cose de Papa Paulo, et in perfectione, secundo mi è facto intendere' (Brown, 'Lorenzo', pp. 98–9).

[169] '[Lorenzo]…dixe che'l non erano in mane sue, ma de Giovanni Tornaboni, et cussì Sua Maestà ge parlete a dicto Zoanne, il quale dixe, ch'el non li havea liberi, et che prima bisognava fare a Roma certi protesti per haverli expediti…' (Brown, 'Lorenzo', p. 99).

[170] Letter of Lorenzo de' Medici to Giovanni Lanfredini, 14 October 1488: 'Giovanni Tornabuoni ha rimandato costì più dì fa tucti e chammei di Monsignore di Mantua' (ASF, MAP, LIX, no. 24), printed in Del Lungo, *Florentia*, p. 301 n. 2; Brown,'Lorenzo', p. 100.

[171] Laurie Fusco kindly drew my attention to the letters of Onofrio Tornabuoni to Lorenzo de' Medici, 10 January 1487: 'Doverete avere auto quelle poche medaglie o intagli di Mantova' (ASF, MAP, LII, no. 21), and 20 January 1487: 'credo che Antonio del Palagio vi chonpiacerà di quelle medaglie d'argento' (ASF, MAP, LII, no. 25). On the tapestries see I 201.

[172] Ludovico Gonzaga to Baccio Ugolini, 26 February 1488: '…ma ch'el voria per prius le robbe in le mane et la vendità di esse dal bancho come di cose proprie, et non come de cose de la heredità del cardinale' (ASP, AGG, b. 41/3, reg. 1, cc. 11^v–12^r), Brown,'Lorenzo', p. 99; also letters to B. Castigati, 9 September, and to G. P. Arrivabene, 13 September 1488, in the same register.

[173] Ludovico Gonzaga to Guizardo Biretta, Ostiano, 22 August 1488: 'Ne scriveno Baccio et Bernardino in nome de messer Zoanpetro che vogliamo operare ch'el signore nostro fratello poni hormai provisione alla vendita de camei, perché a lui è menezato de farlo excommunicare, instando el bancho de Medici alla satisfacione volia dello debito' (ASP, AGG, b. 41/3, reg. 3).

[174] Letter of Onofrio Tornabuoni to Lorenzo de' Medici, 21 January 1489 in ASF, MAP, XXVI, no. 513; Brown, 'Lorenzo', p. 100.

Medici in 1496 was able to raise a loan from Agostino Chigi by repledging the objects deposited by Cardinal Gonzaga's executors.[175] These valuables were now in the hands of several different merchants, who were themselves raising credit on them. In 1497–8 Marchese Francesco Gonzaga was at last trying to buy back the lot, and by April 1498 a deal with Onofrio Tornabuoni was proposed whereby payments would be made in five yearly instalments of 1000 ducats; the gems were meanwhile to be deposited with Ludovico Agnelli.[176] But Onofrio, who may have slightly exaggerated what was at stake and how much of it originated from Paul II's collection,[177] as months passed became exasperated with the slowness of his agent in Mantua; eventually this scheme also failed.

* * *

It is clear that much remained to be done. At some point, probably in 1486, Gianfrancesco Gonzaga and the executors appointed an agent or procurator, Ludovico Cipata, the cardinal's former *spenditore* (W 27), to act on their behalf in collecting moneys and discharging debts,[178] for more creditors kept on emerging. Marchese Francesco Gonzaga also re-entered the scene early in 1486, as though reactivating that clause of the will by which his father had been entrusted with keeping a watch on its administration (W 43). He sent a letter to Ludovico Agnelli, as one of the executors, in support of the claim by the cardinal's chamberlain Carlo Canale, who also had a specific guarantee of non-liability for any debts undertaken on behalf of the cardinal (W 40).[179]

The marchese meanwhile reminded Agnelli that it was laid down in the will that once the debts had been paid, most of the goods of the cardinal had to be divided among the members of the household (W 28). He wrote, too, in support of a claim being pressed by the Genoese bank of the Centurioni,[180] which still

---

[175] Brown, 'Questions of Provenance', p. 104, pointed in 1983 to 'grave errors' in the transcriptions of the list recording this loan (MS BAV, Miscell. Chigi R.V.e.) in Cugnoni, *Chigi*, pp. 114–15, followed in Dacos et al., *Il tesoro*, pp. 125–6; cf. the rather different version printed by Müntz, *Les Collections*, pp. 105–6. Correct transcriptions, including the text of the agreement of 17 May 1496 with Agostino Chigi, are provided in Brown, 'Lorenzo', pp. 88–90. Brown refers (ibid., pp. 90–1) to an 'iron mirror' instead of the 'spechio d'argento' as printed; the inventory reveals that it was not made of silver alone and that the surface was of polished steel (I 567). This mirror and a jasper tondo were evidently the items deposited with the Medici bank in addition to the *tavole* of gems.

[176] Marchese Francesco Gonzaga to Ludovico Agnelli, Mantua, 25 April 1498 (ASMn, AG, b. 2908, lib. 160, c. 69^{r-v}), printed in Brown, 'Lorenzo', p. 101, and to Giorgio Brognolo, Marmirolo, 22 August 1498, he announced this arrangement made with Onofrio Tornabuoni (ASMn b. 2908, lib. 160, fol. 67^{r-v}); Brown, 'Lorenzo', p. 101.

[177] That is, in the passage of a letter to his man in Mantua, Donato Bonsi, Rome, 1 December 1498: '…si truova gioie assai, diamanti, balasci e simile, ma non si troverrebbe già in tutto el mondo simile chose chome sono queste, né credo se puotessino pagare sì grande prezzo che esse non vaglino molto più; costorono a Papa Pagholo un tesoro' (ASMn b. 852 [unnumbered]); Brown, 'Lorenzo', pp. 86, 101.

[178] In November 1486 and March 1488 he was described as the mandatory of the executors (Appendix 3, nos. 25, 27); in September 1491 he himself recorded that he was on a commission from Gianfrancesco to the executors (Appendix 3, no. 29); in a letter of Gianfrancesco Gonzaga of 7 March 1494 he was still 'procuratore electo de li executori testamentarii' (ASMn, AG, b. 1800, c. 329).

[179] Appendix 3, no. 21.

[180] Marchese Francesco Gonzaga to the executors, Marmirolo, 4 April 1486: 'Li Centurioni mercadanti zenovesi ne fanno intendere restano havere de la heredità de la felice memoria del Reverendissimo Monsigniore cardinale nostro come appare per una cedula a loro facta del credito…' (ASMn, AG, b. 2902, lib. 127, fol. 3^{r}).

preoccupied Ludovico Agnelli over a year later.[181] There was also a claim for 1000 ducats that the Venetian Signoria was making as the corporate heir of the *condottiere* Bartolomeo Colleoni. This, so it likewise transpires in a letter of the marchese, was the residue of a loan or series of loans to the value of 6000 ducats, granted many years earlier, which had been underwritten for the cardinal by Marchese Ludovico Gonzaga and now implicated his grandson.[182] Gianfrancesco Gonzaga also referred to this claim in letters written in the winter of 1486–7. In November he was able to insist that the obligation fell upon the marchese, even if the money had to be found from those revenues of the bishopric set aside for the debts. Evidently, Ludovico Cipata had discovered that Marchese Francesco had inherited various debts owed by Marchese Ludovico to the bishopric of Mantua.[183]

Cipata's report, or a copy of it which he addressed to Marchese Francesco, itemizes the moneys owed on account by his grandfather as a lessee of episcopal lands from 1469 onwards.[184] Gianfrancesco therefore notified his nephew, the marchese, that he himself certainly had no obligation beyond what was specifically laid down in the will and that the rest was up to the executors to resolve. In a subsequent letter to the marchese,[185] Gianfrancesco dismissed the latter's argument that because the cardinal had paid off 500 of the 1000 ducats owing to the heirs of Colleoni, and his manager Carlo da Rodiano had had an obligation to pay the rest, he was not liable. Giovan Pietro Arrivabene, back in Mantua on business of the executors, was together with Cipata going to explain in more detail how it was that the marchese owed the bishopric about 1600 ducats. Gianfrancesco ended by tactfully advising the marchese to pay up, so that both would be quit of the matter—not, he again added, that he himself had any liability whatsoever. He seems to have won the argument on principle, because Marchese Francesco sent a letter to Venice the following summer promising that 500 ducats would be sent within a week and the rest shortly afterwards.[186]

Gianfrancesco still could not be free of these cares, however. From all sides the claims continued to be referred to him. There was for instance the claim from the

---

[181] L. Agnelli to Marchese Francesco Gonzaga, 12 September 1487, concerning his attempt to raise a loan for the marchese, in which Domenico Centurione was involved as a surety: 'me ha facto intendere che quando io li facesse pagare ducati 400 quali lui deviva havere della heredità della bona memoria del Reverendissimo Cardinale di Mantua, lui se asectariva ad servirce' (ASMn, AG, b. 847, c. 687).

[182] Marchese Francesco Gonzaga to the executors, 19 April 1486: 'l'habiamo fatta investigare per trarne li conti, et in fine retroviamo essere debito de bona memoria del Reverendissimo Monsignor cardinale nostro barba defuncto, el quale li resta per ducati mille et a principio furono ducati VI^m prestati dal dicto quondam signor Bartholomeo a Sua Signoria cum obligatione dal Illustrissimo quondam Signor nostro avo…ne doleria che mo nui dovessimo essere li pagatori' (ASMn, AG, b. 2902, lib. 127, fols 11^{v}12^r); cf. above, p. 47.

[183] Appendix 3, no. 23.

[184] Cipata to Marchese Francesco, 16 October 1486: 'esendo io Lodovico Cipata mandato da canto di qua da li Reverendi e Magnifici executori testamentarii de la bona memoria del Reverendissimo Monsignor Cardinale barbano di Quella, a vedere e saldare ogni conto pertinente a la heredate di quella, tra le quale aritrovo Vostra Illustrissima Signoria debitrice per resto de le infrascripte anotate partite de libre sedecemiglia seicento e tre soldi sei piccoli 9…' (ASMn, AG, b. 2434, c. 186); cf. above, p. 40. This total represents the balance reached after Cipata had deducted considerable sums which in turn the cardinal had owed to his father.

[185] Appendix 3, no. 24.

[186] Marchese Francesco Gonzaga to the doge, Marmirolo, 13 June 1487: ' … Neque id profecto mea provenit culpa, cum nonnulli debitores Reverendissimi quondam Cardinalis patrui mei qui persolvere tenebantur rem in hanc usque diem distulerint, quod mihi gravissima fuit. Sed ab ipsis nunc quingenti ducati exacti, quos ad sex dies enumerandos istuc transmittam; reliquum debita ita a me procurabitur ut brevi integra fiat solutio…'(ASMn, AG, b. 2902, lib. 129, fol. 70^v).

emperor that 1000 ducats was owing for the legitimization granted to the cardinal's son about ten years previously.[187] In December 1487 Gianfrancesco wrote to the marchese about a loan the cardinal had had from the archbishop of Split, the claim for which he had passed on to the executors.[188] On this occasion, however, he acknowledged that he had had some goods of the cardinal (*certe robbe mobile*) in his own possession, and knowing that the executors wanted to get their hands on these and sell them to raise money, he had sent them to Rome; the executors had promised not to get rid of any items without first telling him, but they had in fact gone ahead and told him he had no right to tie their hands in any way. It is not clear whether this had happened recently or at some earlier stage; in any case, Gianfrancesco declared that he had then washed his hands of any further obligation, except what was laid down in the will, and had told the pope and cardinals it was not within their power to lay any such obligations upon him. He suggested that Cipata could go to Rome to sort things out, but this could only be with the marchese's permission. (It was in this letter that he insisted that all he had bought himself had been properly paid for.)

In February 1488 Gianfrancesco again urged that Cipata should be allowed to go to Rome and get the executors consent to deal with outstanding payments.[189] He repeated this a month later, denying a rumour spread about by various former members of the deceased cardinal's household that Cipata had embezzled money and fled.[190] One of these, Carletto Franzoni, was pressing—so it further emerges in a letter from Agnelli, five years later—for a claim of 1000 ducats and trying to get it offset against money which allegedly the cardinal had been owed in Mantua.[191] At the same time a serious allegation was made by Ludovico Gonzaga, who wanted an *anconetta*, or small religious painting, which had belonged to the cardinal (perhaps one of the two noted in I 598). Cipata had told the master of Ludovico's household, Cristoforo Arrivabene, that his uncle Giovan Pietro had taken it to Rome. Ludovico refused to believe this, threateningly reminded Cipata that he was owed many hundreds of ducats from the cardinal's inheritance and insisted that Cipata himself had the *anconetta* and should hand it over.[192] In November 1490 Gianfrancesco again defended Cipata, who was unable to leave Mantua because of a pending legal case and urged that this should be expedited since the executors had need of him in Rome.[193]

---

[187] Marchese Francesco to Gianfrancesco Gonzaga, Marmirolo, 17 April 1488 (ASMn, AG, b. 2903, lib. 131, fol. 43ʳ); Chambers, 'Cardinalino', p. 7 nn. 18, 31.

[188] Appendix 3, no. 25. This may refer to a loan from Lorenzo Zane, formerly Paul II's treasurer and archbishop of Split (until 1473), who had died in Rome in 1485 (see Weiss, 'Lorenzo Zane').

[189] Gianfrancesco to Marchese Francesco Gonzaga, Bozzolo 18 February 1488, postscript: 'Intendo che la Excellentia Vostra ha facto liberare Lodovico Cipata. La prego adonque gli sia etiam licentia de andarsene a Roma, perché non ha auctorità de pagar alcuno senza licentia di executori, ma bene de scodere e renderne conto' (ASMn, AG, b. 1800, c. 147). A papal brief addressed to the archpriest (Guidotti) of Mantua cathedral, dated 26 February 1489, urged him to enforce payment of the outstanding legacies 'ad pias causas' (ASDMn, Fondo Mensa Vescovile, Pergamene, b. 3, no. 64).

[190] Letter of 26 March 1488 in Appendix 3, no. 27.

[191] L. Agnelli to Marchese Francesco Gonzaga, Rome, 20 March 1493, in Appendix 3, no. 30.

[192] Appendix 3, no. 26; also Ludovico to Cristoforo Arrivabene, Sabbioneta, 1 March 1488: 'sapiamo certo che lui l'ha'(ASP, AGG, b. 41/3, reg. 2, fol. 38ʳ⁻ᵛ).

[193] Gianfrancesco Gonzaga to Isabella d'Este, Bozzolo, 2 November 1490: 'Lodovico Cipata ha assettate multe cose nanti al magnifico consilio di Vostra Excellentia. Gli resta d'essere impedito da uno Jo. Francesco da Ripalta per dinari per havere levati certi conti, come a Quella notificarà, e dovendo transferirse, richiesto da li prefati executori a Roma, prego la Signoria Vostra gli piacia de committere al prefato suo consilio che voglino

Cipata complained in September 1491 that the four executors were enjoying powerful protection which enabled them to avoid paying off the debts, particularly an outstanding portion of the claim by the executors of Colleoni.[194] The liberation of the estate of Bigarello from the *prepositura*, that early provision of the will intended to benefit Francesco 'Cardinalino' (W 5), was still in 1491 a matter for dispute between Gianfrancesco and Protonotary Sigismondo Gonzaga.[195] Sigismondo threatened to appropriate Bigarello and its revenues, notwithstanding the bequest to Francesco 'Cardinalino'; Gianfrancesco insisted that his nephew was in the wrong.[196] For years the legal knots went on tightening. Late in 1492 Gianfrancesco asked the marchese to appoint a professional judge in support of Cipata, so that he could act with more authority,[197] but matters continued to drag on.[198]

* * *

By the 1490s it must have looked rather unlikely that a final settlement would ever be reached. The most active of the executors, Giovan Pietro Arrivabene, was appointed in 1491 to the bishopric of Urbino where he died in 1504; the residual heir, Gianfrancesco Gonzaga, died in 1496, leaving a will rather more generous *ad pias causas* (at least in Bozzolo) than was that of his elder brother, the cardinal.[199] An entry at the end of the inventory made after Gianfrancesco's death suggests that not all the outstanding expenses and claims on the cardinal's estate had yet been settled, the payment to the *prepositura* for the liberation of Bigarello being among them.[200] Maybe those holding on to assets as pledges simply kept

summarie ultimare questa differentia et non tenirlo in tempo a ciò ch'el possa transferirse como ho decto a Roma' (ASMn, AG, b. 1800, c. 208).

[194] Appendix 3, no. 29.

[195] The contentions of both parties, with details of income from 1483 to 1491, are set down in an undated declaration by Benedetto Tosabecci. Gianfrancesco claimed he was owed rather than owing a substantial sum, in view of the late marchese's debt for the leasing of Quistello from the *prepositura*; Sigismondo meanwhile claimed 1014 ducats 58 soldi as income to which he was entitled, 1484–91 (BCG, FDM, b. 15, fasc. 6).

[196] Chambers, 'Cardinalino', p. 10; Ludovico wrote to Tosabecci from Quingentole on 14 June 1491 that Gianfrancesco was 'assai difficile e renitente alla satisfactione de la parte sua…havendo el protonotario riscuosso ducati seicento da Sant'Andrea, quali pervenevano a la heredità…lo signore mio fratello voria si compensassero neli denari ch'el debe exborsare, et poi provedere al resto. Lo protonotario sta forte, dicendo esser liberato da certo breve impetrato, et hinc pendent omnes difficultates' (ASP, AGG, b. 41/4, reg. 6).

[197] Gianfrancesco Gonzaga to Marchese Francesco Gonzaga, Bozzolo, 31 December 1492: '…perché per li reverendi executori del prefato Reverendissimo Monsignor Cardinale hereditarii et per me più anni passati è stato electo et constituito per procuratore de dicta heredità il presente latore Ludovico Cipata per ricavare da chi resta havere la dicta, et fare rendere conto de rebus administrationis et poi per satisfare a qualunque è creditore, prego la Excellentia Vostra per ogni rispecto voglia dare uno iudice o comissario a dicto Ludovico…et accadendo de havere recurso a la prefata per le executione de dicte cause, Quella se digni de haverlo per raccomandato' (ASMn, AG, b. 1800, c. 237).

[198] E.g., Gianfrancesco to Marchese Francesco Gonzaga, Bozzolo 7 March 1494 (ASMn, AG, b. 1800, c. 329); also a letter from Cosimo Strozzi, Mantua, 24 March 1494, about a dispute between the cardinal's heirs and the heirs of Carlo da Rodiano, the cardinal's former estate manager, who had produced a quittance dated in 1469 clearing Carlo of any obligation on the cardinal's behalf (ASMn, AG, b. 2446, c. 400); further developments in letters of Gianfrancesco Gonzaga to Isabella d'Este, 28 September 1495 and 21 June 1496 (ASMn, AG, b. 1800, cc. 395, 422) and Ludovico Cipata to Marchese Francesco Gonzaga, Mantua, 23 June 1495, who urged that the outstanding matters be settled 'essendo dicte cause importantissime sì per beneficio de quella felice anima del difonto, sì etiam per honore de la casa de Gonzaga' (b. 2447, c. 163).

[199] A copy exists in ASMn, AG, b. 1823.

[200] BCG, FDM, b. 23, fol. 72ʳ: heading of addendum dated 8 October 1496 'Debiti de la hereditate presente'; fol. 73ʳ: 'A Sancto Petro de Mantua ducati tre millia et secento ducati passati per la bona memoria del

them, and some of those without any security may never have got anything at all.

It is paradoxical that the cardinal, for all his love and sense of duty towards the Gonzaga family, should have been the cause of so much bitterness and dispute among his nearest and dearest relatives. Gianfrancesco and Ludovico were so anxious to minimize whatever responsibilities they had as beneficiaries to clear up his affairs that they readily implicated their nephew, Marchese Francesco, though neither he nor his brother, the Protonotary Sigismondo Gonzaga, seem to have been too ready to accept the burden. Unreconciled to the disappointment of never getting a cardinal's hat, the inheritance he had really expected, and dismayed to find Sigismondo his rival,[201] Ludovico lurked for years in one or other of his country residences, consoling himself with aesthetic, literary and sporting diversions. Meanwhile, the 'Cardinalino' lived out his marginal and brutish life in the flatlands east of Mantua; with his wife imprisoned (on his insistence) for alleged adultery, and his daughters shut away in a convent, he probably cursed the deviousness of all Gonzaga relatives and courtiers, though he preserved to the end of his life a respect for the memory of his father, in whose tomb he hoped to be buried.[202]

Reverendissimo Monsignor Cardinale/Item per lo interesse se paga ogni anno che sono ducati cento ottanta. Restano havere li preti ducati quatrocento ottanta vel circha/Item per legato del prelibato Reverendissimo Monsignore Cardinale a la prepositura de Sancto Benedicto, ducati tre millia per la liberatione de la possessione da Bigarello como apare nel suo ultimo testamento.'

[201] Marchese Federico was already being encouraged to seek Sigismondo's nomination when he reached the age of 15 in the letter of 7 November 1483 from Stefanino Guidotti (see above, p. 111 n. 75), and Federico started the campaign (e.g., letter to Sixtus IV of July 1484, in ASMn, AG, b. 2901, lib. 120, fol. 61^{r-v}) into which Marchese Francesco put more effort, with ultimate success in 1505.

[202] Chambers, 'Cardinalino', pp. 28–9.

Appendix 1:
The Will of Cardinal Francesco Gonzaga

The will, dated at Bologna, 20 October 1483, is transcribed here from the notarially authenticated copy on parchment (now cut into three sheets) in ASMn, AG, b. 333, cc. 83–5; the same document which was published in part by Eugène Müntz.[1] For ease of reference, paragraph divisions in numbered sequence have been added, abbreviations have been expanded and some punctuation has been introduced. There are other contemporary copies of the will in Modena (ASMod., AEC, Carteggio Principi Esteri, b. 116/1380B) and in Milan (Archivio Storico Civico) in a miscellaneous register relating to Marchese Federico's son Giovanni Gonzaga (1474–1525), a nephew of the cardinal but not one of the beneficiaries.[2]

Cross-references to the inventory have been provided, but notes identifying persons, places, objects etc. have not been added here, since this would have entailed much duplication of material from the introductory chapters; use should be made of the general index.

[1.] In Christi nomine, Amen.
Anno a Nativitate eiusdem millesimoquadringesimo octuagesimo tercio, inditione prima. Die vero lune vigesima mensis octobris pontificatus Sanctissimi in Christo patris et Domini Nostri domini Sixti divina providentia Pape quarti anno terciodecimo ac tempore Serenissimi principis et invictissimi domini domini Federici divina favente clementia Romanorum Imperatoris semper Augusti. Cum inter humanarum rerum experimenta nihil magis constat nihilque magis innotescat quam ut in hoc fluxo ac fragili mundo mors vitam terminet, ut dies hominis claudant ut decet propterea mortalem quemcumque ut quo prudentior est maioribusque fulget honoribus et dignitatibus, eo quoque magis constet ratione movente sibi ac aliis dum potest consulat, rebus suis disponat, et omnia cum effectu ad pacem, quietem, tranquilitatem, animeque salutem dirigat, ut sic corpore naturali vigore penitus destituto, anima ipsa immortalis et letior evolet ad celestia et superne beatitudinis gaudiis celerius perfruatur.
Quocirca, ego Franciscus de Gonzaga, miseratione divina Sancte Marie Nove Sacrosancte Romane Ecclesie diaconus Cardinalis, cathedralium ecclesiarum Mantuane ac Bononiensis administrator, tituli ecclesie Sancti Laurentii in Damaso de Urbe, prepositure Sancti Benedicti de Padolirone ac monasterii Sancte Marie de Felonica mantuane diocesis perpetuus comendatarius, ecclesie collegiate Sancti Andree mantuane primicerius, in civitate Bononie eiusque comitatu et districtu, exarchatu Ravene ac tota provintia Romandiole necnon in civitate Mantue ac toto dominio et territorio Illustris domini Marchionis Mantuani, et in omnibus terris ac locis dominiis Illustrissimorum Dominorum Venetiarum et Mediolanensium Ducum subiectis ac etiam super exercitibus gentium armigerarum dicte ecclesie et eius confederatorum Sedis Apostolice Legatus, terrarum ac locorum Insule, Riparoli, de foris nuncupati, Sablonete, Gazoli, et Belfortis Cremonensis diocesis eorumque pertinentiarum dominus Marchio etc., volens pro recte rationis instinctu anime mee in primis saluti providere et deinde rebus meis ita modum ponere ut nulla unquam rixa, nulla discordia ex illis post mortem meam valeat suboriri, nolens ab intestato

[1] See above, p. 2 n. 7.
[2] Santoro, 'Un manoscritto gonzaghesco', pp. 241, 250, where the will's contents are briefly described.

decedere et cupiens ac vehementer affectans id mearum pietatis erga defunctos parentes singularis dilectionis et affectionis in Illustres dominos fratres meos, amoris in filium benivolentie in consanguineos, animi gratitudinis in omnes que de me benemeriti fuere et liberalitatis in familiares ac domesticos testimonii ac exempli relinquere, quod merito ab omnibus valeat comprobari et executioni demandari, sanus mente et sensu corpore tamen eger, rerum et omnium bonorum meorum dispositionem per presens in scriptis ultimum meum testamentum fatio et condo in hunc modo, videlicet:

[2.] In primis ego idem Franciscus cardinalis testator animam meam omnipotenti Deo et Beate Marie Virgini eius genitrici commendo, rogans suppliciter ut ipse Deus omnipotens mei peccatoris ad eius clementiam toto corde conversi misereatur et ipsa genitrix gloriosa pro remissione peccatorum meorum intercedat. Et tamen iuxta ritum christianum cogitans sepulture corporis mei providere, volo, iubeo et mando quod, adveniente casu obitus mei, corpus meum deferatur ad civitatem Mantue et sepeliatur, cum anullo in digito in quo est ligata quedam turchina quam ego solitus eram deportare, in ecclesia Sancti Francisci in capella ubi Illustres quondam Domini progenitores mei sepulti sunt, et in sepulcro quod tunc fieri mando subtus terram de lapidibus et cemento iuxta archam seu sepulturam Illustris quondam genitoris mei, et desuper ipsum sepulcrum ponatur lapis marmoreus in quo sit insculpta effigies diaconi cardinalis et insignia cardinalatus et domus mee de Gonzaga.

[3.] Item volo, iubeo et mando quidam cooperta mea brochati auri cremesini ricii portetur in exequiis meis et postmodum dimitatur ac relinquatur ecclesie predicte Sancti Francisci mantuani pro mortuario cum cendali nigro circumcirca et cum armis ac insignibus meis depictis [I 361].

[4.] Item volo, iubeo et mando quod omnes et singuli familiares mei quos interesse contigerit celebrationi solemnium exequiarum mearum vestiantur condecenter vestibus nigris secundum consuetudinem et iuxta arbitrium infrascriptorum executorum meorum vel maioris partis eorum.

[5.] Item volo, iubeo et mando quod de legitima que mihi debetur iure nature et omni eo quod alias etiam mihi debetur in bonis paternis et ratione conventionum inter Illustres dominos fratres meos infrascriptos et me per publicum instrumentum factarum, dentur solvantur et numerentur per infrascriptum Illustrem dominum Johannem Franciscum de Gonzaga fratrem meum dilectissimum in benefitium et augumentum prepositure Sancti Benedicti de Padolirone predicte tria milia ducatorum auri. Et per Illustrem dominum Marchionem Mantue solvantur similiter et numerentur in benefitium et augumentum predicta alia quattuor milia ducatorum auri seu quinque milia florenorum Rhenensium que obvenerunt mihi in partem pro dote Illustris quondam domine Barbare genitricis mee et de quibus est debitor meus prefatus Illustris dominus Marchio Mantuanus et hec pro liberatione et affranchatione possessionis Bigarelli eiusdem mantuane diocesis quam de presenti possidet Magnificus miles Franciscus de Gonzaga filius meus naturalis et legitimatus secundum obligationem dicte possessionis Bigarelli; que quidem tria milia et quattuor milia ducatorum auri sic soluta convertantur et expendantur in tot proprietatibus bonis et sufficientibus ad comodum dicte prepositure. Ita quod dicta possessio Bigarelli remaneat penitus exhonerata ab omni obligatione dicti debiti septem milium ducatorum predicto Magnifico Francisco filio meo ut prefertur.

[6.] Item volo, iubeo et mando quod de dicta legitima que mihi debetur iure nature et alias ut supra dentur mile ducenti ducati auri venerabilibus dominis archidiacono et archipresbitero ac capitulo et canonicis dicte cathedralis ecclesie mantuane pro celebrando singulo mense usque imperpetuum in dicta ecclesia mantuana offitio mortuorum pro anima prefati Illustris quondam genitoris mei.

[7.] Item volo, iubeo et mando quod de dicta legitima que mihi debetur iure nature et alias ut supra dentur et alii mile ducenti ducati auri dictis venerabilibus dominis archidiacono et archipresbiteri ac capitulo et canonicis eiusdem cathedralis ecclesie mantuane pro celebrando similiter singulo mense usque imperpetuum in ipsa ecclesia mantuana offitio mortuorum pro anima prefate Illustris quondam domine genitricis mee.

[8.] Item volo, iubeo et mando quod de predicta legitima que mihi debetur iure nature et alias ut supra dentur et alii similiter mile ducenti ducati auri ipsis venerabilibus dominis archidiacono et archipresbitero ac capitulo et canonicis cathedralis ecclesie predicte mantuane pro celebrando etiam singulo mense usque imperpetuum in dicta ecclesia mantuana offitio mortuorum pro remedio et salute anime mee. Teneantur tamen predicti capitulares et canonici ac clerus eiusdem ecclesie cathedralis mantuane in vigilia anniversarii obitus mei ire ad ecclesiam predictam Sancti Francisci processionaliter et illic dicere vesperas ac matutinum mortuorum et in die obitus celebrare missam mortuorum in dicta capella sepulture mee. Que tria milia et sexcentos ducatos auri volo, iubeo et mando solvi per supra, et infrascriptum Illustrissimum dominum Iohannem Franciscum fratrem meum infra spatium quinque annorum a die obitus mei computandorum; et ipsa sic soluta converti et expendi in tot proprietatibus bonis et sufficientibus ad commodum predicte cathedralis ecclesie mantuane et pro causa offitiorum predictorum et interea quod fiet dicta solutio volo, iubeo et mando quod per dictum dominum Iohannem Franciscum dentur, solvantur et numerentur dictis dominis archidiacono, archipresbitero, capitulo et canonicis quindecim ducati singulo mense pro tribus offitiis premissis mortuorum singulo ut prefertur mense in cathedrali ecclesia mantuana predicta et in tribus vicibus celebrandis videlicet quinque pro quolibet offitio, que tria offitia qualibet vice sint de congregatione secundum ritum ipsius ecclesie mantuane.

[9.] Item volo, iubeo et mando quod per predictum Magnificum Franciscum filium meum ut prefertur et illius heredes descendentes ac successores dentur singulo anno in die obitus mei tantum panis, vini et pitantie pro helemosina fratribus predicte ecclesie Sancti Francisci mantuani quod ascendat ad pretium sive valorem trium ducatorum auri, et ipsi fratres teneantur celebrare anniversarium meum in capella altaris maioris ipsius ecclesie Sancti Francisci.

[10.] Item relinquo iure legati imagini gloriose Virginis Marie Votorum nuncupate, posite seu depicte in muro cuiusdam capelle contigue episcopatui et prope cathedralem ecclesiam predictam mantuanam, rubinum meum ligatum in anullo aureo per me solitum deportari. Quem rubinum volo, iubeo ac mando ligari in corona dicte imaginis in parte anteriori frontis ipsius gloriose Virginis et in medio dicte corone [I 577].

[11.] Item iure legati relinquo ecclesie cathedrali mantuane crucem meam argenteam longam, que ratione legationis ante me deferebatur [I 105].

[12.] Item iure legati relinquo ecclesie cathedrali mantuane memorate quoddam candelabrum meum magnum argenteum et deauratum, factum in modum arboris cum imaginibus Adam et Eve [I 106].

[13.] Item iure legati relinquo Illustrissimo principi et Excellentissimo domino domino Alphonso de Aragonia duci Calabrie etc. quamdam corniolam meam magnam, in qua insculpta est facies Julii Cesaris [I 542].

[14.] Item iure legati relinquo Illustri et Potenti domino comiti Hieronimo Forlivii ac Imole etc. Sancte Romane Ecclesie Capitaneo Generali, equum morellum quem alias praefatus dominus comes mihi dono misit.

[15.] Item iure legati relinquo Illustri principi et Excellentissimo domino domino Federico Marchioni Mantue etc. fratri meo honorandissimo, vas illud meum argenteum quod refrescatorium nuncupatur [I 85], quamdam corniolam sive lapidem sardonium ligatam in auro, existentem in quadam capseta argentea [I 564], et saleriam alicorni, existentem in quadam argentea, laborata more greco [I 497], nec non ipsam scatolettam et omnes statuas et imagines meas ex ere seu broncio [I 539].

[16.] Item iure legati relinquo Illustri domino Johanni Francisco praedicto fratri meo dilectissimo, duos gobelletos meos aureos, unum a vino [I 36] et alterum ab aqua [I 35], quibus utebatur.

[17.] Item quia Illustris dominus Rodulfus frater meus dilectissimus in praesentiarum militat ad stipendia venetorum, et propter censuras ac penas a summo pontifice inflictas incapax esset eorum que in huiusmodi meo testamento relinquerentur, idcirco ei nihil relinquo.

[18.] Item iure legati relinquo Reverendo in Christo patri ac Illustri domino domino Lodovico prothonotario apostolico fratri meo dilectissimo, unam bacillam argenteam cum bochali [I 3]. Item et unum bacille a barbitonsore [I 75] cum ramina similiter ex argento [I 78], et missale meum pulcrum, coopertum brochato auri [I 687] ac diamantem parvum ligatum in anullo aureo que solebam in digitis gestare [I 576].

[19.] Item iure legati relinquo Illustri domino Francisco primogenito praefati Illustris domini Marchionis Mantue nepoti meo carissimo, offitiolum meum depictum, coopertum brochato auri [I 691].

[20.] Item eodem iure legati relinquo Reverendo et Illustri domino Sigismundo prothonotario apostolico filio similiter praedicti domini marchionis et nepoti meo carissimo, Decretalem meam in membranis ligatam [I 870].

[21.] Item iure institutionis relinquo dicto Magnifico Francisco filio meo naturali et legitimato ut praefertur, cameram unam sive paramentum integrum pro uno lecto pannorum de rasso ad verduram in campo albo [I 460], quos pannos paulo ante emi feci, nec non et unum capelletum seu sparaverium a lecto terzanelli cremesini [I 461] et unum aliud sparaverium telle cortine, que nuper fieri feci. Item et partem cornu alicorni magnam [I 608].

[22.] Item iure legati relinquo Magnifico Hectori de Gonzaga, filio naturali supradicti Illustris domini Rodulfi, nepoti meo dilecto, tacias duas ex parvis [I 52], scutellas duas [I 40] et tondos duos ex argento [I 41].

[23.] Item iure legati relinquo Spectabili viro domino Johanni Petro Arivabeno sacre penitentiarie scriptori, secretario meo carissimo, calamare meum argenteum [I 73].

[24.] Item iure legati relinquo Francisco de Godinis dicto Botirono, servienti armorum Sanctissimi Domini Nostri pape et mazerio meo dilecto, maziam argenteam quam ante me idem Franciscus deferre consueverat.

[25.] Item iure legati relinquo Johanni Francisco dicto Rattono et Baptistino de Ubertis duobus ragatiis meis, ducatos duodecim pro singulo ipsorum.

[26.] Item iure legati relinquo infrascriptis camerariis meis, videlicet domino Carolo Canali, domino Nicolao Placentino, domino Floramonto Brognollo, domino Johanni Francisco Strate, Ludovico Meliolo, Hyeronimo de Concoregio, Cosmo de Andreasiis, Benedicto Zampo, Leonello de Brollio, Johanni Francisco dicto Bellino et tribus ragatiis, videlicet Alexandro Mangardono, Galvano Qualee dicto Scatolino et Amelio de Trano, omnes vestes meas tam diurnas quam nocturnas, et solitas per me portari [I 121−70, 195−7], excepta quadam turcha damasci cremesini quam iam donavi dicto Hyeronimo de Concoregio. Item mataracios et coopertas ad usum meum quottidianum, non tamen paramenta ad ornamentum deputata. Item camisias, linteamina ac forzerios ad usum camere meae [I 171−94], que omnia dividantur vel vendantur per infrascriptos executores meos, vel maiorem partem eorum, ita quod per ipsos vel ipsam assignetur unicuique camerariorum et trium ragatiorum meorum predictorum equaliter portio suo.

[27.] Item iure legati relinquo camerariis et tribus ragatiis suprascriptis ceterisque istis familiaribus et continuis commensalibus meis, videlicet domino Francisco de Maffeis, domino Aloysio Capre, domino Christoforo de Picolominibus, domino Johanni de la Fera, domino Aloysio Tosabetio, domino Johanni Petro Arivabeno supradicto, domino Stefano Cacie, domino Cesari de Schivenoia, domino Lodovico de Grossis, domino Priori Mellono, domino Jacobo Antonio de Boniciis, domino Francisco Mantenuto, domino

Petro Marso, domino Carolo de Ubertis, Bartholomeo Sanvito, Aurelio Cornicio, Butirono praedicto, Hermeti, Gaspari de Padua, Johanni Aloysio Sicco, Carlino Pavesio, Galeatio Agnello Neapolitano, Vincilao, Alexandro Musono, Spolentino, Nicolao Passarino, Alexandro Passaroto, Francisco de Padua, Johanni Carolo de Canevis, Fregastore, Johanni Antonio Musono, Bartholomeo Bagatelli, Petro Paulo Carmignole, Francisco Cacino, Ludovico de Cipata expensori, magistro Thome de Galessio tonsori, magistro Antonio sartori, Johanni Jacopo credenzario, Bonifatio et Burgognono apparichiatoribus, Gotifredo botigherio, Fratri canevario, Guelfo, Claudio, Damiano et Sebastiano parefrenariis ac Francisco dicto Scarpazono, bocchalia, bacillas, scutellas, tondos, tacias, platellos et reliquum omne argentum meum, tam laboratum quam non laboratum, cuiuscumque maneriei [I 1−72 and *passim*].

[28.] Item et tapezarias [I 198−291], equos, mullos et mullas [I 902−36], paramenta et omnia alia utensilia domus et reliqua omnia bona mea mobilia et se moventia, exceptis argento, libris et aliis, de quibus supra et infra, de quorum bonorum meorum per presens capitulum legatorum pretio primo satisfiat ipsis camerariis, ragatiis et familie pro salariis suis in quibus creditores reperirentur. Reliqua vero dividantur seu vendantur ac distribuantur inter dictos camerarios, tres ragatios et ceteros familiares meos, inspecta qualitate personarum ac servitii meriti et temporis et alias secundum arbitrium et discretionem infrascriptorum executorum meorum vel maioris partis eorum, quorum conscientias honero et quibus stari volo.

[29.] Item confirmo, ratiffico et approbo in quantum expediat et opus sit omnes et singulas donationes per me alias factas supra dicto Magnifico Francisco filio meo ut prefertur tam de possessione Bigarelli premissa et etiam possessione Fossemane mantuane diocesis quam de quibuscumque aliis rebus ac bonis tam mobilibus quam immobilibus et eas omnes vim et robur plenarie firmitatis habere volo, decerno ac declaro et in quantum opporteat ipsas possessiones, res et bona de novo dono seu eidem iure institutionis relinquo.

[30.] Item volo, iubeo et mando quod quedam colana et balassis quam iam pluribus diebus donavi dicto Magnifico Francisco filio meo et quam penes me existentem dedi a paucis diebus citra domino Johanni Petro Arivabeno, secretario meo, ut ipsam pignoraret, sicuti pignoravit, pro ducatis mile auri largis, de quibus iussi fieri satisfieri quibusdam votis meis reluatur de bonis hereditatis mee, et restituatur dicto Francisco, ita quod idem Franciscus nullum damnum sentiat ex ipsa pignoratione.

[31.] Item volo, iubeo et mando quod si supradictus Johannes Franciscus dictus Rattonus stare voluerit ad servitia predicti Magnifici Francisci filii mei [deleted: naturalis et legitimati ut prefertur pupilli] dentur eidem Johanni Francisco per ipsum Franciscum victus prestitus et salarium competens secundum merita et qualitatem eiusdem toto tempore vite sue. Tutores autem prefati Magnifici Francisci filii mei naturalis et legitimati ut prefertur pupilli et in etate puerili constituti elligo, deputo, relinquo et esse volo predictos Reverendum et Illustrem dominum prothonotarium fratrem et Spectabilem dominum Johannem Petrum secretarium meos.

[32.] Item relinquo, deputo et esse volo factorem supradicti Francisci filii mei Antonium de Padua dictum Bonettum in presentiarum etiam factorem eiusdem, cum salario convenienti taxando secundum discretionem et arbitrium prefatorum tutorum. Qui Antonius factor teneatur et obligatus sit reddere rationem singulo anno predictis tutoribus de gestis administratis, solutis ac receptis per eum quousque tamen dictus Franciscus in etate legitima fuerit constitutus, cui tunc similiter ad reddendem rationem ut premittitur ipsum Antonium factorem teneri et obligatum esse volo.

[33.] Item volo, iubeo et mando quod de sexcentum ducatis quos nunc habet in manibus supradictus dominus Franciscus de Maffeis pro pensione sex annorum que mihi reservata est super quandam prepositturam de qua vacante olim per obitum bone memorie Reverendissimi domini cardinalis Hesler fuit mihi provisum, adveniente casu obitus mei restituantur quingenti preposito ipsius prepositure et reliqui centum retineantur pro pensione anni presentis ac deinde ipsi centum dispensentur iuxta voluntatem meam de qua plene informati sunt dominus Aloysius Capra, dominus Johannes Petrus Arivabenus et Aurelius Cornicius suprascripti.

[34.] Item volo, iubeo et mando quod liber Cassiodori super Psalmis, in membranis ligatus, qui est ecclesie Sarsinate et nunc inter libros meos, restituatur ipsi ecclesie et eius episcopo [I 742].

[35.] Item volo, iubeo et mando quod camaini mei, tam ligati in quibuscumque tabulis argenteis, et aliter quomodocumque quam etiam non ligati, nec non vasa cristalina tam similiter ligata quam non ligata, et alia iocalia mea ac libri omnes preter specialiter legatos vendantur per infrascriptos executores meos, vel maiorem partem ipsorum, et de eorum pretio satisfiat creditoribus meis, seu assignentur ipsis creditoribus pro parte vel toto debito quod reperirer habere cum eisdem.

[36.] Item volo, iubeo et mando quod fructus, redditus et proventus possessionum mearum Riparoli et Sablonete cremonensis diocesis seu affictus ipsarum necnon et affictus pischerie Comesadii eiusdem diocesis quot quot et qui qui sint durantibus locationibus de eis factis excepto anno presenti dentur et assignentur per executores meos infrascriptos vel maiorem partem eorum pro satisfaciendo creditoribus et extinguendo debita mea secundum arbitrium eorumdem executorum meorum vel maiorem partem ipsorum. Ita tamen quod si Sanctissimus Dominus Noster concesserit exactionem duodecim milium ducatorum super episcopatu mantuano et prepositura Sancti Benedicti prefatis ut infra, et dicta summa cum aliis rebus in presenti testamento meo ad extinctionem debitorum meorum assignatis satisfieret pro integra solutione tunc et eo casu dicte possessiones et pischeria seu eorum afficitus ex nunc remaneant liberi dicto Illustrissimo domino Johanni Francisco fratri et heredi meo, quod si concessio huismodi non fieret aut ipsa pro minori summa vel aliter et res predicte seu earum pretium non ascenderent ad integram satisfactionem debitorum, tunc et eo casu de dictis possessionibus et pischeria seu illarum afficitibus tantum obligatum remaneat et per ipsum fratrem et heredem meum persolvatur quantum supersit ad dictam integram satisfactionem.

[37.] Item volo, iubeo et mando quod vinea apud Sanctum Sixtum de Urbe et domus post ortum domus habitationis Rome Sancti Laurentii in Damaso apud domum domini Nicolai de Parma et alios suos confines vendantur et illarum pretium exponatur etiam in satisfactione debitorum meorum, quas vineam et domum aliter ego cardinalis testator emi de propriis pecuniis meis.

[38.] Item volo, iubeo et mando quod omne id et totum in quo reperirer creditor tempore obitus mei ratione omnium et singulorum beneficiorum que obtineo in titulum vel commendam sive in pecunia sive in aliis rebus cedat et dispensetur in usum et satisfactionem impensarum funeris et exequiarum ac vestium familie ut supra et etiam aliorum debitorum meorum prout ipsis executoribus meis ut supra videbitur.

[39.] Item volo, iubeo et mando quod fructus seu afficitus anni presentis tam habiti per factores meos et in eorum manibus adhuc existentes quam etiam per fictuarios meos possessionum Sablonete et Riparoli ac pischerie Comesadii suprascriptarum debiti deputentur et exponantur per infrascriptos executores meos vel maiorem partem eorum in sumptibus funeris tam pro exequiis quam pro vestibus familie ut supra vestiende; qui, si ad summam dictorum sumptuum non atingerent, reliquum suppleatur et exigatur de supradictis libris, jocalibus et camainis seu eorum valore pro rata necessaria secundum ordinationem predictorum executorum vel maioris partis ipsorum. Que exequie fiant per ipsos executores ut supra ad imitationem consuetudinis curie romanae pro aliis Reverendissimis dominis cardinalibus.

[40.] Itemque libero, quieto et absolvo dominum Johannem Petrum Arivabenum secretarium et dominum Carolum Canalem camerarium meos predictos a quibuscumque per eos aut alterum eorum gestis administratis solutis et receptis, dicens, asserens et affirmans plene et integre de omnibus per ipsos aut alterum ipsorum gestis, administratis, solutis et receptis ut prefertur redditam fuisse mihi bonam rationem et propterea mando executoribus meis infrascriptis ac heredibus et aliis omnibus et singulis ad quos quomodolibet quacumque ratione vel causa de cetero spectare posset ne aliquo futuro tempore dictos dominos Johannem Petrum et Carolum molestent aut inquietent neque cogant ad reddendam ulterius aliquam rationem de premissis.

[41.] Item volo, iubeo et mando quod per reverendum Lodovicum de Agnellis prothonotarium apostolicum dilectissimum meum et dominum Franciscum de Maffeis de presenti existentes in curia romana petatur suppliciter a Sanctissimo domino nostro papa et Sacro Reverendissimorum Dominorum cardinalium collegio ut Sanctitas et Reverendissime dominationes sue dignentur mihi Francisco cardinali parcere ac veniam dare si quomodocumque in aliquo peccassem vel negligendo vel ommittendo aut alias forte committendo contra mentem et voluntatem prefati Sanctissimi domini nostri et dicti Sacri collegii, et deinde supplicetur vel per dictos dominos prothonotarium Agnellum et Franciscum de Maffeis vel per alios infrascriptos executores meos eidem Sanctissimo domino nostro ut Beatitudo sua ad singularem meam consolationem cui ex nunc etiam supplico, dignetur succedente obitu meo prefato Reverendo ac Illustrissimo domino prothonotario fratri meo de cathedrali ecclesia mantuana providere et imponere super ipsa ecclesia mantuana pro sex annos incohandis post diem obitus mei et ut sequitur finiendis honus solvendi mile ducatos pro quolibet anno et similiter super dicta prepositura Sancti Benedicti simile onus pro sex annis similiter, incohandis et finiendis solvendi mile alios ducatos et pro quolibet anno pro parte satisfactionis debitorum meorum ac concedere et contentari quod omne id et totum in quo reperirer creditor tempore obitus mei ratione omnium et singulorum benefitiorum que obtineo in titulum vel commendam sive in pecunia sive in aliis rebus cedat et dispensetur in usum et satisfactionem impensarum funeris et exequiarum et vestium familie ut supra, et etiam aliorum debitorum meorum prout ipsis executoribus meis ut supra videbitur.

[42.] Item volo, iubeo et mando quod per infrascriptos executores meos vel partem eorum rogetur Illustris dominus Marchio mantuanus frater meus honorandi ut eius Excellentia ad singularem mei consolationem qui ex nunc etiam rogo velit contentari et efficaciter operari quod, succedente obitu meo, provideatur cum effectu per prefatum Sanctissimum dominum nostrum dicto Reverendo et Illustri domino prothonotario fratri nostro comuni de predicta cathedrali ecclesia mantuana.

[43.] Item quo magis et instantius possum supradictum Franciscum filium meum commendo una cum familia et hac ultima voluntate mea eidem Illustri domino marchioni rogans ut sit fautor, defensor et protector dictorum filii, familie et ultime voluntatis, ac ita assistat infrascriptis executoribus meis quod predicta et infrascripta omnis et singula executioni mandari possint per ipsos executores vel maiorem partem eorum.

[44.] In omnibus autem aliis bonis meis immobilibus quondam mihi relictis per recolende memorie Illustrem dominum genitorem meum et in portionem meam vigore conventionum inter Illustres dominos fratres meos et me communiter initarum obventis ac aliis bonis, mobilibus et immobilibus, iuribus, actionibus et nominibus quibuscumque debitorum ore proprio nominando, nomino et instituo heredem meum universalem prefatum Illustrem dominum Johannem Franciscum fratrem meum dilectissimum secundum formam testamenti paterni et facultatem conventionum ut supra initarum.

[45.] Executores autem meos elligo, deputo et esse volo dictos Reverendum dominum Lodovicum de Agnellis sedis apostolice prothonotarium, Venerabiles dominos Franciscum de Maffeis et Alovisium Capram ac Spectabilem dominum Johannem Petrum Arivabenum quibus, vel maiori parti eorum, do, trado et concedo plenam ac liberam potestatem, auctoritatem, arbitrium et bailiam exequendi et executioni mandandi comprehensa et disposita in presenti testamento et ultima voluntate.

[46.] Item volo, iubeo et mando quod si aliquid dubium oriretur in verbis huiusmodi mei testamenti stetur decisioni, terminationi ac interpretationi suprascriptorum executorum meorum vel maioris partis ipsorum.

[47.] Item supranominatis familiaribus et continuis commensalibus meis volo, iubeo et mando addi Antonium dictum parmensem et Antonium de Caietam ortolanum familiares meos quos superius ommiseram ut ipsi pariter participent de bonis per me familie mee ut supra legatis.

[48.] Et hanc volo et assero esse meam ultimam voluntatem quam ut testamentum et testamenti iure valere volo et tenere quod si iure testamenti non valet vel valebit aut infirmari contingat aliqua causa presenti vel futura valeat saltem iure donationis inter vivos vel causa mortis vel iure codicillorum aut alterius cuiuslibet ultime voluntatis ac omnibus melioribus modo via iure causa et forme quibus melius et validius valere poterit.

[49.] Actum Bononie in palatio residentie mee et in camera mea cubiculari, anno, indictione, die, mense ac temporibus quibus supra.

Ego Aurelius Cornitius mantuanus, mandato Reverendissimi domini Francisci de Gonzaga cardinalis mantuanus, propter egritudinem corporalem subscribere impediti, hoc eius testamentum tam heredis institutionem quam cetera in eo contenta suo mandato mea propria manu scripsi, et eo postea presente paginam hanc clausam et ligatam infrascriptis testibus ab eo vocatis et rogatis omnibus simul presentibus offerente et simul asserente id quod in ea continetur suum esse testamentum, et me suprascriptum presentem subscriptionem meam vice et nomine suo et eius mandato apposui et in testimonium me subscripsi, anno, mense et die quibus in testamento.

Ego Johannes Alimentus de Nigris sedis apostolice prothonotarius rogatus et presens una cum omnibus infrascriptis testibus ad omnia et singula in hoc presentis pagine inferiori spatio facta, contenta et scripta simul presentibus et rogatis in ipsam eius utique Reverendissimi domini Francisci cardinalis testamento suo manu mea in testimonium me subscripsi et eam sigillo proprio signavi habente in circulo formam capitis hominis senis barbati quod ad unam ex cordulis suprapositis cere impressi.

Ego frater Apolonius de Placentia ordinis minorum de observantia guardianus loci sancti Pauli in monte rogatus et presens cum suprascripto et omnibus infracsriptis testibus ad omnia et singula in hoc presentis pagine inferiori spatio facta, contenta et scripta simul presentibus et rogatis in ipsam eius utique Reverendissimi domini Francisci cardinalis testamento suo mandato manu mea in testimonium me subscripsi et eam sigillo domini Johannis Petri Arivabeni signari habente in circulo formam capitis hominis quod ad unam ex cordulis suprapositis cere impressi.

Ego Hyeronimus de Ranuciis miles et fisicus bononiensis rogatus et presens una cum omnibus infrascriptis et suprascriptis testibus ad omnia et singula in hoc presentis pagine inferiori spatio facta contento et scripta simul presentibus et rogatis in ipsa eius utique Reverendissimi domini Francisci cardinalis testamento suo mandato manu mea in testimonium meum subscripsi et eam sigillo proprio signavi habente in circulo caput Faustine cum .f. quod ad unam ex cordulis suprapositis cere impressi.

Ego Franciscus Bentius fisicus senensis rogatus et presens una cum omnibus infrascriptis et suprascriptis testibus ad omnia et singula in hoc presentis pagine inferiori spatio facta contenta et scripta simul presentibus et rogatis in ipsam eius utique reverendissimi domini Francisci cardinalis testamento suo mandato manu mea in testimonium me subscripsi et eam sigillo proprio signavi habente arma mee familie id est targam cum lista in transversum eunte in qua sunt tre stelle et in uno quoque spatio tam superiori quam inferiori unum lilium quod ad unam ex cordulis suprapositis cere impressi.

Ego Johannes Antonius Zaita fisicus mantuanus rogatus et presens una cum omnibus infrascriptis et suprascriptis testibus ad omnia et singula in hoc presentis pagine inferiori spatio facta contenta et scripta simul presentibus et rogatis in ipsa eius utique Reverendissimi domini Francisci cardinalis testamento suo mandato manu mea in testimonium me subscripsi et eam sigillo proprio signavi habente in circulo caput hominis barbati et capilati quod ad unam ex cordulis suprapositis cere impressi.

Ego Egidius de Cesena legum doctor rogatus et presens una cum omnibus suprascriptis et infrascriptis testibus ad omnia et singula in hoc presentis pagine inferiori spatio facta, contenta et scripta simul presentibus et rogatis in ipsa eius utique Reverendissimi domini Francisci cardinalis testamento suo mandato manu mea in testionium me subscripsi et eam sigillo proprio signavi habente in circulo formam capitis hominis barbati quod ad unam ex cordulis suprapositis cere impressi.

Ego Leonellus de Victoriis de Faventia fisicus rogatus et presens una cum omnibus suprascriptis testibus ad omnia et singulo in hoc presentis pagine inferiori spatio facta contenta et scripta simul presentibus et rogatis in ipsam eius utique Reverendissim domini Francisci cardinalis testamento suo mandato manu mea in testimonium me subscripsi et eam sigillo proprio signavi habente in circulo formam capitis mulieris que Faustina dicitur quod ad unam ex cordulis suprapositis cere impressi.

[50.] Anno a Nativitate domini MCCCCLXXXIII die XXI mensis octobris coram me notario et testibus infrascriptis ad hoc vocatis specialiter et rogatis Reverendissimus dominus Franciscus de Gonzaga cardinalis mantuanus sanus mente licet corpore eger volens et intendens huic testamento retroscripto clauso subscripto ut dixit manu Aurelii Cornitii familiaris sui et sigillato septem sigillis et subscripto manu septem testium infrascriptorum dari plenam fidem dixit et asseruit illud esse suum ultimum testamentum clausum subscriptum et subscriptum mandato suo manu dicti Aurelii Cornicii familiaris sui de cuius toto tenore in omnibus et per omnia dixit se plenam habere notitiam ac suprascriptum et manibus septem testium illic infrascriptorum [repeats as W49]...etiam ab eo rogatorum ut se subscriberent et sigillarent prout in subscriptionibus eorum continetur quod in mei notarii et testium infrascriptorum presentis tradidit et consignavit dicto domino Johanni Petro secretario suo custodiendum et servandum ac aperiendum et publicandum post mortem eiusdem Reverendissimi domini cardinalis testatoris ac simul confirmavit omnia et singula in eo testamento contenta et scripta et specialiter quoddam legatum quod predicto Aurelio dixit se facere tanquam uni de familia sua secundum arbitrium executorum suorum in predicto eius testamento ut asseruit nominatorum et de predictis omnibus et singulis iussit mihi notario infrascripto unum et plura fieri instrumenta.

[51.] Acta Bononie in palatio residentie prefati Reverendissimi domini cardinalis et legati in camera cubiculari ipsius anno, mense et die suprascriptis indictione vero prima ac pontificatus Sanctissimi in Christo patris et domini mei domini Sixti divine provvidentia pape quarti anno terciodecimo presentibus ibidem fratre Francisco quondam Bartolomei de Feraacantis bononiensis ordinis minorum de observantia et domino Evangelista Zaita laico mantuano legum professore ac Thoma de Zellatis clerico cremonensis diocesis necnon fratre Apollonio, domino magistro Hyeronimo et domino magistro Leonello suprascriptis ac dominis Floramonte Brognolo canonico mantuano et Carolo Cataneo sacre penitentiarie scriptore ipsius Reverendissimi domini cardinalis camerariis testibus ad premissa specialiter vocatis et rogatis.

Nota et rogatio mei Bartholomei quondam Petri de Castigatis de Insula professoris cremonensis diocesis publici Imperiali auctoritate notarii.

[The following additional clause records the opening and publication of the will at Mantua, 29 October 1483]

[52.] Anno a Nativitate Domini millesimo quadringesimo octavigesimo tercio die mercurii XXVIIIIa mensis octobris Illustrissimus dominus Marchio Mantue etc. In camera sua cubiculari castri sui Mantue constitutus retroscriptum testamentum sibi per dominos Aloysium de Capris in utroque [iure] doctorem et Johannem Petrum Ariva- benum secretarium apostolicum, asserentes se esse in dicto testamento executores deputatos presentatum ex ordinacione ut ipsi asseverunt quondam domini testatoris retroscripti legitime clausum et sigillatum, apperiri et publicari mandavit ad eorum requisitionem iuxta mandatum eis factum per bone memorie prefatum dominum testatorem retroscriptum, supplens de plenitudine potestatis etc. et ex certa scientia omnes et singulos defectus solemnitatum si qui intervenirent in apertione et publicatione huiusmodi et illud quo ad apertionem et publicationem huismodi, plenissime auctorizavit cum decreto irritante etc. et cum derogationibus necessariis, ac mandavit mihi Matheo Antimacho secretario suo publico Imperiali auctoritate notario, de premissis unum vel plura conficere instrumentum, presentibus militibus dominis Guidone de Balneo et Eusebio de Malatestis consociis etc. ac Speciali viro Federico de Malatestis camerariorum testibus.

Nota et rogatio mei Mathei Antimachi prefati Illustrissimi domini Marchionis secretarii publici Imperiali auctoritate notarii.

Appendix 2:
The Post-Mortem Inventory of Cardinal Francesco Gonzaga's Possessions

The inventory is transcribed from a paper fascicle measuring 315 x 212 mm and consisting of 20 folios, written recto and verso. It is a separate document in ASDMn, Fondo Capitolo della Cattedrale, serie miscellanea, b. 2/A. To make consultation and reference easier, a numerical sequence has been imposed upon the listed items; notes are inserted beneath individual entries as required. An effort has been made to indicate the various different hands which occur. The inventory as a whole is written almost entirely in the hand of Giovan Francesco Strata, which can be confirmed from his signature near the end (fols 19^r, 20^v), and from an autograph letter to Marchese Federico Gonzaga, dated at Bologna 13 December 1482 (in ASMn, AG, b. 1142). The other two compilers, Cosmo Andriasi and Alesandro Secco or Secho, also appended their signatures near the end of the inventory (fol. 19^r) but otherwise seem to have had little or no part in the writing of it. A pair of additional hands which occur recurrently throughout the inventory, particularly in the marginal annotations but sometimes also amending details within the list, can be identified with two of the cardinal's executors, Giovan Pietro Arrivabene and Alvise Capra. Their autograph signatures appear at the beginning (fol. 1^r) and correspond with their signatures upon a joint letter written on the same day (see Appendix 3, no. 5). To distinguish their insertions from the writing of Strata, the hand of Arrivabene is indicated by italics, and that of Capra by underlining. There seems to be yet another hand annotating the right-hand margins in the list of books between fols 15^r and 18^r, indicating titles which were later in the hands either of Giovan Pietro Arrivabene or Gianfrancesco Gonzaga. This fourth hand might possibly be that of Cosmo Andriasi, but the identity remains uncertain, and it could even be Capra writing more rapidly than usual; it has therefore been signalled with underlining (as for Capra) but with the addition of an asterisk.

Cross-references to the will are indicated by the letter W followed by the number of the relevant paragraph. Modern punctuation has been introduced on a minimal scale, and annotation only provided (indented, in smaller type) where the nature or identity of the object did not seem obvious and well-known (e.g., some book titles and their authors), or where further information might seem to be relevant and useful. Some additional printed sources are cited which are only of relevance to a single entry (particularly with regard to books); these, therefore, have not been included in the general Bibliography. Approximate English equivalents have been supplied in the general Index for some of the more obscure words and descriptive terms, though a few have defeated all efforts at interpretation. Most persons (legatees etc) can also be traced through the Index. In transcribing the inventory, the same practice has been followed here as in textual passages from letters etc, of not correcting or standardising oddities of spelling and grammar, and of not distinguishing (e.g., by the use of italics) Latin words or phrases from those in the vernacular. Since the vocabulary and stock phrases used and promulgated by the chancery secretaries, clergy, notaries etc of the time is so often a medley of the two, such an editorial practice would have been both laborious and pointless. An example of this problem of differentiation is the occurence throughout the inventory of the abbreviated preposition 'cū'; this word has been resolved here as 'cum' rather than the debatable 'cun', which just possibly might have been intended. Another departure from standard Italian philological practice is the retention of spelling exactly as written, e.g., unsounded letters have *not* been removed.

For a more detailed discussion of the original compilation, function and limitations of the inventory see above, Chapter 4 (ii). The lay-out of the original, and the method used here in presenting it, can be best understood by a comparison with the illustrated examples, of fol. 1ʳ (Fig. 11) and fol. 15ʳ (Fig. 12).[1] The columns of numbers to the right of items 1–104, 119 (fols 1ʳ-3ʳ: see Fig. 11) represent weight in *libbre*, *oncie* and *denari*. The unit of weight for precious metals, the *libbra*, was divided into twelve *oncie*, each of twenty-four *denari*, a system apparently universal in Italy, though the actual weight which the *libbra* represented could vary between different cities.[2]

The inventory was evidently used as a checklist of bequests delivered to legatees and of other distributions and sales, and was checked against other lists or inventories, including one made by Giovan Pietro Arrivabene, of objects which he extracted and took with him to Rome early in December 1483. The contemporary annotations, mostly by Capra, Arrivabene and Strata himself, are indicated either by the symbol # (left margin) or ## (right margin), and where a marginal note relates to more than just the one entry immediately following (or beside) it, the sequential numbers are indicated in square brackets. No attempt has been made to reproduce the various gnomic slashes, noughts and crosses etc which are also written in the left margin against individual items; these presumably relate to successive checkings or disposal. It should be noted that references to the deceased marchese (I 539, 564) establish that some of this checking cannot have been before Marchese Federico Gonzaga's death on 14 July 1484.

---

[1] An illustration of fol. 12ʳ is given in Brown, 'Lorenzo', p. 89, fig. 2.

[2] Cf. Florence and Milan, which Mantua may have followed: A. Martini, *Manuale di metrologia...*, Turin, 1883; reprinted Rome, 1976, pp. 207, 336, 351.

[fol. 1ʳ]

Die 27 octobr[is] 1483

Inventario de arienti, zoye, camei, panni de razo, tapeti, panni lini, veste, libri, cavalli, masaritie, et de ogni altre robe restante de la heredità de la bona memoria de Monsignor Cardinale de Mantua scripte per inventario et asignate in man de d. Zohannepetro Arrivabene in presentia de d. Alvise Capra, e de nuy Strata, Cosmo e Secho.

#*Ita est. Ego Jo[hannes] p[etrus] Arrivabenus manu propria*

[1] Doi piatti bianchi grandi de ariento.	15 8 12
[2] Un fiascho de ariento dorato col tesuto.	8 5
#Un bacille col bocale fu dato a Monsignor Prothonotario ratione legati [W 18]:	
[3] Doi bacilli a spichii mezi dorati cum li soi doi bocali.	10 10
[4] Un fiascho de mastice coperto de brochato d'oro verde e guarnito de arzento dorato.	
[5] Una coltellera che sta in pede fornita de coltelli e pironi cum li manichi de arzento.	
[6] Forcine quatro de ariento col manicho retorto.	0 5 12
[7] Un tabernacolo picolino de ariento dorato.	0 8
[8] Un bichero d'ariento col manicho da lucerna.	0 4 12
[9] Un fiaschetino da tenere aqua rosa.	0 4
[10] Doe confetere grande cum li pedi e coppe dorate.	9 10
[11] Una sallera smaltata cum calcedonio.	0 11
[12] Doe nappe dorate a fogliani e animali	1 11 12
[13] Doe nappe bianche granite.	1 9 18
[14] Un perfumatoyo dorato a schaye.	1 2 18
[15] Un gobelletto doppio dorato a schaye.	2 6
[16] Un bichero dorato cum tre animali a piede e col cerchio in mezo.	2 7 12
[17] Un bichero dorato cum tre nynphe ai pedi polito in mezo e cum 3 torre sotto.	3 1 12
[18] Un gobelletto lisso dorato cum arbore in zima al coperchyo.	2 4 6
[19] Un caldarino d'ariento lavorato cum le divise.	10 4

[fol. 1ᵛ]

[20] Tazze xii martellate a bagatini.	19 10
[21] Tazze v cum l'arme aniellate fatti a cavali mezi dorati.	7 9 12
[22] Tazze vi dorate fatte a cavali.	9 3 12
[23] Scutelle vi dorate.	8 9 12
[24] Tondi vi dorati.	7 10 12
[25] Piattelli iiii dorati.	9 5 21
[26] Una coppa granda dorata cum l'arma de Bav[i]era.	5 0

[27] Un gobelletto grande dorato fatto a spichii cum fiore azuro
aperto in cimma.   2 11 6

[28] Un gobelletto alquanto minore dorato lavorato a spichii
col fiore serato in cimma.   2 10 12

[29] Un gobelletto tuto dorato lavorato a borchie e in parte smaltato.   3 7 12

[30] Una coppa lissa tuta dorata cum balla in cimma e lo coperchio
dorato.   2 0 18

[31] Una coppa lissa tuta dorata cum balla biancha granita
in cimma lo coperchio.   2 5 6

[32] Una coppa tuta dorata fatta a cavali torti cum balla a melloni
in cimma lo coperchio.   2 0 6

[33] Pezzi dece d'ariento dorati, cioè piattelletti iiii, scutelle iiii
e scutellini ii.   13 l0 18

#Restituita al Magnifico domino Francesco:

[34] Una pignatella tuta dorata.

[35–6] Legati al Signore Zoan Francesco [W 16]:

[35] Uno bochale d'oro da aqua.

[36] Uno gobelletto d'oro da vino.

[37] Uno cuchiaro d'oro cum un botonzino d'oro.   0 1 11

#[ad rat]ionem? 72:

[38] Una forcheta d'oro cum un fiore aniellato in cimma.   0 0 21

[39] Doe bacille da dare l'aqua a le man.   8 10 6

[40–1] Doe scutelle e dui tondi fureno legati al Magnifico
Hectore [W 22]:

[40] Scutelle xi grande de ariento; nove scutelle vendute.   15 3 8

[41] Tondi xii d'ariento; dece tondi venduti.   12 11

[42] Cuchiari xi d'ariento.   1 1

#al Signor Zoan Francesco una, et le tre vendute:

[43] Forcelle iiii grande de ariento.   1 2

[44] Una tazza dorata col coperchiio da bevere pesata insiema
col pozo mezo dorato.   4 9 18

[fol. 2ʳ]

[45] Una scattolla dorata da confetto.   6 1 17

[46] Un bochale lavorato a giande.   1 10

[47] Una galea grande meza dorata.   6 10

[48] Un quadro longo cum sei balle sotto.   1 11

[49] Una nappa biancha granita vechya.   0 10 15

[50] Piatti sei mezani.   22 7 12

[51] Quadri xxiiii.   15 6

#Doe ne fureno legate al Magnifico Hectore [W 22]:

[52] Tazze viii picole col pede; sei ne fuorono vendute.   8 0

#D. Alvisi Capra:

[53] Un sallino tondo doppio cum vi balle.   0 5

[54] Doe padelle grande cum li coperchii.
 9 10

[55] Una padelletta picola col coperchio.   1 0

[56] Una scudella senza coperchio col manicho longo.   1 1 12
[57] Una ranzera.   1 2
[58] Un ovarolo.   0 9
[59] Una gratusa picola.   0 4 12
[60] Uno coperchio da bichero lisso dorato.   0 3 15
[61] Uno coperchio da bichero lisso biancho.   0 3 3
[62] Uno coperchio da bichero aniellato.
[63] Dui coperchii da bochalina aniellati e dorati.   0 7
[64] Dui coperchii da bochalina dorati lissi.
[65] Dui coperchii da bochalina bianchi lissi cum le ballette dorate.   0 2 18
[66] Candelleri cinque da tavola.   7 3
#D. Aloysio Capra:
[67] Candelleri tre d'ariento tuti dorati.   5 5 6
[68–70 are bracketted; maybe the weight against 69 is a total]:
[68] Bacilla una lissa col bochale suo a la catellana.
[69] Bacilla una lissa col bochale suo a la catellana.   20 8 6
[70] Bacilla una lissa col bochale suo a la catellana.
#Quatro forchete extimate ducati 0 soldi l0:
[71] Forchete xi d'ariento col bichereto a la catelana.   0 11 6
[72] Un caldarino bianco senza coperchio.   2 6 12
#Legato a domino Zoan Petro Arrivabene [W 23]:
[73] Un calamare grande.
[74] Una bacilla d'ariento lissa vechiia.   4 4
#Legato al Reverendo Prothonotario Administrator [W 18]:
[75] Uno bacille da barbero polito cum l'orlo intachato.

[fol. 2ᵛ]
[76] Un bacille da barbero più vechio.   3 2
[77] Un caldarinello da aqua santa col spargolo d'ariento
rotto.   3 2
#*Legata a Monsignor Protonotario* [W 18]:
[78] Una ramina d'ariento.
[79] Un bochale da camara a la catellana senza coperchio.   2 5 12
[80] Una galea picola dorata.   2 0
[81] Dui candelleri per la camera vechii.   2 4 12
[82] Un bochale grande de ariento cum dui manichi mezo
dorato.   15 6
#Habuit dominus Iohannes Petrus et ab eo dominus Electus, Rome:
[83] Quindice tondi d'ariento in parte dorate cum diverse hystoriette   2 3 18
[84] Para xxviii de ancinelli d'ariento dorati.   0 3 22
#Legato al Illustrissimo Signor Marchese [W 15]:
[85] Uno refreschatoyo d'ariento lavorato a figure relevate.
[86] Una bassa d'ariento dorata cum l'alicorno.   3 0 18
[87] Doe bussole d'ariento dorato smaltato.   1 11
#*duplicato infra*:
[88] Uno candellere suxo quatro pedi de faunno.   1 0 18
[89] Una testa d'ariento dorata de serpa cum la lingua.   0 4

[90] Uno soicho d'ariento cum li instrumenti suoi.

> Among his share of Barbara's possessions in her house at San Giorgio, outside Mantua, the cardinal was allotted on 1 December 1481 'uno soio cum bechieri 150' (ASDMn, FCC, misc., b. 2/A, 'Inventario dele cose', fol. 30^r). A *soi*, in Mantuan dialect, was a very large wooden vessel for measuring wine (Arrivabene, *Vocabolario*, p. 746); perhaps, therefore, a silver serving dish, used, say, for wine at banquets, might be intended here, or it might be a type of cooler (cf. *renfrescatoio*).

[91] Una cassa da ochiali d'oro smaltata.   0 1 18

> Among items in the cardinal's house in Mantua after his mother's death in November 1481, 'una cassa da occhiali d'oro' is listed (ASDMn, FCC, misc. b. 2/A, fol. 3^v).

#*data al Reverendissimo Monsignor Protonotario:*

[92] Una anchonetta d'oro cum reliquie.

[93–4] extimati ducati 1 e $^1/_2$ [the manuscript here and below shows $^1/_2$ as ÷]:

[93] Dua para de ancinelli e xii pasetti tondi de ariento dorato.

[94] Una cadenella d'ariento, un sonayno, un bambinetto
et un cadenazolo d'ariento, e alcune altre pezi.   0 2 6

extimati ducati 2$^2/_3$:

[95] Alcuni pezzeti d'oro et un circulo d'oro.   0 0 11

[96] Un campanello d'ariento.   1 7

> Possibly the bell given to Francesco by Cardinal Mella ('Zamorensis') in 1462 (see above, p. 37).

[97] Un candellere d'ariento fatta a la ragonesa col manicho rotto.   0 4 12

[98] Un calice cum la patena dorati.

[99] Doe bochaline d'ariento d'altare.   1 10 18

[100] Una pace de arzento dorata.   1 0

[101] Un piede de croce de arzento.

[102] Lo fornimento d'oro ch'era al tesuto de la tasca
che fu stimato oz. 4 d'oro.   0 4

#venduti 17:

[103] Quadretti xxviii d'arzento havuti dal Zentilisia.   10 7

> On Giancarlo Zentilisio, formerly apprentice to the goldsmith Cristoforo di Geremia, see above, p. 83.

[104] Uno sigillo grande de ariento.   0 7 6

> For the cardinal's seal see above, pp. 83, 92; Fig. 4.

[fol. 3^r]

[105–6] *Assignate a li canonici de San Petro de Mantuoa* [W 11–12]:

[105] La croce dela legatione col manicho longo de arzento.

[106] Lo candellere grande fatto a arbore cum Adam e Eva de ariento dorato.

[107] Una coltelera cum cinque cortelli con manichi de ariento anielati.

[108] Una cortellera cum 3 cortelli cum li manichi negri pontezati de ariento.

[109] Una cortellera cum nove coltelli roti cum li manichi de ariento anielato.

[110] Una cortellera cum doi coltelli cum vere dicono essere de ariento.

[111] Una cortellera a la catellana cum li manichi de ferro.

[112] Doe coltellere cum coltelli cum li manichi tuti de ferro.

[113] Uno arloyo grande in la soa guayna.

[114] Una cortellera cum l'arma suxo el coperchio cum cinque cortelli tra grandi e picoli, forniti de cristallo, e una forcheta.

[115] Cortelli quatro lavorati a la damaschina col manicho d'osso negro forniti de ariento.

[116] Cortelli otto da pane col manicho d'ariento aniellato e dorati verso lo fero.

[117] Forcine quatro de fero dorate.

[118] Doe bacille a la moresca de ramo dorate.

[119] Un guinzaio da chiave de ariento tirato.   0   3   18

[120] Cortelli otto da pane col manicho d'ariento imperfetti excepto uno che ha il manicho aniellato e perfetto havuti dal Meliolo.

> These bread-knives, seven with silver handles, and the eighth finished with inlaid enamel-work, were evidently the work of the goldsmith Bartolomeo Melioli (see above, p. 85).

[fol. 3ᵛ]

#[121–97] *Assignati ai camerieri per legato* [W 26]:

[121] Una turcha de raso cremesino fodrata de zebelini.

[122] Una turcha de damasco cremesino fodrata de zebelini.

[123] Una turcha de damasco lionato fodrata de dossi.

[124] Una turcha de damasco biso fodrata de dossi.

[125] Una turcha de damasco verde scuro fodrata de lupicerveri.

[126] Una turcha de zambellotto pavonazo fodrata de lupiceveri.

[127] Un vestito de pavonazo aperto fodrato de dossi.

[128] Un vestito de rosato fodrato de armelini.

[129] Un vestito de Bruges fodrato de sardeschi bianchi.

[130] Un vestidello de terzanello pavonazo fodrato de pance de varo.

[131] Un copertore de veluto lionato fodrato de martori.

[132] Un copertore de veluto verde fodrato de zibelini.

[133] Un copertore de tafta verde col rechamo fodrato de dossi.

[134] Un copertore de damasco moresco fodrato de armelini.

[135] Un copertore picolo de scorza de bissa fodrato de panze de varo.

[136] Un copertore grande de castroni.

[137] Una fodraya spagnola.

[138] Uno coretto de cendale cremesino fodrato de andesini.

[139] Uno coretto de rosato fodrato de cendal verde.

[140] Uno coretto de rosato fodrato de pignolà biancho rosato.

[141] Quatro squarci de pance de varo.

[142] Doi capironi de armelini.

[143] Quatro capucini fodrati de armelini.

[144] Cinque capucini desfodrati de grana.

[145] Uno capucino de raso cremesino.

[146] Uno capucino de zambelotto pavonazo fodrato de cendal rosso.

[fol. 4ʳ]

[147] Tre capucini de grane fodrati de cendale.

[148] Doi capucini de zambellotto desfodrati.

[149] Una peza bisa fodrata de zibelini.

[150] Una peza cremesina fodrata de avoltore.

[151] Uno fasso de scalfareti de andesini.

[152] Una cappa de zambelotto pavonazo col capirone fodrato de armelini.

[153] Una cappa de zambeloto pavonazo col capirone fodrato de cendal cremesino.

[154] Una cappa de zambelloto cremesino col capirone fodrato de cendal cremesino.

[155] Una cappa de saya pavonaza scura col capirone de armelini.

[156] Uno mantello de zambelloto cremesino.

[157] Un mantello de zambellotto pavonazo.

[158] Un mantello de rosato col suo capuzone doppio.

[159] Una cruzola de saya de rosato col capuzo suo fodrato de cendale cremesino.

[160] Una crozola de saya pavonaza col capuzo fodrato de cendal pavonazo.

[161] Una guarnaza de rosato.

[162] Uno gabano de Bruges col capirone fodrato de raso cremesino.

[163] Uno vestito de Bruges fodrato de sardeschi.

[164] Un gabano de Bruges col capirone fodrato de raso pavonazo.

[165] Un gonello de rosato simplice cum le maniche fodrate de tafta.

[166] Un zipone de damasco verde scuro.

[167] Un zipone de damasco cremesino.

[168] Un par de calce de rosato.

[169] Un par de maniche de samito.

[170] Un par de meze calce de rosato.

[fol. 4ᵛ]

[171] Una coperta de cendale cremesino fodrata de tela verde.

[172] Una coperta de cendale cremesino fodrata cum l'arma in mezo de tela biancha.

[173] Una coperta picola de terzanello azurro cum l'arma in mezo.

[174] Una coperta tuta de tafta bianco.

[175] Una coperta de tela biancha.

[176] Una farsata tinta in grana.

[177] Tre farsate bianche.

[178] Uno matarazo fodrato de raso verde col capezal.

[179] Uno matarazo fodrato de raso alexandrino col capezal.

[180] Uno matarazo fodrato de tafta bianco.

[181] Dui matarazi de pignolà novi.

[182] Tri matarazi vechy de S. Agata.
      See above, p. 104.

[183] Para 23 de lenzoli de cortina e de tela nostrana tra boni e vechii.

[184] Dui lenzoli grandi de uno pezo l'uno.

[185] Tre lenzoli minori de uno pezo.

[186] Alcune fette de lenzolo vechie.

[187] Tre para e $^1/_2$ de lenzoletti picoli da bagno.

[188] Rocheti quattordice tra sancille e cortina.

[189] Camise 10 tra bone e triste.

[190] Una coperta de tovaglia.

[191] Una coperta tuta de cortina.

[192] Una sachoza cumscufioni, maniche vechie e altre cose rotte.

[193] Una sachosa cum alcuni panni de lino malnette.

[194] Forcieri de la camera xviii.

[195] Un capello de bevera negro fodrato de cremesino.

[196] Berete de rosato xvii.

[197] Uno capello de bevera vechiio.

[fol. 5^r]

[198] Doi panni de razo d'oro e de seta de Alexandro.

> These and the following item [I 199] are presumably the cardinal's tapestries of a battle of Alexander the Great so much admired at Bologna in July 1471 (see above, pp. 81–2). The inventory of Gianfrancesco Gonzaga (1496) lists 'uno panello de razo cum figure a la hystoria de Alexandro' (BCG, FMD, b. 23, c. 18^r).

[199] Quatro pezi de razo de Alexandro.

> Cf. I 198.

[200] Uno panno de razo d'oro e de seta vechyo de Solomone.

> A 'Judgement of Solomon' was listed among the Este collection at Ferrara by 1457 (Fortini-Grazzini, *Arazzi*, p. 38).

[201] Quatro pezi de razo vechii d'oro e de seta cum le bandinelle, chiamato lo aparamento del re Alfonso.

> Presumably these pieces had belonged to Alfonso I of Aragon, King of Naples (d. 1458). In a letter from Milan, 5 April 1459, to Marchese Ludovico Gonzaga, Vincenzo Scalona had noted for sale five very fine hangings of 'veluto alexandrino' which had been ordered by Alfonso (C. Magenta, *La certosa di Pavia*, Milan, 1897, p. 56 n. 1). According to a letter of Luigi da Barberino to Niccolò Michelozzi, Rome, 28 April 1487, 'certi amici' (perhaps Giovan Pietro Arrivabene and Agnelli, as executors) 'volevano vendere due panni d'arazzo quali fece già fare el re Alfonso et morì inanzi fussimo finiti tucti, che ne faceva fare parecchi. Vennono quelli erano facti pel duca Borso [d'Este] e di poi pel Cardinale di Mantova, et sono una cosa mirabile secondo intendo' (Pistoia, private collection; printed in De Marinis and Perosa, *Nuovi documenti*, pp. 61–2. I am grateful to Scot McKendrick and Laurie Fusco for these references).

[202] Quatro pezi de razo cum la historia de Joseph.

> A *coltrina* of Joseph, supplied by Rinaldo Boteram of Brussels, was listed among the Este collection at Ferrara by 1457, and often displayed subsequently (Fortini-Grazzini, *Arazzi*, p. 37 and *passim*).

[203] Quatro pezi del aparamento grande de Abraam vechyo.

[204] Quatro pezi del aparamento picolo de Abram novo.

> Ludovico Gonzaga, Bishop-Elect of Mantua, refers to 'la camera nova de Abrahamo' in his letter of 10 August 1484 (Appendix 3, no. 18).

[205] Quatro pezi del aparamento grande vechyo da le damiselle.

[206] Sette pezi de panno de razo da la vindemia.

> Cf. the Este tapestry of *mietitori* seen in 1462 and noted on subsequent occasions (Fortini-Grazzini, *Arazzi*, p. 32).

[207] Doi panni de razo vechii de Jd [Juditta?]

The Este *coltrin* ' of 'Judith and Holofernes', listed by 1457, was recurrently on display (Fortini-Grazzini, *Arazzi*, p. 37 and *passim*).

[208] Doi panni de razo vechii de Ciro.

> No example of Cyrus as the subject of a tapestry is given earlier than 1543 by Roblot-Delondre, 'Sujets antiques'.

[209] Doi panni de razo vechii de Ezichia.

[210] Doi panni de razo vechii a figure.

[211] Panno de razo de Achilles grande.

[212] Panno de razo de Achilles minore ditto del Schirato.

[213] Panetto picolo d'oro e de seta del agnello pascale.

[214] Panetto uno a rivera.

[215] Panetto "Qui sine peccato est".

[216] Panetto de Octaviano novo.

[217] Panno de razo da letto grande de Salamone.

[218] Panetto novo de Salamone da la calza rechamata.

[219] Panno de razo del principio del mondo.

> A tapestry of 'The Creation', mostly woven at Siena, was made for Pope Nicholas V (1447–55) (Roblot-Delondre, 'Sujets antiques', no. 144; information from Scot McKendrick).

[220] Panetto cum Christo in l'orto.

> See Fortini-Grazzini, *Arazzi*, pp. 41–3 (for discussion of a Ferrarese painting 'Christ in the Garden' of c. 1460, thought to be a model for tapestry).

[221] Panetto cum Christo che ha la croce in spalla.

[222] Panetto cum Christo in croce.

[223] Panetto de la Asumptione.

[224] Panno de razo vechyo a figure.

[225] Panno de razo vechyo a figure.

[fol. 5ᵛ]

[226] La spallera de Noè.

[227] La spallera dale vertute.

[228] La spallera dale scientie.

[229] La spallera dai pianeti.

[230] Doe spallera de Santo Antonio.

[231] Una spallera alta a verdure.

[232] Una spallera alta a verdure.

[233] Una spallera alta a verdure.

[234] Un panetto a verdura.

[235] Un panetto a verdura.

[236] Un panetto a verdura.

[237] Un panetto a verdura.

[238] Un panetto a verdura.

[239] Un panetto a verdura.

[240] Banchale un a verdura de br[accia] 6.

[241] Un banchal a verdura de br. 6.

[242] Un banchal a verdura de br. 6.

[243] Un banchal a verdura de br. 6.

[244] Un banchal a verdura de br. 6.

[245] Un banchal a verdura de br. 6.
[246] Un banchal a verdura de br. 6.
[247] Un banchal a verdura de br. 6.
[248] Un banchal a verdura de br. 6.
[249] Un banchal a verdura de br. 6.
[250] Un banchal a verdura de br. 6.
[251] Un banchal a verdura de br. 6.
[252] Un banchal a verdura de br. 4.
[253] Un banchal a verdura de br. 4.
[254] Un banchal a verdura de br. 4.
[255] Un banchal a verdura de br. 4.
[256] Un banchal a verdura de br. 4.
[257] Un banchal a verdura de br. 4.

[fol. 6ʳ]

[258] Un banchal a verdura de br. 8.
[259] Un banchal a verdura de br. 8.
[260] Un banchal a verdura de br. 8.
[261] Un banchal a verdura de br. 8.
[262] Un banchal a verdura de br. 8.
[263] Un banchal a verdura de br. 8.
[264] Un banchale cum 3 arme de br. 8.
[265] Un banchale cum 3 arme de br. 9, cum un altro pezo.
[266] Un banchale cum 3 arme de br. 7.
[267] Un banchale cum 4 arme in dui pezi.
[268] Un banchale over spallera cum doe damiselle e 1 arma.
[269] Un banchale a figure de br. 6.
[270] Un banchale a figure de br. 6.
[271] Un banchale a figure de br. 6.
[272] Un banchale a figure de br. 7.
[273] Un banchale a figure de br. 8.
[274] Un banchal basso a figure de br. 8.
[275] Portera una vechia de razo cum una donna a cavallo.
[276] Portere due de razo de la Anunciata.
[277] Portere due de razo de Perseo.
[278] Portera de razo de Argo.
[279] Portera de razo del ragazo.
[280] Portera de razo de Gedion.
   The story of Gideon was prominent among the tapestries made (1449–53) for Philip the
   Good, Duke of Burgundy, and displayed in the Chapter House of the Order of the Golden
   Fleece at the Hague in 1456 (Roblot-Delondre, 'Sujets antiques', no. 150).
[281] Portera de Octaviano vechia.
[282] Portera de razo del lione.
[283] Portera de razo del franzoso.
[284] Portera de panno verde rechamata a soli.
[285] Portera de panno turchino a fiori de margarita.
[286] Portera de rosato nova rechamata.

[287] Portera pavonaza a melangoli.
[288] Portera pavonaza a tortore.
[289] Portera pavonaza a foiammi.
[290] Portera pavonaza a fiori.
[291] Portera pavonaza a fiori de margarita.

[fol. 6ᵛ]
[292] Una tapeta femina.
[293] Un par de tapeti da terra rasi.
[294] Un par de tapeti da terra longi br. 8.
[295] Un par de tapeti da terra de br. 8.
[296] Un par de tapeti da tera cum l'arma vechya da Gonzaga de br. 7.
[297] Un par de tapeti da terra da compasso novi de br. 7.
[298] Un par de tapeti da terra da compasso de br. 6.
[299] Un par de tapeti da tera da compasso de br. 7.
[300] Un par de tapeti da tera frusti de br. 6.
#Dati a Bellino non venduti:
[301] Un par de tapeti da tera de br. 5.

> The *cameriere* Giovan Francesco, known as Bellino, is named in W 26.

[302] Tapeto grande de Ravenna.
[303] Un tapeto da rose de br. 9 rosegato.
[304] Un tapeto da 4 rote de br. 9.
[305] Un tapeto da la loza de br. 9.
[306] La spallera de tapeto de br. 13.
[307] Un tapeto da la loza de br. 8.
[308] Un tapeto da tavola mezan longo br. 8.
[309] Un tapeto novo cum 5 rote longo br. 8.
[310] Un tapeto novo cum 3 rote longo br. 6.
[311] Un tapeto de 4 rote longo br. 7.
[312] Un tapeto de 2 rote cum lampade de br. 5.
[313] Un tapeto de 3 rose cum lanpade de br. $4^1/_2$.
[314] Un tapeto de lavoreri minuti longo br. 6 dal letuzo.
[315] Un tapeto da la loza de br. 9.
[316] Un tapeto da 3 rose cum lampade de br. 5.
[317] Un tapeto usato de 4 rote de br. 7.
[318] Un tapeto cum 4 moschee de br. $5^2/_3$.
[319] Un tapeto da 2 rote de br. 5.
[320] Un tapeto usato da lavoreri minuti de br. 5.
[321] Un tapeto vechyo grosso de 3 rote de br. 4.
[322] Un tapeto usato de lavoreri minuti de br. $4^1/_2$.
[323] Un tapeto de 4 rote de br. 4.
[324] Un tapeto vechio a lavorer minuti de br. 4.
[325] Un tapeto frusto cum 2 rote de br. 3.

[fol. 7ʳ]
[326] Un tapeto moresco cum una rota de br. 3.
[327] Un tapeto da forciero de br. $2^1/_2$.

[328] Un tapeto da 3 rote da terra de br. 4.

[329] Un tapeto da forciere de br. 3.

[330] Un tapeto novo cum la moschea de br. 3.

[331] Un tapeto da tera da 3 rote de br. 4.

[332] Un tapeto picolo da 2 rote de br. 2.

[333] Un tapeto da forciero de br. 3.

[334] Un tapeto novo cum 2 rote de br. 5 e 3.

[335] Un tapeto a la moresca cum moschea de br. 2 e $^1/_3$.

[336] Un tapeto da forciero de br. 3.

[337] Un tapeto cum moschea de br. 2 e $^1/_2$.

[338] Un tapeto cum moschea de br. 2 e $^1/_3$.

[339] Un tapeto da forciere de br. 2.

[340] Un tapeto picolino.

[341] Tre tapeti picoli da far cossini.

[342] Un tapeto negro novo cum la moschea.

[343] L'aparamento de veluto alexandrino cum stelle d'oro rechamate e cum la sua coperta in dui pezi.

[344] L'aparamento de damasco verde picolo cum la coperta nova et la cortina de cendalino verde.

[345] L'aparamento de brochato d'oro alexandrino in 4 pezi.

[346] L'aparamento de raso verde cum la spallera e due cortine de cendal verde cum quatro cosini.

[347] L'aparamento de damascho biancho cum la spallera e due cortine de cendal biancho cum 4 cossini.

3 Strata; 1 Cornachino; 1 Francesco de Padua; 2 al Fregastora:

[348] Pezi sette de saya rossa depincte.

[349] Pezi [cancelled: otto] sette de saya rossa rechamate.

#D. Hector habuit in recompensum suorum come debitor est Commiss.:

[350] Uno aparamento de tela biancha cum quatro cortine.

> The reference is presumably to Hector, son of Rodolfo Gonzaga, to whom some other items had been bequeathed; this was perhaps a substitution, or in lieu of a sum the executors or their agents owed to him (W 22).

[351] Uno aparamento de tela biancha cum quatro cortine.

[352] Uno aparamento de tela biancha cum quatro cortine cum quatro arme depinte.

[353] Uno aparamento de tafta biancho cum franze d'oro e le dindarelle e cum quatro cortine de seta.

[fol. 7^v]

[354] Un aparamento de cendal verde cum franze d'oro e la testera rechamata cum l'arma e le sue cortine de arete.

[355] Quatro cossini grandi de brochato d'oro alexandrino.

[356] Doi cossini de veluto pavonazo.

[357] Doi cossini de veluto cremesino.

[358] Doi cossini de brochato d'oro verde novi.

[359] Doi cossini de brochato d'oro verde vechii.

[360] Quatro cossini de panno d'oro cremesino.

#<u>Sancto Francesco lassato</u> [W 3]:

[361] Una coperta de brochato d'oro cremesino.

[362] Una vesta over turcha de domasco cremesino nova senza fodra.

[363] Una turcha de raso alexandrino nova senza fodra.

[364] Un vestito de zambeloto pavonazo senza fodra.

[365] Un vestito de zambeloto cremesino senza fodra.

[366] Quatro coperte da cavallo a la divisa cum le arme.

  Regarding I 366–71, cf. I 961–6 below.

[367] Un par de staffe grande dorate.

[368–71] <u>Donati a Cosmo per essere di puocha valuta la cintola sola</u>:

[368] Un par de redene de veluto a la divisa.

[369] Una testera de veluto a la divisa.

[370] Un par de stafili de seta.

[371] Una cintola negra de far la coda.

[372] Una pianeta de brochato d'oro pavonazo cum li frisi d'oro fillato.

[373] Doe dalmatiche de brochato d'oro, una biancha e l'altra rossa cum li frisi d'oro tirato.

#*una*:

[374] Doe cotte, una de tela ortigina, l'altra de cortina.

[375] Un camiso col fornimento de brochato rosso.

[376] Un camiso col fornimento de brochato pavonazo.

[377] Un camiso col fornimento de brochato biancho.

[378] Un amito col friso d'oro tirato *e cum .+. de perle in mezo*.

[379] Un amito de cortina con li cordoni d'oro e de seta biancha.

[380] Un par de cordoni da cinzere d'oro e de seta biancha.

[381] Un par de cordoni da cinzere d'oro e de seta pavonaza.

[382] Un par de cordoni da cinzere ut supra rossi.

[383] Una stolla de brochato d'oro biancho.

[fol. 8ʳ]

[384] Una stolla de brochato d'oro rosso.

[385] Una stolla de brochato d'oro pavonazo.

[386] Un manipulo de brochato d'oro biancho.

[387] Un manipulo de brochato d'oro rosso.

[388] Un manipulo de brochato d'oro pavonazo.

[389] La guayna de corame dale mitre cum doe mitre.

[390] Uno capelleto de brochatello pavonazo d'altare.

[391] Uno palieto de brochatello pavonazo per la sedia.

[392] Uno capelleto de brochatello biancho d'altare.

[393] Uno palieto de brochatello biancho da sedia.

[394] Un palieto de terzanello azuro senza ornamento, fodrà de tela.

[395] Una tavoglia grande de seta azura cum liste incarnate lavorate a la moresca.

[396] Uno missale vechio in carta bona.

[397] Una pianeta de brochatello biancho.

[398] Una pianeta de brochatello pavonazo.

[399] Uno camiso vechyo de cortina.

[400] Una stolla de brochatello biancho.
[401] Una stolla de brochatello pavonazo.
[402] Un manipulo de brochatello biancho.
[403] Un manipulo de brochatello pavonazo.
[404] Un amito simplice.
[405] Doe tovaglie d'altare vechie e grosse.
[406] Una tovaglia d'altare cum li capi lavorati d'oro e de seta.
[407] Una tovaglia de seta d'altare vechia.
[408] Un cordone biancho vechio.
[409] Un palio d'altare de brochatello pavonazo.
[410] Un palio d'altare de brochatello biancho.
[411] Un palio d'altare de brocatello biancho vechio.
[cancelled: un cordone biancho vechyo]
[412] Una pietra sacrata de serpentino.
[413] Una borsa da corporali cum S. Maria e Christo picenino.

[fol. 8ᵛ]
[414] Una borsa de ligno da corporali coperta de veluto alexandrino. rechamata cum Yeshus.
[415] Una meza borsa da corporali cum S. Maria.
[416] Una borsa da corporali cum Yeshus in croce.
[417] Una scatola d'avolio da hostie.
[418] Una anchona d'avolio.
[419] Uno cosinetto de raso verde rotto.
[420] Un fazoleto de seta cum reliquie dentro.
[421] Un fazoleto de seta vechio.
[422] Un collarino de amito de brochatello biancho.
[423] Un scachero d'osso.

> Francesco is recorded playing chess (though nothing is said about this chess-set of carved bone) with Pius II's nephew Cardinal Francesco Todeschini-Piccolomini, in a letter from B. Marasca to Barbara, Rome, 1 May 1462 (ASMn, AG, b. 841, c. 689); Chambers, 'Housing Problems', p. 45, Doc. 6.

[424] Uno letto da piumma.
[425] Doe tovaglie grande da tavola de renso.
[426] Sei tovaglie grande da tavola de renso.
[427] Otto tovaglie mezane da tavola de renso.
[428] Undice tovaglie de renso da sugare le man.
#12 venduti:
[429] Vintiotto tovaglioli de rense da tener denanti.
[430] Meza tovaglia de renso sguarzata cum un mazo de pezi da netare cortelli.
[431] Tre tovaglie grosse da credenza.
[432] Sei peze da sugare ariento.
[433] El pavaglione grande col suo fornimento che donò lo Ill[ustrissi]mo [Alfonso] Duca de Calabria.

> On *padiglioni* (bed canopies or tents) see Thornton, *Renaissance Interior*, pp. 121–7.

[434] Un pavaglione picolo cum le cortine dopie cum li fornimenti soi.

> See above, I 433.

[435] Doe tende da un culo senza ligname.

> These cradle curtains (cf. I 436) had presumably been used for the 'Cardinalino', whose infancy had been spent in the house in Mantua (see above, pp. 24, 104).

[436] Una tenda picola da dui culi cum li ligni.

[437–9] Io. Arrivabenus:

[437] Otto matarazi picoli de terlise de garzatura.

[438] Braza circha 400 de tela grossa.

[439] Lenzoli novi li quali fece fare Zohanne Arrivabene.

#Io. Arrivabe.:

[440] Doe selle vechie consignate per Zohan Antonio Musone.

[441] Coperte 11 da muli da somma.

[442] La coracina de Mons. coperta de raso cremesino cum le fibie de arzento dorato.

fol. 9ʳ

[443] Falda, fianchali, arnise, schenere, la celata cum la bavera invernigate.

> These military items, including a *falda* which was probably a padded garment worn beneath the armour (Newton, *Dress of the Venetians*, p. 166), may well have been part of the cardinal's field equipment in his role as legate during the War of Ferrara. On 25 January 1483 he had written, from Ferrara, to his brother Marchese Federico Gonzaga: 'Nui ne faciamo tanto animosi su questa impresa, che hormai pensiamo de uscire a la campagna et afrontare li inimici gagliardamente quando bisogni. E pur per andarvi più securi, ne pare de ordinarne alcune armature tra le quale havemo commesso a questo maestro Micheletto che procuri farne fare un par de schenere et un par de arnise per la persona nostra, de la quale ne dice che puoteremo essere ben serviti quando cum licentia de Vostra Signoria le possa fare maestro Henrico suo da Milano...' (ASMn, AG, b. 1231, c. 5).

#Canalis:

[444] La coracina coperta de raso verde de Canale.

#Hieronymus:

[445] La coracina coperta de raso verde de Hyeronimo.

#Scatolinus:

[446] La coracina coperta de veluto cremesino de Scatolino.

#Alexander Mongardon:

[447] La coracina coperta de veluto alexandrino de Alexandro.

[448] Uno par de stivalli rossi.

[449] Un par de stivalli negri.

[450] Un par de stivalli aburzachinati reversi.

[451] Tre cossini coperti de corame rosso.

[452] Tre fornimenti da mula pavonazi.

[453] Uno fornimento da mula de rosato.

[454] Dui morsi dorati.

[455] Tre coperte da mulo pavonaze.

[456] Uno pezo de panno verde.

[457] Tre pezi de panno verde picoli .b.c.d.

[458] Uno pezo da panno verde mazor.e

[459] Uno pezo de panno verde mazore.A.

[460–1] d. Francisco vigore legati [W 21]:

[460] Una camera integra e razi bianchi a verdura.

[461] Uno sparavere fornito de tela de rense col suo capeleto novo a la divisa.

> Similar to a *padiglione* (see I 433n), this bed canopy with its top or capping (see Thornton, *Renaissance Interior*, pp. 24, 128) must be the recently ordered *sparaverium* which is also noted (W 21) as a bequest to the 'Cardinalino'. It seems to be the subject of a letter from Eleonora of Aragon, dated at Ferrara, 31 December 1483, to Francesco Gonzaga, the future marchese of Mantua. She wrongly assumed it was intended for the latter rather than for his namesake, the cardinal's son: 'vivendo quella bona et felice memoria del nostro Reverendissimo Monsignore il Cardinale, a sua contemplatione pigliassemo la cura de farli fornire uno sparavero de setta, il quale havemo inteso nel legato ch'el fece a Vostra Signoria nela sua ultima voluntade havere ordinato ch'el sia dato a quella…' She promised to forward it (ASMn, AG, b. 1183).

[462] Una valise pavonaza scura cum l'arme e fiochi.

Fu dato via per essere rotto:

[463] Uno petenatoyo de seta rotto.

[464] Un par de triunphi in una casetina.

> Cardinal Pietro Barbo's inventory of 1457 contains the following entry referring to a gem with the design of a triumphal chariot and figures: 'Item triumphus unus, videlicet duo equi trahentes currum, super quem est juvenis allatus, et ante ipsos equos est senex Gygas nudus…' (Müntz, *Les Arts*, II, p. 245). Possibly this entry is of a similar pair, even if they seem out of place in this section of the inventory.

[465] Un astrolabio e dui quadranti in scatola verde.

[466] Una coperta [corrected above:] tovaglia de seta verde fatta a lavoreri de tovaglia fodrata de tela verde.

[467] Una scatola verde de canne cum dentro sette basiolette de canne de diversi colori lavorate a oro.

fol. 9ᵛ

[I 468−95, 498−516, 518−38 are connected by a long bracket]:

[468] Uno cuchiaro de diaspro fornito de ariento dorato cum meza perla in cimma.

[469] Uno cuchiaro de calcedonio cum manicho de arzento dorato e perla in cimma.

[470] Un cuchiaro de corniola cum manicho de ariento dorato.

[471] Un temperatore col manicho de corniola guarnito de ariento dorato.

> On penknives see Thornton, 'The Study Room', p. 86; also below I 472.

[472] Un temperatore de diaspro guarnito ut supra.

[473] Un manicho de diaspro da cortello.

[474] Doi manichi da cortello de cristallo cum tinta rossa.

[475] Un cuchiareto de cristallo simplice senza manicho.

[476] Un ochio de cristallo simplice.

[477] Un ochiale de cristallo simplice.

[478] Un triangolo de cristallo simplice.

[479] Una sallera de cristallo simplice.

[480] Una balla de cristallo.

[481] Uno vaso de sardonio simplice.

[482] Una sallera de sardonio simplice.

[483] Un pede de diaspro o calcedonio da candellere simplice.

[484] Un cuchiaro de cristallo guarnito de ariento dorato.

[485] Una scatola de diaspro col coperchiio

\# [485–6] guarnite de ariento dorato:

[486] Una scatola de diaspro simile.

[487] Una scutella de diaspro cum dui man[i]chi guarnita ut supra.

[488] Una scutella de meschia de amatisto e de diaspro guarnita d'ariento dorato.

[489] Una scutella de diaspro col manicho guarnita ut supra.

[490] Un candellere de cristallo guarnito de ariento dorato su quatro pedi de faunno.

[491] Un bochaletto de cristallo col coperchio guarnito de ariento dorato.

[492] Un candelereto de cristallo guarnito ut supra.

[493] Doe bochaline d'altare de cristallo guarnite ut supra.

fol. 10ʳ

[494] Una sallera de diaspro fornita d'oro cum sei serpente a pede cum dui ballassi e dui zaffiri e perle nove.

[495] Una sallera dopia de calcedonio cum balle guarnite de ariento dorato.

[496] Una sallera doppia de calcedonio maiore cum le balle guarnite de ariento dorato.

#*habuit Ill. d. marchio* [W 15]:

[497] Una sallera de alicorno cum littere grece intorno, in una caseta de ariento dorato cum l'arma de Constantinopoli.

          See above, p. 161.

[498] Una sallera doppia de cristallo cum un pezo de diaspro ad una, guarnita de ariento dorato.

[499] Una sallera minore de cristallo doppia guarnita de ariento dorato e smaltato.

[500] Un bochal de cristallo de doi pezi guarnino de ariento dorato e smaltato.

[501] Un bochale grande de cristallo de un pezo, col coperchio guarnito d'ariento dorato e smaltato.

[502] Un bochal de cristallo intagliato a papagalli, guarnito de ariento dorato e smaltato cum una perla in cimma.

[503] Una coppa de cristallo col coperchio guarnita de ariento dorato.

[504] Un bochale de diaspro cum dui manichi, col coperchio, col pede e bocha de ariento e una nachara in cimma.

[505] Una coppa de calcedonio col coperchio grande guarnita de ariento dorato.

[506] Una coppa de diaspro col coperchio de ariento dorato e smaltato.

[507] Quatro balle grande de calcedonio.

[508] Doe balle mazore de calcedonio.

[509] Una navesella de cristallo col pede e orlo de ariento.

[510] Una navesella de matreperla guarnita de ariento dorato cum l'arma gonzagesca e brandiburgense.

fol. 10ᵛ

[513] Uno ovarolo grande de cristallo d'ariento dorato, cum tre poste de ovi.

[514] Un vaso de sardonio col pede de arzento dorato, lavorato a fioreti col coperchio guarnito de ariento dorati.

[515] Un vasetto de cristallo longeto cum foiammi guarnito de ariento dorato.

[516] Un refrescatore de diaspro grande fornito de ariento dorato.

#habet d. Electus:

[517] Un bichero de diaspro col coperchio fornito de ariento dorato.

[518] Una busola de corniola in dui pezi guarnita d'oro cum una perla in cimma.

[519] Uno bussolo de diaspro su tre balle guarnito de ariento dorato.

[520] Una lucernetta de calcedonio simplice a l'antiqua.

[521] Una lucerneta de calcedonio e de cameo cum figure de fora de furie marine e spritelli.

[522] Una scudelletta simplice verde, negra, transparente.

[523] Una scudella d'amatisto e de diaspro guarnita de ariento dorato.

[524] Una conchella de plasma guarnita de ariento dorato.

[525] Una conchella simplice de calcedonio cum minera de diamanti.

[526] Un pozo de diaspro guarnito de ariento dorato *o sia tuto oro*.

[527] Una croce de calcedonio, col pomo e col pede de diaspro guarnita d'ariento dorato senza zoye.

[528] Una bissa intortiata de alabastro simplice.

[529] Una cirella schiza dicono essere de alicorno.

[530] Uno ovo de ambro zalo forato e simplice.

[531] Una testa picola de calcedonio simplice.

[532] Quatro cuchiari de cristallo fornite d'ariento dorato de diverse sorte.

[533] Un cuchiaro de vetro de diversi colori col manicho d'ariento.

[534] Doe forchete de cristallo fornite d'ariento dorato.

fol. 11^r

[535] Un pezo de sasso cum minera de rubini.

[536] Doe cappe de matreperla cum una perla per ci[a]schauna.

[537] Lingue xii minore e una mazore de pesce guarnite d'ariento dorato.

> Perhaps these are tongue-stones or 'serpents' tongues', pieces of fossilized sharks teeth, which came mainly from Malta and were used as amulets; they were believed to sweat if near poison. See the entry by J. M. Massing in *Circa 1492: Art in the Age of Exploration*, Exhibition Catalogue, ed. J. A. Levenson, New Haven and London, 1991, no. 12, pp. 129–30.

[538] Un salino de diaspro fornito d'arzento olim dorato.

#habuit Illustris quondam Marchio vigore legati [W 15]:

[539] Tute quante le figure e altre cose de bronzo, che furenno da bona memoria del quondam Reverendissimo Cardinale di Mantua, sono sta' date e consignati per domino Zohanne Petro Arrivabene al Illustrissimo signor Marchese di Mantua, como apare per la scripta over quietanza fatta per Sua Signoria ad esso domino Zohannepetro.

[540–1] Io. pe.:

[540] La testa de papa Paulo ligata in cameo col reverso de uno rubino mazoretto e dui picolini, tre turchine e otto perle picole ligata in ariento dorato.

> Paul II had commissioned 'una corniola cum la testa de papa Paulo cum lo regno in testa et fo facto pacto ducati cento, et la dicta corniola ha Domenico de Piero'; still unpaid for after the pope's death in 1471, Francesco may have have acquired it then (Müntz, *Les Arts*, II, p. 118).

[541] Una Faustina de calcedonio in faza relevata ligata in ariento dorato

#habuit Illustrissimus dux Calabrie vigore legati [W 13]:

[542] Jullio Cesare in corniola cum littere Divi Juli ligato in ariento dorato.

'…el Cardinal de Mantoa a li giorni nostri ave uno camoino antichissimo dove era sculto la immagine di Cexare belissi[m]o, valea 10 milia ducati' was noted by J. Fantaguzzi, *Cura epitaphia repeta* (Ravenna, Biblioteca classense, MS 468, c. 11), quoted by Weiss, *Discovery*, p. 197 n. 4; Brown, 'Lorenzo', p. 90; for similar examples and copies of this cornelian, see also Brown, 'Lorenzo', p. 90 n. 10, p. 93 fig. 4.

[543−63] <u>Jo. pe.</u>:

[543] Una testa col petto de un zovene de calcedonio ligata in ariento dorato.

[544] Un Marte in calcedonio biancho ligato in ariento dorato.

[545] Alexandro Magno incavato in brillo ligato in ariento dorato.

> See I 557n.

fol. 11ᵛ

[546] Antonino in plasma ligato in ariento dorato.

[547] Una testa de corniola cum una laurea ligata in tondo de ariento dorato de un homo.

[548] Una testa de un vechyo senza barba col capo calvo in corniola ligata in ariento dorato.

[549] Una Faustina in aqua marina ligata in ariento dorato cum un cordone verde.

> Maybe Paul II's 'cammeo grande cum una Faustina amantata, la quale lo extima ducati XXXV…el qual cameo dixe…al presente esser nelle mane de Monsignore da Mantua a relatione de Domenico de Piero' (Müntz, *Les Arts*, II, pp. 117−18). See also I 557n.

[550] Uno Alexandro in corniola ligato ut supra.

[551] Uno capo laureato in corniola al longeto ligato ut supra.

[552] Una testa in nicolo al longeto ligata ut supra.

[553] Uno Hercules in niccolo cum una cerva e una cadenella d'ariento dorato.

[554] Un tauro in sardonio ligato ut supra in forma quadra.

[555] Uno calcedonio cum teste cimque e littere 'Aetates' ligato ut supra cum cadenella, e posto in una casetina d'ariento dorato.

[556] Uno sardonio cum testa e petto de un zovene ligato ut supra.

[557] Alexandro Magno in calcedonio biancho ligato ut supra cum cadenella.

> This may be one of the pieces Francesco acquired from Paul II's collection and which were in his hands in November 1471: 'uno calcedonio cum testa de Alexandro…el quale similiter dixe che al presente ha el dicto cardinale de Mantua' (Müntz, *Les Arts*, II, p. 117; Brown, 1989, p. 102 n. 7).

[558] Una figuretta in calcedonio rosso e biancho ligato ut supra.

[559] La testa de Antonino in turchina desligata.

[560] Cleopatra in plasma ligata ut supra cum cadenella e perla e in una casetta d'ariento dorata.

[561] Una figura de homo a la moresca in corniola ligata ut supra cum cadenella e una perla in una casetta d'ariento dorato.

[562] Una testa grande cum li capilli sparti in corniola ligata ut supra, con lo fondo d'ariento e cadenella cum perla in una casetta d'ariento dorato.

[563] Un Marte in corniola col fondo ligato ut supra, cum perla e cadenella in una casetta d'ariento dorato.

fol. 12ʳ

#<u>habuit Illustris quondam Marchio vigore legati</u> [W 15]:

[564] Una corniola cum due figure che se guardano in faza, e una sede e l'altra è in un casamento; e quella che sede ha littere grece di sopra e de sotto; ligata ut supra col fondo cadenella e perla in una casetina d'ariento dorato cum l'Anunciata.

> Apparently the 'Felix gem' (inscribed with the name of its maker, 1st cent. AD), now in the Ashmolean Museum, Oxford. It was noted in Cardinal Pietro Barbo's inventory of 1457 (Müntz, *Les Arts*, II, p. 245) and identified by Pollard, 'The Felix Gem'; see also Brown, 'Questions of Provenance' and the entry (with illustration) by M. Vickers, *Thomas Howard Earl of Arundel*, exhibition catalogue, Ashmolean Museum, Oxford, 1985, no. 75, pp. 73–4; Sheard, *Antiquity*, no. 8; Brown, 'Lorenzo', p. 90.

[565] Tre amatisti grandi desligati in un busoleto de ligno.

[566] Un ambro zallo cum mosche dentro.

> On flies etc enclosed in amber (with references from Martial's *Epigrams* and Pliny's *Natural History*), and the supposed therapeutic properties of amber, see G. Williamson, *The Book of Amber*, London, 1932, esp. pp. 32–40, 141–50).

#<u>Jo. pe.</u>:

[567] Uno spechio quadro de azale ligato in ariento dorato cum otto camei, e col reverso de ariento cum l'arma aniellata.

> Identified by Brown ('Lorenzo', pp. 90–1, who reads 'azale' as iron, but if the word is a derivative of 'acciaio' surely it is steel) as the mirror listed as a pledge in the loan agreement of 1496 between Piero de' Medici and Agostino Chigi: 'uno spechio d'argiento legatovi in esso otto camei' (BAV, MS Chigi R.V.e). For another polished steel mirror, see I 682.

[568] Uno armariolo de ligno coperto de raso cremesino recamato a feste d'oro tirato cum quatro capi de camei de fora e dentro una imagine de Nostra Donna de panno de razo cum oro.

[569] Una tavola de diaspro cum camei otto grandi e sedice minori de intorno, adornata de veluto pavonazo et oro et argento tirato posta in una cassa rossa.

> The second of the tablets listed and valued in the letter of G. P. Arrivabene, 14 February 1486 (Brown, 'Lorenzo', pp. 90–1; see also below, Appendix 3, no. 22).

[570] Una tavola de diaspro maiore cum camei sedice de intorno ligati, adornata de veluto cremesino et oro tirato in una cassa rossa fodrata de veluto alexandrino.

> The first of the tablets G. P. Arrivabene listed in the above letter (ibid.).

[571] Una tavola quadra de plasma cum camei deceotto de intorno ligati, adornata de veluto cremesino et oro tirato in una cassa rossa.

> The third of the tablets Arrivabene listed in the above letter (ibid.).

[572–4] <u>Jo. pe.</u>:

[572] Tavole vinti d'ariento dorate cum camei ligati de diversa sorte a numero centocinquantauno, e tute hanno l'arma e lo nome de la bona memoria de Monsignore, de le quale, che sono in tuto numero vinti, ne sono poste xviii in una cassa de corame negro e due pur in un'altra cassa de corame.

> These twenty silver tablets or trays are described in greater detail in the loan agreement between Piero de' Medici and Agostino Chigi, 17 May 1496 (BAV, MS Chigi R.V.e), cited by Brown, 'Lorenzo', pp. 88–91.

[573] Una casetta de ariento dorata in forma de orloio cum sei capi de camei de fora ligati.

[574] Un tondo de diaspro cum un capo de Pompeo de calcedonio e camei sedice intorno guarnito de veluto alexandrino.

> Among the objects to be deposited with the Medici and pledged in 1496: 'uno tondo di diaspro adorno di velluto alexandrino et d'oro tirato, in esso sedici canmei antichi de più sorte, et una testa de calcidonio et è sanza argiento' (Brown, 'Lorenzo', p. 90 n. 2; see also above, pp. 126–7).

fol. 12ᵛ
Jo. p.:
[575] Camei cinquanta dui picoli e uno grande desligati in un sacheto de terlise.

> These are uncut gems.

#*habuit d. protonotarius vigore legati* [W 18]:
[576] Uno diamante in tavola ligato in anello lavorato a ochy de pavone.
#*Datus Beate Virgini de Votis ex legato* [W 10]:
[577] Un rubino grande in tavola ligato in anello smaltato a tronchi.
[578] Un smeraldo fatto a fazette ligato in oro in anello, el quale ha del tondo.
[579] Doe turchinete ligate in dui anelli smaltati.
[580] Un zaffiro in tavola ligato in anello smaltato.
[581] Una granata in tavola ligata in anello smaltato.
[582] Uno anello d'oro cum l'arma dela bona memoria de Monsignore.
[583] Uno anello d'oro dai contrasigni dele forteze.
[584–6 are bracketted]:
[584] Uno zaffiro disligato forato.
[585] Una vergetina d'ariento già dorato cum caracti dentro, et una turchineta desligata in un busolin de ligno.
[586] Uno anellazo d'otone dorato cum uno rubino contrafatto e arme de papa Paulo.

fol. 13ʳ
#habuit Electus in dono:
[587] Uno pezo de belzoy.

> See above, p. 80.

[588] Una casetina de acipresse cum xi ganette de seta de diversi colori, e quatro spolete cum oro.
[589] Una casetta lavorata de pasta de muschio et oro, cum dentro nove cavoni de seta bianca, et aze sei de seta biancha.
#habuit Bonettus:
[590] Uno cadinello de vetro azuro lavorato ad oro, et in mezo due figure de homini giostranti.

> The beneficiary was presumably Antonio Bonetto of Padua, who was in charge of the affairs of Francesco 'Cardinalino' (W 32).

[591] Un calamaro de ramo in forma de un busolo lavorato a la damaschina.

> On ink-stands, see D. Thornton, 'The Study Room', pp. 74–87; see also I 73.

#habuit Bonettus:
[592] Un refrescatore biancho de vetro lavorato cum oro.

> See I 589.

[593] Un refrescatore de marmore biancho.

#habuit Bonettus:

[594]   Un busoloto de vetro azuro sorofato d'oro.

[595]   Una scatola cum alcuni cavoni de seta de diversi colori.

#Donati per essere rotti:

[596]   Doi cossini de panno rosso rechamati cum un cane.

[597]   Tre cosinetti de pignolato e liste de seta intorno.

[598]   Doe anchonette grece vechie: una cum un crucifixo e l'altra cum Nostra Donna.

[599]   Una scatoletta cum dui marchi da peso e una balanzeta.

#Donata a Jo. Aloysio:

[600]   Una caseta cum artificio da forare perle.

#habuit Episcopus:

[601]   Uno busoleto de cendal verde coperto nel qual dicono esse un dente de Sancta Apolonia.

[602]   Una tasca vechia d'arzone lavorata d'oro tirato cum tesuto d'oro guarnita de ariento aniellato.

[603]   Doi corneti de serpa deli quali uno ha la guayna d'ariento.

[604]   Una saetta; doe petre de rospo; la petra dela bissa; un chuchiaro d'osso antiquo e un pezo de [*cancelled* cristallo] coralo.

[605]   Doi carneri bianchi guarniti d'ariento dorato

#*Restituta Sacristie Sancti Petri*:

[606]   Una tovaglia da tavola azura lavorà a oro a la morescha.

[607]   Un'altra tovaglia tuta lavorata a oro a la moresca cum cordoni pendenti.

#*Datum Magnifico d. Francisco ex legato* [W 21]:

[608]   Un pezo de alicorno

> This piece of 'unicorn' was presumably less valued than the item on an ornamental stand (I 86; see also pp. 80–1, 124 and index, s.v.). On the amuletic properties against poison and on legends associated with 'unicorn' or narwhal, i.e., arctic whale horn, see Massing (as above, I 537), no. 7, p. 126, citing G. Schönberger, 'Narwal-Einhorn: Studien über einen seltenen Werkstoff', *Städel-Jahrbuch*, 9, 1935–6, pp. 167–247, and J. W. Einhorn, *Spiritalis unicornis: Das Einhorn als Bedeutungsträger in Literatur und Kunst des Mittelalters*, Munich, 1976.

[609]   La pietra dal asino in una guayna negra.

fol. 13ᵛ

#habuit Cosmus dono:

[610]   Un calzatore de corno fornito d'ariento.

[611]   Tre rocheti de tela ortigina lavorati d'oro.

[612]   Una tovaglia de seta azura lavorata a la perusina.

[613]   Tre cintole moresche de diversi colori.

[614]   Uno colare da cane de brochato d'oro guarnito d'ariento.

[615]   Uno borsoto zenovose d'oro cum botoncini.

[616]   Uno borsoto a la veneciana de raso cremesino lavorato a la damaschina.

[617]   Una tascha rechamata d'oro e seta, cum dui corni de abundantia col tesuto brochato d'oro e lo fornimento d'oro.

[618]   Uno cosinetto fatto a tellarolo d'oro e de seta pieno de lavanda.

[619]   Sei panaselli o tovagliete ligate insiema da confetere lavorate de seta e oro.

[620]   Tovaglioli 8 de rense cum li capi negri.

#D. Aloysio Tosabezo d[ono]:

[621] Doi lassi da can de seta.

[622] Doa para de guanti de lana.

[623] Doa para de guanti de capreto forniti de seta e oro.

[624] Una scatola de avolio cum un pezo de ambra.

[625] Una cintola a la moresca cum li capi d'oro.

[626] Cinque cintole de cortina cum li capi d'oro e de seta, e parechii pezi de tela de cortina e seta, in una casetta de acipresso straforata.

[627] Uno lenzolo de sancille lavorato d'oro ale cuseture.

[628] Uno cavezo de tela nova nostrana de br. 55.

[629–30] in una sachoza:

[629] Paneselli quadri sei.

[630] Paneselli longi dece.

[631–3] in una sachoza:

[631] Decenove capi tra tovaglie e tovagliole.

[632] Quatro peze da barbero.

[633] Uno mazo de peze da rocheti strazate.

fol. 14^r

[634–40] *Data camerariis duplicata*: ##in una fodreta:

[634] Parechie maniche de rocheti in una sachetina.

[635] Quatro cuffioni.

[636] Mudande in una sacheta.

[637] Sacheta da supplicatione.

[638] Fodrete vechie in una sachella.

[639] Dui cosineti de piumino da stomacho.

[640] Una sachella de fasse.

[641–2] in una fodreta:

[641] Doi cosinetti pieni de rose profumate.

[642] Uno pezo de veluto de più colori.

#duplicato:

[cancelled] Uno guinzayo da chiave d'ariento tirato.

[643] Una cintola pavonaza d'oro.

[644] Una cintola verde d'oro.

[645] Una cintola de cremesi usata.

[646] Una vesica de muschio.

[647] Una tovaglia de seta cum oro cum franze d'oro.

[648] Uno panesello quadro cum lavoreri a la moresca.

[649] Un panesello cum capi lavorati d'ariento cum le cere.

[650] Un panesello cum li capi lavorati a la moresca de seta biancha.

[651] Un panesello grande cum 3 lavoreri de seta a la moresca.

[652] Uno panesello quadreto cum li capi lavorati de seta senza cere.

[653] Uno panesello lavorato, li capi d'oro e de seta cum cere.

[654] Un panesello de sancille, cum li capi lavorati d'oro e de seta, e cerre d'oro.

[655] Uno panesello cum capi d'oro e le cerre.

[656] Uno panesello quadro cum li capi d'ariento senza cere lavorato a la moresca.

[657] Uno panesello longo cum li capi senza cere lavorato de seta biancha a la mores[c]a.

[658] Uno panesello cum franza d'oro a spinapesse.

[659] Dui paneselli de seta lavorati d'oro e seta cremesina.

[660] Doi paneselli de sancille cum li capi lavorati d'oro e seta.

fol. 14ᵛ

[661] Uno petenatoyo de sancille lavorato d'oro e seta.

[662] Un altro petenatoyo lavorato tuto d'oro cum tremolanti.

[663] Una tavoglia de seta lavorata a stelle e fiori.

[664] Sei pannelli cum li capi lavorati de seta biancha.

[665] Un panesello grosso cum capi lavorati de straforo.

[666] Doi paneselli quadri da confetere, uno zalo cum oro l'altro pavonazo.

[667] Uno aguchiarolo de ramo smaltato.

[668] Para sei de fodrete da cossini.

[669] Paneselli nove sutili cum li capi lavorati de filo.

[670] Paneselli dece più grosseti cum li capi bianchi vergati.

[671] Paneselli undice mezani cum li capi lavorati de filo.

[672] Paneselli cimque grossi.

[673] Uno rotolo de parechii paneselli insiema.

[674] Un altro panesello.

[675] Tovaglie otto de renso.

[676] Tovagliole picole tre de renso.

[677] Tovaglioli sei de renso cum li capi negri, et uno cum li capi bianchi.

[678–86 are bracketted]:

[678] Uno sole d'oro cum razi rechamato.

[679] Uno colaro da cane fatto a tellarolo d'oro cum figure.

[680] Uno paro de guanti de lana bianchi lavorati d'oro.

[681] Una sachoza rechamata de seta et oro cum zavatole dentro.

[682] Uno spechio de azale cum la cassa intarsiata.

> Cf. I 567. On polished steel mirrors see Thornton, 'The Study Room', pp. 104, 111, 133.

[683] Uno cosinetto cum cendal verde intorno.

[684] Uno orologio da sabione guarnito d'oro tirato cum perle.

[685] Tagli de drapo d'oro beretino per pianeta, tunicella e dalmaticha.

[686] Quatro zochi da capelleto.

fol. 15ʳ

#habuit Reverendus d. protonotarius Administrator vigore legati [W 18]:

[687] Un messale grande coperto de brochato d'oro e guarnito de ariento senza serame.

> Almost certainly the large illuminated missal still extant (Mantua, Museo diocesano), originally commissioned by Giovan Lucido Gonzaga to be illuminated by Belbello of Pavia (started c. 1448), which Barbara of Brandenburg wanted completed in 1461; probably the same large missal which she sent to Francesco in 1467, and the one which he declared he always took with him whether at Rome or Marino (see above, pp. 57–8, for bibliography etc).

[688] Un breviario da camera coperto de brochato d'oro.

[689] Un breviario da camera coperto de veluto cremesino.

#*Iop.**:

[690] Un breviario portatile picolino.

#*habuit Illustris d. Franciscus* [W 19]:

[691] Un officiolo de diverse oratione miniato, historiato e coperto de brochato d'oro cremesino.

#Iofra. Ca.[?]*:

[692] Un officiolo de la Donna coperto de brochato alexandrino.

[693] Un libro in capreto de la confessione.

[694] La Bibia grande in un volume in carta.

> Probably the 'Bibia grande' valued at 50 ducats, one of the eight of his mother's books allotted to the cardinal in 1481 (ASDMn, FCC, ser. misc., b. 2/A, 'Inventario de le cose', fol. 14^r).

\# [695–6] IoF.*:

\#\# [695–6] in bona carta cum la guayna de corame:

[695] Prima parte de la Bibia.

[696] Seconda parte de la Bibia.

[697] Doi volumi de la Bibia a stampo.

[698] Bibia portatile coperta de veluto negro.

[699] Bibia portatile coperta de verde.

[700] Fioreti de la Bibia in papiro in vulgare.

[701] Augustino De Civitate Dei.

[702] Postilla super Evangellium Luce et Marci.

[703] Versi in vulgare de Vita Christi in papiro.

[704] Un libreto de Reliquie cum cordoni *chiamato de devotione e statione*.

[705] Opere de San Bernardo.

[706] Un volume de le Vite di Sancti Patri.

[707] Quatro volumi de la Summa Antonina.

> St Antonino OFM, Bishop of Florence, *Summa moralis theologiae*. See S. Orlandi, *Bibliografia antoniniana*, Vatican City, 1962, pp. 25–64, 295–305.

[708] Speculum Vite humane in papiro.

[709] Un Psalmista in papiro *a stampo*.

[710] Vita de Sancta Agnese.

> For hagiographical literature concerning St Agnes, see P. Franchi de' Cavalieri, 'S. Agnese nella tradizione e nella leggenda', *Römische Quartalschrift*, Supplementheft X, Rome, 1899.

[711] Opera antiqua de le parabole de Salamone.

[712] Opera de fra Jacopone.

> Presumably the *Laude* of Jacopone da Todi; Barbara of Brandenburg had possessed a 'Jacoponus' according to the inventory of her possessions in 1481 (ASMn, AN, Estensioni, R. 78, Cornice).

[713] Sermone de Sancto Augustino Ad Heremitas in papiro.

> Perhaps from the anonymous Pseudo-Augustine, *Libellus sancti Augustini episcopi de vita heremetica vel solitaria distinctus per sermones quos fecit fratribus suis heremiticis*, as in BAV, MS Vat. Lat. 11446 (see J. Ruysschaert, *Bibliotheca Vaticana codices vat. lat. 11414–11709*, Vatican City, 1959, pp. 70–1). A book of the same title belonging to Barbara of Brandenburg passed to the cardinal in 1481, valued at 1/2 a ducat (ASDMn, FCC, ser. misc. b. 2/A, 'Inventario de le cose', fol. 14^r).

#Iop.*:
[714] Un libreto de Meditatione de la Passione de Christo.

> See M. Jordan Stallings, *Meditationes de Passione Christi olim Sancti Bonaventurae attributae*, Washington D.C., 1965.

[715] Psalmista coperto de damaschino rosso.

[716] Psalmista vechio [cancelled: *de littera moderna.*]

> Presumably Paris, BN, MS Lat. 772, a fourteenth-century psalter with the cardinal's arms on fols 100^v, 137^v (Meroni, *Mostra*, p. 35 n. 71). Among Barbara's books allotted to the cardinal in 1481 (as in I 694) was a 'salmista in carta bona vechio', valued at 1 ducat (ASDMn, FCC, ser. misc. b. 2/A, 'Inventario de le cose', fol. 14^r); also noted in the inventory of goods in the cardinal's house in Mantua after Barbara's death were 'psalmiste duo, unus novus et alter vetus' (ASMn, AN, Estensioni, R. 78, Cornice 1481, inventory, fol. 4^r).

#*Restituta episcopo mantuano*:
[717] *Biblia in versi.*

> See Petrus Riga, *Aurora. Biblia Versificata. A Verse Commentary on the Bible*, pars I, ed. P. E. Beichner, Notre Dame, 1965.

fol. 15^v

[718] Hyeronimo sopra Matheo.

> Jerome, *Commentarius in Evangelium secundum Matthaeum* (*PL*, XXVI, cols 15–228).

[719] Libro de le Sententie.

> Presumably the *Sententiarum libri quatuor*, or *Sentences* of Peter Lombard (d. 1160), a comprehensive and standard textbook of theology (*PL*, CXCII).

#Iop.*:
[720] Opera del Filelfo de Sacerdotio Christi.

> Franciscus Philelphus, *De Jesu Christi sacerdotio ad Sixtum Quartum*; there was also a printed edition of this work: Rome, Stephan Plannck, 1476 (*BMC*, IV, 94).

[721] Somnia Daniellis.

> See *Somniale Danielis… A Medieval Latin Dream Interpretation Handbook*, ed. Lawrence T. Martin, Frankfurt am Main etc, 1981.

#Iop.*:
[722] Libreto de la passione de Christo in versi de vescovo de Rezo.

> Possibly an unrecorded work by Gentile Becchi (Bishop of Arezzo, 1473–97), on whose writings see *DBI*, s.v.; P. O. Kristeller, *Supplementum Ficinianum*, II, Florence, 1937, p. 340. Lorenzo de' Medici had attempted to to use Francesco's good offices to have Becchi made a cardinal, writing to him in February 1477 (Lorenzo de' Medici, *Lettere*, II, no. 250, p. 313).

[723] La passione de Christo in papiro *a stampo*.

> Possibly N. Cicerchia, *La passione di Gesù Christo*, Florence, S. Jacopo a Ripoli, before 8 April 1483 (GW 6702).

[724] Vita beati Gregorii.

> Probably Johannes Diaconus, *De vita Gregorii* (*PL*, LXXV, cols 59–242; ed. H. Goll, Freiburg, 1950).

#Iop.*:
[725] La vita de Christo in papiro.

> Probably Ludolph of Saxony (d. 1378), *Vita Christi* (modern edition by L. M. Rigollot, 4 vols, Paris, 1878).

[726] Libro de confessione in vulgare coperto de montanina zala.

[727] Dialogo de San Gregorio.

> One of St Gregory the Great's *Dialogorum libri IV* (*PL*, LXXVII, cols 144–430). In the inventory of Barbara of Brandenburg is also listed a 'Dialogus Sancti Gregorii' (ASMn, AN, Estensioni, R. 78, Cornice 1481, inventory, fol. 4^r).

#Iop.:

[728] La vita de fra Zoanne da Capistrano in papiro.

> Teofilo da Como, *Vita del beato Giovanni de Capistrano*. There was also a printed edition: Como, Baldassare da Fossato, 1479 (*BMC*, VII, 1025).

[729] Eusebio de hystoria ecclesiastica.

> Eusebius (c. AD 260–340), Bishop of Caesarea, *Ecclesiastical History*, transl. Rufinus.

[730] Liber de nativitate Virginis Marie.

#Iop.*:

[731] Libro in papiro de profecia de Sancta Brigida.

> A copy of the *Revelationes* of St Bridget of Sweden (c. 1303–73) had been ordered from Rome in 1392 for the Gonzaga library (R. Zucchi, 'Ottonello De Scalzi e il "De viris"', *Italia medioevale e umanistica*, 17, 1974, p. 484); this, however, appears to have been a vernacular version, perhaps a copy of the one written at Siena in 1398 (C. Nordenfalk, 'St Bridget of Sweden as Represented in Illuminated Manuscripts', *De Artibus Opuscula XL: Essays in Honor of E. Panofsky*, ed. M. Meiss, New York, 1961, pp. 371–93, esp. p. 382). St Bridget may have held a particular interest for the cardinal because of her association with the palace which he inhabited in Rome adjoining San Lorenzo in Damaso. She had allegedly waited for a year (?1349) in her room there which had a direct view of the high altar, until visited a second time by the angel speaking Swedish who gave instructions for her new order of nuns (Schiavo, *Cancelleria*, pp. 28–30).

[732] Opereta de San Bernardo cum la vita de Virgilio.

> Unspecified work of St Bernard probably bound with Donatus, *Vita Vergilii*.

[733] Le confessione de Sancto Augustino.

[734] La 2a parte di Morali de San Gregorio.

> Books VI–X of Gregory the Great's *Moralium libri* (*PL*, LXXV, cols 730–952).

[735] Augustino De Civitate Dei vulgare.

[736] Prediche de fra Ruberto in papiro.

> Roberto Caracciolo, OFM (1425–95), Bishop of Aquino (1475) and of Lecce (1484), was a celebrated preacher. The cardinal might have first appreciated his preaching of the crusade in 1464; more recently, he had invited him to Mantua, according to a letter of Ludovico Gonzaga, Bishop-Elect, to Stefanino Guidotti, Mantua, 16 December 1483: 'Se ben mi ricordo, lo reverendo vescovo de Aquino, chi è frate Roberto, essendo la bona memoria del Reverendissimo Monsignor Cardinale mio fratello a Roma, e ritrovandose lui in ragionamento cum Suoa Signoria Reverendissima che lo richiedeva ad venire a predicare a Mantuoa per la quadragesima proxima futura, ge promise de farlo' (ASP, AGG, b. 41/3, reg. 1, fol. 24^r). Various collections of Roberto's sermons were made in the 1470s; these included a first printed edition of the *Sermones quadragesimales*, Milan, 1474. See *DBI*, s.v.; S. Bastanzio, *Fra Roberto Caracciolo predicatore del sec. XV*, Isola del Liri, 1947.

[737] Prediche de frate Antonio de Betonda.

> Antonio da Bitonto, OFM (c. 1385–1465), another active preacher (also involved in crusade preaching, 1459–64), whose *Sermones domenicales per totum annum* were, for example, copied before 1436, revised by Fra Filippo da Rodigò and printed in 1495. See *DBI*, s.v.; C. Piana, 'Antonius de Bitonto OFM, praedicator et scriptor saec. XV', *Franciscan Studies*, 13, 1953, pp. 178–97. In the inventory of Barbara of Brandenburg in 1481 a 'Predicationes fratris Antonii de Betunto in bona carta' is listed (ASMn, AN, Estensioni, R. 78, Cornice 1481, inventory, fol. 3^v).

[738] Papalista.

> Barbara of Brandenburg had owned a *papalista* (list of popes), which passed to the cardinal in 1481, valued at 6 ducats (cf. I 694 etc).

#Iop.*:

[739] Repetitione de negligentia prelatorum in papiro.

> Possibly a title in canon law.

[740] Epistole de San Hyeronimo in un volume.

> The letters of St Jerome (*PL*, XXII, cols 325–1191).

[741] Epistole de San Hyeronimo contra Iovinianum.

> St Jerome's *Adversus Jovinianum libri II* were directed to a monk (d. 405) who doubted the values of sexual abstinence and virginity (*PL*, XXIII, cols 221–352).

#*habuit Episcopus Sarsinas* [W 34]:

[742] Cassiodoro su li psalmi.

> Cassiodorus, *Expositio Psalmorum* (*PL*, LXX, 9–1056; Stegmüller, 1894; modern edition by M. Adrien, Turnhout, 1958). The marginal note seems to signify that the book had been returned to the Bishop of Sarsina (near Cesena)—or rather to his cathedral library (see W 34: 'qui est ecclesiae Sarsinatae et nunc inter libros meos'), having been borrowed formerly from his predecessor, namely Fortunato or Fortunatus de Pelacanis (Eubel, II, p. 254), who had briefly been Francesco's *luogotenente* in the legation of Bologna. He had written to Marchese Ludovico of his arrival there on 15 October 1471 (ASMn, AG, b. 1141, c. 214); the cardinal mentioned his death in a letter to Marchese Ludovico Gonzaga, Rome, 2 January 1475: 's'el poveretto del vescovo de Sarsina, qual morse questi dì e già fu mio locotenente, fussi vivo, l'haria aviato' (b. 845, c. 339).

[743] Doi volumi de la Summa Rayneriana.

> Raniero (Giordani) da Pisa, O.P. (b. 1348), *Panteologia*, first printed as *Summa et nucleus theologiae*, Nuremberg, 1474.

[744] Le vite di santi in carta coperto de veluto pavonazo guarnito de ariento dorato.

[745] El cirimoniale de corte in carta.

> Perhaps the *Liber ceremoniarum curiae* of Antonius Rebioli, or one of the compilations by Guido de Busco or Petrus Burgensis (see F. Wasner, 'Tor der Geschichte. Beiträge zum päpstlichen Zeremonienwesen im 15. Jahrhundert', *Archivum historiae pontificiae*, 6, 1958, pp. 113–62, at pp. 124–36; B. Schimmelpfennig, *Die Zeremonienbücher der römischen Kirche im Mittelalter*, Tübingen, 1973, pp. 134–40) or even an early version of the *Caeremoniale romanum* of Agostino Patrizi, papal master of ceremonies from 1468. Although Sixtus IV had, soon after his accession, commissioned this work, the final version may not have been written before the end of 1484 and completed in 1488; Patrizi's *Sacrarum caeremoniarium…libri tres* was printed in 1510 (photostatic reprint, Ridgemount NJ, 1965). See Patrizi, *Cérémonial papal*, I, pp. 24–30, 85. See also above, pp. 6–7.

#Iop.*:

[746] Lo martirologio coperto de cremesino.

#Io. fr.*:

[747] Vite di pontifici del Platina a stampo.

> Bartholomeus [Sacchi] de Platina, *Vitae pontificum*, John of Cologne and Johannes Manthen, Venice, 1479 (*BMC*, V, 235).

[748–9] Io. F.*:

[748] Libreto da canto coperto de brochato d'oro.

> Cf. inventory of Gianfrancesco Gonzaga, 1496: 'uno libreto de Rason de canto coperto de brocha d'oro et fornito de argento' (BCG, FDM, b. 23, fol. 10ᵛ).

[749] Libreto de chiromantia coperto de raso leonato.

Cf. inventory of Gianfrancesco Gonzaga, 1496: 'uno quinterno de ghiromantia' (BCG, FDM, b. 23, fol. 15^r).

[750] *Lo missale dela capella.*

> Cf. I 396, 687.

fol. 16^r

#IoF.*:

[751] Dite Cretense miniato, historiato e coperto de cremesino, cum le chiavete d'ariento dorato.

> Dictys Cretensis, *Ephemerides belli troiani libri a Lucio Septimio ex graeco in latinum sermonem translati* (modern edition by W. Eisenhut, Leipzig, 1958). This must be Chester Beatty Library, Dublin, Western MS 122, in which, although the *stemma* is erased, there is [fol. 3] a miniature of the cardinal's enigmatic device of the lynx and pyramid (see above, p. 85; and Fig. 3), which also appears on the reverse of his medal by Sperandio (Alexander, 'Notes', p. 20 n. 44; Chambers, 'Virtù militare', pp. 221–3 and n. 68; de la Mare, 'Florentine Scribes', app. III, no. 2, p. 285). Cf. also the inventory of Gianfrancesco Gonzaga, 1496: 'uno libro ghiamato Cretensio de bello troyano' (BCG, FDM, b. 23, fol. 10^v).

[752] Un Terentio in carta.

> One or more of the plays of Terence.

[753] Un Salustio in carta.

> Presumably one or more of Sallust's historical works, the *Bellum Catilinae*, the *Bellum Iugurthinum*, or possibly the (ascribed) *Invectiva in Ciceronem*.

[754] La Eneide in carta.

> Virgil's *Aeneid*, the only work by him listed in the inventory.

[755] Ovidio mazore in carta.

> This is presumably Ovid's *Metamorphoses*, but as the book is described as the 'larger' Ovid it is difficult to identify it with Paris, BN MS Lat. 10311, the surviving, small copy of the *Metamorphoses* (much damaged, with the *stemma* and most decorated initials cut out), which is nevertheless signed at the end [fol. 164^v]: 'IULIANUS.PRO.D.F.PROTONO-TARIO.ET.MAR.', i.e., written for Francesco by Giuliano da Viterbo before December 1461 (Meroni, *Mostra*, pp. 59–60; C. Samaran and R. Marichal, *Catalogue des manuscrits en écriture latine portant des indications de date*, III, 1974, 635; F. Munari, *Catalogue of the Mss. of Ovid's Metamorphoses*, Uppsala and London, 1957, no. 266, p. 53).

[756] Le Epistole de Ovidio in carta.

> Presumably Ovid's *Heroides* rather than the *Epistulae ex Ponto*.

#*habuit mutuo d. protonotarius*:

[757] Libro da li Insomnii in carta.

> Probably Hippocrates, *De insomniis*, an edition of which (translated by Andrea Brenta of Padua) was printed in Rome by Oliverius Servius, in 1481 (*BMC*, IV, 130). Alternatively it might be the work by William of Aragon, *Liber de pronosticationibus sompniorum*. See Thorndike, *History*, II, pp. 290–312 ('Ancient and Mediaeval Dreambooks').

[758] Un altro in papiro.

[759] Lucano in carta.

> Presumably Lucan, *Bellum civile* or *Pharsalia*, an epic poem about the civil wars between Caesar and Pompey.

[760] Lo canzonero in carta.

> This is more probably a song-book (cf. I 748, 818, 853) than the vernacular sonnets etc of Petrarch (Cf. I 762), which were not commonly known as the 'Canzoniere' at this date, although the title was diffused in some early printed editions.

#R[estitu]ti:

[761] Apologi de B[artolomeo] Scala in carta.

> Bartholomeo Scala, *Apologi centum*, dedicated to Lorenzo de' Medici il Magnifico in 1481; modern editions by C. Müllner, Vienna, 1897, and in the forthcoming: Bartolomeo Scala, *Humanistic and Political Writings*, ed. A. Brown. On the cardinal's recent wish for a copy of this work see the reference to a draft letter from Scala to Jacopo Guicciardini at Ferrara, 14 April 1483: '…ingegneròmmi satisfare alla volontà di Monsignore legato delli apologi, o vogliamo dire fumee secondo il Mellino' (ASF, Dieci, Missive Leg. Comm. 5, fol. 223r), quoted by Brown, *Scala, Chancellor of Florence*, p. 199 n. 18; see also pp. 278–88, *passim*.

#*habuit mutuo d. protonotarius*:

[762] Un Petrarca coperto de veluto verde.

> This must be either the *Sonectorum & Cantelenarum Liber*, BAV, MS Urb. lat. 681 (see Fig. 7, and M. Vatasso, *I codici petrarcheschi della Biblioteca Vaticana*, Studi e testi 20, Rome, 1908, p. 93), written by Antonio Sinibaldi (signature fol. 190r), or—more probably—BL, Harley MS 3567, the *Rime* and *Trionfi* written by Matteo Contugi of Volterra, with interlinear annotations by Bartolomeo Sanvito and miniatures (apart from the first one) doubtfully attributed to Pietro Gundaleri da Cremona. The latter appears to be by the 'Master of the Vatican Homer', i.e., possibly Gaspare of Padua (Meroni, *Mostra*, pp. 57–60; C. E. Wright, *Fontes Harleiani*, London, 1972, p. 167; de la Mare, 'Florentine Scribes', app. III, no. 22, p. 288). Both these MSS bear the arms of a Gonzaga cardinal. While Wright was probably correct (according to the marginal note against this entry, shown above) in his guess that the Harley MS belonged to Sigismondo Gonzaga, protonotary and later cardinal, he seems to exclude the likelihood that it belonged originally to Francesco, and after his death passed to his nephew (the *stemma* with the cardinal's hat would have served again for Sigismondo after his promotion in 1505). That Francesco also owned the copy of Petrarch's *Rime* now in the Victoria and Albert Museum Library (see below, Manuscripts and Unpublished Sources) is less certain; although this too is decorated with a cardinal's hat, it does not show the Gonzaga arms.

[763] Un libreto de sonetti coperto de pavonazo.

> Possibly another copy of Petrarch's sonnets (cf. I 762) but equally they may well have been by other authors.

[764] Libro de la ventura a stampo coperto de verde.

> Possibly the first version of the fortune book by Lorenzo (Gualtieri) 'Spirito', *Libro della ventura*, Vicenza, 1473, which the author subsequently revised (autograph MS, dated 10 January 1482, Venice, Biblioteca Marciana, cl. Ital. 87 [6226]; printed Brescia, 1483–4). See G. B. Vermiglioli, *Biografia degli scrittori Perugini*, II, Perugia, 1829, pp. 296–300; Kristeller, *Iter*, II, p. 272.

[765] Lo Mesue coperto de montanina in papiro per littera.

> Johannes Mesue, *Antidotarium* or *Grabadin medicamentorum compositorum*; see Sarton, *Introduction*, I, pp. 728–9 (see also I 770).

[766] La carta da navigare.

> Possibly a portolan map.

[767] La Pedia de Ciro tradutta dal Filelfo in papyro.

> Francesco Filelfo wrote to the cardinal on 9 October 1469 that he was sending him his Latin translation of Xenophon's *Cyropaedia*, which he had dedicated to Paul II (*Epistolarum…libri*, fol. 214v). In 1470, when Giovanni Andrea Bussi, Bishop of Aleria, proposed a printed edition, Filelfo wrote to him that the best copy was that possessed by the cardinal (ibid., fol. 225r); see also *DBI*, s.v.

[768] Tragedie de Senecha.

> Some or all of the nine tragedies by Seneca the Younger.

[769] Ysagoge Leonardi Aretini.

L. Bruni, *Isagogicon moralis disciplinae ad Galeottum Ricasolanum* (modern edition in Leonardo Bruni, *Humanistisch-philosophische Schriften*, ed H. Baron, Leipzig and Berlin, 1928; reprint Wiesbaden, 1970, pp. 20–40).

[770] Mesue in vulgare.

This may be the vernacular version of I 765, entitled *Delle medicine semplici solutive* and printed rather than manuscript; the first printing was at Modena, Johannes Vurster, 1475 (see Sarton, *Introduction*, I, p. 729; *BMC*, VII, p. 1059); Barbara of Brandenburg had owned a 'Mesue impressus' (ASMn, AN, Estensioni, R. 78, Cornice 1481, inventory, fol. 3^v); the same, valued at half a ducat, passed to the cardinal (ASDMn, FCC, ser. misc., b. 2/A, 'Inventario de le cose', fol. 14^r).

[771] Columella.

The incomplete work on agriculture, *De re rustica*, of this writer (1st cent. AD) who reputedly had estates near Albano. Pomponio Leto wrote a commentary. (Modern edition: Columella, *Opera quae extant*, ed. W. Lundström, Göteborg, l966–8.)

#Io. p.*:

[772] Opera de d. Mario Filelfo coperta de raso pavonazo.

Perhaps Giovan Mario Filelfo's *De communis vite continentia*, in which the cardinal is an interlocutor (see above, p. 66). G. M. Filelfo's autograph copy, with a dedication to Sixtus IV, is in MS BCM, 79 (A III 15); this had until 1806 been in the possession of the Arrivabene family (G. Andres, *Catalogo di manoscritti della famiglia Capilupi di Mantova*, Mantua, 1897, pp. 77–8). The *stemma* on fol. 1 is, however, neither that of the Gonzaga nor of the Arrivabene families.

[773] Cronicha q[uondam] Samuellis de rebus Veronensibus.

No Veronese chronicler of this name is known, but a possible supposition (for which I thank Gianmaria Varanini) is that there was a chronicle in the possession of the painter and antiquarian Samuele da Tradate, himself a Veronese, which might have passed to the cardinal. Samuele had died in the cardinal's house in Rome in October 1466 (letters of G. P. Arrivabene and Marasca to Barbara of Brandenburg, Rome, 8 October 1466, in ASMn, AG, b. 843, quoted by Signorini, *Opus hoc tenue*, p. 110).

[774] Colecte multarum rerum coperta di biancho.

[775] Colecte multarum rerum in papiro.

#Io.*:

[776] Colecte multarum rerum in papiro coperta de verde.

#Io.p.*:

[777] Libro de le virtute e vicii coperto de cremesino.

Possibly a version of the vulgarization by Jacopo de Agello OFM of Guillaume Peyraut (Peraldus), *Summa de vitiis et virtutibus*; see Farenga, '"Indoctis viris"', pp. 405–6.

[778] Tullio De Oficiis in forma piccola.

Cicero, *De officiis*.

[779] Paulo Orosio in montanina verde.

Presumably Orosius (a pupil of St Augustine), *Historiae adversus paganos*, concerning the history of the world up to 417 AD (modern edition by C. Zangemeister, Vienna, 1882).

[780] Nonio Marcello.

Presumably Nonius Marcellus (early 4th cent. AD), *De compendiosa doctrina*, a compilation combining grammar and other miscellaneous information (modern edition by W. M. Lindsay, 3 vols, Leipzig, 1903).

[781] Epistole Senece coperte de corame rosso.

The Younger Seneca's collection of fictitious letters entitled *Epistulae morales*.

[782] Plauto.

One or more of the comedies of Plautus.

fol. 16ᵛ

[783] Libro a stampo [erased: 'manichis'] de machinis bellicis in papiro.

> Presumably R. Valturio, *De re militari*, Iohannes ex Verona Nicolai filius, Verona, 1472 (*BMC*, VII, p. 948). No early printing is known of Mariano Taccola, *De rebus militaribus* (1449), later entitled *De machinis* (modern edition by E. Knobloch, Baden-Baden, 1984).

[784] Petrarcha De Vita Sollitaria in papiro.

> The only prose work of Petrarch listed in the inventory.

#Io. p.*

[785] De conservatione sanitatis a stampo in papiro.

> Benedetto de' Riguardati da Norcia, *De conservatione sanitatis*, Rome, G. F. de Lignamine, 1475, or Bologna, Domenico Lapi per Sigismundo de Libri, 1477 (*BMC*, IV, 34 and VI, 814; Farenga, 'Le prefazioni', pp. 147, 171).

#Iop*

[786] Libro de calculatione coperto de rosso.

[787] Pomponio Mela.

> Pomponius Mela, *De chorographia*, a geographical survey of the world in the 1st cent. AD, based on Strabo.

[788] Marco Polo in papiro.

> This is unlikely to be a version of the original French text of the *Livres des merveilles*, supposedly based on the dictated travel memoirs of the Venetian merchant Marco Polo (c. 1254–1324); it might possibly be a copy of the Latin translation by Francesco Pipino, or else the Tuscan translation from the so-called 'Ottimo' text of Niccolò dell'Ormanni (1309). For the problems see L. Foscolo Benedetto, *Il Milione di Marco Polo*, Florence, 1928; Ruggiero M. Ruggieri, *Marco Polo il Milione*, Florence, 1986.

[789] Marco Polo in papiro.

> See I 788.

[790] Colecte multarum rerum.

[791] Invective contra Catelina.

> Presumably Cicero's Catilinarian orations.

[792] Terentio col comento a stampo.

> One of several printed editions of the *Comœdiae* with the commentary of Aelius Donatus (Venice, 1476–82, Treviso, 1477–81); see *BMC*, V, 272; VII, 1027; see also I 752.

[793] Scripto de la poetria de Oratio.

> This might be Horace's *Ars poetica*, but the word 'scripto' suggests a commentary (cf. I 803) although, admittedly, the word 'comento' is specifically used elsewhere (e.g., I 792, 813). One might also have expected a Latin title, since known commentaries on Horace's poetry were in Latin, including the recent one by Cristoforo Landino; the ancient commentaries by Helenius (pseudo-)Acron (2nd cent. AD) and Pomponius Porphyrion (3rd cent. AD) were included with an early printing of Horace's works (Venice, 1481), but it is tempting to suggest this entry may refer to a copy of Landino's commentary, written in 1481–2; it was already printed—with an ode by Poliziano—in Florence, August 1482, and in Venice, 1483 (Cristoforo Landino, *Scritti critici e teorici*, ed. R. Cardini, I, Rome, 1974, pp. 195–202). On the other hand, it cannot be excluded that this might be a lost commentary by Niccolò Perotti or some other academic luminary (see G. Curcio, *Q. Orazio Flacco studiato in Italia dal secolo XIII al XVIII*, Catania, 1913, pp. 53–4).

[794] Declamatione de Senecha in papiro.

> Unless this is a scribal error for the *De clementia* of the younger Seneca, it is perhaps part of the *controversiae* and *suasoriae* of the Elder Seneca in his *Oratorum sententiae*.

[795] De mulieribus illustribus Bocacii coperto de rosso.

> This cannot, presumably, be identified as any one of the known copies of Boccaccio's *Lives of Famous Women* as none of these is noted as decorated with the cardinal's *stemma*;

see Boccacio, *De mulieribus claris*, ed. V. Zaccaria, 2nd edn, Milan, 1970, pp. 455–8. Giovan Filippo de Lignamine wrote to Marchese Federico Gonzaga, Rome 25 August 1479, that he would send to Margherita of Bavaria, or possibly Barbara ('alla… marchesana') 'uno libro chiamato Boccacio de claris mulieribus' (ASMn, AG, b. 846, c. 356).

[796] [cancelled]: un altro Tullio De Officiis in forma picola [substituted]: *Rhetorica Nova.*

Presumably the *Rhetorica ad Herennium*, formerly attributed to Cicero.

[797] Alberto Magno De Mineralibus.

Albertus Magnus (d. 1280), the Dominican scholar and writer of commentaries on many of Aristotle's works, made perhaps his most original contribution to learning with this book (see Introduction by C. Wyckoff to Albertus, *Book of Minerals*).

[798] Iuvenale e Perseo.

The *Satires* of Juvenal and Persius.

[799] Africha Petrarce in papiro.

Petrarch's unfinished Latin epic, *Africa*.

#Io. p.*:

[800] Traductione de Homero in papiro *a stampo*.

Probably the *Aliqui libri ex Iliade Homeri*, translated by Nicolò della Valle, printed by Giovan Filippo de Lignamine, 1474 (*BMC*, IV, 33; Farenga, 'Le prefazioni', p. 170). See also above, pp. 60–3, on the incomplete ('Vatican') Homer, missing from the inventory.

[801] Cicerone De Claris Oratoribus.

Cicero's *Brutus*.

#*fuit restitutus principi*:

[802] Helio Sparciano.

Aelius Spartianus was supposedly one of the authors known as the *Scriptores historiae Augustae*, a collection of biographies of Roman emperors, dating from the 4th cent. AD. The book listed here is probably the same one, with illustrated heads of the emperors, which was requested as a loan in November 1466 from Marchese L. Gonzaga and granted rather reluctantly (see above, p. 58). The note that only now (i.e., after the cardinal's death) was the original (MS Turin, BN, E III 19, damaged by fire in 1904) restored to the main Gonzaga library might suggest that a copy was never made, though one in Rome (MS BN, Vitt. Em. 1004) rubricated by Sanvito, may have been made for Francesco; the owner's arms are erased (Alexander, *Illuminations*, p. 67; de la Mare, 'Florentine Scribes', app. III, p. 289, no. 26.)

[803] Scripto sopra l'oratione de Tulio in papiro.

Unidentifiable commentary either upon Cicero's *De oratore* or on one or more of his orations.

[804] Plinio.

Presumably the Elder Pliny's *Historia naturalis*, of which Marchese Ludovico Gonzaga had a famous exemplar (MS Turin, BN, I. i. 22–3, much damaged by fire in 1904; see Meroni, *Mostra*, pp. 27, 56, 80–1). Many of the subjects discussed by Pliny (e.g., stones) would have been of particular interest to Francesco.

[805] Alberto Magno De Proprietatibus Rerum.

Albertus Magnus's commentary on the pseudo-Aristotelian *De causis proprietatum elementorum*. See the modern edition by P. Hossfeld in Albertus Magnus, *Opera omnia*, V (2), Münster, 1980, pp. 47–106.

[806] La terza Decca de Livio.

The third decade of Livy's history of Rome *Ab urbe condita*.

[807] Tre Decce de Livio in un volume

The first, third and fourth decades (i.e., all the parts then known) of Livy's history.

[808] La seconda Decca de Livio.

> Obviously not the lost second decade of Livy's history, this is perhaps a copy of the third decade (i.e., the second in sequence, as presumably in I 807); just conceivably it might be Leonardo Bruni's *Commentaria primi belli Punici*; as Bruni points out in his 'Proœmium' (1421), the First Punic War was the subject of the second decade ('cuius libri si exstarent, nihil opus erat novo labore'); see Bruni, *Humanistisch-philosophische Schriften* (as above, I 769n), pp. 122–3. I owe this suggestion to Giuseppe Frasso, but it seems odd there should be no attribution here to Bruni.

[809] Romuleon.

> A compilation by Benvenuto da Imola dedicated to Cardinal Albornoz. See F. Zambrini, 'Saggio sul Romuleon di Benvenuto da Imola', in *Prose e rime edite e inedite d'autori imolesi del secolo XIV*, Imola, 1846, pp. 1–37; G. Guatteri, *Il Romuleon di Benvenuto da Imola volgarizzato nel buon secolo*, Bologna, 1867.

[810] Fulgentio.

> St Fulgentius (468–533), Bishop of Ruspe, had various works of St Augustine attributed to him, of which this is most probably the *De fide*.

[811] Tullio De Oratore.

> Cicero's *De oratore*, the complete text of which had been discovered at Lodi in 1422.

[812] Historia Mantuana d. Guidonis.

> Presumably MS BAV, Vat. Lat. 2960, entitled (fol. 35a) 'Mantuane Urbis gestorum liber' (Frasso, 'Oggetti', p. 144), which is a contemporary account (unedited) of Mantua and the fortunes of war c. 1390–8, illuminated with an unidentified portrait. It is inscribed in a later hand 'Guido de gestis mantuae', linking it perhaps to the protonotary Guido Gonzaga (see above, pp. 26n, 39, 57 and I 815). It also bears the autograph signature 'Jo. petri Arrivabeni' (fol. 1ʳ), so was presumably among the cardinal's books which passed, either by purchase or appropriation, to his former secretary and executor. However, there is no marginal note here to indicate that it was one of the items Arrivabene had extracted and taken to Rome in December 1483 (see above, p. 113).

#Io. fr.*:

[813] Comento de Marso a stampo in papiro *sopra Tullio De Officiis*.

> Pietro Marsi's commentary on Cicero's *De officiis*, with dedication to Cardinal Gonzaga, printed at Venice, Baptista de Tortis, 1481, 1482. (*BMC*, V, 321; GW 6950, 6952). On Pietro Marsi (c. 1440–c. 1510), see above, p. 66; Della Torre, *Paolo Marsi*, esp. pp. 97–8, 224–5, 275.

[814] Sonetti de d. Filippo da Nuvolone.

> On Filippo Nuvoloni (1432–78) of Mantua and his writings, see Zonta, *Filippo Nuvolone e un suo dialogo*; Perosa, 'Filippo Nuvolone'; Faccioli, *Mantova*, II, pp. 85–112; Signorini, 'Contributo', suggests there was perhaps a link between the poet and Francesco, before the latter became a cardinal.

[815] Iosepho et Egesippo.

> This is almost certainly MS London, British Library, Harley 3691, which is inscribed (fol. 222ᵛ): 'Scripsit Julianus de Viterbio pro domino Guidone de Gonsaga protonotario Anno domini millesimo quadringentesimo quinquagesimo septimo' (1457 was also the year Giuliano wrote I 835). It could have passed to Francesco with other books formerly belonging to Guido (see above, pp. 56–7 and I 812). The MS, a large volume (37 x 26.5 cm) with fine decorations of initial letters etc, contains much of the *Antiquitates* (Books I–XVI) in the 'Cassidoran' (6th century) translation, most of the *Bellum Judaicum* and Hegesippus, *Historia* (F. Blatt, *The Latin Josephus*, I, Copenhagen, 1958, pp. 41–2). The principal works of Josephus (born c. AD 37–8) are thus combined with the Christianized (4th century) version of the *Bellum* attributed to 'Hegesippus', on whose text and disputed identity see *Hegesippi qui dicitur Historiae libri V*, ed. V. Ussani, Corpus scriptorum ecclesiasticorum Latinorum, 66, Vienna and Leipzig, 1932; reprint 1960; H. Feldman, *Josephus and Modern Scholarship*, Berlin etc, 1984, pp. 40–7.

fol. 17^r

#Io. p.*:

[816] Tractato di Mantua de d. Leonardo de Arezo.

> Treatise (about the Etruscan origin of Mantua) in the form of a letter dated 27 May 1418 from Leonardo Bruni to Gianfrancesco Gonzaga, capitano of Mantua and the cardinal's grandfather (Leonardo Bruni, *Epistolarum libri*, ed. L. Mehus, II, Florence, 1741, pp. 217–29 [X.xxv]). Copies of this text, in both Latin and Italian, were noted in Florentine libraries by F. P. Luiso, 'Due omonimi di Leonardo Bruni nel secolo xv', *Giornale storico della letteratura italiana*, 32, 1898, p. 150 n. 7.

[817] Vita de M[arco] Antonio e Bruto.

> Presumably the two *Lives* by Plutarch.

#Io. fr.*:

[818] Canzone del Si[gnor] Malatesta.

> Many copies survive of at least sixty-eight sonnets and other *canzoni* composed by Malatesta Malatesta of Pesaro (d. 1429), a relative of the cardinal's paternal grandmother, Paola Malatesta (see D. Trolli, *Malatesta Malatesti: Rime*, Parma, 1982). The title 'Cantiones domini Malateste' appears among the books of Barbara of Brandenburg in the cardinal's house in Mantua in November 1481 (ASMn, AN, Estensioni, R. 78, Cornice 1481, inventory, fol. 4^r).

[819] Opereta in papiro de la Vita del Turcho.

> No life of the Ottoman Sultan Mehmed II, the Conqueror (1432–81) is known to have been written in Italian by this date; nor does the title suggest Pius II's *Epistola ad Mahumetem*, written c. 1461, a copy of which might well have been expected among Cardinal Gonzaga's books. There is a remote possibility that this 'opereta' might refer to the preface to Gian Maria Filelfo's *Amyris*, a long Latin poem in praise of Mehmed; this preface, by Othman Lillo Ferducci, an Anconitan merchant at Gallipoli, contained a biographical outline and was dedicated to Galeazzo Maria Sforza, Duke of Milan. See R. Schwoebel, *The Shadow of the Crescent*, Nieuwkoop, 1967, p. 149.

#Io. fr.*:

[820] Matheo Palmero a stampo.

> Presumably (since no other work of Palmieri's had been printed by 1483) his version, with continuation up to the 1440s, of Eusebius's *Chronicon*, printed at Milan 1475–6, or even the Ratdolt printing, Venice, 1483 (Hain, 6716). See M. Palmieri, *De temporibus*, ed. G. Scaramella, *RIS*, XXVI (i), Città di Castello, 1906, pp. xxii–xxiii.

#Io.F.*:

[821] Libro de le Antiquitate de Chiriaco de Ancona.

> The title 'de le Antiquitate' suggests that this was a copy of the lost *Commentarii* of Ciriaco (c. 1391–post 1453) or sylloge of classical inscriptions which Ciriaco had collected in Italy (Frasso, 'Oggetti', p. 144). Marchese Ludovico Gonzaga had hoped to borrow in 1461 the copy in the Sforza library at Pavia, when Francesco was studying there; just possibly this was a copy of the same (a letter of 10 February 1461 refers to 'un libreto dove sono scripti molti epigrammati tolti a Roma per Chiarico d'Ancona': see R. Sabbadini, *Classici e umanisti da codici ambrosiani*, Florence, 1933, pp. 1–52, esp. pp. 44–6; Weiss, *Discovery*, p. 109; E. W. Bodner, *Cyriacus of Ancona and Athens*, Brussels, 1960, p. 71). See also above, p. 77, concerning an extant sylloge of inscriptions—specifically collected in Rome but apparently not by Ciriaco—which it has been suggested might have belonged to Francesco (MS Utrecht, University Library, 764).

[822] Praticha Jo. Jostre.

> Possibly a treatise on 'practical medicine' or surgery; the author's name is unidentified, unless it is a corruption of Joannes Jamarus or Jamatus, a scholar from southern Italy (fl. c. 1230–52) who wrote a work entitled *Cyrurgia* (Sarton, *Introduction*, II, p. 654).

[823] Bosadrello in carta de sonetti per la ventura.

Baldassare da Fossombrone, *Il Menzoniero* or *Bosadrello*, a collection of fifty-seven sonnets first printed at Ferrara, Severino da Ferrara, 1475 (Hain, 7310). Baldassare (born c. 1400–10) was a secretary of Marchese Ludovico Gonzaga and wrote or put together his *Bosadrello* at the request of Barbara of Brandenburg (see G. Crocioni, 'Baldassare da Fossombrone e il suo Menzoniero o Bosadrello alla corte dei Gonzaga', *La Rinascita*, 6, 1943, pp. 224–57; also *DBI*, s.v.).

[824] Lectura super Platone ad Timeum.

This is probably the commentary on Plato's *Timaeus* (On Nature) by Calcidius, written to accompany his translation c. AD 400, of which many MS copies survive (text in *Plato Latinus*, IV: *Timaeus a Calcidio Translatus Commentarioque Instructus*, ed. J. H. Waszink, London and Leiden, 1975).

[825] Euclide.

Presumably a Latin version of the *Elements*. A printed version had recently appeared: *Liber elementorum Euclidis perspicacissimi in artem Geometrie*, Venice, Ratdolt, 1482.

[826] Libro de Alberto Magno in papiro.

Possibly a duplicate of the *De mineralibus*, but probably one of Albertus's numerous other works (see I 797; Albertus Magnus, *Book of Minerals*, pp. xxvi–xxvii).

[827] Libro de le virtù e vicii coperto de corame rosso.

Cf. I 777.

#Iop.*:

[828] Opere de papa Pio a stampo.

No comprehensive collection of the writings of Pius II had been printed by 1483; this item might have been one of various editions of his *Epistolae*, or of several other titles perhaps bound together (e.g., Hain, 147–261; see also I 819n.).

[829] Guielmo in cirugia in papyro.

Guglielmo da Saliceto (d. c. 1280), *Chirurgia* (Thorndike, *History*, 1141; Sarton, *Introduction*, II, 1078–9).

[830] Registro in papiro de l'intrate de la giesia.

This appears to be the compilation, with a faded *stemma* of Cardinal F. Gonzaga on the frontispiece, in MS Valencia, Biblioteca central universitaria 615. It has been listed with the title *Taxae vel emolumenta ecclesiastica* (Meroni, *Mostra*, p. 59), but this appears to be a modern description, not appearing on the manuscript, which has no title page and simply begins 'IN CIVITATE Romana sunt quinque ecclesie que Patriarchales dicuntur…', followed by a list of the cardinal bishoprics, presbyteral and diaconal churches, and then, alphabetically under bishoprics, of bishoprics and religious houses throughout western Christendom and *in partibus infidelium*. Possibly the purpose was to list benefices subject to provision by the pope and cardinals in consistory, with taxation figures and some updated revisions. These corrections are generally from the earlier fifteenth century and not beyond the pontificate of Pius II, though a bull of 1466 is cited (see above, p. 39).

[831] Lapidarium Dioscoridis.

Dioscorides, *Materia medica* (available in various Latin translations from the Greek), lib. V (concerning stones).

#Io. p.*:

[832] Opereta del vescovo de Vintimilia.

Among the shorter works of Battista Giudici da Finale, O.P. (Joannes Baptista de Iudicibus de Finario, Bishop of Ventimiglia 1471–84), those most likely to have interested Cardinal Gonzaga were the *De migratione Petri cardinalis S. Sixti*, the *Apologia Iudaeorum etc* (concerning the supposed murder of the infant Simone of Trent), the *Invectiva contra Platinam* and the *De canonizatione Beati Bonaventurae*, lib. 2 (1479). The 'opereta' may be any of these. See Quaglioni, *Apologia etc*, 1987, and on the author, Kaeppelli in *DHGE*, XXI, pp. 51–2.

#R[estitui]ta:

[833] Opereta de d. Zoan Lucidio Catanio super obitu Mar[chionissae].

Giovanni Lucido Catanei, *Oratio in funere illustrissimae Barbarae Marchionissae Mantue* (November 1481), was printed by Angelus Ugoletus, Parma, 1493, together with his funeral orations for Marchese Federico Gonzaga and the cardinal (*BMC*, VII p. 945; GW 6219). MS Holkham Hall 496, from the Gonzaga (but obviously not Francesco's) library (Meroni, *Mostra*, p. 37), also includes these orations. On Cattanei (*sic*) see *DBI*, s.v.; Faccioli, *Mantova*, II, pp. 384, 407–8.

#Io.p.*:

[834] Opereta de d. Benedetto Morando.

Probably a presentation MS of the *Oratio de laudibus Bononiae contra Senenses*, which was dedicated to the cardinal and is throughout addressed to him, in which Morandi (a distinguished Bolognese who held the office of secretary to the Anziani; d. 1478) mainly argues the superiority of Bologna to Siena. It was printed at Bologna by Ugo de Rugeriis, with the date 12 April 1481 (*BMC*, VI, p. 806; G. Fantuzzi, *Notizie degli scrittori bolognesi*, VI, Bologna, 1788, pp. 107–9).

#*Data al magnifico d. Francisco*:

[835] La gramatica del quondam Monsignore.

Tractatus grammaticalis editus a puero per me Franciscum Gonzagum protonotarium: MS Modena, Biblioteca Estense, α.F.2.26 (Lat. 1101). This elementary Latin grammar was probably composed by Francesco's tutor Marasca and includes some particular exercises involving the noun 'protonotarius'. There are some marginal annotations, including (fol. 11ʳ: 'De superlativis') one which is probably in Francesco's autograph. It also contains (fols 41–6) Guarino's *Carmina differentialia*. The MS was written by Giuliano da Viterbo (dated 30 May 1457, on fol. 39ʳ). The frontispiece shows portraits at their writing desks of both master and pupil and bears Francesco's arms as protonotary. (Meroni, *Mostra*, nos 20–1, pp. 80–2, tav. 109, 110; Chambers and Martineau, *Splendours*, no. 21; see above, p. 56; and Figs 1, 2).

#Io.p.*:

[836] Opera de d. Lionello Chiaregato.

Leonello Chieregato (1443–1506), Bishop of Arbe, a member of Cardinal Marco Barbo's household, had written before 1483 various orations, poems etc and translated a work entitled *De causis divisionis et dissensionis Graecorum a Latinis* as well as an oration of Isocrates and a dialogue of Lucian (see *DBI*, s.v.).

[837] Versi de d. Agapito, vescovo de Camerino.

Agapito Cenci Rustici (Bishop of Camerino, 1463–4) wrote *Carmina ad Carolum Gonzagam* (Carlo Gonzaga, the cardinal's uncle, who died in exile at Ferrara), which may be the work listed here (R. Sabbadini in *Enciclopedia italiana*, s.v.).

[838] Apuleio De herbis cum le picture.

Herbarium Apulei Platonici, a herbal prescription book based on Dioscorides, spuriously attributed to Apuleius (F. Hunger, *The Herbal of Pseudo-Apuleius*, Leiden, 1935). This is identifiable as MS BL, Add. 21115, with the Gonzaga arms and an *impresa*, and dedicatory letter to Francesco by Giovan Filippo de Lignamine. Written by Pietro Orsoleo (information from Professor A. de la Mare), it appears to be a copy from the printed edition produced by Giovan Filippo (c. 1481–2) with the same dedication (a version was also printed with a dedication to Cardinal Giuliano della Rovere; *BMC*, IV, pp. 131–2; Farenga, 'Le prefazioni', pp. 158–9; Chambers and Martineau, *Splendours*, no. 27).

[839–41] Jo.p.*:

[839] Una opereta de Emilio in versi.

The *Carmina* of Emilio Boccabella, lib. II and lib. V of which were dedicated to Cardinal Gonzaga and contain eulogistic verses addressed to him and to members of his household; almost certainly this is the cardinal's presentation copy which bears his arms and is entitled: *Carmina Divo. F. Gonzaga Card. Mantuano Aemilius Romanus*, MS Venice, Biblioteca Marciana, Lat. cl. XII 178 (4025). Lib. II is also included in the incomplete collection dedicated to Sixtus IV (MS BAV, Ottob. Lat. 2280), and both lib. II and lib. V in the one dedicated to Girolamo Riario (MS Weimar, Landesbibliothek, Q. 114). See also Tissoni-Benvenuti, *L'Orfeo*, pp. 47–8.

[840] Libreto in papiro ranarum et murium.

Probably a copy of the Latin translation of the pseudo-Homeric *Batrachomyomachia* by Carlo Marsuppini (c. 1398–1453): see Zippel, 'Carlo Marsuppini', p. 204.

[841] Libreto de versi dil Prindilaqua.

Francesco Prendilaqua of Mantua (c. 1430–post 1509), author of a *Vita* of Vittorino da Feltre and secretary to the cardinal's uncle Alessandro Gonzaga (d. 1466), wrote several other works (including a consolatory oration on the death of Dorotea Gonzaga, cf. I 842), but verses by him are not elsewhere recorded (see Faccioli, *Mantova*, II, pp. 28–9).

[842] Versi de Calimacho De Morte Sororis.

Filippo Buonaccorsi (1437–96), known as Callimaco Esperiente, secretary to Cardinal Roverella and an associate of Pomponio Leto, wrote an ode on the death of Cardinal Francesco's sister Dorotea (d. 1467), who had been rejected in marriage by Galeazzo Maria Sforza, heir to the duchy of Milan, on account of her alleged deformity. See above, p. 23; for the text see Callimaco, *Epigrammatum libri*, pp. 105–11 (II, 143); Kumaniecki, 'Epicedion in Dorotheam Gonzagam'; see also Garfagnini, *Callimaco Esperiente*.

[843–7] Io.p.*:
[843] Versi Stelle Benadusii.

Although nothing appears to be known about Stella, the Benadusi were a fairly prominent Mantuan family; Arrivabene Benadusi, a leading court physician under Marchese Ludovico Gonzaga, shared a house with his brother Paolo, according to the chronicler Andrea Schivenoglia (MS BCMn, 1019, fol. 2^v).

[844] Versi Tome Marasce.

Similarly the Marasca family, but without mention of a Tomà Marasca, is listed by Schivenoglia (ibid., fol. 58^v); just possibly the name given here is a diminutive of Bartolomeo Marasca, the cardinal's tutor and master of his household until 1469, though he is not known to have written verses.

[845] Versi del Platino.

Cf. below, I 843. On the life and works of Piattino Piatti, a friend of Giovan Pietro Arrivabene, see Simioni, 'Un'umanista milanese'.

[846] Versi de Nicodemo Folengo.

Nicodemo, whose father was Giacomo Folengo, a prominent Mantuan notary who entertained Cardinal Isidore of Kiev in his house in 1459, and whose mother was a niece of Vittorino da Feltre, was educated by the latter's successors (in particular by Colombino da Verona) and composed epigrams and miscellaneous verses (some still unedited). Marchese Federico Gonzaga, his godfather, wrote a letter recommending him to the Cardinal of Genoa (Paolo Campofregoso) on 5 July 1482, when he apparently went to Rome in search of a patron. Whether or not Cardinal Gonzaga took him in is unclear, but presumably the verses named here are from about this date and may correspond to the collections addressed to Federico di Montefeltro, Duke of Urbino, entitled *Nicodemi Folengi musarum cultoris Elegiarum liber* (MS BAV, Urb. Lat. 747), or the *Carmina* in MS Bologna, Biblioteca universitaria, 595, X, fasc. 1, fols 12–26^v, or those sent to Lorenzo de' Medici (MS Florence, Biblioteca Laurenziana, XXXV. 41) See G. Billanovich, *Tra Don Teofilo Folengo e Merlin Cocaio*, Naples, 1948, pp. 1–9 (Nicodemo was the uncle of Don Teofilo Folengo); Kristeller, *Iter*, I, p. 23; Nicodemo Folengo, *Carmina*, ed. A. Perosa, Pisa, 1990.

[847] Ciccho de Ascole in papiro.

Almost certainly *Acerba*, the best-known astrological work of Cecco (Francesco) Stabili d'Ascoli (1269–1324). Two copies had been in the Gonzaga library in 1407. See the modern edition by C. Censori and E. Vittori, '*L'Acerba*'. *Secondo la lezione del Codice Eugubino dell'anno 1376*, Ascoli Piceno, 1971. See also C. Ciociola, 'Rassegna Stabili-ana' (Postille agli Atti del Convegno del 1969), *Lettere italiane*, 30, 1978, pp. 97–123; 'Nuove accessioni acerbiane: cartoni per la storia della tradizione', *Rendiconti… dell'Accademia nazionale dei Lincei*, Classe di scienze morali, storiche, filologiche, 8th ser., 33, 1978, pp. 491–508, esp. pp. 490–8. Barbara of Brandenburg also had a 'Cecus de Esculo' among the books in the cardinal's house in Mantua listed after her death (ASMn, AN, Estensioni R. 78, Cornice 1481, inventory, fol. 4^r).

fol. 17^v

#Iop.*:

[848] Plutarco De Liberis educandis.

> Presumably the Latin translation by Guarino da Verona of Plutarch's treatise on Greek methods of education (part of his *Moralia*).

[849] Epistole de Tullio.

> Either or both of Cicero's letter collections *Ad familiares* and *Ad Atticum* (Petrarch's major discovery).

[850] Prisciano.

> Priscianus (6th cent. AD), *Institutiones grammaticae.*

[851] Libro de certi re e regine in vulgare.

> This text, perhaps a chivalric romance, is hardly identifiable from the description; a similar Latin title 'Liber certorum regum et reginarum in bona carta' appears among the books of Barbara of Brandenburg listed in the cardinal's house in Mantua after her death (ASMn, AN, Estensioni, R. 78, Cornice 1481, fol. 4^r).

[852] Lo Dante hystoriato.

> A 'Dante in carta bona cum figure' (valued at 8 ducats)—presumably the *Divina commedia*—was among the eight books of Barbara of Brandenburg which passed to Cardinal Gonzaga after her death (ASDMn, FCC, b. 2/A, 'Inventario de le cose', fol. 14^r).

#Io. fr.*:

[853] Canzone spagnole in papiro.

> The 'Cantiones spagnole in bona carta', listed among Barbara of Brandenburg's books in the cardinal's house after her death (ASMn, AN, Estensioni, R. 78, Cornice 1481, inventory, fol. 3^v), was presumably the same 'Canzon spagnole' (valued at half a ducat) among eight of her books allotted to the cardinal (ADMn, FCC, ser. misc., b. 2/A, 'Inventario de le cose', fol. 14^r).

[854] Dante col commento a stampo in papiro.

> This may have been either the edition of the *Divina commedia* (with commentary by Benvenuto da Imola) printed by Vindelinus of Speyer, Venice 1477 (*BMC*, VI, p. 248; GW 7964), or that (with commentary by Martino Paolo) printed by Ludovico and Alberto Piemontesi and Guido de Terzago, Milan, 1478 (*BMC*, VI, p. 738; GW 7965), or (with commentary by Cristoforo Landino) that printed by Nicolò di Lorenzo, Florence, 1481 (*BMC*, VI, p. 628; GW 7966).

[855] La Instituta picola.

> The *Institutes*, a textbook of Roman civil law, which formed part of the *Corpus iuris civilis* compiled for the Emperor Justinian in the sixth century AD.

[856] Lo Codico.

> The code of imperial rescripts (*Codex*) forming part of the *Corpus iuris civilis* (see I 855).

[857] Lo Volumme.

> The 'Volumen parvum', a name given to the third part of the *Corpus iuris civilis*, which includes the *Codex* (see I 856), *Institutiones*, *Authenticum* and *Libri feodorum.*

[858] Lo Digesto Novo.

The *Digest*, the longest and most important part of Justinian's *Corpus iuris civilis*, containing precepts and *consilia* of Roman jurists, was for convenience divided into several parts. This is the final part, i.e., *Digestum*, xxxix–l. See I 864–5.

[859] Cynno sul Codico.

Cinus (Cino Sighibuldi) of Pistoia (1270–c. 1336), *Lectura super codice*, the commentary on Justinian's *Code* by this jurist and poet. See C. Zaccagnini, *Cino da Pistoia*, Pistoia, 1919; F. Calasso, *Medio evo del diritto*, Milan, 1954, esp. pp. 570–2.

[860] Odofredo sul Codico.

Odofredus (d. 1265), the Bolognese jurist, whose *Lecturae in codicem* were to be printed at Lyons, 1489. (See also I 856).

[861] Repertorio de rasone canonica per alfabeto.

[862] La Tiberiade de Bartolo coperta de verde.

Bartolus de Saxoferrato, *Tractatus Tiberiadis*, c. 1355 (see F. Calasso in *DBI*, s.v.).

#Iop.*:
[863] Opereta de d. Hyeronimo di Preti sopra la Instituta.

This simplified version of the *Institutes* (see I 855), written by Francesco Gonzaga's first law tutor (see above, pp. 50–1, 56) is in MS Reggio Emilia, BC, vari E.27, with dedication to the protonotary dated 1459, and his arms (fol. 1ʳ). See Kristeller, *Iter*, II, p. 85; B. Fava, 'Elenco descrittivo di 30 codici quattrocenteschi della Biblioteca municipale di Reggio Emilia', *Atti e memorie per le antiche provincie modenesi*, 8th ser., 7, 1955, p. 178.

[864] Digesto Vechyo.

That is, the first part of the *Digest* (see I 858): *Digestum*, i–xxiv (2).

[865] L'Inforzato.

The *Digestum infortiatum* was the curious name given to the second part of the *Digest* (see I 858, 864), i.e., xxiv(3)–xxxviii.

[866] Bartholo sopra ff. vechio.

Bartolus of Sassoferrato, *Lectura super Digesto veteri* (see I 864 and, on Bartolus, *DBI*, s.v.). The *Digest* is often abbreviated as 'ff.'

[867] Casi de Bernardo de la Decretale.

Bernard of Parma, *Casus Longi super quinque libros decretalium*, i.e., a commentary on the *Decretals* (see I 870). It already had had a first printing in 1475 (GW 4092). On Bernard, see P. Ourliac in *Dictionnaire de droit canonique*, ed. A. Villien et al., I, Paris, 1924, p. 782; J. F. von Schulte, *Die Geschichte der Quellen und Literatur des canonischen Rechts von Gratian bis auf die Gegenwart*, II (2), Stuttgart, 1875, pp. 114–15.

[868] Casi del Decreto in versi.

Presumably versified extracts from the *Decretum*, the basic textbook of early common law, also known as the *Concordantia discordantium canonum*, compiled by Gratian c. 1140 and forming part of the *Corpus iuris canonici*. (Cf. I 869, of which this may be simply another copy.)

#Iop.*:
[869] Casi del Decreto in versi cum la giosa.

Presumably Ludovico Bolognini, *Compendium decretorum* in verses, with brief commentary (a copy exists in MS Rome, Biblioteca Corsiniana, Cors. 64 [40. F.I]: Kristeller, *Iter*, II, pp. 108–9) and dedication to Francesco; he is addressed as 'Felsinee princeps urbis, pater unice cunctis', from which has been inferred a date soon after Francesco became bishop in July 1476 (Caprioli, *Indagini*, p. 140 n. 3). It was printed as *Syllogianthon idest collectio florum*, Bologna, 1486 (GW 4637; Schulte, *Die Geschichte* [as in I 867n], p. 347); Bolognini claimed he began it when first teaching civil law at Bologna in 1472. On him see also *DBI*, s.v., and above, p. 55.

#*Data Reverendo et Illustri d. Sigismundo*: [W 20]
[870] Decretale.

The six books of decretals published by Pope Gregory IX in 1234, forming part of the *Corpus iuris canonici*.

#*Restituta Episcopo mantuano*:

[871] Compillatione antiqua del Decreto.

[872] Li Soliloquii de Augustino vulgare.

A vernacular ˙ ersion of St Augustine, *Soliloquia* (*PL*, XXXII); probably the same as the 'Siloloquia Sancti Augustini' which Barbara of Brandenburg had possessed in 1481 (ASMn, ANA, R. 78, Cornice).

[873] Un almanach a stampo.

[874] Guido Bonatto in papiro.

Guido Bonatti of Forlì, *Liber introductorius ad iudicia stellarum*, or *De astronomia tractatus* (printed edition: Ratdolt, Augsburg, 1491). See B. Boncompagni, *Della vita e delle opere di Guido Bonatto, astrologo ed astronomo del secolo XIII*, London, 1851; Sarton, *Introduction*, II, pp. 988–9; *DBI*, s.v.

[875] Introductorium Alcabicii arabici in papiro.

Alcabitius ('Abd al-Aziz ibn 'utman al-Kabisi), Moslem astrologer of the tenth century to whom many works are attributed, was particularly well-known for his *Introductorium*, translated into Latin by John of Seville, with commentary by John of Saxony. A printed version was already available: *Introductorium Alchabitii Arabici ad scientiam judicialem astronomiae*, transl. Mattheus Moretus de Brescia, Bologna, Johannes Vurster, 1473 (Sarton, *Introduction*, I, p. 669).

[876] Alpetragio et Almagesto de Ptolomeo.

Al-Bitrugi (Alpetragius), Moslem astronomer of the twelfth century, was the author of a major work translated by Michael Scot (1217) as *De motibus celorum* (modern edition by F. J. Carmody, Berkeley and Los Angeles, 1952); this was evidently bound here with a Latin version of the *Almagest*, the mathematical treatise of Ptolemy.

[877] Amoar de Nativitatibus in papiro.

Omar or Umar ibn al Farrukhan (Alfraganus Tiberiadis), *De nativitatibus*, was translated by John of Seville (Sarton, *Introduction*, II, p. 170).

[878] Le tavole de Bianchino in papiro.

Giovanni Bianchini (dates uncertain) compiled *Tabulae astronomiae* or *Canones super tabulas* presented to Leonello d'Este in 1436; many copies survive: a finely illuminated one was made for Borso d'Este to give to Emperor Frederick III in 1452, when Bianchini was ennobled; *DBI*, s.v.; G. Boffito, 'Le tavole astronomiche di G. B. da un codice della collezione Olschki', *La bibliofilía*, 9, 1907–8, pp. 378–88, 446–60.

[879] Alcabitio cum altre opere de astrologia.

Cf. I 875.

[880] Jullio Firmico in papiro.

Julius Firmicus Maternus's astrological treatise (4th cent. AD), entitled *Mathesis* (modern edn W. Kroll, F. Skutsch, E. Ziegler, *Matheseos libri VIII*, 2 vols, Leipzig, 1897–1913).

fol. 18ʳ

[881] Messala De Revolutionibus Annorum et alii.

Mashallah (known through Latin translations as Messahala; d. c. 815–20), was the author of *De scientia motu orbis* or *De revolutione annorum mundi* (Sarton, *Introduction*, I, p. 531; II, p. 170).

[882] Tavole de Alfonso.

The astronomical tables drawn up for Alfonso the Wise (1221–84), King of Castile and Leon, c. 1272 (Sarton, *Introduction*, II, p. 837).

[883] Hyginio in carta bona hystoriato coperto de raso cremesino

> Probably the *Astronomica* attributed to Hyginus, a writer of uncertain identity (Sarton,
> *Introduction*, I, p. 226; modern edition by E. Chatelain and P. Legendre, Paris, 1909).

[884] Introductorio de astronomia in papiro.

> Possibly yet another copy of Alcabitius; cf. I 875, 879.

[885] Quadripartito de Ptolomeo in papiro.

> Presumably the *Tetrabiblos* (treatise on astronomy) of Ptolemy (cf. I 876).

[886] Tavole de Bianchino in papiro.

> Cf. I 878.

[887] Hyginio in papiro.

> Cf. I 883.

[888] Summa anglicana in papiro.

> Possibly Bartholomaeus Anglicus, *De proprietatibus rerum*, of which an Italian translation
> by Vivaldo Belcazar of Mantua was made by 1309 (Sarton, *Introduction*, II, pp. 586–8).

[889] Libro de Natura Cellorum in papiro.

> Presumably the title should have 'coelorum', but this is not enough for identification.

[890] Marco Manilio in versi De Astrologia *in papiro a stampo*.

> Four printed editions of Marcus Manilius's *Astronomicon* are known before 1483: Nürem-
> berg, Johannes Müller, c. 1471–4 (Hain, 10703; *BMC*, II, 456); Bologna, Ugo Ruggeri and
> Donnino Bertochi, 1474 (Hain, 10707; *BMC*, VI, 805); Naples, 1476. Another edition,
> dated 1480, is in BCMn (Hain, 10702). Cf. C. Ferrarini, *Incunabulorum quae in civica
> bibliotheca mantuana adservantur catalogus*, Mantua, 1937, p. 129 n. 747.

[891] Summa Hali Habel Raghel.

> Ali ibn abi-l-Rijal (known as Hali Abenragel al Hasan), who flourished at Cordova c.
> 1016–40, was famous for his work on horoscopes, translated from a Castilian version into
> Latin by Aegidius de Tebaldis and Petrus de Regio under the title *De iudiciis astrorum*
> (first printed at Venice, 1485). See Sarton, *Introduction*, I, pp. 715–16.

#Iop.*:

[892] Libellus astronomicum ymaginum Iebith.

> Probably Thabit ibn Qurra (second half of 9th cent.), *De imaginibus astronomicis* (Sarton,
> *Introduction*, II, p. 170; see F. J. Carmody, *The Astronomical Works of Thabit ben Qurra*,
> Berkeley and Los Angeles, 1960).

[893] Libro mazore De geomantia manu Sanviti.

> This may be the book sought by the cardinal's brother Ludovico in June 1484 (see above,
> p. 122). The anonymous *Ars completa geomantiae* in MS London, Victoria and Albert
> Museum Library, L. 2464–1950, has been ascribed to Bartolomeo Sanvito (Alexander, 'A
> Manuscript', p. 39 n. 37); the damaged arms, however, in no way suggest those of the
> cardinal.

[894] Libro minore de geomantia *manu d. Iuliani*

> That is, copied in the hand of Giuliano da Viterbo, so presumably the book had been in
> Francesco's possession for many years (see also above, p. 122).

[895] Libro de arithmetica e giometria coperto de pavonazo.

[896–7] *Restituti principi*:

[896] Librezolo picolo vechio de giomantia.

[897] Un altro libreto vechio de giomantia.

[898] Antonio Musa De Herbis antiquo.

> The *De herba vetonica* was a spurious treatise attributed to this Roman physician (Sarton,
> *Introduction*, I, p. 231).

[899] Una opereta a stampo in carta bona de Io. Filippo de Lignamine.

Giovan Filippo de Lignamine, *Opuscula*, including *Dicta...Sybillarum etc*, Rome, 1481 (*BMC*, IV, p. 131). This copy (BAV, Incun. IV. 29) was bought by Giovan Pietro Arrivabene (Farenga, 'Le prefazioni', p. 172).

[900] L'Etica de Aristoteles in papiro cum altri libri.

[901] Le Pandete de medicina.

Mattheus Silvaticus, *Liber pandectarum medicinae*. The dedication by the editor, Matteo Moretti of Brescia, in the edition printed at Bologna, Johannes Vurster, 1474 (*BMC*, VI, p. 803) is to Cardinal Gonzaga.

[902] La mula Liarda.

#habuit d. Aloysius Capra

[903] La mula Alfana.

[904] La milanese.

[905] La marchesana.

[906] La ragona.

[907] La cancellera.

[908] La fiorentina.

[909] La mula bisa.

#Data a chi la volse:

[910] La morella vechiia.

[911] La bastarda.

[912] La mula che cavalchò d. Alvise.

That is, the mule which Alvise Capra rode (before he had I 903), unless this refers to another person, perhaps Alvise Tosabecci.

[913] La mula scarpazona.

[914] La mazacrocha.

[915] El cavallo reale.

[916] El morello todesco.

[917] El frison.

[918] El cavallo del priore.

Probably the same individual as 'domino Priori Mellono' (W 27), unless it is Ludovico Aldegati (d. 1486), the cardinal's suffragan bishop and prior of San Marco, Mantua.

[919] El balon.

[920] El cavallo che cavalcava el Meliolo.

That is, the horse ridden by either Bartolomeo (the goldsmith) or by Ludovico Melioli (treasurer at Bologna).

[921] El cavallo de Hermes.

The horse ridden by the Paduan goldsmith Hermes de Bonis.

[922] El cavallo del Pasarotto.

[923] El cavallo de maestro Thomas.

'Maestro Thomas' (cf. I 959–60) was probably Tomasso Gallesio named in the will as 'tonsor' (W 27) and as 'Thomasino barbiere' among the cardinal's former retainers—together with Strata, Cosmo [Andreasi] and others—in Bishop-Elect Ludovico Gonzaga's household, according to a letter from the same to Ruffino Gablonetta, Bracciano, 9 June 1484 (ASP, AGG, b. 41 [3], fol. 168ᵛ).

[924] La chinea.

[925] El cavallo vechio del spenditore.

One of the horses of (perhaps) Ludovico Cipata (cf. I 926–7).

#era del spenditore:

[926] El cavallo che menò el spenditore da Mantua (cf. I 925).

[927] El cavallo cavalcava al presente el spenditore (cf. I 925–6).

[928] El cavallo del Strata.

> The horse ridden by Gian Francesco Strata, compiler of the inventory.

[929] El mulo da Fuligno.

[930] Un altro mulo morello.

[931] El mulo Leardo.

[932] El mulo Malatesta.

fol. 19^r

[933] El mulo Pelegrino.

[934] El mulo Martino.

[935] El mulo da la Poreta.

> Cardinal Gonzaga had been most recently at the baths of Porretta in July 1483 (see above, pp. 96, 103; see also Table of Itineraries).

#Dato de gratia:

[936] El mulo Ciccho.

[937] Una cassa de corame negro cum 5 colti dentro de medaglie de metale, che sono in tuto per numero 414.

[signatures]

Ioannesfranciscus dela Strata

Cosmus de Andriassiis

Alesander Siccus

[938–40] Io.pe.:

[938] In la cassa d'ariento del orilogio medaglie d'oro 47.

[939] Item, d'ariento in diversi colti computata una dorata medaglie 35.

[940] Item, in un cartozeto medaglie 11.

[941] In la scatola de ligno fatta al torno medaglie picole d'ariento 281.

[942] Item, la grande de Constantino 1.

> This was almost certainly not antique, but probably a cast derived from the famous medallion, made by a northern French or Burgundian goldsmith, which Jean Duke of Berry acquired in 1402 (Hill, *Medals of the Renaissance*, pp. 20, 131, pl. 24, 1; see also R. Weiss, 'The Medieval Medallions of Constantine and Heraclius', *Numismatic Chronicle*, 7th ser., 3, 1963, pp. 129–44). Gianfrancesco Gonzaga's inventory of 1496 records he had 'una medalia grande de Constantino de argento de forama' (BCG, FMD, b. 23, fol. 9^v); maybe it was the same one. Cristoforo di Geremia had copied an image of Constantine for his medal of 1468 commemorating peace and the visit of Frederick III to Rome (Hill, *Corpus*, no. 755), but this seems an unlikely alternative.

[943] In la scatola de carta biancha diverse medaglie in dui colti, e lo terzo è vacuo, sono tute d'ariento, medaglie 39.

#Io.pe.:

[944] In uno busoleto picolino medaglie d'ariento dorato 12.

[945] In uno sachetino de damasco alexandrino diverse medaglie d'ariento 417

Nota de camei e corniole desligate in una cassa che ha quatro colti:

[946–7] Io. p.:

[946] In quelli de sotto camei grandi 12.

[947] In lo colto sequente de diverse sorte desligati camei 41.

fol. 19ᵛ

[948–53] Io. p.:

[948] Item doi cum le panizole d'oro 2.

[949] Item un grande in calcedonio che ha figura integra de homo sedente, ligato in cerchio de ariento dorato 1.

[950] In l'altro colto camei 20.

[951] In lo 4º colto 34 desligati tra camei e corniole e 3 ligati in circuli dorati; sono in summa 37.

[cancelled:] In sachetino de tela…

[952] In scatola de carta dorata tra grandi e picoli, in tuto 107.

[953] In la scatola de corame in otto anguli, 14 anelli d'oro cum camei e corniole e uno de ottone; anelli 15.

[signature] Iohannesfranciscus de la Strata

fol. 20ʳ [blank]

fol. 20ᵛ

Robe che manchavano in questo, e cavate del inventario de d. Zohannepetro
Arrivabene:

#in pagina 8a: Jo.pe.:

[954] Una casetina de corame negro, lavorata e ligata cum 5 sigilli ut supra, cum dentro 24 mazeti de diverse petre, mazorete, mezane e minore, ligate in oro e scolpite, che son in tuto a numero 103.

#in eadem pagina: [955–6] Jo. pe.:

[955] Una casetina longeta in 8 anguli de coramo, lavorata a la damaschina ligata e sigillata ut supra, cum dentro 4 didali cum anelli in tuto 14 d'oro, cum diverse petre de sculptura, e ultra li predicti un anello de ramo cum un intaglio in vetro.

[956] Una perla ligata in ariento, chi è de li ornamenti de la pace, de ariento dorato.

#In XXa pagina:

[957] Doe maniche de samito fodrate de canzante.

#in XXXVII pagina:

[958] Tre pezi de corame da tavola e da muro.

#in XXXVIII pagina:

[959] Un coperta de rosato da mula.

#in eadem; habuit magister Thomas:

[960] El stuzo da barbero che havea maestro Thomas.

> This was perhaps the barber's *astuccio* (box or case for instruments). On 'Thomas' see I 923n.

[signature] Johanesfranciscus de la Strata

Item. Robe che manchano:

#Reperti in uno folio de mea manu: et duplicati…

[961] Quatro coperte da cavallo a la devisa, extimati ducati 6.

[962] Uno par de staffe grande dorate.
[963] Un par de redene de veluto a la devisa.
[964] Una testera de veluto a la divisa.
[965] Un par de staffili [de] seta.
[966] Una cintola negra da far la coda.
[signature] Johannesfranciscus de la Strata

Appendix 3:
Letters Relating to the Cardinal's Death and Post-Mortem Affairs

For an explanation of the conventions adopted, see the second paragraph of the introductory section to Appendix 2 (above, pp. 142–3).

1. ASMn, AG, b. 1142 (unnumbered)
Giovan Pietro Arrivabene to Marchese Federico Gonzaga, Bologna, 22 October 1483 (damaged; date and sender's name are missing, but the hand is Arrivabene's).

Illustrissimo Signor mio, commendatione. Fu mandata questa nocte la dolorosa noticia de la morte de la bona memoria de Monsignor Cardinale, a le quatro hore de nocte, per messo a posta, adrizato verso Revero, dove intendeva deversi trovare la Excellentia Vostra, che sapiamo ne haverà conceputo quello immenso dolore, che convene a la singulare fraterna carità era tra vui doi. Dio li habia fatto misericordia a l'animo come son certo, attenta la summa contritione con la qual è mancato e lo buon intellecto de che Dio li fece gratia fin a l'ultimo. Hora, per satisfare a la voluntà suoa, d. Aloisio Capra et io, deputati per suoa Signoria executori testamentarii, communicato lo tuto cum Monsignor protonotario vostro fratello, connoscendo lo bisogno de questo corpo non richiedere dilatione longa, cussì etiam consigliati da' medici, siamo astretti de levarne de qui domane col corpo, qual, posto in una cassa secundo usanza, faremo portar in una carretta honoratamente acompagnato da tuta la famiglia.

E compartimo le giornate a questo modo, che domane Deo dante andaremo a Modena, l'altro dì, che serà vèneri, a Coreza, sabbato stamo ambigui se a Gonzaga o Borgoforte; e se de questo a tempo puoremo havere rispuosta resolutiva da Vostra Signoria, qual viagio sia più de suo parere, che quello seguiressimo; ma quando la rispuosta non ce puotesse essere ad hora, nui ne adrizaressimo pur a Gonzaga. E dominica intraressimo in Mantuoa, de che n'è parso per questo messo speciale dare noticia a la Excellentia Vostra, la qual pregamo se digni ordinare a' suoi officiali o de Borgoforte o de Gonzaga, secundo dove haveremo a capitare, che, andando inanti li nostri sescalchi, ne faciano fare commoditate de le stantie.

Io, in executione de la commissione che Vostra Signoria me dede a Goido, ho scritto subito a Roma a la Sanctitate de Nostro Signore de la provisione del vescovato per Monsignor protonotario, e similiter al Signor conte ad Imola, che voglia con suoe lettere favorire et aiutare la cosa de là, e già ne ho rispuosta che ha scritto efficacissimamente. Restaria mo, puo' che lo caso è seguito, che Vostra Signoria ne facesse, piacendoli, una lettera particulare a Nostro Signore, cum exprimerli la voluntà suoa circa ciò, a confirmatione del mio scrivere, la qual mandandonela incontra, nui subito adrizaremo a Roma. E per non havere io tempo, li supplico voglia fare communicare lo mio scrivere de sopra al Signor […]llo, dove ello serà, et a la buona gratia suoa me raccomando. Bononie […]

2. ASMn, AG, b. 1142
Giovan Pietro Arrivabene to Marchese Federico Gonzaga, (outside) Bologna, 23 October 1483.

Illustrissimo Signor mio, commendatione. Questa matina, su le xii hore, montando nui a cavallo, sopragionse un cavallaro nostro con la littera de heri de Vostra Excellentia, in la qual me dice la suoa deliberatione de mandare lo Reverendo et Illustre Monsignor protonotario suo figliolo cum quell'altra comitiva, designandoci la via da Modena a Carpi, la qual omnino non svaria molto dal nostro pensiere, per lo qual già havemo scripto a Coreza, e mandato là lo sescalcho nostro ad apparichiare per domane, e scritto a quelli signori; e pensamo che, havendolo Vostra Signoria intieso, haverà drizato per quella via dicto Monsignor protonotario a la qual nui pur ne adrizaremmo, essendo mo cussì dato l'ordine. E penso che domane sera habiamo a trovarlo lì. Intenderemo li ordini e modi che Vostra Signoria harà deliberato se servino per riponere lo corpo in la sepultura, la qual se ha electo la bona memoria de Monsignor mio in la capella vostra in San Francesco in terra presso a la sepultura grande. E per nui designavamo intrare dominica sera a nocte, e fare che a la porta de la terra fusse el clero cum le religione, et che a drittura lo portassimo a San Francesco nel casson proprio, reponerlo in la capella; p[uoi?] farli un deposito, fin che la sepultura fusse finita. E puoi, posto ordine a le cerimonie consuete, se faranno le exequie sollenne in San Francesco, secundo la consuetudine di cardinali, existimando perhò che la Signoria Vostra serà contenta fare commandare gientilhuomini, doctori e citadini per portarlo da la porta a San Francesco. Questi sono discorsi de d. Aloiso Capra e mio come executori, communicati perhò cum Monsignor protonotario vostro fratello. Tamen et hec omnia e la designatione del tempo, quando se haveranno a cominciare le exequie, se regularanno al commandamento de Quella, a la qual anche supplicamo che se digni farne dare tute le instructione a ciò conveniente. Et insieme havere raccommandata tuta questa famiglia sconsolata et abandonata come la gloriosa memoria de Monsignor mio ge la raccommandò nel suo ultimo, e me, Signor mio, in ispecie, derelicto da tanto bene e gratioso patron mio. A Roma fu scripto per doe mie in buona forma. E finché Monsignor de Aragona passò, intiesi già a Roma essere facti li designi del vescovato e prepositura conformi a la voluntà vostra. Me [raccomando a la] buona gratia de Vostra Signoria. Ex hospicio citra Bononie ad 4 miliaria xxiii° octobris 1483.

        Excellentie Vestre   servitor Jo. P. Arrivabenus.

3. ASMn, AG, b. 1321
Giovan Pietro Arrivabene to Marchese Federico Gonzaga, Correggio, 24 October 1483.

Illustre Signor mio, commendatione. El se manda Sanvito sescalcho inanti informato di pensieri e modi che a nui occorreriano de servarsi per la introductione de dominica del corpo de la bona memoria de Monsignore mio in Mantuoa. E cerimonie se haveriano a fare per quella sera, ad fine che del tuto dia noticia a la Signoria Vostra. E che successive se faciano li ordinamenti secundo lo potere e commandamento de Quella, a la qual integramente ugni cosa se remette. La Signoria Vostra consideri in quanta perdita e dolore sia rimasa questa povera famiglia. E de tuto se digni havere compassione e pigliarne in se speciale protectione per memoria de la benedetta anima de Monsignore mio, el qual tanto teneramente l'amava. Et io ne son optimamente conscio. Cussì ge la raccommando tuta non omettendo di me in specialitate, che li supplico voglia cum la gratia suoa ristorarmi e consolarmi de tanto affanno. Et a Quella me raccomando. Ex Corigia xxiiii° octobris 1483.

Illustris Dominationis Vestre   servitor Jo. P. Arrivabenus

4. ASMn, AG, b. 2105 (unnumbered; registered, with some spelling variations, in ASMn, AG, b. 2900, lib. 115, fols 73^v–4^r)
Francesco Gonzaga to Marchese Federico Gonzaga, Mantua, 25 October 1483.

Illustrissimo Signor mio patre. Hogii, quamprimum hebi la lettera de Vostra Excellentia, spaciai mio messo al Reverendo Monsignore Protonotario mio barba et maestro Zo.Petro Arrivabeno, significandoli quanto Quella mi commandava. Doppo è gionto qui Sanvito seschalcho, mandato per li prefati Monsignore et maestro Zo.Petro informato de quanto li occorreria de servarsi per la introductione del corpo del quondam Reverendissimo Monsignore Cardinale, quale debbe essere dimane dreto le xxiiii hore. Lui s'è ridutto a me facendomi intendere li modi si servono in corte di Roma, quali qui presso dirò, cioè circa l'introductione del corpo, che per anchora non s'è ragionato d'altro. Tuti quelli de la famiglia segueno el corpo, cominciando a li più degni. Prima vanno auditori, secretarii, capellani, camerieri, poi scuderi; a questi si dànno per compagni li primi parenti del defuncto, et successivamente finché gli ne sono. Doppo si gli metteno de li gentilhomini fin'al compimento. In questo caso dicono ch'el prefato Monsignore protonotario, ultra ch'el sii fratello, per essere familiare, ché a questo se ha respecto, serà lo primo, et io li serò per compagno. Hector, figliolo del Illustrissimo Signor messer Rodulfo mio barba [serà] el secundo, et Monsignore Protonotario mio fratello si gli darà per compagno; et cussì per ordine secundo la dignità de li famigliari et propinquità de sangue. Cento doppieri serano col corpo fin a San Francesco, et dimane, come ho dicto, dretto le xxiiii hore se levarà da Sancto Biasio fuora de la porta da Cerese, che lì se fermarà fin a quell'hora, perché, essendo gionto hogii a Gonzaga, da matina se aviarà passando a Saviolla, dove ho scritto si gli ritrovino li porti de Burgoforte, et si condurà nanti la dicta hora. S'è preso partito che da matina si trovino insieme Sanvito, Zoan Arrivabene, el massaro et Be de li Agnelli, et faciano la lista de tuti et pongano ordine per quelli si gli debeno ritrovare. Ho voluto per mia satisfactione significare el tuto a Vostra Excellentia, in buona gratia de la quale continuo me raccomando. Mantue, xxv octobris 1483.

Illustrissime Dominationis vestre filius et servitor Franciscus.

5. ASMn, AG, b. 2430, c. 646
Alvise Capra and Giovan Pietro Arrivabene to Marchese Federico Gonzaga, Mantua, 27 October 1483.

Illustrissimo Signor nostro, commendatione. La Excellentia Vostra haverà intieso lo nostro arivare qua heri sera col corpo de la bona memoria de Monsignor nostro, acompagnato da la famiglia suoa derelicta e dolorata, el qual honoratissimamente fu portato e reposto in la chiesia de San Francesco secundo la institutione suoa, adiungendoseli l'amorevele ordinatione de Vostra Signoria, la qual in nome de tuta la famiglia summamente ringratiamo. E perché quella, fin da Bologna, per lettere de me Zoan Petro, intiese del testamento fatto e serato, et havendose mo a procedere a la apertione de esso per exequire la voluntà suoa, stavamo tuti doi in pensiere de transferirne domane a la Excellentia Vostra, sì per dare forma a ciò, non puotendo avanti tal aprimento renunciare alcuna particularità del testamento, sì per exponerli quanto la benedetta anima de questo Signore nostro ne commise in voce. Ma essendone ditto che quella serìa qui domane, suspendessimo lo pensiere nostro. E perché mo, al tardo, la venuta suoa e lo tempo ne sono posti in dubio, n'è parso de drizare prima questa nostra lettera a Vostra Signoria, e pregarLa che la se digni farne intendere se la vole l'aspettiamo qui, o che e quando veniamo [?da] Lei, perché, secundo lo suo commandamento, ne governaremo, significandoli interim che dal protonotario Agnello e d. Francesco Maffei ho io, Zoan Petro, questa sera lettera de xxiii cum un capitolo del tenore incluso, che è in rispuosta de le mie prime, che scrissi a Roma quando viddi lo caso desperato circa la provisione di beneficii de qua secundo la voluntà de Vostra Signoria, de che tra domane e l'altro ne aspettamo anche piú particulare rispuosta per quello che fu replicato là statim post obitum. Et a la bona gratia de Vostra Signoria ne raccomandiamo. Mantue xxvii octobris 1483.

        Excellentie Vestre servitores Aloysius Capra & Jo. Pe. Arrivabenus executores testamentarii.

6. ASMn AG b. 2105 (unnumbered)
Francesco Gonzaga to Marchese Federico Gonzaga, Mantua, 27 October 1483.

Illustrissimo Signor mio patre. Benché fusse ordinato ch'el corpo del quondam Reverendissimo Monsignore mio barba giongesse a San Biasio, et de lì se levasse, nondimeno, parendo a li deputati a questo la via essere molto longa fin a San Francisco, fu condutto a Sancta Magdalena fuora da la Predella per la via de Levata. De lì, heri sera, dreto le xxiiii hore, secundo l'ordine, fu levato, portandosi adrittura sul ponte de San Jacomo et de lì a San Francisco. Si servò in accompagnar[lo] il modo ch'io scrissi a Vostra Excellentia et si gionse presso li familiari et parenti uno gentilhomo […] andavano tre in pari. Nanti el corpo erano li mazeri cum le maze, et il portatore del capello. Niuno lì era accappato. Tuta Mantua lì concorse. Gionto ch'el fu in San Francisco, se lì cantò suso un bon pezo, poi lo portorono in la capella nostra. De lì partendosi feci compagnia a Monsignore protonotario mio barba fin mezo la piacia, che de lì si driciò in vescoato et io in corte, che erano le iii hore. Dicono che da dimane ad otto giorni cominciaro le cerimonie consuete farsi a cardinali. M'è parso per mio debito significare questo a la Signoria Vostra, in bona gratia de la quale de continuo me raccomando. Mantue xxvii octobris 1483.

      Illustrissime Dominationis vestre   Filius et servitor Franciscus.

7. ASMn, AG, b. 847, c. 16
Giovan Pietro Arrivabene to Marchese Federico Gonzaga, Rome, 26 December 1483 (written as 1484, i.e., Mantuan style).

Illustrissimo Signor mio, commendatione. La principal casone che più me facesse accelerare la mia ritornata fu per essere non mancho observatore de vera fede a la bona memoria del patron mio morto che me fussi stato in vita suoa, come sempre in tute opere mie me son forzato fare constare ad ugniuno. E questo era per consultare cum li compagni qui executori del testamento insieme deputati, e dare forma praecipue al pagamento di debiti, parendomi lo più importante articulo li fusse per honore del Signore defuncto. Et a questo non era per manchare in cosa alchuna de quanto pertinesse ad me.

        Arivato, trovo essere spazato per lo reverendo domino lo arciprete un breve directivo a Vostra Excellentia, secundo la richiesta fatta in nome suo, dove a quella se dà cura de esser superintendente a questa executione de testamento insieme con li executori o alcuni de essi o deputati da lor, tanto per la satisfactione di debiti, quanto di legati cum acopiarli insieme doe persone come nel breve, del qual ho copia, se contiene, la qual cosa, per riverentia de Vostra Signoria, me move a starmi prima ad intendere la ordinatione e commandamento suo, per pigliare la forma de la voluntà suoa, la qual non solo amorevele a l'honore e nome de Monsignore mio, ma etiam per la auctorità son certo disponerà providamente sopra questa cosa, in correspondentia de quella fede che la benedetta anima de Monsignor mio in extremis, secundo lo suo consueto perhò, piglioe de la Excellentia Vostra, raccommandandoli precipuamente quella suoa ultima voluntà. Né altro per hora me accade, se non che devotamente me raccomando a la bona gratia de Vostra Signoria, que diu feliciter valeat. Rome xxvi decembris 1484

Excellentie Vestre   Servitor Jo. P. Arrivabenus.

8. ASMn, AG, b. 847, c. 21
Ludovico Agnelli, Francesco Maffei and Giovan Pietro Arrivabene to Marchese Federico Gonzaga, Rome, 21 January 1484.

Illustrissime Princeps ac excellentissime domine, domine noster singularissime, humilem commendationem. Habiamo ricevuta una lettera de Vostra Illustrissima Signoria et in quella inclusa la copia del breve di Nostro Signore sopra la exequutione del testamento della bona memoria de Monsignor nostro Reverendissimo cardinale, alla quale rispondemo che semo presti ad obedire quanto quella ne commanda circa la supersessione della exequutione del predicto testamento, et cusì facemo. Daremo anche ordine di mandarli lo inventario de tutte le robe tanto di quelle che sono di qua, quanto di quelle di là. Et perché ne richiede prefata Vostra Illustrissima Signoria debiamo venire o vero substituire qualchuno in vice nostra, saremo insieme, et non possendo venire personalmente ordinaremo quanto ne commanda Vostra Excellentia, et ad Quella ne daremo notitia, afinché la possa fare in quella cosa quanto sarà necessario. Ci racommandamo alla Excellentia Vostra, que diu felicissime valeat. Rome xxi Januarii mccccclxxxiiii.

Eiusdem Illustrissime Dominationis Vestre devoti servitores L. Agnellus protonotarius   F. de Maffeis protonotarius   Jo. Pe. Arrivabenus.

9. ASMn, AG, b. 847, c. 26.
Gaspare da Padova to Marchese Federico Gonzaga, Rome, 28 February 1484.

Illustrissime et Excellentissime Domine, Domine mi observandissime, post debitam commendationem etc. Perché la rason e'l bisogno mi constringe a scrivere a la Illustrissima Signoria Vostra, pertanto io mi ricorerò a Quella come a signore che sempre li piacque ch'el fusse facto iusticia a chi pretende di havere ragione. La casone di questa è che, essendomi ritenuti ducati xxii da d. Johanne Pietro Arrivabene del salario che me avanzava con la bona memoria de lo Reverendissimo cardinale, dicendo lui ritenermeli per mesi xi ch'io steti absente da la Signoria sua Reverendissima, cioé perché non andai con Quella quando la se partì di qua per andare a Ferrara, et a ciò che la Signoria Vostra Illustrissima intenda el tutto, quando lo Reverendissimo cardinale bone memorie si partite di qua, io supplicai a sua Signoria Reverendissima che mi volesse concedere ch'io ristasse qui per alchuni zorni per rispecto de alchune mie importante facende, se Quella non haveva bisogno di me, et che presto andaria a trovarla. Me rispuose che haveva grato ch'io ristasse et detemi alchune commissione fra le quali me commisse ch'io dovesse sollicitare uno Juliano de Scipio che facesse una masenina di porphido per tridare sapore, et oltra questo procurasse di trovare qualche medaglia o altre cose antiche, et ch'io gi le dovesse mandare. Dapoi non molti zorni vène qui Agnolo Maffei, el quale fra pochi dì ritornò a Ferrara, et per lui mandai a sua Signoria Reverendissima alchune medaglie d'argento e di bronzo, et scrissi a Quella che se volesse dignare de farmi intendere se la voleva ch'io andase a trovarla, o vero ch'io ristasse qui et l'avisai comme la masenina non era finita, per rispecto del maestro che era amalato. Sua Signoria Reverendissima mi fece scrivere ch'io ristasse qui et che non haveva de bisogno di me a Ferara et che io li mandase qualche corniola anticha et ch'io sollicitasse che la masenina si fornisse, et sopra ciò più lettere mi fece scrivere. Et io dicendo questo a d. Johanne Pietro, me rispose ch'io ne dovesse parlare con li altri executori, li quali me risposeno che per la parte sua erano contenti ch'el mi fussero dati li predicti xxii ducati. Dapoi, essendo stati molti zorni amalato d. Johan Pietro, gliene ho riparlato. Me ha risposto che in questa facenda non può far niente et che, se la Illustrissima Signoria Vostra li scrive, ch'el lo farà. Volgio che la Signoria Vostra intenda come son stato anni xvi e più servitore de la bone memoria del Reverendissimo cardinale, et non ho havuto altro che la provisione, cioé ducati doi el mese, onde [me] doglio che la mia longa servitù meriti questo premio da li executori. Pertanto ricorro da la Signoria Vostra Illustrissima, pregando Quella che si degni di far scrivere qui a lo ambasciatore suo, o vero a d. Johanne Pietro, che questo poco di salario aquistato in xi mesi a le mie spese non mi sia ritenuto e facto questo torto. Io seria venuto a trovare la Signoria Vostra Illustrissima, ma el Camerlengo ch'è successo patrone de la casa che fu de la bona memoria di Monsignore mio Reverendissimo mi trov[ò] qui in casa, et non mi ha voluto lasare partire. Ma voglio che la Signoria Vostra Illustrissima intenda che sempre serò servo di Quella et de la casa di Gonzaga, et possendo io far cosa grata a la Signoria Vostra supplico a Quella mi volglia commandare et che exaudisca li mie iuste dimande. A la quale di continuo mi raccomando. Rome xxviii februarii 1484.

Eiusdem Vestre Illustrissime Dominationis servitor Gaspar de Padua.

10. ASMn, AG, b. 847, cc. 5ʳ–6ʳ

Giovan Pietro Arrivabene to Marchese Federico Gonzaga, Rome, 14 March 1484.

Illustrissimo Signor mio, commendatione. Dissi ultimamente a la Excellentia Vostra per una mia che, essendo per la gratia de Dio riducto in buona sanitate, attenderia a far fare copia de l'inventario de tutte le robbe a messere Alviso Capra e a me consignate in Mantuoa de la hereditate de la bona memoria de Monsignor mio. Et non havendo fin qui havuto persona idonea, hora la mando per questo parafreniero del Reverendissimo Monsignor protonotario in man del dicto domino Alviso, a ciò che, per mezo suo, desiderando Vostra Signoria altra informatione, Ella ne possa essere da lui pienamente instructa. E qui inclusa serà specialmente una lista de quelle cose che io portai cum me, cussì invitato et confortato a fare per littere commune del protonotario Agnello e de domino Francesco Maffei. De quelle che sono rimase a Mantuoa, Zohanne mio fratello ne haverà mostrato l'inventario. E perché la bona memoria de Monsignor faceva lo legato distincto e li camerieri per sé, e puoi a li camarieri e famiglia insieme , divisamente da quello de che voleva fussero pagati li debiti, come nel testamento se contiene, nui a li camerieri assignassemo lo suo, e similiter a la famiglia, la qual volse restasse depositato presso di me finché se vendesse. Et tamen per farne la vendita a fine se facesseno li pagamenti e distributione tra lor che lo testamento ordinava, fecero electione de tre, li quali concoresseno cum nui a li precii e venditione de le robbe. E cussì se procedette. Et io ne ho de tuto lo bello conto chiaro e disteso, a cosa per cosa, qual se mostrarà sempre dove bisognarà e Vostra Signoria ordinarà. E de quanto a me sian restato in mane se renderà buon conto.

L'è vero che quando domino l'arciprete a nui executori de qua assignò quella littera de Vostra Excellentia cum la copia inclusa del breve, essendo io in quello tempo gravemente infirmo, fu ricordato che per essere di qua in Roma lo più forte di debiti, et a li creditori seria stranio venire a Mantuoa a liquidare li suoi crediti et a dimandare denari, pareria buono, quando cussì piacesse a Vostra Signoria, che Quella deputasse qui uno a suo nome, el qual havesse ad intervenire a legitimare et acceptare questi debiti, et che le robbe deputate a pagamento di debiti se mandassino de qua, non volendole Vostra Signoria o tute o parte per sé, dove haveriano migliore precio et, o se vendessero o dessero in pagamento a' creditori, li quali forsi le contariano a magiore valuta per conseguirne la suoa satisfactione. E cussì pregammo domino lo arciprete, che lo scrivesse, non puotendo né volendo nui procedere più inanti senza l'auctorità de Vostra Signoria, el deputato de la qual puoria saltem in hoc principio intender et informarLa. E certo, per satisfactione de chi aspetta, non se voria darli più indusia. E tamen, per anticipare, mando pur a domino Alviso un desgrossamento d'alcuni debiti, li quali sono più chiari. Alcune altre petitioni sono ben fatte, le quale non pare a nui de qua senza l'auctorità de Vostra Signoria e scientia de lo herede, de cuius interesse agitur, devere absolutamente acceptare. Perhò pareva buono e necessario mezo che qui fusse uno chi intervenisse a nome di quella. E speraria, che presto presto a tuto se daria buona forma.

In questi creditori sono li Medici de corte, li quali deveno havere da ducati 3500, per li quali alcuni de casa et io insieme cum lor siamo fideiussori obligati *in forma Camere*. E volendo mo lor, per trarne lo suo denaro, procedere contra de nui a le censure, è stato necessario assecurarli sopra li camei, che non è parso inconveniente, attento che la hereditate è obligata a relevare nui de ugni danno etc. E di questo, quasi statim dopo lo mio arivare, ne fui da lor assaltato e molestato, subiungendo che lo Magnifico Lorenzo li tuoria sempre in pagamento a iusto precio, e forsi a lui, ultra che sia huomo qual molto se ne dilecta, se contariano a più valuta, attento che non haveria cussì a sborsarne lo denaro. Immo ne retraria lo suo, ma tuto, se intende, quando Vostra Signoria non li havesse l'animo per sé, de che m'è parso avisarnela.

Qui anche sono in pigno già 4 anni le confectiere, doe grande de cristallo, per 300 ducati, e de li interessi pro 50, le quale costarono 500. Seria da finirle per non lasciarle a l'interesse. Sónoli le gioie, che ha in man domino Francesco Maffei, de le quale domino l'arciprete deve havere dato informatione a la Signoria Vostra. E similiter esso domino Francesco ha in suo potere lecti, massaricie e molte altre robbe che erano qui in casa, de le quale non ha dato a nui inventario alcuno. Penso che forsi l'haverà mandato a Vostra Signoria. Item ha li denari de quella pensione, quali Monsignor, per scarico de la conscientia suoa, ordina che se restituiscano. Se haveranno cum l'auctorità de Vostra Signoria a ritrare e farne quello effecto, puo' che né lui né Hieronymo non hanno potuto, etiam cum molta instantia, obtenere dal papa che restassino a Hieronymo. E Suoa Beatitudine me lo disse, allegando che non voleva ne restase circa la conscientia del cardinale. Aspettaremo adonque intendere in omnibus la voluntà de Vostra Excellencia, la qual volendo in cosa alcuna havere lo parere e consentimento di executori, puoterà chiedere lì domino Alviso, el qual da me, fin a principio, in la partita mia fu sustituito. Et in nome suo e mio serà sempre obediente a tuti commandamenti de quella, a la gratia de la qual humelmente me raccomando. Rome xiiii° Martii 1484.

Excellentie Vestre servitor   Io. P. Arrivabenus.

11. ASMn, AG, b. 847, c. 137
Stefanino Guidotti to Marchese Federico Gonzaga, 19 March 1484.

Illustrissimo Signor mio singularissimo etc. Ultra le altre mie za scritte a la Excellentia Vostra, che hano importantia circha i fatti soi, me fi fatta instantia da tuti i creditori qua de la bona memoria del Reverendissimo quondam cardinale di Mantua che la Signoria Vostra si digni per lo interesse e di loro e de la heredità de diputar in loco suo uno che possa legitimare e saldare i conti loro e pigliar ordine e modo ch'el se gli satisfaza li executori per lo interesse de la heredità. Supplicano quello medesimo che Vostra Signoria sia contenta o deputi chi gli piace che le robe mobile di casa che perdano conditione de la vendita come più indusiano, come sono letti e simel drapamenti, che si deliberi venderli. Item, perché messer Francesco Maffeo tiene pur quelle zoie, cioé quello diamante di pretio de ducati mille e altre assai, e non se ne po cavar construtto, perché il monstra volerle tener per sua secureza per certo suo credito, e perdano tempo, bisognarìa ch'el fussi qui homo di Vostra Excellentia che de le cose che non si possono liquidar là a Mantua havessi facultà per la rata sua di liquidarle, legitimarle, probarle e fare quanto in essa expeditione bisognassi, maxime in quelle cose che habelmente non si posseno tratar di là. Promisi a tuti di scriverne a la Signoria Vostra. Quella mo' deliberi il parir suo quando l'habia il tempo di deliberare circha queste cose, oltra le più urgente e necessarie che gli tochano a Lei, e a la gratia Sua sempre me racomando. Rome 19 martii 1484.

Illustrissime Dominationis Vestre Servitor Stephaninus Guidotti.

12. ASMn, AG, b. 847, c. 35
Gaspare da Padova to Marchese Federico Gonzaga, Rome, 29 March 1484 (sender's signature is destroyed, but the hand is the same as no. 9 above).

Illustrissime et Excellentissime domine, domine mi observandissime, post debitam commendationem etc.

Ho riceputo da lo Ambasator de la Vostra Excellencia la letera che è ad risposta de la mia ch'io scripsi a Quella, la quale me è stata di summa consolatione, considerando che essa Vostra Excellencia se habia degnata di exaudire le supplicatione mie, et rispondermi con tanta benignitate, la quale me constringe ad esser in perpetuo servo di Quella. Poi, intendendo che la Excellencia Vostra harebbe chara quella masenina che fo principiata in nome de la bona memoria de lo Reverendissimo vostro fratello, andai subito a trovare el maestro, lo quale pregai che la volesse finire, perché la Illustrissima Signoria Vostra la torria, et così ordinassimo insieme che lui la finisse, ma con più bella forma et con altri ornamenti di quello che prima era stata ordinata, et perché el ditto maestro non fece mai merchato né pacto con la bona memoria de lo Reverendissimo Monsignore di cosa che lui li facesse, questo medesimo vole fare con la Excellencia Vostra, et dice che quando la serà fornita che la rimeterà al iudicio e discricione mia, e fo[r]nita che la sia, farò per la Excellencia Vostra tanto quanto merita la servitù ch'io ho con Quella. Poi circa al facto de le cose antiche che me ha dicto lo oratore di Vostra Excellencia in nome di Quella, io starò attento et con diligentia procurerò che Quella haverà qualche cosa excellente.

Ulterius, vedendendo per la littera de la Excellencia Vostra che Quella me rimette a domino Jo. Pietro Arrivabene, dicendo che oportune li scrive et commanda ch'el me debia satisfare, son stato con lui, et non havendo operato dicta littera niente, mi è necessario replicare et ricorrermi da chi mi puo aiutare, e di ciò me rincrese e duole ch'el me bisogni affannare tanto la Excellencia Vostra, ma pur vedendo che li executori non l'anno potuto piegare, mi è forza di ricorrere a l'u[lti]mo refugio. In conclusione, lui me ha risposto che per la littera di Vostra Excellencia non ha aucturità di potermi dare lo avanzo mio, et ch'el bisogna che la Signoria Vostra Illustrissima commeta a qualchuno di qua il voto di Quella, et che poi lui iudicherà s'io ho ad havere questi dinari o no.

Ho etiam monstrato a lo Ambasciatore le littere che mi fece scrivere la bona memoria del Cardinale da Ferrara, per le quale Sua Reverencia ha compreso ch'io ho rasone. Non ho altro obstaculo che maestro Jo. Pietro, lo quale al principio ch'el vene a Roma mi domandò certo Homero che mi è rimasto ne le mane, et non n'è fornito di scrivere né de miniare; et io, avendolo mandato con certe mie robe fuora di chasa per salvarle quando achadete la morte de la bona memoria de Cardinale, disi che io gi lo daria et perché subito non gi lo portai, ha preso sdegno, et volmi premiare in questo modo de la mia longa servitute. Et vedendo io che le provision de gli altri servitore del quondam Reverendissimo sono stato pagate per sue mane senza l'aucturità de li altri executori, et volendo el consenso de li ditti per questo facto mio, et poi che lui lo hebbe, me rimesse a Vostra Excellencia, poi non la vole obedire. Non so che partito mi pilgiare si non suplicare di gratia ha Vostra Excellencia che si degni commettere questa mia causa di qua a persona che ministre iusticia et che habia podestà di fare ch'io sia satisfacto havendo rasone, a ciò ch'io non habia più a molestare con mie littere la Vostra Excellencia, a la quale di continuo me ricomando et supplico a Quella che exaudisca con celerità le mie iuste dimande, perché dito domino Jo. Pietro fato Pasqua si parte da Roma. Rome, XXVIIII marcii 1484.

Et Vestre Illustrissime Dominationis
[damaged] serv[itor Gaspar] de [Padua] ca[merario?]

13. ASMn, AG, b. 1800, c. 89
Gianfrancesco Gonzaga, Count of Rodigò, to Marchese Federico Gonzaga, Bozzolo, 25 May 1484.

Illustrissime princeps et excellentissime domine frater et domine mi horandissime. Mando da vostra Illustrissima Signoria Antonio Cattaneo, lator presente, per alchune littere haute da Roma per lo quale, havendo inteso Quella essere liberata per breve de la Sanctità de Nostro Signore da quelle cose del quondam Reverendissimo Monsignore nostro, parendomi che Vostra Excellentia, sotto li oghii de la quale me sono sempre ripossato, non ne pilliarà più altro impazo, ho deliberato, se cossì a Quella parerà, dopo che questo peso ha a remanere a le spalle mie, de tore per inventario presso de mi tute quelle cose, et per questo mando esso Antonio, al quale Vostra Celsitudine credera quanto a me proprio, et etiam, accadendo, se dignarà dargli ogni aiuto necessario. Et a la bona gratia de Quella continue me ricomando. Datum Bozuli die 25 maii 1484.

Illustrissime et excellentissime et vostro servitor et frater Johanes Franciscus de Gonzaga Marchio Rotinghique comes etc.

14. ASP, AGG, b. 43/1, reg. 1, fols 172^r–3^v
Ludovico Gonzaga, Bishop-Elect of Mantua, to Gianfrancesco Gonzaga, Count of Rodigò, Bracciano, 9 June 1484.

Illustris etc. Scio che lo Magnifico messer Zoan Piero Arrivabeno, affectionatissimo a Vostra Signoria et a me, chi hora se ritrova a Napoli, dove fu mandato già parechii dì da la Sanctitate de Nostro Signore per oratore suo, ha tra li debiti che se hanno ad pagare de la bona memoria del Reverendissimo Monsignor nostro fratello duoi che li premono, a li quali non se puoteria dare dilatione senza graveza e carico suo et anche mio, come intenderà la Signoria vostra. L'uno è per li panni negri tuolti a li funerali da Juliano Borgi per termino de aprile proxime passato, per li quali crede perhò sia pagata una buona parte. L'altro è di mille ducati accattati a Bologna nel ultimo del prefato Monsignore sopra la collana del puttino nostro nepote, a termine per tutto magio o giugno. Per la redemptione de la collana se fece sempre designo sopra li denari che havevanno ad entrare de le fictanze de Sabioneta, Riparolo e Comesazo deputati a debiti per commessione del prelibato Monsignore, come denari più vivi. Per li panni c'è la assignatione facta nel testamento, che è pur principalmente sopra esse fictanze. Quod urget est lo dubio se ha, che dicta collana non se perdesse, o lo pupillo in modo alcuno non ne patesse, quale precipuamente è raccomandato sotto la protectione e tutoria mia, et anche del predicto messer Zohannepetro. Prego adonque la Signoria Vostra, come amico chi sono a messer Zoan Piero e tutore del fanciullo e debbo condignamente havere cura de le cose suoe, sia contenta a lasciare correre quelli pagamenti, e convertirli ut supra, e maxime per la collana, che si possa riscuotere e renderla al pupillo, che certo me pareria pur troppo carico che quello ne patesse et havessine lesione alcuna. Serà questo a me gratissimo, e riceverollo per satisfactione de messer Zoan Piero e sgraveza de la conscientia mia a singulare complacentia da Vostra prefata Signoria, a la quale me raccomando et que feliciter valeat. Brachiani viiii Junii 1484.

15. ASP AGG b. 41/3 reg. 1 fols 192^v–4^v
Ludovico Gonzaga, Bishop-Elect of Mantua, to Ruffino Gablonetta, Bracciano, 26 June 1484 (extract and postscript).

Lodovicus etc. Nui havemo molto bene intieso quanto ne dite per la vostra de heri, maxime circa lo ragionamento facto cum lo Reverendissimo Monsignor de Parma in causa liberationis, de la quale seressimo certissimamente tanto cupidi de riportarne effectuale gratia, particulariter et specialiter a nui concessa da la Sanctitate de Nostro Signore quanto che de cosa quale per mo puotessimo desyderare…

Ricevuta che hareti questa nostra, andareti ad ritrovare Suoa Reverendissima Signoria facendoli noto quanto a nui haveti scritto, e questa rispuosta nostra. E per levare ugni dubio e sinistro concepto che forsi havesse facto la Sanctitate de Nostro [Signore], e per la pura e mera veritate, diretili per parte nostra, che ex nunc nui li certificamo, che quando la bona memoria del Reverendissimo Cardinale nostro observandissimo fratello e patre fece lo suo testamento, nui non ne eravamo puncto informati né lo sapessimo donec fu publicato, e manche de ciò anche ne era informato lo Signor marchese. Il che, se vero sia state e sia, l'ha dimonstrato la impetratione facta per la liberatione del figliolo, cuius onerationis per la prepositura che l'ha de San Benedetto iudicet ipsa si consensit vel non, essendosi impetrata tal liberatione. Di nui non vogliamo dire, perché omnibus constat che non ne sapevamo coelle, nisi postquam apertum fuit testamentum. Ratificatione nostra non ne appare doppo, né ne gravaressimo se non ch'el ne pare essere iniusto e factone torto, che nui soli senza utilità debiamo patire graveza. Lo Reverendo domino Sigismundo facilmente fu exhonerato per le rasone che intendereti per la copia del breve quale qui inclusa ve mandiamo, le medesime se puoteriano addure e exprimere per nui dal patronato in fuora.

Sapemo bene che da pagare li debiti lo modo c'è molto bene, e che la prelibata memoria dum conderet eius testamentum disse che la ligitima sua valeva da 60 in 70^m ducati, che seria una grossissima posta che facto lo computo a portione de l'intrate reusceria pur a quella quantitate de sessanta in settanta milia ducati. Sònoce più, ultra quelli cinque milia fiorini de Rheno, ultra tre milia de la dote materna, quattro milia etiam fiorini, al credere nostro, che deveva havere esso Reverendissimo Monsignor nostro fratello dal Re de Dacia, e molti beni mobeli, quali soli seressimo de opinione che, spacciandose per lo denaro de la vagliuta, che voressimo perhò fusse a migliori tempi, extinguiriano gagliardissimamente tutti li debiti, et avanzariane anche qualche cosa. Queste ragione apparente e chiarissime militano per nui. Non ne seria facto grande torto se soli fussimo oppressi; lo Reverendo domino protonotario Sigismundo ha li beneficii liberi; perché a nui deveriano essere obligati? Lo Illustre Signor Zoanfrancesco è herede; ha e deve havere quanto dicemo di sopra; non ha oblligatione de più che settemilia ducati ultra la satisfactione di debiti, quali, come havemo ditto, seressimo de opinione che li beni mobeli a lui lasciati pagariano, cur ergo hoc nobis honus obligationis fructuum ecclesie nostre mantuane relinquere debet…

[Postscript]

A ciò che precisamente e secundo la mera veritate intendiati la summa di debiti che ha ad pagare lo Illustre signor Zoan Francesco nostro fratello, per vigore del testamento e de la hereditate, sapiati che essa summa non excede deceotto o vintimilia ducati, et cum li funerali, ultra la satisfactione del legato de la famiglia, la robba de la quale se ritrovava in mane de Zoan Arrivabeno in nome de domino Zoan Petro, [e che] esso signor Zoan Francesco novamente ha havuta, come deveti havere intieso, che vale molto bene quatrimilia ducati e più, secundo che dicono molti de la famiglia. Lui ha questa in suo arbitrio e potestà. Sònoce li camei che costorono a la bona memoria de Monsignor da XXm ducati. Poniamo che vagliano da Xm li ligati e li disligati mille. Sònoce tanti vasi de cristallo, calcedonio et altra sorte, che ne vagliono domilia. Sònoce libri per mille, gioie per domilia. Li tremilia fiorini de la dote materna, ultra li cinque milia assignati ad liberare la possessione de Bigarello per lo puttino e pupillo de Monsignore, li quatromilia pur fiorini del re de Dacia, li fructi de la prepositura de l'anno passato, chi cum Sancto Andrea pigliano gagliardamente tre milia ducati e più; e le possessione lasciate per esso Monsignor, che ne daranno de intrata forsi più de domilia cinquecento. Ultra che ve ne sono o do o tre milia che hebbe la suoa Signoria doppo la morte immediate dil prefato Reverendissimo Monsignor per certa condennatione facta facta a l'Isola, terra de suoa Signoria Reverendissima. Le quale poste fariano cussì a la grossa una summa de più de trentasei milia ducati. L'è ben vero che ultra li debiti gli è la liberatione de la possessione de Bigarello per settemilia, per la quale se gli assignano li cinque milia fiorini de Rheno sopradecti, chi deve darli lo illustre Signor marchese. De' vedeti se, ultra la legitima, c'è da pagare e d'avanzo. Puoi che, come da vui e non da parte nostra, senza monstrare né la littera né questa poliza, altramente hareti comunicato el tutto cum Monsignor de Parma, brusareti l'una e l'altra, e non sia fallo. Non manchareti ut, pro vobis et in buona forma, habiamo lo intento nostro. *Ut in litteris.*

16. ASMn, Fondo D'Arco 85, fol. 40

Ludovico Gonzaga, Bishop-Elect of Mantua, to Gianfrancesco Gonzaga, Count of Rodigò, Bracciano, 14 July 1484.

Illustris etc. La optima disposetione de Vostra Signoria verso il puttino che ciascuno de nui deve tractare e riputare come figliolo, per rispetto e riverentia de la bona memoria del Reverendissimo Monsignore Cardinale nostro fratello è summamente da commendare; cum domino Zohannepiero, quale aspetto qui, e dice de volere venire, facto che l'harà lo debito suo cum Nostro Signore, participarò quanto me scrive Vostra prefata Signoria e circa li funerali e circa la redemptione de la collana. Se quella volesse da me l'inventario di libri, e de quelli puochi argenti quali tuolsi da Zoan Arrivabeno, cum obligatione o de restituirli o de pagarli, prout ipse scit, mandarògelo di buona voglia, quando se vogliano mettere a conto de li mei ottocento ducati, col nome de Dio. Me raccomando a la Signoria Vostra, que feliciter valeat. Brachiani xiiii° Julii 1484.

17. ASMn, Fondo D'Arco 85, fols 72–3

Ludovico Gonzaga, Bishop-Elect of Mantua, to Gianfrancesco Gonzaga, Count of Rodigò, Bracciano, 26 July 1484.

Illustris etc. Fu qui luni passato, che fu a li xviii° del presente, insieme cum l'oratore de Vostra Signoria lo spectabile messer Zoanpiero Arrivabeno, chi partì questa matina a buon hora, per demonstrare la integrità e vera fede cum la quale lui sempre è ito e va cum la prefata Vostra Signoria, et anche per fare constare in mia presentia coram oratore vestro ch'el vole venirsene liberamente e fare l'officio de buono servitore come ex nunc testifico e facio fede che egli è verso di Quella, da la quale gli duole bene che non sia connosciuta la sincera servitù suoa. Siamo più volte l'oratore, esso messer Zoanpiero et io, stati insieme per pigliare assetto a le cose de Vostra prelibata Signoria, e maxime per lo facto di camei, et habiamo havuto diversi e longi ragionamenti. Ho sempre trovato promtissimo dicto messer Zoanpetro maxime ad fare relaxare e devenire in mane de Quella, o de l'oratore suo, dicti camei, quando tamen sit ipse liberatus et exhoneratus penitus ab obligatione di tremilia e cinquecento ducati che se ha col bancho de'Medici, ad quorum satisfactionem tenetur et astrictus est in forma Camere. Sa la Signoria Vostra che cosa è ad essere obligato in forma Camere; lui non voria per quanto l'ha a questo mundo essere excommunicato, né anche voria se li procedesse ad capturam, che si può fare, senza notificargelo altramente. Essendo sgravato, subito daria li camei. Offeriscese de operare e fare questo col bancho: ch'el restarà contento che per duoi mesi essi camei siano reposti presso di me, a ciò che Vostra Signoria fra quello mezo possi tractare col bancho o de satisfarlo o de contentarlo e perché lui sia liberato, il che subsequendo, causarà lo effecto che ella desidera, cioé che illico l'haverà li camei. Mai sì che, passati li duoi mesi, né essendo lo bancho contentato, né dicto messer Zoanpetro liberato, vole che essi camei siano dati a lui per secureza suoa e per attasentare lo bancho. Quando questo mezo piacia a Vostra prefata Signoria, io pigliarò decti camei presso di me, hac conditione che, passato lo termino de duoi mesi, habbia, non essendo contento lo bancho né exhonerato in tutto messer Zoanpetro, ad dargli a lui, prout supradictum est. De questo et altri partiti proposti lo ambasciatore suo, chi tutti li ha intiesi, gli ne scriverà diffusamente. Non serò adonque più prolixo, rimmetendome al scrivere de esso, e io a Quella me raccomando que feliciter valeat. Brachiani, xxvi Julii 1484.

18. ASMn, Fondo D'Arco 85, fols 125–6

Ludovico Gonzaga, Bishop-Elect of Mantua, to Gianfrancesco Gonzaga, Count of Rodigò, Bracciano, 10 August 1484.

Illustris etc. L'è stato qui questa matina Aloyso Vismarra ad farme intendere lo bisogno de li denari suoi de' quali è creditore de la bona memoria del Reverendissimo Monsignore Cardinale nostro fratello e lo singulare desiderio che haveria de esserne satisfacto, o che, se li pigliasse tal partito, che l'havesse ad fare restare contento. Diceme che le robbe de qua non fanno puncto a proposito suo, né che de' camei o de gioe non se ne saperia valere, mai sì che de le cose di là che ha in mano la Signoria Vostra ne acceptaria bene per tanto precio che pigliasse la summa de quanto lui deve havere. Sònoli li duoi panni de Alexandro, ègli la camera nova de Abrahamo, e sònoli altre cose che lui

tuoria voluntieri, offerendose ad stare contento che essi panni e cose fussero puoste
presso di me, e quando de ciò se ne contentasse etiam la Signoria Vostra e le desse
liberamente per la stima che ne fusse facta de quietare e liberare quella, come herede de la
prefata memoria, dal debito che hora se ha cum lui. Scio in vero dicto Aloyso essere
continuamente stato servitore et affectionatissimo de la prelibata memoria, de tutta la casa
et in specie de essa Vostra Signoria. Scio ch'el credito suo non è per interessi né per
usure. Per satisfactione suoa et per acquietarlo me induria, quando cussì fusse in
beneplacito de la Signoria Vostra, ad tuore appresso di me le robbe che lui voria. Piacia a
Quella de notificarme lo parere e la intentione suoa, perché quemadmodum illa volet, et
ego ita volam. Me raccomando a Vostra Signoria, que feliciter valeat. Brachiani X
Augusti 1484.

19. ASMn, AG, Fondo D'Arco 85, fols 131–2
Ludovico Gonzaga, Bishop-Elect of Mantua, to Gianfrancesco Gonzaga, Count
of Rodigò, Bracciano, 10 August 1484.

Spectabilis etc. Per ugni commodità et occorrentia suoa puoteria certissimamente non
mancho valersi di me e de tutte cose mie lo Illustre Signor Zoanfrancesco mio honorando
fratello, che di sé e de le suoe proprie, per ricercare cussì convenientissimamente lo
amore e la convictione fraterna che mi dà tanto magiore ardire de chiedere
confidentissimamente ne li bisogni mei la subventione de Suoa Signoria cum indemnità et
incommodità di Quella. È apresso a domino Zoanpetro o a lo bancho de' Gaddi certa
quantità de denari, de robbe vendute de la hereditate de la bona memoria del
Reverendissimo Monsignor Cardinale mio observandissimo fratello e patre, che avanzoe
doppo lo pagamento facto de le page a la famiglia. Havendo de proximo ad andare a
Mantuoa, haveria bisogno al mancho de trecento ducati. Credo che quella quantità
ascenda forsi a tale summa. Quando vui me ne volesti compiacere e servire, riceverialo
prima per singulare complacentia. Puoi per indemnità de lo prefato Illustre Signor
Zoanfrancesco, patrono vostro, me obligaria per altritanti o al bancho de' Medici o ad
Aloysio Vismara, chi me rendo certo me acceptaria di buona voglia per debitore. Se
puoteti compiacerme, fatelo, ché ve ne prego strettamente che non dubito puncto lo Signore mio fratello ne haverà piacere grandissimo e restaranne contentissimo, e vui me ne
fareti cosa acceptissima. Offerendome di continuo parato a li beneplaciti vostri. Bene
valete. Brachiani X Augusti 1484.

20. ASMn, AG, b. 847, cc. 484^{r-v}
Giovan Pietro Arrivabene to Marchese Francesco Gonzaga, Rome, 2 January
1486.

Illustrissimo Signor mio, commendatione. Respondendo ad un capitolo de la littera de
Vostra Excellentia de li xi del passato, in una mia de xxviiii mandata per le poste circa'l
fatto de' camei, me remisi de scrivergene più isteso in la venuta del cavallaro. Havendose
debito per resto d'un conto vechio col bancho di Medici o sia cum Zohanne Tornabuoni,
zio del Magnifico Lorenzo, el qual alhora governava el bancho qui, de 3500 ducati, per li
quali lo protonotario Agnello et io e alcuni altri de casa eramo, come fideiussori, obligati
in forma Camere, lo bancho qui cominciò ad volere usare actione contra li beni che se
ritrovavano de la hereditate de la bona memoria de Monsignor lo cardinale, cum farli
vendere a trasatto, come se suole in simel casi, o farseli adiudicare in pagamento per
quello ne offereva lui. Et interim insieme voleva procedere contra nui in farne publicare

excommunicati per casone de tal obligo ad fine de tanto più presto consequirne lo pagamento suo. Unde per schiffare questo et per non giettare le robbe, fu necessariamente preso partito de aquietarli cum assecurarli su la consignatione de le XX tavole de camei ligati in ariento, e de altre robbe che li furono date ne le mane, cum condicione che havesseno a tenerli fin al Natale 1485, che mo è l'anno, al qual tempo, non essendo satisfatti, fusse lor licito, premoniti perhò nui de un mese avanti, metterle in vendita e trarne lo denaro per conto suo.

La cosa rimase suspesa, per la pratica faceva Lorenzo de comprarle, fin a la tornata mia de Lombardia lo marzo passato, de la qual, trovandolo alhora un puocho indisposto de la persona nel mio passare da Firenza, non puoti tractarne seco al longo, e lui me remise a farne cum Zoanne Tornabuoni che stava qui in quello tempo. Et tandem successive la pratica se continuò col mezo de Bacio Ugolini per lo qual infine Lorenzo se risuolse non volere de tute quelle cose, de le quale lo Illustrissimo signor Zo[hanne] Francesco può mostrarne a Vostra Signoria la lista che è presso de lui, dare se non 4100 ducati, lo qual precio, parendo a li executori molto piccolo, non se li prestarono orechie.

La peste prima, mo la guerra, hanno fatto che fin qui la cosa se tiene sopita né altramente se insta. Et anche un Antonio Tornabuoni, che governa mo el bancho qui, et ha la cura speciale de questa materia, è stato molto infirmo et è de presenti. L'è vero che credo non habiamo andare molto in longo che tornaranno su la instantia prima, o de la vendita o del pagamento. Per me ho sempre desiderato che queste cose cussì egregie, ornate del nome e de l'arme de la casa de Gonzaga, restino in la casa et non vadano in man d'altri. E la Excellentia Vostra faria cosa gloriosa e digna de l'animo suo generoso a pigliarle e conservarle a perpetua memoria, ché sempre faciano ad ugni signore che ve capitasse a casa una mostra honorevele.

El bisogno seria per questo principio, che la Signoria Vostra pagasse a' Medici li suoi ducati 3500; puoi, per lo residuo, conveneriase del precio con lo herede e con li executori. E come fussero cavate da' Medici, le se puoriano mandare in man de quella che, ultra la informatione qual interim ge ne può dare e lo prefato signor Zo[hanne] Francesco e lo Reverendissimo Monsignor electo, cum relatione etiam de Zo[hanne] Aluiso de Boneto e de Hermes, li quali ne sono instructissimi, puoteria puoi cum l'ochio vederle e iudicarle, benché alias cussì de grosso le vedesse. Questa è la informatione la qual me occorre de darli. E la Signoria Vostra sopra ciò deliberaramo quello li parirà. Et a me commandarà quanto vorà se facia. Et io a la gratia suoa me raccomando, que feliciter valeat. Roma ii Januarii 1486.

Excellentie Vestre   servitor Io. P. Arrivabenus.

21. ASMn, AG, b. 2902, lib. 125, fols 65^{r–v}

Marchese Francesco Gonzaga to Protonotary Ludovico Agnelli, Mantua, 23 January 1486.

Reverendo Monsignore. La Signoria Vostra debbe essere meglio informata de nui qual fusse l'intentione del Reverendissimo Monsignor Cardinale quondam nostro barba circha li debiti che se havevano a pagare doppo la morte de Sua Reverendissima Signoria. Sapiamo anchora non gli sia nascosto de un debito de otantatre ducati contracto ad instantia del prefato Reverendissimo Monsignore Cardinale per messer Carlo Canale, scriptore penetentiero, e constare ad plenum a Vostra Signoria questo essere vero per libri de mercadanti che se pretendeno creditori de tal summa. Debbeli anchor essere noto quello se havesse ad exequire de la robba de Sua bona memoria, che pagati li debiti se havesse a dividere fra la familia, attendo bene il tempo e qualità de servitù de ciaschuno. De queste cose credemo dicto messer Carlo non meritare essere lasiato in travalio et inremunerato del longo e fidel servitio suo, ni essere necessario che siamo prolixi in questa materia cum Vostra Signoria, ma solum restrinzerne in quello che è nostro precipuo desyderio per l'affectione havemo al prefato messer Carlo. Unde li diremo e pregaremo di cuore Vostra Signoria che, se may la crede farne cosa grata, li piaqua interponersi presso li altri executori testamentarii cum omne sua auctoritate e gratia a fare provisione che esso maestro Carlo rimangni libero da quello debito de ottantatre ducati, constandoli, come dicto, essere vero che'l fusse contracto a nome del prefato Monsignor Cardinale nostro, ché altramente non ne pareria conveniente ni honesto; e poi la compensi ch'el merito de la servitù sua non è de sorte che ne habia a sperare et conseguirne ingratitudine. Confidamose in la Signoria Vostra che in questo, per la prudentia e circumspectione sua non procederà cum minor caldo e maturità quanto sia co[n]sueta fare in qualunche acto dove l'habia ad intervenire, e tanto più che speramo le racomandatione nostre non essere de pocha auctoritate presso lei in le cose che concerneno honestà e debito. Messer Zo. Petro Arrivabene, nostro oratore, etiam de commissione nostra rescaldarà cum Vostra Signoria questo effecto a ció cum più brevità de tempo se gli dia fine e silentio per esso messer Carlo, quale, havuta la votiva expeditione, è necessitato ritornare dal canto di qua. Racomandiamone a Vostra Reverenda Signoria. Mantue 23 Januarii 1486.

22. ASMn, AG, b. 847, cc. 496^{r-v}

Giovan Pietro Arivabene to Marchese Francesco Gonzaga, Rome, 14 February 1486.

Illustrissimo Signor mio, commendatione. Ho visto la rispuosta de Vostra Excellentia factami circa la deliberatione suoa de pigliare quelle XX tavole de camei et altre robbe che sono in mane de' Medici, de la qual resto in me molto consolato, havendo sempre summamente desiderato che una cosa tanto preciosa, e de tanta memoria, rimanesse in la vostra Illustrissima casa. Come quello chi governa lo bancho di Medici sia ridutto d'una suoa longa infirmità in qualche convalescentia, per modo che attenda a facende, ricercandomi del credito suo, li farò intendere questo pensiere de Vostra Signoria et a lei ne darò aviso. Et tamen interim non starò de ricordarli cum ugni riverentia che, havendo Quella l'animo a ciò, seria forsi a proposito migliore de anticipare de trovare el modo de pagarli questi 3500 ducati, per cavarli lor le robbe de mane, e ridurle in libertà de Quella, perché ho connosciuto pur lo Magnifico Lorenzo appetitoso de queste cose, e non voria che, vedendose guastare lo designo de haverle, ce constringesse, sotto brevità de tempo, o ad darli lo conto suo o liberargele, o che da canto facesse saltare suso qualche creditore chi procurasse de arestarle per altro credito. Paremi debito mio de fare intendere el tuto a Vostra Signoria, la qual puoi habia a deliberare quanto li piacerà.

De le doe tavole de diaspro et una de plasma adornate de camei, che credo siano da 58 in tuto, molto belli, stretti da creditori, le demmo in pagamento ad un mercadante milanese per un suo credito de ducati 1259 de carlini, che sono ducati 1100 d'oro largi, secundo la estima ne era fatta qui da persone intendente, ma volemmo che, piacendo a Vostra Excellentia de tuorle per lo precio estimato ut supra, lui fusse obligato a darle, e per tal condicione apposta. Lui ne ha pregato che ne diamo aviso a Quella per intendere se la le vole, e che fra doi mesi ne voria havere lo chiaro, perché altramente, quando Lei non dispuonesse de tuorle, ne pigliaria partito cum altri, non havendo intentione de ritenerle lì morte, et è persona che tuoria lo precio a Milano. Sì che anche de queste la Signoria Vostra puorà deliberare e rispondere, notificandoli che le doe tavole de diaspro sono in sé excellentissime e lustre come un spechio, e fanno la facia naturale. Una è de diaspro puro, estimata solum la pietra cento ducati, l'altra ha del diaspro e chalcedonio e mixtura, estimata 30, e la plasma 100. E per più informatione mando qui inclusa una scritta de la particulare estima. Et a la gratia de Vostra Signoria me raccomando, que feliciter valeat. Rome XIIIIº februarii 1486.

Excellentie Vestre Servitor Io. P. Arrivabenus.

La tavola de diaspro magiore estimata per sé ducati 100 cum camei 16 estimati ut infra:

70. 15. 20. 8. 15. 20. 10. 10. 25. 8. 8. 15. 30. 8. 15. 15. = 392

La tavola minore de diaspro, chalcedonio e mixtura estimata per sé ducati 30 cum camei 24 estimati ut infra:

20. 20. 20. 20. 8. 8. 20. 8. 8. 15. 10. 8. 20. 30. 15. 20. 20. 15. 20. 10. 8. 25. 10. 8. = 396

La tavola de plasma estimata per sé ducati 100 cum camei 18 estimati ut infra:

15. 10. 10. 10. 15. 20. 15. 15. 15. 20. 15. 10. 8. 10. 10. 10. 15. 10. = 333

[Total] 333 +396 + 392 = 1121

23. ASMn, AG, b. 1800, c. 107ʳ

Gianfrancesco Gonzaga, Count of Rodigò, to Marchese Francesco Gonzaga, Bozzolo, 8 November 1486.

Illustre et excelso Signor mio. Questa sera ho havuto una di Vostra Excellentia per la quale Quella me scrive voglia pigliare qualche compositione cum li executori de li ducati mille richiedono per la Illustrissima Signoria de Venetia, in nome de l'illustre quondam Bartolomeo Collione. Ad che rispondendo a la Signoria Vostra gli notifico como a questi dì passati li offitiali suoi hanno inteso multo bene da Ludovico Cipata, mandato da li executori testamentarii del quondam Reverendissimo Monsignor cardinale mio fratello, di quali dinari se debbono pagare questi ducati mille, et ha lo facto constare per li conti de lo episcopato che per il ficto teneva la bona memoria de lo Illustrissimo signor mio genitore et avo di quella, postea successive si doveano pagare per il quondam Illustrissimo signor marchese genitore d'epsa et mio honorando fratello, et sic successive per Vostra Excellentia, et quando bene non gli fusse questo modo, facio noto como io non seria obligato a la Signoria Vostra prefata se non de quanto me ha obligato il prefato quondam Reverendissimo Monsignor cardinale mio per il testamento suo. Del resto lasso tutto il carico a li executori di sua Reverendissima Signoria, quali hanno tutta la robba ne le mane, et in tuto ne sonn excluso, sì che la Signoria Vostra intenderà da li suoi offitiali medesimi questo essere la verità, et quando obligato a questo fusse non creda la prefata fusse stato a quest'hora a providergli per honore de la casa nostra et del defuncto. A la cui gratia una cum la Illustre mia consorte et figli sempre me raccomando. Bozuli viii novembris 1486.

Illustris dominationis vestre patruus Ioannes Franciscus de Gonzaga Marchio Rotingique comes etc.

24. ASMn, AG, b. 1800, cc. 112ʳ⁻ᵛ (damaged)

Gianfrancesco Gonzaga, Count of Rodigò, to Marchese Francesco Gonzaga, Bozzolo, 19 January 1487.

[Illustrissimo] et excellente Domine: nepos et domine honorate. Questa sera ho visto quanto la Excellentia Vostra me rescrive per il pagamento de li ducati mille del illustre quondam Bartholomeo Collione, et la accomodata risposta facta per quella a la Illustrissima Signoria de Venetia; et heri sera ritornò Jacobo de Piscenino et me refferse la excusatione faceva la prefata et anco li suoi offitiali, como la non era obligata ad tale pagamento, perché la bona memoria di Monsignor Cardinale mio fratello già havea facto pagare ducati cinquecento et poi ordinato al quondam Carlo da Rodiano il compito pagamento etc. Di che, ritrovandose qua messer Ioanpetro Arrivabene per altre occurrentie pertinente a la heredità del prefato quondam Reverendisimo Monsignore mio fratello ne ho parlato cum sua magnificentia et me confirma questo essere la verità, ma che Sua Reverendissima Signoria havea ordinato che, prima se vedesseno li conti de lo Illustrissimo Signor patre di Vostra Excellentia et mio honorato fratello, et trovandose debitore de lo episcopato di tanti dinari che questi, fusseno pagati e questa fu sua intentione. Benché mai ne fusse facto…ne se potesse allora assettare li conti, per modo che né l'uno né l'altro ha facto tale satisfactione, como etiam più amplamente farà constare a Vostra Excellentia o a suoi offitiali esso messer Ioanpetro che domani vene lì a Mantua, et similmente Ludovico Cipata in nome de li executori farà videre como Vostra Signoria per li suoi libri resta debitrice de lo episcopato de circa ducati 1600. Sì che la prefata potrà fare videre se la resta debitrice aut non; et, restando, me pareria honesto et ragionevole che anco Quella satisfacia, et maxime essendo già stati deputati questi dinari ad tale pagamento; tamen la Excellentia Vostra facia como gli parrà et piacerà, et se digni de fare administrare ragione sumaria et expedita a dicto Ludovico Cipata, in nome de questi executori contra tutti quelli restano debitori de lo episcopato, et favor[ire questo] conto, che senza dubio gli serà de pagare magiore summa de dinari et la Signoria Vostra serà scarichata et anco io, benché non gli habia alcuna obligatione, et questo peso ho lassato a li executori. Né altra risposta facio a la prefata, se non reccomendarme a Quella sempre. Bozuli, xviiii Januarii mccccIxxxvii.

Illustris Dominationis Vestri patruus Ioannes Franciscus de Gonzaga Marchio Rotingique Comes etc.

25. ASMn, AG, b. 1800, c. 138

Gianfrancesco Gonzaga, Lord of Rodigò, to Marchese Francesco Gonzaga, Bozzolo, 21 December 1487.

Illustrissimo Signor mio. Hogi ho havuto la littera de Vostra Excellentia insieme cum una de la Illustrissima Signoria de Venetia in recommendatione del Reverendo Monsignore Archivescovo de Spalatro per certa summa de dinari già prestati al Reverendissimo quondam Monsignore Cardinale mio fratello, ad che, Signore mio, farò breve risposta a la prefata et dico che assai me dole che questo Reverendo Monsignore et li altri creditori del prefato quondam Monsignore Cardinale non siano pagati et satisfacti de li crediti loro, per honore de la Illustre casa nostra et per discarico del defuncto. Ma havendo la sua Signoria Reverendissima per legato dato la auctorità a li executori de rescodere et pagare ognuno et alcuno gli sia superiore, non posso farne altro. Bene so che, havendo io certe robbe mobile ne le mani, loro la volseno per pagare li debiti et gli la mandai fin a Roma, et benché dicesseno non dispensarla senza mia saputa, tamen la hanno distribuita come è parso a loro, dicendo che io non poteva ligargli le mane, et che loro erano li executori et che farianno che ognuno rimarria satisfacto senza che io me ne impazasse. Allora me ne liberai in tutto et mandai a dire a la Santità de Nostro Signore et a li Signori cardinali che, una volta era liberato, che non era in potestà di Sua Beatitudine de più obligarme, salvo quanto nel testamento contenia. Nondimeno, per reverentia de Vostra Signoria, scriverò de novo a li executori a ciò che vedano la instantia ne fa la Signoria et la prefata. Piacendogli, gli mandarò ambe le lettere, et per questo ritengo quella de la prefata Signoria de Venetia, et cussì ne expecto la sua voluntà. Benché lì a Mantoa gli sia

Lodovico Cipata, et non so quello se facia, bene pare che senza licentia de Vostra Excellentia non possa partirse et già ho pagata tutta la robba comprata per me da la heredità et benissimo. Poi notifico a la prefata che io ho ad essere l'ultimo como herede richiesto et, quando quello che ha testato il defuncto non bastasse, che credo la Excellentia Vostra sapia essergli de superchio exequendose il testamento. A la cui gratia me raccomando sempre. Bozuli, xxi Decembris mcccclxxxvii.

Patruus Iohannes Franciscus de Gonzaga Marchio Rotingique comes etc.

26. ASP, AGG, b. 41/3, reg. 2, fol. 38ʳ
Ludovico Gonzaga, Bishop-Elect of Mantua, to Ludovico Cipata, Sabbioneta, 1 March 1488.

Nobilis amice carissime. Havendovi facto rechiedere per messer Christophoro Arrivabene nostro maestro di casa quella anchoneta che fuoe de la felice memoria del quondam Reverendissimo Monsignor Cardinale nostro fratello, esso ne ha rispuosto vui allegare che non l'haveti, et che messer Zoanpetro Arrivabene la portoe a Roma, il che sapiamo certo non essere vero, et non bisogna che cum nui usiati questi termini, né ce meniati el capo intorno cum simile parole, perché sapeti bene che si connosciamo. Non aspectavamo già da vui tal rispuosta, perch'el vi è pur noto che debiamo havere de la hereditate del quondam prefato Reverendissimo Monsignor Cardinale parechii centenara di ducati, per il che ce la potevate mandare sicuramente, che non puocho ne siamo maravigliati. Per tanto di novo scrivemo al prefato messer Christophoro debba richiedervi per parte nostra la predicta anchonetta. Pregamovi ge la vogliati dare liberamente, senza altra exceptione, che non obstante debiamo havere e grossamente (come è dicto) de la prefata hereditate, nihilominus, ne offerimo et prometemo ex nunc de pagarla. Et in questo ne fareti singulare complacentia. Bene valete. Sablonete 1 Martii 1488.

27. ASMn, AG, b. 1800, c. 148
Gianfrancesco Gonzaga, Count of Rodigò, to Marchese Francesco Gonzaga, Bozzolo, 26 March 1488.

Illustrissimo Signor mio. Per essere Lodovico Cipata richiesto da li executori de la heredità de la bona memoria de Monsignore Cardinale mio fratello, che per grande bisogno de dicta heredità dovesse transferirse a Roma per tri o quatro mesi per expedire alcune vendite e satisfare a certi creditori che ancora gli sono, esso Ludovico mèrcuri passato fu da me a tòrre licentia de l'andare suo. Io gli la dette di bona voglia a ciò che etiam a Roma se satisfacesseno quelli creditori, et che poi tornasse a la expeditione de quella. Intendo hora che Carletto di Franzone, cum alcuni altri de la famiglia del prefato Monsignore Cardinale mio, hanno supplicato a la Excellentia Vostra che dicto Lodovico se ne asportava multi dinari e fugiva, che non è il vero et non va se non cum bona licentia. Sì che prego la Signoria Vostra la se digni farlo liberare a ciò ch'el possa andare et tornare per ultimare queste cose de la heredità, secundo la voluntà de li executori, et che io ogni dì non habia questo stimulo, né che sia dato tedio a Vostra Excellentia, la quale me ne farà cosa grata. A la cui gratia me raccomando. Bozuli xxvi Martii Mcccclxxxviii.

Patruus Ioannis Franciscus de Gonzaga Marchio Rotingique comes etc.

28. ASP, AGG, b. 41/3, reg. 3 (unnumbered)
Ludovico Gonzaga, Bishop-Elect of Mantua to Giovan Pietro Arrivabene, Sabbioneta, 12 January 1489.

Reverende etc. Per satisfare a quanto da Roma mi è scripto, mandovi per via de' banchi lo alicorno fu della bona memoria del Cardinale. Per giocar più securo, né a Comino corero lo volsi dare, sapendo quello esser di bon pretio et che in man sue non seria stato senza periculo, havendo a reger li cani ge ho dati per lo Signore Francesco. Ad me non è parso de farlo dividere, tamen perché da molti mi era dissuaso, tam etiam perché, re vera, quando fosse in dui pezzi, non seria a veruna delle parte molto honerevole né di quello pretio è, essendo in uno pezzo; ma più presto ho voluto drizarlo in man vostre, col mezo di Onofrio Tornaboni, cussì integro, del qual vui ne disponereti al modo vostro, perché io ex nunc vi do vices meas et tuta quella auctorità ne fu data per la felice recordatione del Cardinale circa res suas, et quanto fareti de dicto alicorno, si tenerà per facto. Quando allo Reverendissimo Cardinale Andegavensis piacia di haverlo, a vui starà a deliberarlo como vi parerà. Pregovi ben charamente che a Sua Reverendissima Signoria faciati intendere questo alicorno non esser mio, et che quando el fosse ne faria uno dono a quella, per signo della fede et vera servitù mia in lei.

Et per Dio, messer Zoanpetro mio, quando non mi fosse costato, se no uno centenaro de ducati, io l'harebbe comprato per fare questo effecto. Ma havendomi facto intendere Boneto nostro che uno merchadante venetiano ge ha dicto de farli dare cinquecento ducati, tuta volta che lo voglia vendere, mi ha facto stare retirato. Vui sapeti como sto et perhò non dirò altro nisi che di questo alicorno faciati alto e basso como vi pare et [a] vui me ricomando. Sablonete 12 Januarii 1489.

29. ASMn, AG, b. 848, c. 497
Ludovico Cipata to Marchese Francesco Gonzaga, Rome, 5 September 1491.

Illustrissime princeps et excelse domine, domine mi singularissime et cum ogni debite reverentie: con ricore a Quella notificando che già sei mesi pasati fue mandato da lo Illustrissimo signor domino Zoan Francesco barbano di Vostra Illustrissima Signoria a Roma, cum lictere directive a' Reverendissimi Signori cardinali et a li Reverendi quattro executori testamentarii dil quondam bona memoria dil cardinale de Gonzaga etc., ad effecto de fare che tuti li creditori di la heredità di quella fusseno satisfacti a beneficio de l'anima del difonto e per honore de la casa di quello; vedendo essere dispiacuto e menato in longo da li predicti executori, quali sono favoriti ne la corte di Roma, per tal modo che li creditori non seria[n] mai satisfacti, et praecipue li magnifici signori executori dil quondam Bartholomeo Collioni, quali restano habere ducati ducento de la obligatione e promissa sopra de li cinque millia ducati de le quale ne appare littera del quondam Illustre signor marchese, havo paterno di quelli, sotto dì xii di octobre 1[47]3, dove per questo supplico et prego Vostra prefacta Illustrissima Signoria se digni per sua clementia et gratia scrivere qua a lo ambasiatore de quella che me voglia prestare aiuto e favore contra a li predicti executori, a rexone e non altramente, a ciò che li creditori siane satisfacti como è debito, et, considerato che essi hanno havute tute le robe e beni hereditari, como ne appare per inventario et scripte di loro manne, et, facendo questo Vostra Illustrissima Signoria, ne resultarà beneficio de quella benedeta anima dil defonto et honore e utile a la casa. A la qual di continuo mi aricomando. Rome V^to Septembris 1491.

Eiusdem dominationis vestre servus vester fidelissimus Lodovicus de Cipata cum iterata aricomandatione etc.

30. ASMn, AG, b. 849, c. 381
Ludovico Agnelli to Marchese Francesco Gonzaga, Rome, 20 March 1493.

Illustrissime Princeps et excellentissime domine, domine singularissime, humili commendatione premissa. Già per lo passato per una sua Vostra Excellentia me recommandò Carletto de li Franzioni di Mantua, ché essendo io uno de li executori del testamento de la bona memoria del Reverendissimo Cardinale nostro de Mantua, et essendo lui creditore di ducati mille, volessi essere insieme cum li altri executori e fare ch'el fussi satisfacto. Qual cosa haveramo facta liberamente quando ce fussi suto el modo per omne respecto, e maxime ad contemplationem de Vostra Excellentia, ad la quale prefato Carletto hora ha refugio. Vedendosi non havere potuto consequire di qua quanto seria stato il debito, e retrovandosi di là certi debitori del quondam Monsignore Reverendissimo de Mantua, me ha pregato che io vogla scrivere questa in sua recommendatione ad Vostra Excellentia, e pregare Quella che li vogla essere favorevole et permettere ch'el se faci executione contra dicti debitori, cum conditione che lui habia a essere uno de li primi satisfacti. Il che, motus bono zelo, facio multo voluntiera per alevamento et scaricho de l'anima di quella bona memoria, et per li meriti de la longa servitù che continuamente dicto hebe cum quella, et etiam per satisfactione del debito che, ultra sia debito, serà ancora assai honesta elemosina, che prefata sia satisfacto del credito suo, come più ad plenum referirà ad Vostra Excellentia el venerabile messer Georgio preposito mantuano, il quale ad unguem è informato del tutto. Unde lo recommando ad Vostra Excellentia grandemente, pregando Quella che in questa honesta occurentia se digni prestarli tutti quelli honesti favori et adiuti che seranno opportuni et convenienti, che lo receverò ad gratia singulare da epsa Vostra Excellentia, a la cui bona gratia sempre me racommando. Rome, xx martii mcccclxxxxiii.

E Vestre Excellentie   devotus servitor L. Agnellus prothonotarius.

Illustrations

Fig. 1: MS Modena, Biblioteca Universitaria Estense, α.F.2.26 (Lat. 1101), Latin grammar treatise written for Protonotary Francesco Gonzaga, 1457: illuminated frontispiece. The upper portrait shows Francesco, aged thirteen, and the lower shows his master, Bartolomeo Marasca (or possibly the scribe Giuliano da Viterbo). (See I 835)

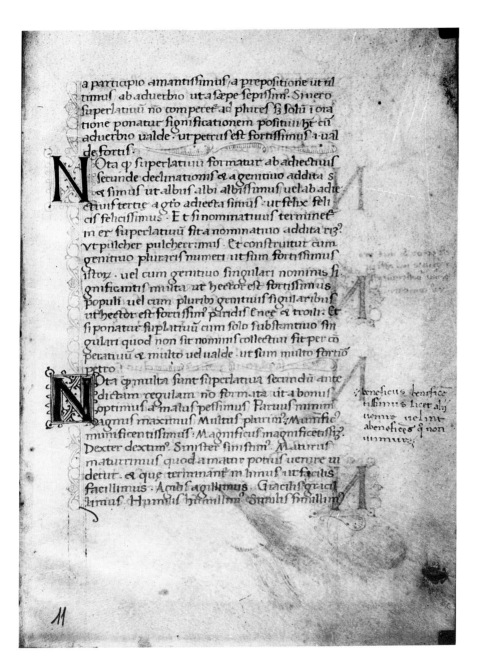

Fig. 2: MS Modena, Biblioteca Universitaria Estense, α.F.2.26 (Lat. 1101), fol. 11^r. Passage of text, written by Giuliano da Viterbo, showing annotation probably in the hand of Protonotary Francesco Gonzaga (later Cardinal).

Fig. 3: MS Dublin, Chester Beatty, W.122, fol. 3 (Dictys Cretensis, *Ephemerides belli troiani*). Illuminated initial, showing the same device as in Fig. 6. (See I 751)

Fig. 4: ASDMn, FCC, Pergamene, b. 23, no. 2591: wax impression of seal, attached to official letter of Cardinal Francesco Gonzaga, 3 October 1474. (See pp. 83, 92)

Fig. 5: Sperandio Savelli, medal commemorating Cardinal Francesco Gonzaga. Obverse, with portrait head of the Cardinal (?1483). (See p. 85)

Fig. 6: Reverse, with the device of a lynx, signifying vigilance, beside a pyramid on which the word 'ENIGMATA' is legible on some examples, with martial equipment (a breast-plate, shield, quiver etc.) on the ground and in the sky. (See p. 85)

Fig. 7: MS Vatican City, BAV, Urb. Lat. 681 fol. 11[r]. Petrarch, Sonnets (scribe, Antonio Sinibaldi; illuminator unknown). (See I 762n)

Fig. 8: MS Vatican City, BAV, Vat. Gr. 1626 fol. 1ᵛ. 'The Vatican Homer': *Iliad* (Greek text), written by Johannes Rhosos; illumination by ? Gaspare da Padova. Note the pyramid device in lcft margin; cf. Figs 3, 6. (See pp. 60–3)

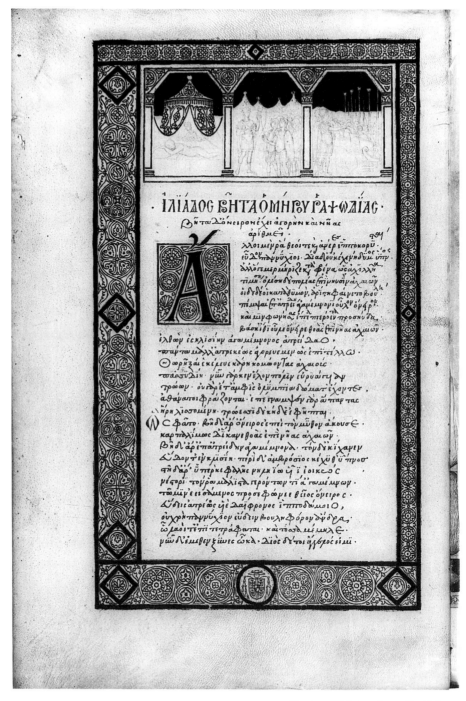

Fig. 9: MS Vatican City, BAV, Vat. Gr. 1626 fol. 17ᵛ. 'The Vatican Homer': *Iliad* (Greek text), written by Johannes Rhosos; uncompleted illumination.

ILIADOS SECVNDVS HOMERI CONGLVTINATIONIS·
SECVNDVS VERO SOMNIVM HABET CONCIONEM ET NAVES
ENVMERAT·

LII QVIDEM DII ET VIRII INEQVIS ARMATI
Dormiebant p̃ tota noc̃ te ioue uc̃o ñō tenebat cõtinens somnus.
Sed ille considerabat in mente ut achillem
Honor& pdat uc̃o multos in nauibus achiuor̃.
Hoc uc̃o ipsi in aīo optimũ uidebatur consiliũ
Mittere ad atrida agamemnone pnitiosũ somniũ
Et illud cũ uocaṡ& uerba uolatilia dicebat
Eia ualde pnitiosũ somniũ ueloces ad naues achiuor̃.

A ccedens uero ad tentorium agamemnonis atridæ
O mnia ualde congrue dicas ut iubeo
A rmare ipsum dicas capitibus comantes achiuos.
C um toto exercitu nunc ᴎ expugnabit urbe latas uias habentem
T roianor̃ non ᴎ amplius bifaria olympias domos colentes
I mmortales consulunt flexit ᴎ omnes.
I uno precans a troianis uero dolores pendent.
S ic fatus est iuit uero somnium postq̃ uerbum audiuit.
C ito uero accessit ueloces ad naues achiuor̃.
I uit uero ad atridam agamemnonem hunc repperijt
D ormientem in tentorio circa uero ipsũ diuinus effusus fuit somnus.
S tetit uero supra caput nelei filio similis
N estori quem maxime senũ honorabat agamemnoᴎ.
H uic simile effectum eum allocutũ est diuinum somnium.
D ormis atrei fili prudentis equitis.
N on oport& per totam noc̃ tem dormire consultorem uirum:
C ui populi commissi sunt & tot sunt in cura·
M odo uero me cognosce cito: iouis aũt tibi nuncius sum.

Fig. 10: MS Vatican City, BAV, Vat. Gr. 1626, fol. 18ʳ. 'The Vatican Homer':
Iliad (Latin translation), written by Bartolomeo Sanvito, illuminated by (?)
Gaspare da Padova. (See Fig. 9, opposite)

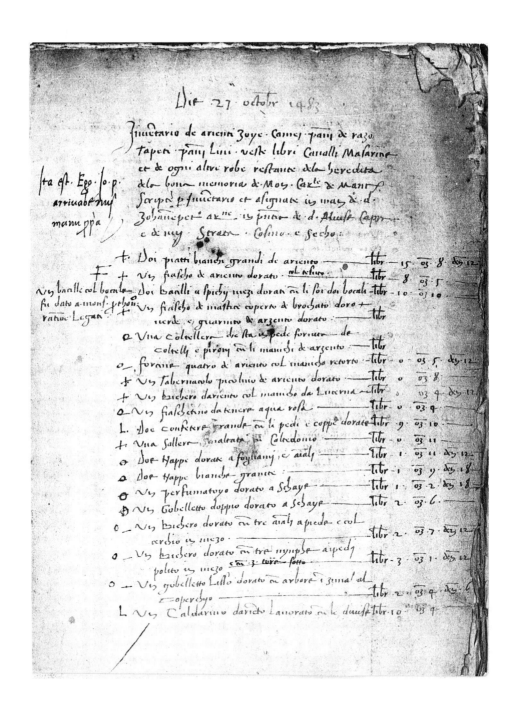

Fig. 11. Post-mortem inventory of Cardinal Francesco Gonzaga, fol. 1ʳ. (See Appendix 2)

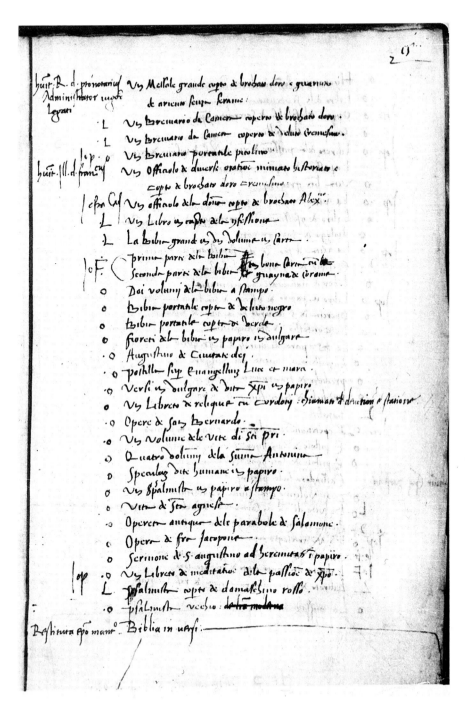

Fig. 12. Post-mortem inventory of Cardinal Francesco Gonzaga, fol. 15ʳ. (See Appendix 2)

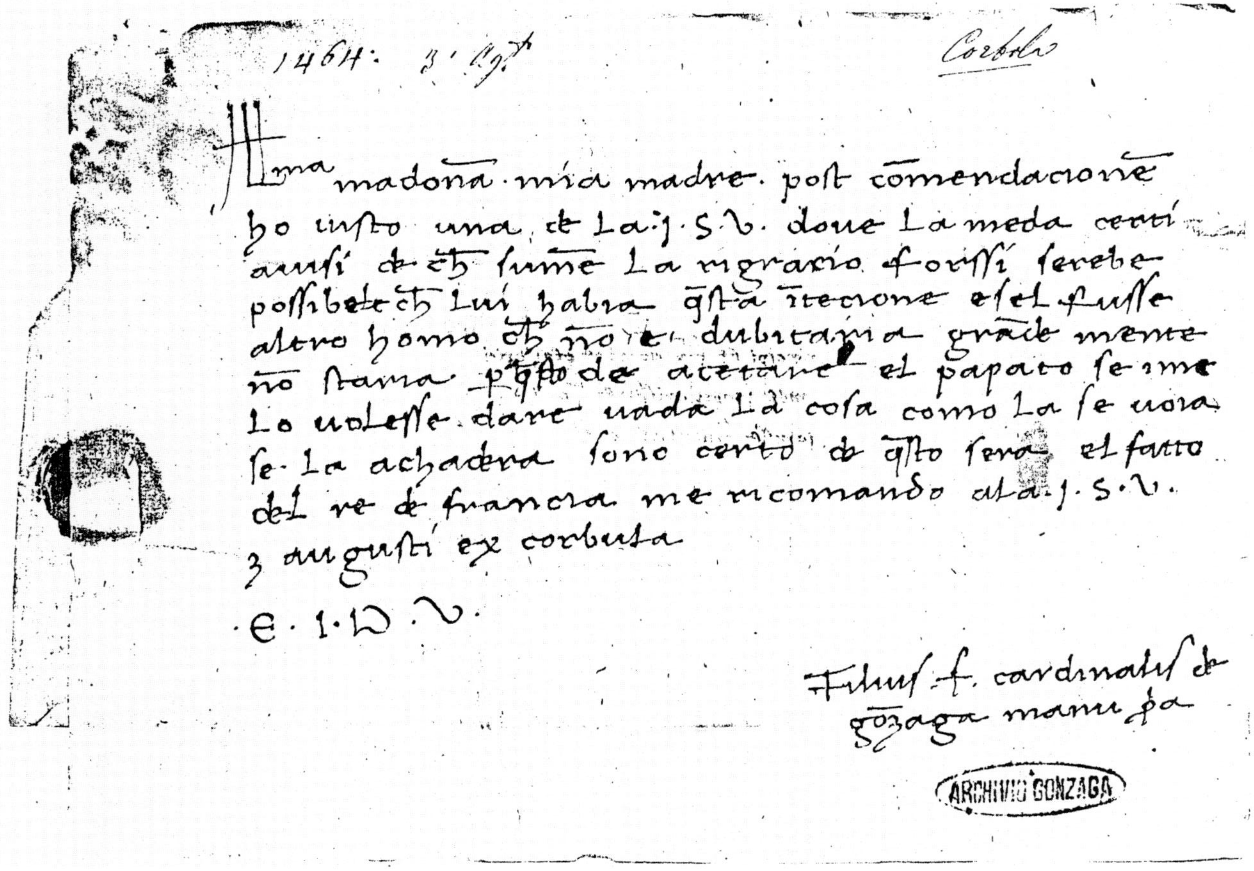

1464: 3 Agt

Corbole

Ill.ma madona mia madre. post comendacione
ho visto una de la I. S. V. doue la me da certi
auisi de che summe la ringracio et cussi serebe
possibele che lui habia questa itencione et sel fusse
altro homo che non e dubitaria grandemente
non stanta per questo de acetare el papato se ime
lo volesse dare vada la cosa como la se vora
se la achadera sono certo che questo sera el fatto
del re de francia me ricomando ala I. S. V.
3 augusti ex corbula
E. I. D. V.

Filius F. cardinalis de
gonzaga manu propria

ARCHIVIO GONZAGA

Courtesy, Ministero dei Beni Culturali, Protocollo no. 2237/V.9, parere n. 38/91

Fig. 13: ASMn AG, b. 2098 (unnumbered). Autograph letter of Cardinal Francesco Gonzaga to his mother, Barbara of Brandenburg, dated at Corbola (on the river Po) 3 August [1464].

Manuscripts and Unpublished Sources

NOTE: Manuscript books extant which belonged to Cardinal Francesco Gonzaga are indicated in the following list by an asterisk [*]; a cross-reference to the inventory is given for titles which can be identified there. Manuscripts which may possibly have been made for him are indicated thus [?*]. Those which were written or rubricated by Bartolomeo Sanvito are noted [Sanvito]; those which contain illumination by 'the Master of the Vatican Homer' (*alias* Gaspare da Padova?) are noted thus [#]. These identifications depend on the findings of Alexander and de la Mare, as indicated.

Boston, Mass., Public Library
>> f. Med. 126 (1548): Marcantonio Aldegatti, *In Cinthiam libri tres*; [*]

Cesena, Biblioteca Malatestiana
>> XXIX. 8 (Leonardo Montagna, *Carmina*)

Dublin, Chester Beatty Library
>> W 122: Dictys Cretensis, *Ephemerides belli troiani*; [Sanvito]; contains *imprese*; [*]

Florence, Archivio di Stato (ASF)
> Archivio Mediceo avanti il Principato (MAP)
>> XIX, 450; XXVI, 513; XXXVIII, 134; XXXIX, 192A, 205, 227, 308, 346; XLVI, 397, 413; LII, 21, 25; LV, 7, 15, 28−9, 37, 55, 357; LIX, 24; LXXIII, 357; CXXXVIII, 227.[1]

Forlì, Biblioteca comunale
>> Autografi Piancastelli, fasc. 121 (two official letters from Cardinal F. Gonzaga's chancery)

Guastalla, Biblioteca civica Maldotti (BCG)
> Fondo Marani Davolio (FMD)
>> b. 15, fasc. 6
>> b. 23 (Inventory of Gianfrancesco Gonzaga, 1496)

London
> British Library (BL)
>> Harley 3567: Petrarch, *Rime e trionfi*. [Contugi; Sanvito's rubrications] arms; #(frontispiece); [?*I 762]
>> Harley 3691: Josephus, *Antiquitates*, *Bellum Judaicum*; Hegesippus, *Historia* [Giuliano da Viterbo]; [*I 815]

---

[1] Transcripts of the following were kindly provided by Laurie Fusco: XXVI, 513; XXXIX, 192A, 205, 227, 308, 346; LII, 21, 25; LV, 7, 15, 28−9, 37, 55, 357; LIX, 24; LXXIII, 357; CXXXVIII, 227.

Harley 5790: Greek Gospels; [Rhosos]; [*]
Additional 21115. Herbal of Pseudo-Apuleius; [*I 838]
Additional 14085: Terence (belonged to A. Maffei)

Victoria and Albert Museum Library
L.101–1947 [KRP E.16]: Petrarch, *Rime*. Cardinal's hat; defaced arms, not Gonzaga. [Sanvito?];[2] [?*I 762]
L. 2464–1950 [KRP D.17]: *Ars completa geomantiae.* [Sanvito?];[3] [?*I 893]

Mantua

Archivio di Stato (ASMn)
Archivio Gonzaga (AG)[4]
20 (Divisioni degli stati)
282 bis (Maloselli, *Vacheto*)
333 cc. 83–5 (will: see above, Appendix 1)

544 (Innsbruck e Graz: inviati e diversi)
834 (Brevi papali ai signori di Mantova)
841–50 (Roma: inviati e diversi)
1085 (Firenze: Lettere della Signoria e dei Medici ai Gonzaga)
1099–1102 (Firenze: inviati e diversi)
1141–1142 (Bologna: inviati e diversi)
1228 (Ferrara: Lettere degli Estensi ai Signori di Mantova)
1231 (Ferrara: inviati e diversi)
1321 (Correggio: inviati e diversi)
1339 (Mirandola: inviati e diversi)
1367 (Parma: inviati e diversi)
1402 (Trento: Lettere dei Principi Vescovi ai Gonzaga)
1413 (Lettere dei D'Arco e Castelbarco ai Gonzaga)
1431bis (Venezia: inviati e diversi)
1599 (Brescia: Lettere ai Gonzaga)
1621–22, 1629 (Milano: inviati e diversi)
1800 (Bozzolo: Lettere dei Signori di Bozzolo e Sabbioneta)
1812 (Bozzolo: inviati e diversi)
1823 (Pergamene residue del Archivio di Bozzolo-Sabbioneta: Principi)
2095–8, 2101, 2104–5 (Lettere originali dei Gonzaga)
2187 (Minute della Cancelleria)

---

[2] Alexander, 'A Manuscript', *passim* and esp. p. 39 n. 37.

[3] Ibid.

[4] Numbers shown below refer to *buste* (see Luzio-Torelli, *L'Archivio Gonzaga*). The *carte* in most *buste* are numbered in sequence, but a few have to date not been numbered (e.g., 850, 1102, 1142); some have been re-numbered (e.g., 1101). One (843) has recently been numbered and then twice re-numbered; so, to avoid confusion, no numbers have been cited from this *busta*.

2393, 2397–400, 2402, 2409, 2413–16, 2422, 2424,
2426, 2430, 2432, 2434, 2447–8 (Lettere ai Gonzaga da
Mantova e Paesi dello Stato)

Gonzaga letter registers 2883–2908 (Copialettere):
2883 lib. 14, 19
2886 lib. 32, 34–5, 37
2887 lib. 41–2
2888 lib. 46–7, 49
2889 lib. 51–2, 54
2890 lib. 56, 59
2891 lib. 65
2894 lib. 81
2896 lib. 96 (register of Cardinal F. Gonzaga)
2899 lib. 111, 113
2900 lib. 114 (register of Cardinal F. Gonzaga) 116, 117
2901 lib. 120
2902 lib. 125–7, 129
2903 lib. 131, 134–5
2908 lib. 160

3328 (*Prepositura* di San Benedetto)
3351 (Register of Cardinal Francesco Gonzaga)
Libri decretorum 21
Autografi, b. 7
Archivio notarile (ASMn AN)
Estensioni, R. 78 (Antonio Cornice, 1481: includes
summaries of Barbara of Brandenburg's will
and inventory of possessions in Cardinal's
house in Mantua)
Estensioni, R. 80 (A. Cornice, 1483)
Fondo d'Arco
b.85 (letter register, 1483–4, of Protonotary Ludovico
Gonzaga, Bishop-Elect of Mantua)

Archivio storico diocesano (ASDMn)
Fondo Capitolo della Cattedrale (FCC)
Serie miscellanea: b. 2/A (includes inventory of
Cardinal Francesco Gonzaga, 1483: see above,
Appendix 2); 'Inventario de le cose de la
heredità' (lists, noting distributions
among Barbara's heirs, 1481); inventory
showing contents of Barbara's houses at
S. Giorgio, Sachetta and Fossamana, 1481;
'Terminationes commissariorum' (further details of
administration by Barbara's executors)
Pergamene: b. XXIII, 2588; 2590–1 (official letters of
Cardinal Gonzaga's chancery)

Fondo Mensa vescovile
Pergamene: b. 2 nos 33–45; b. 3 nos 46–64 (papal
letters)

Biblioteca comunale (BCMn)
79 (A III 15) (G. M. Filelfo, *De comunis vite
continentia*)
909 (H I 35) (Bessarion, *Orationes*; Perotti, *Epistola*)
1019 (I I 2) (A. Schivenoglia, *Cronaca*)

Museo diocesano
Missal of Barbara of Brandenburg; [*I 687]

Milan
Archivio di Stato, (ASMil)
Archivio ducale Visconteo Sforzesco (Sforzesco)
cart. 62, 68, 69, 70, 74, 80, 88 (Potenze Estere: Roma)
cart. 178 188 194 (Potenze Estere: Romagna, i.e.,
Bologna)
cart. 329 396 (Potenze Estere: Mantova)
Autografi
cart. 28, 68

Biblioteca Ambrosiana
Sp. 13. Book of Hours [Sanvito];[5] [?*]

Modena
Archivio di Stato (ASMod)
Archivio Cancelleria ducale Estense Segreto (AEC)
Ambasciatori, Roma, b. 1
Carteggio Principi Esteri (cardinali), b. 1380B/116

Biblioteca universitaria Estense
α.F.2.26 (Lat. 1101): *Tractatus grammaticalis*, also
Guarino, *Carmina differentialia*; [Giuliano da
Viterbo]; arms, etc.; [*I 835]
α.N.7.28 (Ital. 1155). Felice Feliciano, *Canzoni* etc

New York, Pierpont Morgan Library
946: Martial, *Epigrammata*; [Sanvito];[6] [?*]

Paris, Bibliothèque nationale (BN)
Lat. 772: Psalter (14th cent.); arms; [*I 716]
Lat. 10311: Ovid; [Giuliano da Viterbo]; [*I 755]

---

[5] Alexander, 'A Manuscript', pp. 33–4, and esp. p. 39 n. 34
[6] This was said to belong to Cardinal F. Gonzaga by De Ricci, *Census*, II, no. 1719 n. 4; Meroni, *Mostra* p. 38, reported it 'ora irreperibile'; Kristeller, *Iter*, V, p. 335, cites *16th report to Fellows of Pierpont Morgan Library 1969–71*, p. 21, New York 1973: 'for a member of the Gonzaga family'; cf. de la Mare, 'Florentine Scribes', app. III, no. 23, who notes unidentified arms and *putti* with protonotary's hats. It is therefore more probable that the MS was made for either of the protonotaries Ludovico Gonzaga or Ludovico Agnelli.

Lat. 15814: Suetonius, *Vitae imperatorum*; [Sanvito];[7] [?*].

Parma, Archivio di Stato (ASP)
Archivio Gonzaga di Guastalla (AGG)
b. 41/3 reg. 1; reg. 2; reg. 3; b. 41/4 reg. 4; reg. 6 (letter registers of Ludovico Gonzaga, Bishop-Elect of Mantua, 1484–91)

Reggio Emilia, Biblioteca Municipale
Vari E. 27: Girolamo Preti, *Summarie divisiones titulorum institutionum*; [*I 863]

Rome
Biblioteca Corsiniana
Corsin. 64 (40.F.1): L. Bolognini, *Compendium decretorum*

Biblioteca nazionale (BN)
1004: *Scriptores historiae Augustae*; [Sanvito rubrications];[8] [? *]

Turin, Biblioteca nazionale (BN)
E.III.19 Aelius Spartianus, *Scriptores historiae Augustae*
I.i.22–3 Pliny, *Historia naturalis*

Utrecht, Bibliotheek der Rijksuniversiteit
764 (I. D. 4). *Inscriptiones urbis Romae latinae*; Gonzaga arms, but without cardinal's hat;[9] [?*]

Valencia, Biblioteca central universitaria
615: *Taxae ecclesiae*; arms; [*I 830]

Vatican City
Archivio Vaticano (AV)
Reg. Vat. 402, 526, 536, 543, 554, 582, 632, 635
Obligationes et solutiones 83, 84
Diversa cameralia 37
Arm. XXXIX reg. 16, 16a (brevia)

Biblioteca Apostolica Vaticana (BAV)
Urb. Lat. 681: Petrarch, *Sonectorum et cantilenarum liber, Triumphorum liber*; arms; [?*I 762]
Vat. Lat. 1670: verses of Porcellio Pandoni
Vat. Lat. 2874: G. A. Campano, *Epigrammata*
Vat. Lat. 2934: fragmentary writings of Pomponio Leto
Vat. Lat. 2960: Guido Gonzaga, *Mantuane urbis*

---

[7] Alexander, *Renaissance Illuminations*, pp. 66–7, pl. 13–14. But cf. de la Mare, *Florentine Scribes*, p. 287, app. III no. 12; also above p. 58 for the cardinal's statement that he had no copy of Suetonius, which would suggest, if this MS was his, it was made after 1476.

[8] de la Mare, 'Florentine Scribes', app. III, p. 289 no. 26.

[9] Van der Horst, *Medieval Manuscripts*, p. 48, no. 178, and information from Judith Pollmann. See I 821.

> *gestorum liber*; [*I 812]
> Vat. Lat. 3611: Antonio Geraldini, *Carmina*
> Vat. Gr. 1626: Homer, *Iliad* [Greek, Rhosos; Latin, Sanvito]; arms, *imprese*; [*]
> Vat Gr. 1627: Homer, *Odyssey* [Greek; Rhosos]; arms; [*]
> Chigi H VII. 228: Quintus Curtius Ruffus, *De gestis Alexandri Magni*; arms; [*]
> Chigi J VII 260: (contains Porcellio, *De iucunditate de situ Sanctae Agathe*)
> Ottob. Lat. 2280: Emilio Boccabella, *Carmina*
> Regin. Lat. 1911: contains Porcellio Pandoni, *Epigrammata*
> Ross. 1129: G. A. Campano, *Epigrammata*

Venice, Biblioteca Marciana
> Lat. cl. XII 178 (4025): Boccabella, *Carmina*; arms; [*I 839]

Weimar, Landesbibliothek
> Q. 14: Boccabella, *Carmina*

Bibliography

NOTE: This bibliography does not list works cited in the list of abbreviations nor all of the works cited in the inventory.

Acta pontificum Danica, III (1431–71), Copenhagen, 1908

Ady, C. M., 'Francesco Puteolano maestro dei figlioli di Giovanni II Bentivoglio', *L'archiginassio*, 30, 1935, pp. 156–7

—— *The Bentivoglio of Bologna*, Oxford, 1937; reprint 1969

Albertus Magnus, *Book of Minerals*, trans. D. Wyckoff, Oxford, 1967

Alexander, J. J. G., 'A Manuscript of Petrarch's Rime and Trionfi', *Victoria and Albert Museum Yearbook*, 2, 1970, pp. 27–40

—— *Italian Renaissance Illuminations*, New York and London, 1977

Alexander, J. J. G. and de la Mare, A., *The Italian Manuscripts in the Library of Major J. R. Abbey*, London, 1969

Aliano, A. Esposito, 'Testamento e inventari per la ricostruzione della biblioteca del cardinale Guglielmo d'Estouteville' in *Scrittura, biblioteche*, 1980, pp. 309–42

Alidosi, G. N. P., *Instruttione delle cose notabili nella città di Bologna*, Bologna, 1621

Ammannati, Jacopo (Iacobus Picolominus Cardinalis Papiensis), *Epistolae et commentarii*, Milan, 1506

Antonovics, A. V., 'A Late Fifteenth-Century Division Register of the College of Cardinals', *Papers of the British School at Rome*, 35, 1967, pp. 87–101

—— 'The Library of Cardinal Domenico Capranica' in *Cultural Aspects of the Italian Renaissance*, ed. C. H. Clough, Manchester and New York, 1976, pp. 141–59

Arrivabene, F., *Vocabolario mantovano-italiano*, Mantua, 1882

Avesani, R., 'Epaeneticorum ad Pium II Pont. Max. Libri V' in *Enea Silvio Piccolomini Papa Pio II*, ed. D. Maffei, Siena, 1968, pp. 15–97

Battaglia, S., *Grande dizionario della lingua italiana*, Turin, 1961–

Bazzotti, U., 'Imprese gonzaghesche a Palazzo Te' in *Giulio Romano e l'espansione del Rinascimento* (Convegno, 1989), Mantua, 1991, pp. 155–68

Begani, O., ed., *Breve chronicon monasterii Mantuani Sancti Andreae*, RIS, XXIV, 13, Città di Castello, 1908

Bellincioni, Bernardo, *Le rime*, ed. P. Fanfani, Bologna, 1876

Berselli, C., 'Il messale miniato del duomo di Mantova', *Civiltà mantovana*, n.s., 4, 1984, pp. 21–43

Biadego, G., 'Leonardo di Agostino Montagna letterato veronese del secolo xv', *Il propugnatore*, n.s., 6, 1973, part I, pp. 295–398; part II, pp. 39–111

Bianca, C., 'La formazione della biblioteca latina del Bessarione' in *Scrittura, biblioteche*, 1980, pp. 103–65

—— 'La biblioteca romana di Niccolò Cusano' in *Scrittura, biblioteche*, 1983, pp. 669–708

—— '"Auctoritas " e "veritas": il Filelfo e le dispute tra Platonici e Aristotelici' in *Francesco Filelfo nel quinto centenario della morte*, (Convegno, Tolentino, 1981), ed. R. Avesani et al., Padua, 1986, pp. 207–47

Bianca, C. et al., 'Materiali e ipotesi per le biblioteche cardinalizie' in *Scrittura, biblioteche*, 1980, pp. 73–84

Billo, L., 'Le nozze di Paola Gonzaga a Bolzano', *Studi trentini*, 15, 1934, pp. 3–22

Bonatti, B., 'La Dieta di Cremona', *Archivio storico lombardo*, 35, 1908, pp. 258–67

Braghirolli, W., 'Leon Battista Alberti a Mantova. Documenti e notizie inediti', *Archivio storico italiano*, 3rd ser., 9, 1869, pp. 3–31

—— *Della manifattura di arazzi a Mantova*, Mantua, 1879

Brown, A., *Bartolomeo Scala (1430–97), Chancellor of Florence. The Humanist as Bureaucrat*, Princeton, 1979

Brown, C. M., 'Little Known and Unpublished Letters concerning Andrea Mantegna, Bernardino Parentino, Pietro Lombardo, Leonardo da Vinci and Filippo Benintendi', *L'arte*, 6, 1969, pp. 140–64; 7–8, 1970, pp. 182–214

—— 'Cardinal Francesco Gonzaga's Collection of Antique Intaglios and Cameos: Questions of Provenance, Identification and Dispersal', *Gazette des beaux-arts*, 125, 1983, pp. 102–4

Brown, C. M., with L. Fusco and G. Corti, 'Lorenzo de' Medici and the Dispersal of the Antiquarian Collections of Cardinal Francesco Gonzaga', *Arte lombarda*, 90–1, 1989, pp. 86–103

Byatt, L. M. C., 'The Concept of Hospitality in a Cardinal's Household in Renaissance Rome' in *A Tribute to Denys Hay*, ed. D. S. Chambers and J. E. Law = *Renaissance Studies*, 2, 1988, pp. 312–20

Callimaco (Buonaccorsi), Filippo, *Epigrammatum libri duo*, ed. C. F. Kumaniecki, Warsaw, 1963

Campana, A. and Meldioli Masotti, P., ed., *Bartolomeo Sacchi il Platina* (Convegno, 1981), Padua, 1986

Canart, P., 'Scribes grecs de la Renaissance', *Scriptorium*, 17, 1963, pp. 56–82

Canensi, Michele, *see* Gaspare da Verona

Caprioglio, P. Farenga, *see* Farenga, P

Caprioli, S., *Indagini sul Bolognini: Giurisprudenza e filologia nel '400 italiano*, Varese, 1969

Carnevali, S., 'Un culto parallelo del sangue di Cristo nella cattedrale di Mantova' in *Storia e arte religiosa a Mantova: Visite di pontefici e la reliquia del Preziosissimo Sangue*, Mantua, 1991, pp. 73–82

Catalogue of Books Printed in the Fifteenth Century Now in the British Museum, London, 1908–

Cattanei, Giovanni Lucido, (Joannes Lucidus Cataneus Mantuanus Iuris Doctor), 'Oratio funebris pro Reverendissimo in Christo patre et Illustris[simo] D. D. Francisco Gonzaga Marchione etc Cardinale Mantuano' in *Orationes variae*, Parma, 1493

Cavazza, F. G., 'Il Palazzo del Comune in Bologna', *Giornale storico dell'arte*, 3, 1890, pp. 107–18

Celani, E., 'La venuta di Borso d'Este in Roma l'anno 1471', *Archivio della Società romana di storia patria*, 13, 1890, pp. 361–450

'Cena e rappresentazione data dal Cardinale Gonzaga', *Archivio storico lombardo*, 2nd ser., 15, 1888, pp. 194–5

Chambers, D. S., 'The Economic Predicament of Renaissance Cardinals', *Studies in Medieval and Renaissance History*, 3, 1966, pp. 289–313

—— 'The Housing Problems of Cardinal Francesco Gonzaga', *Journal of the Warburg and Courtauld Institutes*, 39, 1976, pp. 21–58

—— 'Sant'Andrea at Mantua and Gonzaga Patronage, 1460–72', *Journal of the Warburg and Courtauld Institutes*, 40, 1977, pp. 99–127

—— 'Francesco "Cardinalino" (c. 1477–1511): The Son of Cardinal Francesco Gonzaga', *Atti e memorie della Accademia virgiliana*, n.s., 48, 1980, pp. 5–55

—— 'Giovanni Pietro Arrivabene (1439–1504): Humanistic Secretary and Bishop', *Aevum*, 58, 1984, pp. 397–438

—— 'A Defence of Non-Residence in the Later Fifteenth Century: Cardinal Francesco Gonzaga and the Mantuan Clergy', *Journal of Ecclesiastical History*, 36, 1985, pp. 605–33

—— 'Il Platina e il Cardinale Francesco Gonzaga' in Campana and Meldioli Mazzotti, *Platina*, pp. 9–19

—— 'Virtù militare del cardinale Francesco Gonzaga' in *Guerre, stati e città, Mantova e l'Italia padana del secolo XIII al XIX*, (Atti delle Giornate di studio in omaggio a Adele Bellù), Mantua, 1988, pp. 215–29

—— 'Cardinal Francesco Gonzaga in Florence' in *Florence and Italy: Renaissance Studies in Honour of Nicolai Rubinstein*, ed. P. Denley and C. Elam, London, 1988, pp. 241–61

—— 'Bartolomeo Marasca: Master of Cardinal Gonzaga's Household (1462–1469)', *Aevum*, 63, 1989, pp. 265–83

—— 'Mantua and Trent in the Later Fifteenth Century', *Il Trentino e la dominazione veneziana* (Convegno, Rovereto, 1989) in *Atti dell'Accademia roveretana degli Agiati*, 6th ser., 28, 1988, pp. 69–95

Chambers, D. S. and Martineau, J., *Splendours of the Gonzaga* (Exhibition Catalogue, Victoria and Albert Museum), London, 1981

Cherubini, P., 'Giacomo Ammannati Piccolomini: libri, biblioteca e umanisti' in *Scrittura, biblioteche*, 1983, pp. 175–256

Chittolini, G., 'Un problema aperto: la crisi della proprietà ecclesiastica fra quattro e cinquecento: locazioni novenalli, spese di migliorie ed investiture perpetue nella pianura lombarda', *Rivista storica italiana*, 80, 1973, pp. 353–93

—— ed., *Gli Sforza, la chiesa lombarda, la corte di Roma. Strutture e pratiche beneficiarie nel ducato di Milano*, Naples, 1989

Clergeac, A., *La Curie et les bénéficiers consistoriaux*, Paris, 1911

Coffin, D., *The Villa in the Life of Renaissance Rome*, Princeton, 1979

Corpus chronicorum Bononiensium, ed. A. Sorbelli, RIS, XVIII (1), IV, Bologna, 1924–30

Cortesi, M., 'Il vescovo Johannes Hinderbach e la cultura umanistica a Trento' in *Bernardo Clesio e il suo tempo*, ed. P. Prodi, Città di Castello, 1988, pp. 477–502

Cortesi, Paolo, *De cardinalatu*, Casa Cortese, 1510

Covi, Dario A., 'A Documented Tondo by Botticelli', *Scritti di storia dell'arte in onore di Ugo Procacci*, Milan, 1977, pp. 270–2

—— 'Nuovi documenti per Antonio e Piero del Pollaiuolo e Antonio Rosellino', *Prospettiva*, 12, 1978, pp. 61–72

Cruciani, F., *Teatro nel Rinascimento. Roma 1450–1550*, Rome, 1983

Cugnoni, G., *Agostino Chigi il Magnifico*, Rome, 1878

Curtius, E. R., *European Literature and the Latin Middle Ages*, New York, 1953; reprint Princeton, 1973

da Campagnola, Stanislao, 'Le vicende della canonizzazzione di S. Bonaventura' in *San Bonaventura francescano: Convegni del Centro di studi sulla spiritualità medievale, XV*, Todi, 1974, pp. 211–55

Dacos, N. et al., *Il tesoro di Lorenzo il Magnifico, I: Le gemme*, Florence, 1972

D'Amico, J., *Renaissance Humanism in Papal Rome*, Baltimore, 1983

D'Arco, C., *Delle arti e degli artifici di Mantova. Notizie*, 2 vols, Mantua, 1857–9

Davari, S., *Notizie storiche intorno allo studio pubblico di Mantova*, Mantua, 1879

—— 'Ancora della chiesa di S. Sebastiano in Mantova e di Luca Fancelli', *Rassegna d'arte*, 1, 1901, pp. 93–5

Degenhart, B., 'Ludovico Gonzaga in einer Miniatur Pisanellos', *Pantheon*, 30, 1972, pp. 193–210

De Kunert, S., 'Un padovano ignoto ed un suo Memoriale de' primi anni del cinquecento (1505–1511)...', *Bullettino del Museo civico di Padova*, 10, 1907, pp. 1–73

de la Mare, A. C., 'The Florentine Scribes of Cardinal Giovanni of Aragon', *Il libro e il testo* (Atti del Convegno), ed. E. Questa and R. Raffaelli, Urbino, 1984, pp. 245–89

—— 'New Research on Humanistic Scribes in Florence' in *Miniatura fiorentina del Rinascimento*, ed. A. Garzelli, I, Florence, 1985, pp. 393–573

Della Torre, A., *Paolo Marsi da Pescina*, Rocca San Casciano, 1902

Del Lungo, *Florentia, uomini e cose del Quattrocento*, Florence, 1897

De Marinis, T. and Perosa, A., *Nuovi documenti per la storia del Rinascimento*, Florence, 1970

De' Medici, Lorenzo, *Lettere*, I, II (1460–74; 1474–78), ed. R. Fubini, Florence, 1977; III, IV (1478–79; 1479–80), ed. N. Rubinstein, Florence, 1977–8

De Ricci, S., *Census of Medieval and Renaissance Manuscripts in the United States and Canada*, II, New York, 1940; *Supplement*, ed. C. U. Faye and W. H. Bond, New York, 1962

Dionisotti, C., *Gli umanisti e il volgare fra quattro e cinquecento*, Florence, 1968

Diplomatarium diocesis Lundensis, IV, Monumenta Scaniae historica, Copenhagen, 1909

Donesmondi, I., *Storia ecclesiastica di Mantova*, 2 vols, Mantua, 1612–16; reprint Bologna, 1977

Esch, A., 'Mauern bei Mantegna', *Zeitschrift für Kunstgeschichte*, 47, 1984, pp. 293–319

Evans, J., *Magical Jewels in the Middle Ages and the Renaissance*, Oxford, 1922

Eubel, C., *Hierarchia catholica medii aevi sive summorum pontificum s.r.e. cardinalium ecclesiarum antistum series*, II, Münster, 1901

Faccioli, E., *Mantova. Le lettere*, I–II, Mantua, 1959–62

Farenga, P., '"Indoctis viris… mulierculis quoque ipsis": cultura in volgare nella stampa romana?' in *Scrittura, biblioteche*, 1980, pp. 403–15

—— 'Le prefazioni alle edizioni romane di Giovanni Filippo de Lignamine' in *Scrittura, biblioteche*, 1983, pp. 135–74

—— '"Monumenta memoriae". Pietro Riario fra mito e storia' in *Un pontificato e una città. Sisto IV (1471–84)*, eds M. Miglio et al., Vatican City, 1986, pp. 179–216

Ferrari, M. and Zanata, I., 'La capella del "Sangue di Christo" nella cattedrale di Mantova', *Storia e arte religiosa a Mantova. Visite di pontefici e la reliquia del Preziosissimo Sangue*, Mantua, 1991, pp. 83–98

Ferraù, G., '"Historia urbis Mantuae Gonzagaeque familiae"' in Campana and Meldioli Mazzotti, *Platina*, pp. 21–38

Filelfo, F., *Epistolarum familiarium libri XXXVII*, Venice, 1502

Florio, John, *A Worlde of Wordes*, London, 1598; reprint Hildesheim, 1972

Foligno, C., 'Di alcuni codici Gonzagheschi ed Estensi appartenuti all'abate Canonici', *Il libro e la stampa*, I.3, 1907, pp. 69–75

Forti Grazzini, N., *Arazzi a Ferrara*, Ferrara, 1982

Franchini, D. et al., *La scienza a corte*, Rome, 1979

Frasso, G., 'Oggetti d'arte e libri nell'inventario del cardinale Francesco Gonzaga' in *Mantova e i Gonzaga nella civiltà del Rinascimento*, Mantua 1977, pp. 141–4

—— 'Un poeta improvvisatore nella "familia" del cardinale Francesco Gonzaga: Francesco Cieco da Firenze', *Italia medievale e umanistica*, 20, 1977, pp. 35–40

Frittelli, U., *Gianantonio de' Pandoni detto il "Porcellio"*, Florence, 1900

Garfagnani, G. C., ed., *Callimaco Esperiente, poeta e politico del '400*, Florence, 1987

Garin, E., ed., *Il pensiero pedagogico dello umanesimo*, Florence, 1958

Gaspare da Verona, *De gestis Pauli II P.M.*, in *Le vite di Paolo II di Gaspare da Verona e Michele Canensi*, ed. G. Zippel, RIS, III, 16, Città di Castello, 1904–11

Gaye, G., ed., *Carteggio inedito d'artisti dei secoli XIV, XV, XVI*, I, Florence, 1839

Gesamtkatalog der Wiegendrucke, Leipzig, 1925–

Gherardi, Jacopo (Iacopus Volaterranus), *Il Diario romano… dal 7 settembre 1479 al 12 agosto 1484*, ed. E. Carusi, RIS, XXIII, 3, Città di Castello, 1904–11

Ghirardacci, C., *Della historia di Bologna*, ed. A. Sorbelli, RIS, XXXIII, 1, Città di Castello, 1915–32

Ginelli, C., *Codices Vaticani*, Vatican City, 1950

Goldthwaite, R., 'The Empire of Things: Consumer Demand in Renaissance Italy' in Kent and Simons, eds, *Patronage, Art and Society*, pp. 153–75

Hain, L., *Repertorium bibliographicum*, 2 vols, 1826–38; Supplements, 1892–1910

Haubst, R., 'Der Reformentwurf Pius' des Zweiten', *Römische Quartalschrift*, 49, 1954, pp. 188–242

Hausmann, F. R., 'Die Benefizien des Kardinals Jacopo Ammannati Piccolomini', *Römische historische Mitteilungen*, 13, 1971, pp. 27–80

Hay, D., *The Church in Italy in the Fifteenth Century*, Cambridge, 1977

Hill, G., *A Corpus of Italian Medals before Cellini*, London, 1930

—— *Medals of the Renaissance*, rev. G. Pollard, London, 1978

Hoberg, H., *Taxae pro communibus servitiis ex libris obligationum ab anno 1295 usque ad annum 1455 confectis*, Studi e testi 144, Vatican City, 1949

Hobson, A., *Humanists and Bookbinders*, Cambridge, 1989

Hofmann, W. von, *Forschungen zur Geschichte der Kurialen Behörden*, 2 vols, Berlin, 1914

Hollweg, W., *Dr Georg Hessler. Ein kaiserliche Diplomat und römischer Kardinal des 15 Jahrhunderts*, Leipzig, 1907

Huelsen, C., et al., *S. Agata dei Goti*, Rome, 1924

Ilardi, V., 'Eyeglasses and Concave Lenses in Fifteenth-Century Florence and Milan: New Documents', *Renaissance Quarterly*, 29, 1976, pp. 341–60

Johnson, E., *S. Andrea at Mantua*, London, 1975

Kent, F. W. and Simons, P., eds., *Patronage, Art and Society in Renaissance Italy*, Oxford, 1987

Kristeller, P., *Andrea Mantegna*, Berlin and Leipzig, 1902

Kristeller, P. O., *Iter Italicum*, 6 vols, London and Leiden, 1963–91

Kumaniecki, C. F., 'Epicedion in Dorotheam Gonzagam', *Studies in Honour of B. L. Ullmann*, II, Rome, 1964, pp. 365–73

Labowsky, L., *Bessarion's Library and the Biblioteca Marciana: Six Early Inventories*, Rome, 1979

Lanconelli, A., 'La biblioteca romana di Jean Jouffroy' in *Scrittura, biblioteche*, 1980, pp. 275–94

Landucci, L., *Diario*, ed. I. de Badia, Florence, 1883

Lee, E., *Sixtus IV and Men of Letters*, Rome, 1978

Lightbown, R., *Mantegna*, Oxford, 1986

Lublinsky, W., 'Le Semideus de Caton Sacco', *Analecta medii aevii*, 2, 1927, pp. 95–118

Luciani, A. G., 'Minoranze significative nella biblioteca del cardinale Domenico Capranica' in *Scritture, biblioteche*, 1980, pp. 167–82

Lugano, P., 'La basilica di Santa Maria Nuova al Foro Romano (Santa Francesca Romana)', *Rivista storica benedettina*, 13, 1922, pp. 139–53

Lunt, W. E., *Papal Revenues in the Middle Ages*, 2 vols, New York, 1934; reprint 1965

Luzio, A. and Renier, R., 'Del Bellincioni', *Archivio storico lombardo*, 2nd ser., 6, 1888, pp. 709–11

—— 'Il Platina e i Gonzaga', *Giornale storico della letteratura italiana*, 13, 1889, pp. 430–40

—— 'I Filelfo e l'umanismo alla corte dei Gonzaga', *Giornale storico della letteratura italiana*, 16, 1890, pp. 119–217

—— *Mantova e Urbino. Isabella d'Este ed Elisabetta Gonzaga nelle relazioni famigliari e nelle vicende politiche*, Rome, 1893

Luzio, A. and Torelli, P., *L'Archivio Gonzaga di Mantova*, 2 vols, Verona, 1920–2

McKendrick, S., 'Classical Mythology and Ancient History in Works of Art at the Courts of France, Burgundy and England (1364–1500)', PhD diss., University of London, 1988

Maffei, Raffaele (Raphaelis Volaterranus), *Commentariorum Urbanorum libri XXXVIII*, Rome, 1506

Magenta, C., *I Visconti e gli Sforza nel Castello di Pavia*, 2 vols, Milan, 1883

Marani, E. and Perina, C., *Mantova. Le arti*, II, Mantua, 1961

Marinangeli, B., 'La canonizzazione di S. Bonaventura e il processo di Lione', *Miscellanea francescana*, 17, 1916, pp. 65–86, 105–20, 165–74

Mazzoldi, L., *Mantova. La storia*, II, Mantua, 1960

Meneghin, V., *Bernardino da Feltre e i monte di pietà*, Vicenza, 1974

Meroni, U., *Mostra dei codici gonzagheschi 1328–1540*, Mantua, 1966

Messina, M., 'Francesco Accolti, umanista, giureconsulto, poeta del secolo XV', *Rinascimento*, 1, 1950, pp. 293–321

Meuthen, E., *Die letzten Jahre des Nikolaus von Kues*, Cologne, 1958

Miglio, M., '*Vidi thiaram Pauli papae secundi*' in his *Storiografia pontificia del quattrocento*, Bologna, 1975, pp. 119–53

Milham, M. E., 'The Manuscripts of Platina's "De honesta voluptate" and of its Source Martino', *Scriptorium*, 26, 1972, pp. 127–9

—— 'New Aspects of "De honesta voluptate ac valitudine"' in Campana and Meldioli Mazzotti, *Platina*, pp. 91–6

Mitchell, C., 'Felice Feliciano antiquarius', *Proceedings of the British Academy*, 47, 1962, pp. 197–221

Motta, E., 'Un pranzo dato in Roma dal Cardinale di Mantova agli ambasciatori di Francia', *Bolletino storico della Svizzera italiana*, 6, 1884, pp. 21–2

Müntz, E., 'Le Musée du Capitole et les autres collections romains à la fin du xve siècle et au commencement du xve siècle', *Revue archéologique*, n.s., 24, 1882, pp. 24–36

—— *Les Arts à la cour des papes pendant le 15e et le 16e siècle*, 3 vols, Paris, 1882

—— *Les Collections des Médicis au 15e siècle*, Paris, 1888

Nasalli Rocca di Corneliano, E., 'Il cardinale Bessarione legato pontificio in Bologna 1450–55', *Atti e memorie della R. deputazione di storia patria per le provincie di Romagna*, 4th ser., 20, 1930, pp. 17–18

Newton, S. M., *The Dress of the Venetians, 1495 to 1525*, Aldershot, 1988

Norman, D., 'The Library of Cardinal Oliviero Caraffa', *The Book Collector*, 36, 1987, pp. 354–490

Partner, P., *The Pope's Men: The Papal Civil Service in the Renaissance*, Oxford, 1990

Paschini, P., *Lodovico Cardinal Camerlengo*, Rome, 1939

—— *Il carteggio fra il cardinale Marco Barbo e Giovanni Lorenzi*, Vatican City, 1948

—— 'I benefici ecclesiastici del cardinale Marco Barbo', *Rivista di storia della chiesa in Italia*, 13, 1959, pp. 335–54

Pastor, L. von, *Storia dei Papi*, II (revised Italian version ed. A. Mercati), Rome, 1961

Pastore, G. and Manzoli G. C., *Il messale di Barbara*, Mantua, 1991

Patetta, F., 'Di una raccolta di componimenti e di una medaglia in memoria di Alessandro Cinuzzi Senese, paggio del conte Girolamo Riario', *Bulletino senese di storia patria*, 6, 1899, pp. 151–76

Patrizi, Agostino, *L'Œuvre de Patrizi Piccolomini ou le cérémonial papal de la première Renaissance*, ed. M. Dykmans, 2 vols, Studi e testi, 293, Vatican City, 1980

Pecorari, F., 'Il palazzo del cardinale Francesco Gonzaga', *Civiltà mantovana*, n.s., 9, 1985, pp. 9–34

Pellegrini, M., 'Ascanio Sforza: la creazione di un cardinale "di famiglia"' in Chittolini, *Gli Sforza, la chiesa lombarda*, pp. 215–89

Piccolomini, Aeneas Sylvius, *see* Pius II

Piccolomini, Giacomo, *see* Ammannati, Giacomo

Piccolpazzo, C., *Li tre libri del vasaio*, ed. G. Conti, Florence, 1976

Piccolrovazzi, P., *La contrastata nomina del cardinale Francesco Gonzaga al vescovado di Bressanone*, Trento, 1935

Picotti, G. B., *La giovinezza di Leone X*, Milan, 1928; reprint Rome, 1981

—— *Ricerche umanistiche*, Florence, 1955

Pirrotta, N., *Li due Orfei. Da Poliziano a Monteverdi*, 2nd edn, Turin, 1981

Pius II, *Commentarii*, ed. A. von Heck, 2 vols, Vatican City, 1984.

—— *Commentarii*, transl. F. A. Gragg, *Smith College Studies in History*, 22, 25, 30, 35, 43, Northampton, Mass., 1937–57

Platina (Sacchi, Bartolomeo), *De honesta voluptate et valitudine*, Venice, 1475

—— *Historia urbis Mantuae*, RIS, XX Milan, 1731, cols 16–862

—— *Liber de vita Christi ac omnium pontificum*, ed. G. Gaida, RIS, III, 1, Città di Castello, 1913–32

—— *De principe*, ed. G. Ferraù, Palermo, 1979

Poliziano, Angelo, *Stanze per la giostra; Orfeo; Rime*, ed. B. Maier, Novara, 1968

Pollard, G., 'The Felix Gem at Oxford and its Provenance', *The Burlington Magazine*, 119, 1977, p. 574

Praticò, G., 'Lorenzo il Magnifico e i Gonzaga', *Archivio storico italiano*, 107, 1949, pp. 155–71

Prendilacqua, Francesco, *Dialogus* in Garin, *Il pensiero pedagogico*, pp. 552–667

Pronti, S., 'Nuove acquisizioni documentarie e critiche sul tondo Botticelli del Museo di Piacenza', *Bollettino storico piacentino*, 88, 1988, pp. 1–20

Quaglioni, D., ed., *Apologia Iudaeorum; invectiva contra Platinam. Propaganda antiebraica e polemiche durante il pontificato di Sisto IV, 1471–81*, Rome, 1987

Resti-Ferrari, M. P., 'Spigolature. Aggiunte al codice diplomatico mantegnesco del Kristeller', *Atti e memorie della R. Accademia virgiliana di Mantova*, n.s., 19–20, 1926–7, pp. 263–80

Robertson, I., 'The Signoria of Girolamo Riario in Imola', *Historical Studies: Australia and New Zealand*, 15, 1971–3, pp. 88–117

Roblot-Delondre, R., 'Les Sujets antiques dans la tapisserie', *Revue archéologique*, 5th ser., 5–6, 1917, pp. 296–309; 7–8, 1918, pp. 131–50; 9, 1919, pp. 48–63, 294–332

Rosmini, C. de, *Vita di Francesco Filelfo da Tolentino*; *Supplemento*, Milan, 1808

Rossi, U., 'I medaglisti del Rinascimento alla corte di Mantova. I: Ermes Flavio de Bonis', *Rivista italiana di numismatica*, 1, 1888, pp. 25–40

—— 'Cristoforo di Geremia', *Archivio storico dell'arte*, 1, 1888, pp. 404–10

Rossi, V., 'Niccolò Lelio Cosmico, poeta padovano', *Giornale storico della letteratura italiana*, 13, 1889, pp. 101–58

Rubinstein, N., 'Il "De optimo cive" del Platina' in Campana and Meldioli Mazzotti, *Platina*, pp. 137–44

Ruysschaert, J., 'Recherche des deux bibliothèques romaines Maffei des XVe et XVIe siècles', *La bibliofilía*, 60, 1958, pp. 306–55

—— 'Miniaturistes "romains" à Naples' in T. de Marinis, *La biblioteca napoletana dei re d'Aragona*, Supplemento I, Verona 1969, pp. 263–74

Sacchi, Bartolomeo, *see* Platina

Santoro, C., 'Un manoscritto gonzaghesco nell'Archivio storico civico di Milano', *Archivio storico lombardo*, 88, 1961, pp. 237–51

Sarton, G., *Introduction to the History of Science*, I–II, Baltimore, 1927–31

Schiavo, A., *Il Palazzo della Cancelleria*, Rome, 1964

Scriptores rerum Danicarum medii aevi, eds J. Langebek et al., VIII, Copenhagen, 1934

Scrittura, biblioteche e stampa a Roma nel Quattrocento: Aspetti e problemi (Atti del seminario, 1979), eds C. Bianca et al., Vatican City, 1980

Scrittura, biblioteche e stampa a Roma nel Quattrocento (Atti del 2° seminario, 1982), ed. M. Miglio, Vatican City, 1983

Sella, P., *Glossario latino-italiano: Stato della Chiesa, Veneto, Abruzzi*, Studi e testi, 109, Vatican City, 1944

Sheard, W., *Antiquity in the Renaissance*, Northampton, Mass., 1979

Sighinolfi, L., 'Francesco Puteolano e le origini della stampa in Bologna e in Parma', *La bibliofilía*, 15, 1913–14, pp. 263–6, 331–44, 383–92, 451–67

Signorini, R., 'Contributo alla biografia di Filippo Nuvoloni', *Civiltà mantovana*, 6, 1972, pp. 318–23

—— 'L'elevazione di Francesco Gonzaga al cardinalato': appendix to 'Federico III e Cristiano I nella Camera degli Sposi', *Mitteilungen des Kunsthistorischen Institutes in Florenz*, 18, 1974, pp. 247–9

—— 'Lettura storica della Camera degli Sposi di Andrea Mantegna', *Journal of the Warburg and Courtauld Institutes*, 38, 1975, pp. 109–35

—— 'Due sonetti di Filippo Nuvoloni ad Andrea Mantegna' in *Studi in onore di Rafaelle Spongano*, Bologna, 1980, pp. 165–72

—— 'Ludovico Muore', *Atti dell'Accademia nazionale virgiliana*, n.s., 50, 1982, pp. 91–129

—— *'Opus hoc tenue': La Camera dipinta di Andrea Mantegna*, Mantua, 1985

—— 'Baldassare Soardi dedicatorio della "Vita" di Vittorino da Feltre del Platina' in Campana and Meldioli Masotti, *Platina*, pp. 153–207

—— 'La malattia mortale di Barbara di Brandeburgo Gonzaga, seconda marchesa di Mantova', *Civiltà mantovana*, n.s., 15, 1987, pp. 1–39

Simioni, A., 'Un'umanista milanese: Piattino Piatti', *Archivio storico lombardo*, 4th series, 2, 1904, pp. 5–50, 226–301

Sottili, A., 'Il palio per l'altare di Santa Caterina e il dossier sul rettorato di Giovanni di Lussemborgo', *Annali di storia pavese*, 18–19, 1989, pp. 77–102

Spallanzani, M., *Ceramiche orientali a Firenze nel Rinascimento*, Florence, 1978

Strnad, A. A., 'Francesco Todeschini Piccolomini. Politik und Mäzenatentum im Quattrocento', *Römische historische Mitteilungen*, 8–9, 1964–6

—— 'Der Apostolische Protonotar Dr Georg Hessler', *Römische Quartalschrift*, 65, 1970, pp. 29–53

Swain, E., 'Faith in the Family: the Practice of Religion by the Gonzagas', *Journal of Family History*, 8, 1983, pp. 177–89

Tenenti, A., *Il senso della morte e l'amore della vita nel Rinascimento*, Turin, 1957

Tesori d'arte nella terra dei Gonzaga, Exhibition Catalogue, Mantua, 1974

Thieme, U. and Becker, F., *Allgemeines Lexikon der bildenden Künstler von der Antike bis zur Gegenwart*, 37 vols, Leipzig, 1907–50

Thorndike, L., *A History of Magic and Experimental Science*, II, New York, 1923

—— 'Some Unpublished and Minor Works Bordering on Science Written in the Late Fifteenth Century', *Speculum*, 39, 1964, pp. 85–95

Thornton, D., 'The Study Room', PhD diss., University of London, 1990

Thornton, P., *The Italian Renaissance Interior 1400–1600*, London, 1991

Tissoni-Benvenuti, A., 'Il viaggio di Isabella d'Este a Mantova nel giugno 1480 e la datazione dell'*Orfeo* del Poliziano', *Giornale storico della letteratura italiana*, 158, 1981, pp. 368–83

—— 'Due schede per il Platina' in Campana and Meldioli Masotti, *Platina*, pp. 209–13

—— *L'Orfeo del Poliziano*, Padua, 1986

Tomasoni, P., *Lapidario estense*, Milan, 1990

Torroncelli, A., 'Note per la biblioteca di Marco Barbo' in *Scrittura, biblioteche*, 1980, pp. 343–52

Ullmann, B. L., 'Codices Maffeianai' in his *Studies in the Italian Renaissance*, Rome, 1973, pp. 373–82

Vaccari, P., *Storia della Università di Pavia*, Pavia, 1957

Vaini, M., 'La collegiata di Sant'Andrea, la prepositura di San Benedetto Po e la politica ecclesiastica dei Gonzaga', *Sant'Andrea di Mantova e Leon Battista Alberti* (Atti del Convegno, 1972), Mantua, 1975, pp. 335–9

Valtieri, S., 'La fabbrica del palazzo del Cardinale Raffaelle Riario', *Quaderni dell'Istituto di storia dell'architettura*, 27, 1982, pp. 3–24

—— *La Basilica di San Lorenzo in Damaso nel Palazzo della Cancelleria a Roma attraverso il suo archivio ritenuto scomparso*, Rome, 1984

Vasić Vatovec, C., *Luca Fancelli architetto: Epistolario gonzaghesco*, Florence, 1979

Venturi, A., 'Sperandio da Mantova', *Archivio storico dell'arte*, 1, 1888, pp. 385–97

Verde, A. F., *Lo studio fiorentino, 1473–1503*, II, Florence, 1973

Vitalini, V., 'A proposito della datazione dell' "Orfeo" del Poliziano', *Giornale storico della letteratura italiana*, 146, 1969, pp. 245–51

Volaterranus, Jacopus, *see* Gherardi, Jacopo

Volaterranus, Raphaelus, *see* Maffei, Raffaele

Volta, Z., 'Catone Sacco e il collegio di sua fondazione a Pavia', *Archivio storico lombardo*, 8, 1891, pp. 562–600

Wardrop, J., *The Script of Humanism*, Oxford, 1963

Weil-Garris, K. and D'Amico, J. F., *The Renaissance Cardinal's Ideal Palace: A Chapter from Cortesi's De cardinalatu*, Rome, 1980

Weiss, R., *Un umanista veneziano: Papa Paolo II*, Venice, 1958

—— 'Lorenzo Zane arcivescovo di Spalato e governatore di Cesena', *Studi romagnoli*, 16, 1965, pp. 163–9

—— *The Renaissance Discovery of Classsical Antiquity*, Oxford, 1969

Zabughin V., *Giulio Pomponio Leto*, 3 vols, Grottaferrata and Rome, 1909–12

Zambotti, B., *Diario ferrarese*, ed. G. Pardi, RIS, XXIV, 7, Bologna, 1934–7

Zippel, G., ed., *Le vite di Paolo II di Gaspare da Verona e Michele Canensi*, RIS, III, 16, Città di Castello, 1904–11

—— 'Un apologia dimenticata di Pietro Riario' in *Scritti di storia, di filosofia e d'arte: Per nozze Fedele de Fabritiis*, Naples, 1908, pp. 329–46

—— 'Carlo Marsuppini d'Arezzo. Notizie biografiche' in his *Storia e cultura del Rinascimento italiano*, ed. G. Zippel, Padua, 1979, pp. 198–214

—— 'La morte di Marco Barbo cardinale di San Marco' in his *Storia e cultura del Rinascimento italiano*, ed. G. Zippel, Padua, 1979, pp. 483–93

Zucchi, R., 'Per una storia della biblioteca dei Gonzaga, signori di Mantova', tesi di laurea, Università Cattolica, Milan, 1966–7

Index

The references in this index of persons, objects, places etc, are to pages, or, where preceded by the letters W, I or L respectively, to paragraphs in the cardinal's will (Appendix 1), items in the Inventory (Appendix 2), or selected letters (Appendix 3).

The index serves on a limited scale also as a glossary. Thus, where an object is described in the documents with an Italian or Mantuan word the meaning of which is not obvious, a presumed English equivalent is provided in all but a few intractable cases. Some generic terms are also indexed in English, e.g. 'tapestry', with cross-references to the appropriate Italian words. It must be borne in mind that few of the objects survive and only minimal clues are given about their appearance; moreover, there is often no consensus among experts as to the meaning, and little reason to asssume consistency in fifteenth-century usage, of many of the descriptive words supplied for particular items. This applies particularly to the objects of *pietra dura*, rock-crystal, silver and other metals. For example, a *bochale* (*boccale*) was obviously a vessel with a mouth from which to pour or drink liquid and might have had a handle and sometimes a cover or lid; the English equivalent offered is 'jug', but in some cases 'ewer' might be more appropriate, in others perhaps 'tankard' or 'flagon'.[1] There can be little hope of precision, therefore, in this sort of vocabulary,[2] though for words describing types of tapestry work and clothing there may be rather more standardisation.[3] However, particular furs and textiles have not generally been separately indexed or translated, since these words can be easily found in dictionaries.[4]

Common-sense has sometimes overruled consistency. For instance, precious stones and metals have generally been differentiated, but because so many objects in the inventory are of silver or silver-gilt, silver does not have a generic entry. Cameos and intaglios, impossible to distinguish in most references, are classified together as 'gems'. There is only a limited breakdown of the books under subject categories, though authors, where known, are listed. The Table of Itineraries and the place-names cited in footnotes as the provenance of letters etc have not been separately indexed. For obvious reasons there is no general entry under the name of Cardinal Francesco Gonzaga.

---

[1] Florio, *Worlde of Wordes*, s.v., suggests, among other things 'pot, drinking vessel....also an Ewer'.

[2] Note some acute remarks in Spallanzani, *Ceramiche orientali*, pp. 40–1, a work which takes many fifteenth-century inventories into account, as does Thornton *Italian Renaissance Interior*, which is invaluable for furniture, fabrics and furnishings. For terms used to describe ornamental dishes and drinking vessels, Piccolpazzo, *Li tre libri* is also useful. Although no ceramic items are recorded in Cardinal Francesco Gonzaga's possesssion, the same words to describe an object's form might be used regardless of what it was made of.

[3] I am grateful to Scot McKendrick for advice on English terms relating to tapestry. Some 'equivalent' English words for articles of clothing are borrowed from Newton, *Dress of the Venetians*. Also useful for garments and miscellaneous items is the annotated list of Elisabetta Gonzaga's dowry (1488) in Luzio and Renier, *Mantova e Urbino*, pp. 293–306.

[4] Among the most useful should be noted: Florio, *Worlde of Wordes*; Arrivabene, *Vocabolario mantovano-italiano*; Sella, *Glossario*; and Battaglia, *Grande dizionario*, I–XV (in progress).